The Arden Guide to Renaissance Drama

The Arden Guide to Renaissance Drama

An Introduction with Primary Sources

Brinda Charry

Bloomsbury Arden Shakespeare
An imprint of Bloomsbury Publishing Plc

B L O O M S B U R Y
LONDON • OXFORD • NEW YORK • NEW DELHI • SYDNEY

Bloomsbury Arden Shakespeare

An imprint of Bloomsbury Publishing Plc

Imprint previously known as Arden Shakespeare

50 Bedford Square   1385 Broadway
London   New York
WC1B 3DP   NY 10018
UK   USA

www.bloomsbury.com

BLOOMSBURY, THE ARDEN SHAKESPEARE and the Diana logo are trademarks of Bloomsbury Publishing Plc

First published 2017

© Brinda Charry, 2017

British Library Cataloguing-in-Publication Data
A catalogue record for this book is available from the British Library.

ISBN: HB: 978-1-472-57225-7
        PB: 978-1-472-57224-0
        ePDF: 978-1-472-57227-1
        eBook: 978-1-472-57226-4

Library of Congress Cataloging-in-Publication Data
Names: Charry, Brinda, author.
Title: The Arden guide to Renaissance drama : an introduction with primary sources / Brinda Charry.
Description: London ; New York : Bloomsbury Arden Shakespeare: Bloomsbury Arden Shakespeare, 2017.
Identifiers: LCCN 2017003695 | ISBN 9781472572240 (paperback) | ISBN 9781472572257 (hardback) | ISBN 9781472572271 (ePDF) | ISBN 9781472572264 (ePub)
Subjects: LCSH: English drama—Early modern and Elizabethan, 1500–1600—Study and teaching (Higher) | English drama—17th century—Study and teaching (Higher). | Renaissance—England—Study and teaching (Higher) | BISAC: LITERARY CRITICISM / Drama. | LITERARY CRITICISM / Renaissance.
Classification: LCC PR653 .C46 2017 | DDC 822/.309–dc20 LC record available at https://lccn.loc.gov/2017003695

Cover design: Dani Leigh
Cover image © Landscape with the Fall of Icarus, c.1555 (oil on canvas), Bruegel, Pieter the Elder (c.1525–69) /Musées Royaux des Beaux-Arts de Belgique, Brussels, Belgium / Bridgeman Images

Typeset by RefineCatch Limited, Bungay, Suffolk
Printed and bound in Great Britain

To find out more about our authors and books visit www.bloomsbury.com. Here you will find extracts, author interviews, details of forthcoming events and the option to sign up for our newsletters.

For my teachers

Contents

Part II

x   **Contents**

List of Illustrations

List of Extracts

Chapter 1: Politics and Society

Chapter 2: Men and Women

Chapter 3: Travel and Trade

Chapter 4: Humanism

Chapter 5: The Stage

Chapter 6: Authors, Books and Readers

Chapter 7: Genre

Chapter 8: Language and Style

Preface

Renaissance plays are among the world's most valuable literary artifacts. They are also historical documents, ideological statements, philosophical reflections and theatrical scripts. This book attempts to help students know and appreciate the plays in all these manifestations.

The political, social, cultural and literary contexts examined in each chapter in Part I help place the plays in their moment of production. To fully understand that moment, students are invited to consider events and issues ranging from conceptualizations of kingship to the Protestant Reformation, humanist learning to censorship, international travel to staging practices, patronage and book printing. That most famous of Renaissance writers, William Shakespeare, described plays as 'the abstract and brief chronicles of the time' (*Hamlet*, 2.2.524–25). Of course, the relationship between the 'text' and its 'time' is not a straightforward one. Plays don't just reflect or reproduce reality, and 'reading' drama is not simply a matter of looking for simple correspondences and connections between a play and history. Plays can also participate in history by creating a culture's sense of itself. Renaissance drama also conceptualizes and challenges, or at least unsettles, the realities and dominant ways of thinking of its time. Besides, reading and interpreting the plays in the twenty-first century is also perhaps a way of engaging with our own moment in history.

Excerpts from historical documents are reproduced in each chapter. They are from a variety of genres – political tracts, prayer books, learned treatises, diaries, travelogues and so forth. The idea behind these documents is to encourage students to see them in intertextual relationship with the plays and to encourage reflection on how these so-called historical texts, like the literary ones, do not offer a simple, unmediated access to reality – They too have to be interpreted and analysed. Students are invited to ask questions about the nature and function of these documents and the plays: What genre do the historical documents belong to and how does that impact the way they relate to and reflect on the historical moment? Are they examples of 'literature' too? Are the plays just one among many social and political texts? Or are they different from the documents, even special and unique, because of their status as 'fiction' and because they subsequently came to be conceived as 'literature'? These are questions that make the study of Renaissance drama in relation to its context complex and stimulating.

Part II of this book studies fourteen Renaissance plays. Each (necessarily brief) chapter draws attention to important themes and key issues raised by the text. The questions that follow the discussion of each play provide teachers and students the opportunity to further discuss the language of the plays and the complexity of the text–context relationship and to read the plays in relation to the events, movements and issues described in Part I. The plays in Part II represent a variety of genres and are drawn from the work of a number of playwrights. All of these plays, even the less canonical ones, are taught in modern classrooms, indicating that the Renaissance literary canon has been subject to reinterpretation like the Renaissance itself.

The debate around the term 'Renaissance' reflects some of the re-conceptions of the time period. 'Renaissance', as used first by scholars in the 1800s, understands the era as one of cultural renewal and growth. The term 'early modern', preferred by many scholars today, implies that the era is a crucible of those ideas and social structures that are characteristic of the 'modern' age – the period is very much the precursor of our own moment in history. While the term 'Renaissance' is used in this book, largely because it is still the more familiar term, it is evoked with a full consciousness of the complexities and contradictions of the era.

Acknowledgements

Thank you to all the teachers who taught me to understand, appreciate and ask questions of Renaissance drama. This book is dedicated to them. A note of special gratitude to Dympna Callaghan, dear mentor and friend. Thanks also to Margaret Bartley, whose idea this was and who has offered steady support and encouragement, Emily Hockley, whose insightful comments have been simply invaluable, and Emma Smith, who has been generous with her time and expertise and whose suggestions have made this a better book. Thanks also to Venkat Sadasivan for his thoughtfulness, patience and sense of humour, to Gitanjali Shahani, Meriem Pages and Amy Burnette for dealing with my numerous queries and to Premi Shankavaram for stepping in when I most needed it. Through my students I relive the pleasure and wonder of reading these plays – thank you.

Part I

1

Politics and Society

The Central Asian emperor Tamburlaine is the subject of the two-part play
Tamburlaine the Great (first published 1590) by the English Renaissance
author Christopher Marlowe. Marlowe dramatizes the military and political
exploits of that sovereign: energetic, restlessly ambitious, uncannily intelligent,
bloody but also somehow heroic. The play's prologue urges us to 'View but his
picture in this tragic glass, / And then applaud his fortunes as you please' (Part
One, Prologue, 7–8).[1] The story of Tamburlaine is turbulent and grand. It is the
natural stuff of theatre. Echoing oft-repeated statements of drama as holding
a mirror up to 'nature' or reality, Marlowe's play claims to be a 'glass' that reflects
the actuality behind the text. But the reality itself is unstable and largely
inaccessible and the play is more a 'picture' that refashions and represents the
real in dramatic and concentrated form, combining fact and fable to create
something new and distinct. The members of the audience were participants
in this new reality, as well as witnesses and judges. Like Marlowe, other
Renaissance dramatists, along with their spectators and their readers, engaged
in complicated ways with kings and nations, rulers and the ruled and the
politics of the past and of their own day.

It was truly a time of great political change in England. In the year 1485,
King Henry VII's victory over Richard III had effectively ended the War of
the Roses and Henry had become the first monarch of the Tudor dynasty.
His son Henry VIII had further consolidated Tudor power. After Henry
VIII, his only son Edward and his first daughter Mary had each ruled
briefly, until Henry's second daughter Elizabeth became queen. The reign of
Queen Elizabeth I and that of her nephew and successor, the Stuart ruler
King James I, saw the growth and increased popularity of a professional
English drama.

The many accounts of Elizabeth's life and reign represent her as an
intelligent, capable ruler who was also indecisive and difficult. Her era

certainly had its highs and lows. The 1590s onwards were marked by bad harvests, low wages and English involvement in expensive military conflicts in France and the Netherlands. The fact that the queen stayed unmarried and bore no children meant that the question of who would succeed her remained unresolved almost until her death. However, there were gains in certain economic sectors and England achieved a famous victory over the Spanish Armada, enhancing the political prestige of the country and raising the pride and self-confidence of the English people.

James, who had been king of Scotland, succeeded Elizabeth and inaugurated Stuart rule in England. James has been subject to varying treatment by historians. He has been read as a prudent and sensible king, or as foolish and weak in spite of his claims to learning. What is quite clear is that his belief in the absolute authority of the monarch alienated Parliament and the early years of his reign were marred by charges of corruption as the king promoted his favourites in court. However, James did succeed in securing peace with Spain and his reign also saw the continued growth of art and literature.

It was certainly a period of turbulence and change. Five monarchs sat on the throne of England in the Tudor period alone; there were three changes in state religion followed by sectarian strife and several socio-economic upheavals. But the drama flourished, both because interesting times are fodder to a writer's imagination and also because it was, in spite of everything (and somewhat miraculously perhaps), still a time of relative stability allowing for rich cultural and artistic production. While few plays dealt directly with controversial political issues, political and social questions were alluded to indirectly or shaped writers' thematic concerns in complex but discernible ways.

Kingship

Drama regularly took up the theme of kingship: How did one assume power? What were its limits? Who was a legitimate king? Centuries before the Renaissance, the Magna Carta sealed by King John in 1215 had declared that the supremacy of the monarch was conditional. This meant that political authority would be exercised by the king as well as by Parliament. In practice, noblemen who were powerful feudal lords had also exercised considerable power. The Tudor era, however, saw an increased centralization of power. By a series of acts of Parliament between 1531 and 1534, Henry VIII not only severed the English Church from Rome but also proclaimed 'this realm of England an empire', 'governed by one supreme head and king'.[2] Consequently, the monarch became the central authority who unified the national community and protected it from internal dissent and external threat. While he or she was advised by the Privy Council and by the two houses of Parliament, the monarch still selected members to serve on the Privy Council and also retained the right to call Parliament. Writers like Sir Thomas Smith (*De Republica* Anglorum [1583]) and Richard Hooker (*Of the Laws of Ecclesiastical Policy* [1594]) continued to insist that government be participatory. The king had supreme authority, wrote Hooker, but he 'hath no power to do without consent of the Lords and Commons assembled in Parliament'.[3] In spite of such urgings, the reality was that the monarch was the single most powerful force in England.

The English monarchs emphasized the theory of 'the divine right of kings', according to which the king's power was God-given and the king need not be subject to any human authority. Political power thus legitimized itself by claiming heavenly sanction. While Elizabeth was a pragmatic ruler who claimed divine authority even as she negotiated and sometimes compromised with Parliament, James was more insistent on the absolute and divine authority of kings. As he stated in a 1609 speech to Parliament: 'The State of the Monarchy is the supremest thing upon earth: for Kings are not only GOD's lieutenants upon earth, and sit upon GOD's throne, but even by GOD himself they are called gods.'[4] The monarch's divinity clearly invested him with absolute power, but it also required him, in his role as a 'lieutenant' of God, to administer justice, reward good, punish evil and work for the public welfare. In other words, the 'godly prince', as described in James's writing, had weighty responsibilities even as he had great privileges.

Rulers also had to engage in sophisticated public relations exercises to win the admiration and loyalty of the people. For instance, the 'cult of Elizabeth' was a clever public relations strategy that projected Queen Elizabeth as a goddess as well as a Protestant heroine and a Protestant substitute for the Virgin Mary. Elizabeth made use of the medieval discourse of chivalry, describing her courtiers as her knights and herself as the mistress they served. She also represented herself as the wife of her nation and mother of her people. As she said in response to repeated urgings to marry and bear children: 'I am already bound unto an husband, which is the kingdom of England' and 'everyone of you, as many as are English, are my children and kinsfolk'.[5] Elizabeth also recognized that kingship was theatrical and involved the successful performance of a public role. While James was irked by the need to stage himself for the public eye, complaining that 'a King is as one set on a stage, whose smallest actions and gestures, all the people gazingly do behold',[6] Elizabeth revelled in performance. Her public appearances were carefully orchestrated and marked by display. If this was the great age of theatre, the Queen was perhaps its principal performer.

London, the capital where these games of power were being played, was a rapidly growing city. Its population increased from 120,000 in 1550 to 200,000 by 1600. It attracted people from other parts of the country and from Europe and became the centre where professionals, tradesmen, apprentices, criminals and rogues congregated, even as it was the site of power and leisure for the elites. It was in this urban milieu that the public theatre arose. London's status as capital city also encouraged drama in other ways. The royal court was an important site for political advancement, intrigue, fashion as well as artistic performance, and actors were drawn into its orbit. Both Queen Elizabeth and King James delighted in plays and had them enacted at court. William Shakespeare's acting company received the patronage of the king in 1603, even as the players were subject to government control through a licensing and censorship office, as will be discussed in Chapter 6.

Kings as represented in drama are fascinating figures – god-like and awe-inspiring yet morally complex. Marlowe's *Tamburlaine* acknowledges the glamour of kingship: Tamburlaine longs for 'The sweet fruition of an earthly crown' (Part I, 2.7.29) and the captain Theridamas says that 'a god is not so glorious as a king. / I think the pleasure they enjoy in heaven / Cannot compare with kingly joys on earth' (Part 1, 2.5.57–59). Shakespeare's history plays represent the monarch as central to the nation's history and celebrate outstanding kings. In its valorization of kingship the theatre can be read as a politically conservative institution, perhaps even as an instrument used by the state to further its own interests. But the stage also exposed the contradictions of power. Marlowe's Tamburlaine is a successful world-conqueror, but he is also a megalomaniac who seizes power through trickery and brutal violence. Richard in Shakespeare's *Richard III* (c. 1591) is duplicitous and murderous and Shakespeare's Henry V too does not hesitate to betray his old friends. Drama depicted royal power as complex in other ways. The tragedy *Gorboduc* (1561) tells of the disasters that result when a king disregards his councillors. In all history plays the monarch's personality, with both its frailties and strengths, was rendered all too human. Edward II in Marlowe's play of the same name is a weak king who loses the affection of his people and comes to a brutal end. *Edward II* (1593) also recognizes that power is illusory and transient – 'But what are kings, when regiment is gone, / But perfect shadows in a sunshine day?' (20, 26–27), wonders Marlowe.[7]

Critics of the theatre worried that even depicting kings on stage was an irreverent act. As the anti-theatrical commentator Stephen Gosson wrote, 'For a mean person to take upon him the title of a Prince with counterfeit port and train, is . . . within the compass of a lie.'[8] By playing kings on stage, actors actually drew spectators' attention to the fact that a large component of power was successful performance. In doing so, they stripped kingship of its sacred aura. In Shakespeare's *King Lear* (c. 1603–06) the old, mad, frail king who realizes that he is all too human and 'smells of mortality' is a reminder of the non-divinity of kings (4.6.129).

The excesses of power also fascinated playwrights. The Italian political philosopher Niccolò Machiavelli had famously argued that 'virtue' in kings was not to be equated with traditional morality but meant prowess and cunning. Machiavelli's ideas were admittedly more complex than stated here, but remorseless Machiavellian rulers were represented and even caricatured on the Renaissance stage. Besides, a number of 'tyrant plays' depicting despotic rulers were staged. The issue of tyranny was a fraught one. Many thinkers, notably John Ponet (*A Short Treatise of Political Power* [1556]) argued that no community should tolerate dictators who should be deposed and, if necessary, killed, while others were of the opinion that the consent of the public is necessary for rule but kings cannot and should not be deposed by the people. On stage, Caesar in Shakespeare's *Julius Caesar* (1599) is a dictator, but the play holds that deposing of an existing government is an even greater evil. In Shakespeare's *Macbeth* (c. 1606), Macbeth, once he becomes Scottish king, is described as a 'tyrant' who deserves to be killed. The emperor Tiberius in Ben Jonson's *Sejanus* (1603) is frighteningly despotic, and other tyrant kings – Mustapha, Selimus and Solimon, for example – also ranted and raved and indiscriminately killed on Renaissance stages.

Many plays, especially Jacobean ones like John Webster's *The Duchess of Malfi* (1612–13), John Marston's *The Malcontent* (1603), Thomas Kyd's *The Spanish Tragedy* (c. 1585–89) and Thomas Middleton's *The Revenger's Tragedy* (c. 1606), depict the royal court as a corrupt and unjust place. So when it comes to the depiction of monarchy, while drama was conservative and propagandistic in some ways, it cannot, as David Bevington reminds us, be equated with official propaganda. The better playwrights questioned and deconstructed power and their audiences had diverse responses to the plays, ensuring that the 'drama possessed a vitality of independent expression.'[9]

From Niccolò Machiavelli, *The Prince* (1532). Trans. Daniel Donno, 1966.
(© Random House)

The Italian thinker Niccolò Machiavelli's famous political treatise *The Prince* (1532) was widely read across Europe. In this well-known excerpt, Machiavelli argues that a king need not necessarily be virtuous.

Therefore a prince will not actually need to have all the qualities previously mentioned, but he must surely seem to have them. Indeed, I would go as far as to say that having them all and always conforming to them would be harmful, while appearing to have them would be useful. That is, it will be well for him to seem and, actually, to be merciful, faithful, humane, frank, and religious. But he should preserve a disposition[10] which will make a reversal of conduct possible in case the need arises. It must be understood, however, that a prince – especially a prince who has but recently attained power – cannot observe all of those virtues for which men are reputed good, because it is often necessary to act against mercy, against faith, against humanity, against frankness, against religion in order to preserve the state. Thus he must be disposed to change according to the winds of fortune and the alterations of circumstance dictate. As I have already said, he must stick to the good so long as he can, but, being compelled by necessity, he must be ready to take the way of evil.

Hence a prince must take care never to utter a word that is not implicit with the five above-mentioned qualities; and he must never appear to be anything but the very soul of clemency,[11] faithfulness, frankness, humanity, and religion to all who see and hear him. But of all the qualities he must seem to have, none is more important than the last. Generally, men judge by the eye rather than the hand, for all men can see a thing, but few come close enough to touch it. All men will see what you seem to be; only a few will know what you are, and those few will not dare to oppose the many who have the majesty of the state on their side to defend them. In all men's acts, and in those of princes most especially, it is the result that renders the verdict when there is no court of appeal. Let the prince conquer a state, then, and preserve it; the methods employed will always be judged honourable, and everyone will praise them. For the mob is always impressed by appearances and by results; and the world is composed of the mob. . . . A certain ruler of our time, whom it is better not to name, preaches nothing but peace and faith, yet he is the extreme enemy of both; and if he had been true to either of them, he would more than once have lost either power or reputation.

The English Reformation

The religious plays of the Middle Ages – the miracle, mystery and morality plays – preceded the secular public drama of the Renaissance. In 1576 church authorities complained that these medieval plays contained many elements 'which tend to the derogation of the Majesty and glory of God, the prophanation of the sacraments and the maintenance of superstition and idolatry'.[12] The objection to the moralities was the result of a revolutionary religious movement that swept across Europe – the Protestant Reformation.

Religion was central to Renaissance society. It shaped an individual's understanding of the universe, of self, society, life, death and the divine. It also provided inspiration for art and influenced the drama. Renaissance Christianity was however marked by contest and conflict. In the early 1500s the German priest Martin Luther spearheaded the public critique of the Roman Catholic Church. He was concerned with what he saw as the Roman Catholic Church's corruption and financial abuse and also emphasized his objections to certain aspects of church practice including the worship of idols and the granting of indulgences as remission of punishment for sin. Luther also believed that the Catholic Church had lost sight of the original Christian doctrine that salvation is attained through faith in God and Christ. Luther's ideas gathered energy and became a movement that came to be called the 'Reformation' because, from the perspective of the protestors, the church needed to be 're-formed' or returned to what it was in its earliest years before the 'papists' (as Roman Catholics were called) took control over it. The Reformation soon spread from Germany to other parts of northern Europe and other thinkers, including the Swiss theologian John Calvin, also protested against the Roman Catholic Church.

The English king Henry VIII passed a series of laws in the 1530s to break away from the 'Church of Rome' and to establish himself as head of the 'Church of England'. As the historian Christopher Haigh points out, without the royal initiative, English Protestantism might have been crushed at a very early stage: 'It was politics which made the difference, politics which provided the dynamic for change'.[13] It is important, however, to remember that the English Reformation did not happen overnight or in a revolutionary fashion. Neither was the English Reformation a simple forward movement. As Haigh writes, 'In England such events did not come in a swift and orderly sequence, as consecutive steps of a preplanned program or a protest movement: they came (and went again) as the accidents of everyday politics and the consequences of power struggle'.[14] Henry's own commitment to the new religion varied in intensity depending on the political situation, but he gradually made decisions and passed laws that resulted in the rejection of the authority of the Pope, the reduction of the power of priests, the suppression of Catholic monasteries and the introduction of new and simplified forms of worship. Material objects of religion like images, rosaries and altars were perceived by Protestants as superstitious remnants of the nation's Catholic past and Henry's government stripped the churches of these features. Protestants felt that they were going back to the old, true church of the early Christians, even as they enthusiastically proclaimed the rise of a brave new order. As the Earl of Derby wrote in 1539, 'Englishmen have forsaken Satan, his satellites and all works of darkness and dedicated themselves to Christ's words and faith, and to the works of light'.[15]

Under Henry's son Edward there was a sweeping programme of Protestant reform, but when Edward's sister Mary came to the throne she restored the nation to Catholicism and many ardent Protestants were executed while others went into exile in Europe. When Elizabeth ascended the throne in 1558 she once again declared Protestantism the national religion. The Elizabethan Settlement of 1559 called for uniformity of worship across the country. The Act of Uniformity abolished the mass and reinstated the Protestant church service centred around the Book of Common Prayer. Individuals could be punished by fines or even imprisonment for engaging in other forms of worship and in unlicensed preaching. While this might seem very rigid and dictatorial, in reality the Elizabethan religious settlement was a compromise between the older religion and Protestantism. The Queen was no religious zealot but a practical politician who wanted order and political loyalty. She did not hunt down Catholic heretics in a deliberate fashion and never did (nor indeed could) police people's inner beliefs. She looked instead for outward conformity and let local parishes work out their own compromise between Catholic and Protestant practices. The Act of Uniformity modified the Book of Common Prayer, first produced during Edward's reign, to soften its more starkly Protestant features, allowed priests to wear special attire when celebrating communion (even though lavish

Catholic priestly vestments were disallowed) and retained a few ritualistic elements of worship. The Queen did not specifically forbid the retention of images in churches and while she banned religious processions, she cited practical reasons for doing so (saying they created public disorder) and even allowed a select few.

Elizabeth's reformation was successful because of her pragmatism and also because of her long reign. Besides, many Englishmen, due to political conflicts with Spain, became vehemently anti-Spanish and consequently anti-Catholic. By the 1580s most positions of power in Parliament and court were occupied by Protestants and the 'gradual consolidation of the Anglican Church must ... be numbered among the achievements of this versatile age'.[16] James I, in his turn, was also a religious moderate although radical Catholics engineered the unsuccessful Gunpowder Plot in an attempt to assassinate him in 1605, and in the second part of his reign serious divisions arose in the English Church between moderate and extremist Protestants.

From 'An Act for the Uniformity of Common Prayer' passed by Parliament in 1559.
(Courtesy of the University of Virginia Press and The Folger Shakespeare Library)

A significant part of the Elizabethan Religious Settlement, 'An Act for the Uniformity of Common Prayer' enforced the use of the *Book of Common Prayer* in church service. The first *Book of Common Prayer* was published in 1549 during the reign of Edward and included a calendar of worship and the forms of prayer to be used in Protestant worship. In 1552 it was slightly re-edited by Thomas Cranmer, Archbishop of Canterbury. Elizabeth I reintroduced it in 1559 with a few modifications.

And further be it enacted by the Queen's Highness, with the assent of the lords and commons in this present Parliament assembled and by authority of the same, that all and singular ministers in any cathedral or parish church or other place within this realm of England, Wales, and the marches of the same, or other the Queen's dominions, shall, from and after the Feast of the Nativity of Saint John Baptist[17] next coming, be bounden to[18] say and use the matins,[19] evensong,[20] celebration of the Lord's Supper, and administration of each of the sacraments, and all their common and open prayer, in such order and form as is mentioned in the said book so authorized by Parliament in the said fifth and sixth year of the reign of King Edward the Sixth, with one alteration or addition of certain Lessons to be used on every Sunday in the year, and the form of the Litany altered and corrected, and two sentences only added in the delivery of the Sacrament[21] to the communicants,[22] and none other or otherwise. And that if any manner of person,[23] vicar, or other whatsoever minister that ought or should sing or say common prayer mentioned in the said book, or minister the sacraments, from and after the Feast of the Nativity of Saint John Baptist next coming, refuse to use the said common prayers or to minister the sacraments in such cathedral or parish church or other places as he should use to minister the same, in such order and form as they be mentioned and set forth in the said book, or shall willfully or obstinately standing in the same use any other rite, ceremony, order, form, or manner of celebrating of the Lord's Supper openly or privily,[24] or matins, evensong, administration of the sacraments, or other open prayers than is mentioned and set forth in the said book (open prayer in and throughout this Act is meant that prayer which is for other to come unto or hear, either in common churches or privy chapels or oratories,[25] commonly called the service of the Church) or shall preach, declare, or speak anything in the derogation or depraving[26] of the said book or anything thererin contained, or of any part thereof, and shall be thereof lawfully convicted according to the laws of this realm by verdict of twelve men, or by his own confession, or by the notorious evidence of the fact: shall lose and forfeit to the Queen's Highness, her heirs and successors, for his first offense the profit of all his spiritual benefices or promotions coming or arising in one whole year next after this conviction. And also that the person so convicted shall for the same offense suffer imprisonment by the space of six months without bail or mainprise.[27] And if any such person once convict of any offense concerning the premises shall after his first conviction eftsoons[28] offend and be thereof in form aforesaid lawfully convict, that then the same person shall for his second offense suffer imprisonment by the space of one whole year and also shall therefore be deprived, *ipso facto*,[29] of all his spiritual promotions.

. . .

And it is ordained and enacted by the authority abovesaid, that if any person or persons whatsoever after the said Feast of the Nativity of

Saint John Baptist next coming, shall in any interludes, plays, songs, rhymes, or by other open words, declare or speak anything in the derogation, depraving, or despising of the same book or of anything therein contained or any part thereof, or shall by open fact, deed, or by open threatenings compel or cause or otherwise procure or maintain any parson, vicar, or other minister in any cathedral or parish church or in chapel or in any other place to sing or say any common and open prayer or to minister any sacrament otherwise or in any other manner and form than is mentioned in the said book, or that by any of the said means shall unlawfully interrupt or let[30] any parson, vicar, or other minister in any cathedral or parish church, chapel or any other place to sing or say common and open prayer or to minister the sacraments of any of them in such manner and form as is mentioned in the said book, that then every such person being thereof lawfully convicted in form abovesaid shall forfeit to the Queen our sovereign lady, her heirs and successors, for the first offense a hundred marks.

. . .

And that from and after the said Feast of the Nativity of Saint John Baptist next coming, all and every person and persons inhabiting within this realm, or any other the Queen's Majesty's dominions, shall diligently and faithfully, having no lawful or reasonable excuse to be absent, endeavor themselves to resort to their parish church or chapel accustomed, or upon reasonable let thereof to some usual place where common prayer and such service of God shall be used in such time of let upon every Sunday and other days ordained and used to be kept as holy days. And then and there to abide orderly and soberly during the time of the common prayer, preachings, or other service of God there to be used and ministered, upon pain of punishment by the censures of the Church. And also upon pain that every person so offending shall forfeit for every such offense twelve pence to be levied by the churchwardens of the parish where such offense shall be done, to the use of the poor of the same parish, of the goods, lands, and tenements[31] of such offender, by way of distress. . . . And be it further enacted by the authority aforesaid that all laws, statutes, and ordinances[32] wherein and whereby any other service, administration of sacraments, or common prayer is limited, established, or set forth to be used within this realm or any other the Queen's dominions or countries, shall from henceforth be utterly void and of none effect.

Figure 1.1 'An Act for the Uniformity of Common Prayer', from the *Book of Common Prayer*, 1559, Benton 1.95 (Courtesy of the Trustees of the Boston Public Library/Rare Books).

But what about the common people? Religious change on this scale is surely not only about laws and proclamations. It 'also included the response of millions of men, women and children, whose names we will not know, but whose presence and participation are acts of history'.[33] While some of the common people devoted their energies and even gave their lives to defending and propagating the new movement, the English Reformation was such a gradual event that many of the commoners living in the midst of it did not realize that a revolutionary 'Reformation' had even happened. Of course, they noticed changes in forms of worship and the fact that church service was now conducted in English. But they still did not make any dramatic choice of religion at any particular moment. Instead, they took a series of smaller decisions regarding ritual and worship. The religious orientation of students at the universities was the first to change and a young generation of intellectuals became interested in Protestant ideas. Urban folk and tradesmen also gravitated more quickly to the new religion since they were more likely to be literate and to be introduced to it through books.

However, because religion was interwoven with family practices and local customs, Catholic practices lingered far into the Reformation. Altars, rosary beads, holy water, images and saint worship did not entirely disappear. Some people actually remained Catholic. These post-Reformation Catholics were either gentry households with regular access to a priest or isolated families who practised their faith in secret. Catholic missionaries or 'seminary priests' (usually of the Jesuit order) also travelled to England in secret after the 1570s to sustain those English families who remained in the Catholic fold. There is evidence of individuals who continued to ask for Catholic burials and others who refused to go to Protestant worship saying they wanted to stay in the faith they were born into. Government officials complained that many people 'contrary to all good order solemnly keep and observe ... old superstitious holy days and fasting days long since abrogated and forbidden'.[34] Some of these Catholics were vehemently against the Queen and even concocted murder plots against her; others wanted to combine two loyalties: to their queen and to the old religion.

While it is important to acknowledge that the English Reformation was a piecemeal, uneven process, the fact is it did happen. It might not have been popular among the masses at first, but it appealed to an influential minority of people, and eventually most people were Protestants. Some of them had converted to the new religion and others were pressured into it; some simply fell into it and others were born into it. For several people the new religion offered personal fulfilment and solace; for many others adapting to the new order was simply a matter of survival. Gradually, and perhaps naturally, they adjusted to the new order. Many of them realized, in the words of William Perkins, 'it is safest to do in religion as most do.'[35] This is not to imply that there was no uncertainty or confusion. People under thirty in 1559 had spent their childhoods being barraged by contradictory religious messages and 'each generation's experience of the Reformation produced new uncertainties and challenges that had to be negotiated without maps, for they were travelling where their parents had never been.'[36] For many individuals the banishing of Catholic institutions meant the loss of familiar rituals built into the texture of communal life. The new religion with its emphasis on personalized, inner faith could not fully make up for this loss. The suppression of Catholic monasteries also meant that old schools, hospitals, relationships and hierarchies vanished.

The Reformation meant the loss of certain choices – like that of becoming a celibate monk or nun, for instance. It did divide families with older people often remaining loyal to the old faith and youngsters moving away from it though most families and communities did continue to coexist in spite of these differences. In fact, people got more accustomed to a degree of religious diversity. Eventually, families made up new family mythologies and memories stressing the martyrdom of the first generation that had converted to the new faith, while Catholics told tales of their ancestors as heroically resisting the imposition of Protestantism. Protestantism also opened up new venues: people could choose a form of worship free of ceremonies; priests could marry; women could approach God directly without the close supervision of a male priest. The Protestant emphasis on duty and hard work led to entrepreneurship and the growth of business and industry. Interestingly, Protestantism also encouraged political resistance because even though every Englishman owed obedience to the monarch, the new faith said that one should ultimately listen to one's conscience. Eventually, the spirit of questioning and critique extended to new thinking in political theory, philosophy and science. Gradually, by the time James came to the throne, the Catholic past had become a distant memory for many people. In the words of Eamon Duffy, this new generation knew nothing but the reformed religion and 'did not look back at the Catholic past as their own, but another country, another world'.[37]

Puritans

Ironically, the greatest threat to the Anglican Church eventually came from conflicts within English Protestantism itself. By the 1580s, Puritans – certain groups of very committed reformed Christians who were often described as the 'hotter sort of Protestants' – began to complain that Elizabethan reform had not gone far enough. They complained that Roman Catholic rituals such as priestly garments and accessories, kneeling during communion and the use of organ music persisted in Anglican services. In a letter to Parliament in 1572 a group of Puritans wrote, 'we in England are so far from having a church rightly reformed, according to the precept of God's word, that as yet we are scarce come to the outward face of the same'.[38] The Puritans were also appalled by what they perceived as the 'popishness' of the majority of English Protestants. One influential Puritan, William Perkins, complained that 'the reminder of popery yet stick in the minds of many of them, and they think to serve God is nothing else but to deal truly with men and to babble a few words morning and evening, at home or in church, though there be little understanding'.[39]

So the Puritans launched a campaign to influence the government to enact further reform and also worked within parishes to get the people to be committed to the new religion. Religion, they said, was not just about attending church service – life was a continuous act of worship. Perkins's *The Foundation of the Christian Religion* (1590) urged people to apply prayers 'inwardly to your hearts and conscience and outwardly to your lives and conversations'.[40] The Puritans set up high religious standards for the people to follow, expected informed commitment and were very critical of moral or spiritual failings in others. In certain communities Puritan vicars refused communion to half their parishioners because they thought they were ignorant of religion.[41] Many Puritans found even the use of the Common Prayer Book and the few rituals it prescribed as unnecessarily restraining and advocated for an even simpler style of preaching and prayer. Local puritan authorities also called for the suppression of drinking, dancing, gambling, sports, stage plays and fairs, all of which they saw as 'carnal', 'worldly' and 'wicked'.

The early Puritans still worked within the Anglican Church, but the divide between Puritans and mainstream Protestants gradually grew and the former became a force unto themselves. Elizabeth deflected the Puritan campaign quite successfully, so the Puritans relaunched their campaign once

James came to the throne. Their hopes that James would be more sympathetic to their cause were dashed when the new king turned out to be as uncomfortable with dissent and extremism as his predecessor. James also disapproved of Puritan magistrates outlawing sports and dancing and issued an order known as the 'Declaration of Sports' (1618) protecting the right to dance and to practise archery and other athletic activities. He also refused to accede to Puritan demands in the Hampton Court Conference of 1604, creating a group that stayed embittered and felt marginalized from the national mainstream.

Before one dismisses Puritans as a lunatic fringe or merely general killjoys (though they were surely something of the latter), it is important to remember that many of them were high-standing churchmen, lawyers and officials who had influential positions. They denounced excessive greed and the practice of usury; they engaged in public works and had something to do with the establishment of the Elizabethan Poor Law to aid the less fortunate. Because they did not hesitate to challenge government, they created an anti-authoritarian climate. They also had a far-reaching historical influence – some of them settled in what is now the United States and played a role in the founding of that country. Further, years after James's death and shortly after the English Civil War, they became a major political force within England.

The Reformation and drama

What about the impact of the Reformation on literature, particularly drama? Anglicanism and Puritanism alike were truly 'religions of the book'. In fact, the Reformation owes part of its success to the fact that it coincided with the advent of printing in Europe. The English Protestant writer John Foxe wrote that 'God hath opened the press to preach, whose mouth the Pope is never able to stop'.[42] Printed books spread the message of the Reformation and indeed, many of the early Protestant printers put their lives at risk for the new cause. Top on the Reformers' agenda was making the Word of God accessible to the common man. This meant that they actively supported the translation of the scriptures from Latin to the 'vernacular' languages. William Tyndale translated the Bible into English in 1525–26; the 'Great Bible' translated by Bishop Miles Coverdale was authorized by Henry VIII in 1539; the Geneva Bible was translated by exiled English communities in Geneva in 1560; the Bishop's Bible was produced under the authority of the Elizabethan Anglican Church in 1568. In 1604 the Puritans requested King James for a new translation of the

Bible. This was one of the few Puritan demands he accepted, and the King James Bible, one of the finest pieces of writing in the English language, was commissioned by him and completed in 1611 by a committee of scholars and theologians. The widespread demand for the Bible is evidenced by that fact that there were eighteen editions of the Bishop's Bible, ninety-one of the Geneva Bible and 140 of the King James Bible![43] These translations of the Bible into English enhanced the prestige of the English language and encouraged literary writing in English, as we will see in a later chapter.

Apart from the Bible, a number of other books were produced by the Reformers: the Book of Common Prayer, which was to be used in Anglican worship, Foxe's *Acts and Monuments* (1563), a multi-volume history of the English Church and those Englishmen who martyred themselves to the Protestant cause, and multiple editions of the state-sanctioned *Book of Homilies*, which were distributed across the country to be used in religious service. Apart from these very well-known books, there were hundreds of treatises critiquing Catholicism, catechisms offering religious education to the masses and pious chapbooks and broadsides.[44] About 50 per cent of the books registered at the time were in fact religious, and the Reformation was truly a battle fought with books.[45]

While the Protestant translations of the Bible into the vernacular enhanced the prestige of writing in English, some scholars argue that Protestant hostility towards theatre actually impeded the development of English drama. It is true that the mystery plays and morality plays of the Middle Ages were revised or entirely suppressed due to 'popish' elements in them. However, Henry VIII's advisor, Thomas Cromwell, actually felt theatre could potentially serve to spread the Protestant message because (in the words of Cromwell's secretary Richard Morison) 'into the common people things sooner enter by the eyes than the ears: remembering more better that they see than they hear'.[46] Playwrights in the reign of Henry and Edward adapted the medieval morality plays to the Reformation climate. So, for example, the 'Vice' of medieval drama became a Roman Catholic priest and humour was directed against Catholic prayers and rituals. Some of the popular plays that came out of this emerging tradition of Protestant drama included *New Custom*, which features two aged Catholic priests in conflict with two young, dynamic Reformed preachers who naturally win the day, and *King Johan* (c. 1538) by John Bale, which depicts foreign Catholic powers trying to get control over England. Other plays, including *Mary Magdalene*, *Lusty Juventas* and *Nice Wanton*, add elements of dramatic tension and human complexity to the religious content.

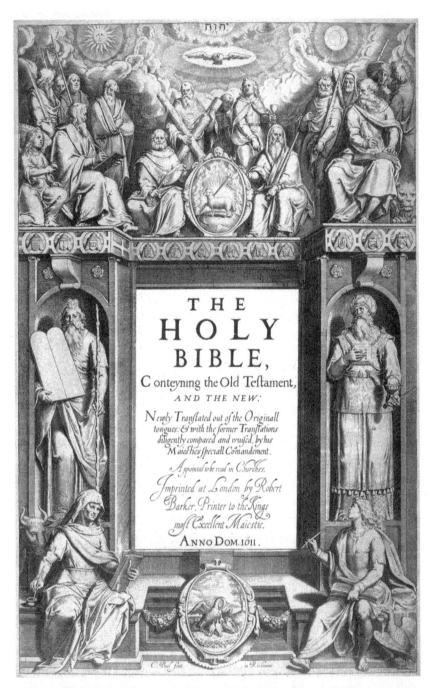

Figure 1.2 Frontispiece to the King James Bible, 1611, which shows the Twelve Apostles at the top. Moses and Aaron flank the central text. In the four corners sit Matthew, Mark, Luke and John, authors of the four gospels, with their symbolic animals. At the top, over the Holy Spirit in the form of a dove, is the Tetragrammaton 'יהוה' ('YHWH').

However, the Elizabethan era began with a royal proclamation to ban all plays that dealt with religious or contemporary political matters (a similar Act to Restrain Abuses of Players was enacted in 1606). Drama did take a secular turn after this though there are indications that the old Edwardian Protestant plays were revived in the 1570s and – going by the titles of plays enacted by the Lord Admiral's Men playing company – there were a few other new biblical plays written in the 1590s, perhaps to appeal to the moderately devout members of the audience. Only two texts of biblical plays performed for the Elizabethan public theatre survive – they are *A Looking Glass for London* (1594) by Thomas Lodge and Robert Greene and *David and Bethsabe* (1599) by George Peele. They both steer away from representing God on stage and the latter reads almost like a history play.

We will read more about hostility to the theatre in Chapter Five. For now it will suffice to point out that Puritans were among the most vocal in their expression of anti-theatre sentiment. Philip Stubbes's *The Anatomie of Abuses* (1583), William Prynne's *Histrio-mastix* (1633) and other Puritan writings accused plays of drawing people away from church and of being 'bawdy', 'wanton', 'scurrilous' and generally immoral and corrupting. The stage was a visual medium and so associated with Catholic idolatry. According to Prynne, the theatre offered a particularly sensual experience as 'the lively action of players' makes them 'pierce into the spectators' eyes, ears, and lewd affections'.[47] Acting was also equated with lying and hypocrisy. Because they took on a variety of personas and roles, actors were accused of being constantly deceptive. Due to the Puritan hostility to entertainment in general and to theatre in particular, the term 'puritan' was nearly always an unflattering one in plays. The priggish and pompous Malvolio of Shakespeare's *Twelfth Night* (1602) is described as a 'puritan' and Jonson satirizes Puritans through Tribulation Wholesome in *The Alchemist* (1610) and Zeal-of-the-Land Busy in *Bartholomew Fair* (1614). Puritans were also mocked by Thomas Nashe and John Lyly in plays debunking the Puritan tracts known as Martin Marprelate pamphlets (1589–90) that attacked the Anglican church.

Anti-theatrical rhetoric must have kept a few puritanical individuals away from the theatre, but the professional drama still flourished. It was very different from the religious theatre of the Middle Ages or the early Reformation years, but it was not 'secular' in the modern sense. Instead religion pervaded the stage in more ways than one. Thomas Dekker's *The Whore of Babylon* (1607) and Thomas Middleton's *A Game of Chess* (1624) are obviously anti-Catholic. Shakespeare's *King John* (c. 1595) is perhaps more moderate in its anti-Catholicism but depicts the clergy and the English king in conflict. At one level Marlowe's *Doctor Faustus* (performed *c.* 1594) follows the structure of a morality play and even represents Faustus as a Protestant hero who boxes the Pope's ear in one farcical scene. Even plays with more worldly concerns were influenced by religion. Biblical allusions were used for ornamentation and general moralism, and the solemn, graceful language of the Bible was 'a rich and infinitely varied source of imaginative and formal inspiration'.[48] Many playgoers most likely understood the religious allusions and consequently were able to see plays in a new, more profound light. Stage props with religious associations added to the visual interest and Philip Henslowe's inventory of props belonging to his company include a 'hells mouth', an 'altar' and a 'pope's mitre'.[49] In fact, the hat of Cardinal Wolsey, the English Catholic cardinal in the years preceding the Reformation, might have eventually fallen into the hands of a playing company and become a stage prop![50] Actors and playwrights also defended their pursuit on moral grounds. For example, Thomas Heywood, in his *An Apology for Actors* (1612), wrote that plays could reform even hardened sinners by revealing 'unto them the monstrousness of their sin' and providing models of exemplary moral behaviour.[51]

Christian themes also made their way into the plays. God or 'Providence', rather than a blind fate, determined the course of human events. The Protestant preoccupation with sinfulness, divine punishment and repentance recurred. Bosola in *The Duchess of Malfi* wrestles with 'a guilty conscience', which 'is a black register, wherein is writ / All our good deeds and bad' (4.2.342–43)[52] and *A Woman Killed With Kindness* (1603) by Thomas Heywood depicts a penitent adulteress intensely soul-searching and is very much in the didactic and homiletic tradition.[53] The stage was filled with characters praying, contemplating the meaning of virtue, vice, life and death. As William Hamlin puts it, Renaissance drama contains 'the most searching moral philosophy of the age'.[54] The disruption and uncertainty caused by the Reformation raised questions regarding good and evil and the meaning of human life and history, all of which were subjects of stage tragedy. Protestantism also encouraged intense self-scrutiny and one was encouraged to constantly examine oneself and one's mind and soul – this surely influenced the sometimes obsessive introspection that is so characteristic of tragic heroes. What David Kastan writes of Shakespeare probably applies to many of the playwright's contemporaries too: 'Religion is central to the plays, but Shakespeare is not a religious playwright'.[55] Besides, the best works were characterized by doubt, conflict and scepticism rather than by clear-cut religious messages. In Jonson's *Sejanus* and in Thomas Middleton's *A Game of Chess*, religion is used by those in power to further their own ends, and Barabas in Marlowe's *The Jew of Malta* (*c.* 1589–90) states quite forthrightly that religion is 'but a childish toy' (Prologue, 14).[56] Marlowe was actually accused of being atheist, though 'atheism' in the period did not necessarily mean godlessness as such but could simply imply heterodoxy, or deviation from or challenging the accepted order, a trait seen in all of Marlowe's heroes. So drama could support the new religion but also more subtly subvert, or at least call into question, all religion. In any case, the Protestant Reformation was an important influence on drama. Religion was a personal experience, a social phenomenon and a political issue. The religious experience was accompanied by joy and tranquillity and also by doubt, anxiety and terror. It had tremendous dramatic potential and it is no small wonder that the stage was inspired by it.

The nation

The nation is not only a political unit but also a community with a sense of its distinctive identity. This does not imply that the people of a nation are alike or homogenous. What it means is that there is a sense of a shared 'national' identity and culture in spite of internal diversity and differences. The modern political philosopher Benedict Anderson has described the nation as an 'imagined' community – imagined because we will never see or never know all members but still feel a sense of affiliation with them.[57] Many historians locate the beginnings of nationalism in the Renaissance, and some of them specifically in Renaissance England. In fact, Leah Greenfeld goes so far as to say that 'The original modern idea of the nation emerged in sixteenth-century England, which was the first nation in the world.'[58] It is true that the term 'nation' was rarely used in the modern sense during the Renaissance. Instead, in the case of England, the terms evoked were 'realm', body politic', 'state', or 'commonwealth'. But patriotism was gradually replacing other kinds of loyalty and we can talk of an emerging English national consciousness. The Tudor nation was neither homogenous nor democratic, but it was still characterized by a new kind awareness of itself as a community of many participants who had a sense of pride in their English identity, a pride reflected in the English Bishop John Aylmer's 1558 statement that 'God is English.'

In 1534 Henry VIII declared that 'this realm of England is an empire . . . without restraint or provocation to any foreign princes or potentates of the world'.[59] The word 'empire' implied that England was now an independent and separate unit with its own identity. The Reformation thus initiated the rise of English nationalism. Eventually, the Act of Uniformity, which gave people a homogenous form of worship, offered all citizens a common cultural experience. The nation was perceived as a godly Protestant community and religious and national identity began to be seen as interconnected. Hooker wrote that 'there is not any man in the Church of England but the same man is also a member of the commonwealth; nor any man a member of the commonwealth which is also not of the Church of England'.[60] The conflict with Catholic Spain also intensified nationalism and books such as Foxe's *Acts and Monuments* helped create the sense of a national community born out of a struggle between the forces of good and evil, the true and the false church. The scholar William Haller has argued that Foxe projected the English as God's chosen people and England as an 'elect nation'.[61] This has been complicated by later scholars who argue that, for Foxe, England was still part of a larger international Protestant community. But whatever the case, Foxe did depict England as a Protestant nation with a unique destiny.

There were other factors that facilitated the rise of national feeling. England was less politically divided than other European countries and all its inhabitants shared a common language. The centralized government with a fixed capital, London, was a force of national integration. There were more points of contact between the central authority and local communities through common systems of taxation and law. The common law was a particularly 'important socializing force inculcating both law-abiding behaviour and a sense of national identity'.[62] Edmund Dudley, advisor to Henry VII, wrote in his treatise *The Tree of Commonwealth* (c. 1509) that 'The commonwealth of this realm or the subjects or inhabitants thereof may be resembled to a fair and mighty tree growing in a field or pasture, under the covert or shade whereof all beasts, both fat and lean are protected and comforted from heat and cold as the time requireth.' Dudley's metaphor of the commonwealth as a protective tree implies that justice, equality and peace were promised and provided to all inhabitants of the nation.[63]

No discussion of English national identity in the Renaissance can ignore the question of British identity. James I dreamt of England and Scotland united as 'one commonwealth ... in lovely and perpetual peace' and pushed his agenda in Parliament.[64] Even before James's political plans, William Camden had written *Britannia* (1586), a massive work that described the geography and history of both England and Ireland. Camden said that his wish was 'to restore antiquity to Britain and Britain to antiquity' and so to give 'Britain' a sense of collective history and identity. John Speed's 1611 collection of maps of England, Scotland, Wales and Ireland was titled *Theatre of the Empire of Great Britain* and was the product of James's wish for a united Great Britain. However, in spite of these constructions of Britain, Parliament rejected the union of England and Scotland, and Britain as a political unit was not to materialize until a much later date. The opening act of Shakespeare's play *Henry V* (1599) mentions the Scots as enemies who might raid England, but eventually the most loyal of soldiers in the 'English' army are a Scotsman, an Irishman and a Welshman. The play can be read as projecting a united kingdom of four countries though it is also possible to see Irish, Scottish and Welsh identities subsumed or taken over by English identity. In any case, as David Baker writes, *Henry V* is a play 'set between nations'.[65] In general, it is important to see English nationalism in the Renaissance in relation to Scottish, Irish and Welsh identities.

English nationalism was complicated in other ways. As we have seen, Puritanism created sharp divides in English society. Besides, for all the patriotism and the fear and dislike of foreigners, it was feared that the English had no distinct identity and were imitative of other cultures (the scholar Roger Ascham in his 1570 work *The Scholemaster* famously complained that Englishmen travelling to Italy were taking on Italian fashion and manners). Nationalism was a sentiment probably experienced more by the upper classes and the urban middle class. The idea of nationhood permeated the rural areas and the poorer sections of the population much more slowly.

Modern scholars agree that no nation, including England, was simply 'discovered' by its people; instead, a sense of shared national identity was gradually created.[66] Books played a special role in this. Renaissance historians Edward Hall (*The Union of the Two Noble Families of Lancaster and York*, 1548) and Ralph Holinshed (*Chronicles of England, Scotland and Ireland*, 1577) stressed a shared past, and social commentators like William Harrison (*The Description of England*, 1577) emphasized a sense of an English society with certain defining features. Chorographers or map-makers gave people an idea of the nation as a territorial unit with defined boundaries.[67] Writers such as Richard Hakluyt who compiled accounts of English travels abroad helped define the nation in competition with and contrast to foreign nations. In fact, voyages to distant lands were projected by Hakluyt, writing in 1582, as a patriotic enterprise 'to advance the honour of our country'.[68] Travel writing helped shape the idea of 'racial' and 'cultural' difference and England was placed in the context of a global system. All these books and institutions led to a gradual but fairly clear shift towards national consciousness.

English writers were also acutely aware of the great literary traditions of ancient Greece and Rome and those of contemporary Italy, France and Spain, and strove to develop their own. There was increasing emphasis on an English literary past with the medieval poets Geoffrey Chaucer and John Gower described as the first English poets. Renaissance writers like Edmund Spenser consequently saw themselves as continuing a great tradition. The popular drama, on the other hand, had no such clear agenda but still contributed to the new discourse of nationalism. Heywood, in his *Apology*, evoked the language of patriotism to respond to those hostile to theatre. Theatre, Heywood wrote, enhanced the status and glory of any nation. So, for instance, the ancient Romans, 'in the noon-tide of their glory, and height of all their honour, they edified their Theatres, and Amphi-theatres: for in their flourishing commonweal, their public Comedians and Tragedians most flourished'.[69] Heywood implied that England should follow the Roman example. The mixed audience made up of various social classes and the blend of native English influences with classical ones also made the vibrant popular theatre of the day – in the words of Walter Cohen – 'the drama of a nation' in more ways than one.[70] In fact, Robert Weimann has argued that the unique social milieu of the theatre where the lowborn clowning actor communicated with the aristocratic spectator has its origins in rituals of a past era when society was less divided and held the promise of a future era in which the national community was conceived in terms of equality.[71]

History plays were set in the English past and narrated the stories of English kings and their deeds. They too created the sense of a shared past marked by great men and heroic feats. Heywood emphasized the patriotic and inspirational function of these plays: 'To turn to our domestic histories, what English blood seeing the person of any bold Englishman presented and doth not hug his fame and honey at his valor … what coward to see his countryman valiant would not be ashamed of his own cowardice?'[72] The character John of Gaunt in Shakespeare's *Richard II* (1595) famously celebrates England as 'this scept'red isle' and 'This precious stone set in the silver sea' (2.1.40, 46) and *Henry V* mentions the word 'England' and 'English' more than a hundred times.[73] Several comedies also built on nationalistic sentiments. Bess Bridges of Heywood's *The Fair Maid of the West* (Part 1, 1597–1603, Part 2 *c.* 1627) is a brave young woman (clearly meant to be reminiscent of Queen Elizabeth) who unites men of different classes into one community, sets out to fight the rapacious Spanish and take on the lustful Moors. English virtue is clearly set up in contrast to foreign vice in this play. In Robert Greene's *Friar Bacon and Friar Bungay* (*c.* 1589), England becomes a utopic space where beautiful English milkmaids marry aristocrats and humble scholars reaffirm English prestige through their learned pursuits. So Bacon, an English magician, promises to build a wall of brass around England to ensure that foreigners 'shall not touch a grass of English ground' (2.61).[74]

However, this patriotic flavour does not mean that history plays did not display any awareness of the complexities of nationhood. As discussed earlier, kings were not always heroic in these plays and the national past was not always glorious but marked by error and wrongdoing. Plays also asked subtle questions about the nation: is it simply identified with the king? How inclusive is it? 'What ish my nation?', asks MacMorris in *Henry V* (3.2.124), a question that had no clear answer. It is, of course, debatable as to whether all members of the audience picked up on the complexities of the historical narratives. They might well have overlooked the plays' conflicts and more subtle messages and simply responded with patriotic pride. In fact, history plays, specifically those by Shakespeare, continue to be read as expressions of English patriotism.

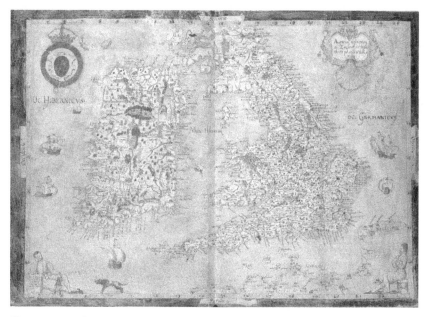

Figure 1.3 'General Description of England and Ireland' by Laurence Nowell, *c.* 1564 (© The British Library Board).

Social rank

Social rank and status was an important issue in the context of Renaissance England's emerging national consciousness. While the more modern word 'class' did not exist in the period and some historians would argue that one cannot talk of class in an era before capitalism, people were still organized into 'estates', 'ranks' and 'orders' and there was certainly an awareness of and occasionally resentment at inequality.

Even as the various sections of society were seen as mutually interdependent, it was clearly not a relationship of equals. Instead, society was organized hierarchically, and this hierarchy was viewed as a feature of the cosmos and nature and as divinely ordained. Consequently, revolting against the order was seen as challenging God. The almost obsessive emphasis on social order and rank implies that there was tremendous fear that it would break down. As D.E. Underdown writes, 'fears of an impending breakdown of the social order have been common in many periods of history' but never 'were they more widespread, or more intense, than in early modern England'.[75] Much energy was thus expended in reinforcing order through education, sermons and laws.

From 'A Homily on Disobedience and Wilful Rebellion' (1571).

The Book of Homilies is a two-volume collection of sermons issued in several editions (1547, 1563, 1571). The sermons were written by Protestant bishops and scholars and distributed throughout the country to be delivered by local preachers. 'A Homily on Disobedience and Wilful Rebellion' delivers an important message on the evils of political disobedience. It is an example of the government using the church to spread political messages.

As God the Creator and Lord of all things appointed his angels and heavenly creatures in all obedience to serve and to honour his Majesty: so was it his will that man, his chief creature upon the earth, should live under the obedience of him his Creator and Lord: and for that cause GOD, as soon as he had created man, gave unto him a certain precept and law, which he (being yet in the state of innocency and remaining in Paradise) should observe as a pledge and token of his due and bounden[76] obedience, with denunciation[77] of death if he did transgress and break the said law and commandment. And as God would have man to be his obedient subject, so did he make all earthly creatures subject unto man, who kept their due obedience unto man, so long as man remained in his obedience unto God: in the which obedience if man had continued still, there had been no poverty, no diseases, no sickness, no death, nor other miseries, wherewith mankind is now infinitely and most miserably afflicted and oppressed. So here appeareth the original kingdom of GOD over Angels and man, and universally over all things, and of man over earthly creatures, which GOD had made subject unto him, and with all the felicity[78] and blessed state which Angels, man, and all creatures had remained in, had they continued in due obedience unto GOD their King. For as long as in this first kingdom the subjects continued in due obedience to God their King, so long did God embrace all his subjects with his love, favour, and grace, which to enjoy is perfect felicity. Whereby it is evident that obedience is the principal virtue of all virtues, and indeed the very root of all virtues, and the cause of all felicity.

. . .

And, as God himself, being of an infinite Majesty, power, and wisdom, ruleth and governeth all things in heaven and in earth, as the universal Monarch: and only King and Emperor over all, as being only able to take and bear the charge of all: so hath he constituted, ordained,[79] and set earthly princes over particular Kingdoms and Dominions[80] in earth, both for the avoiding of all confusion, which else would be in the world, if it should be without such governors, and for the great quiet and benefit of earthly men their subjects, and also that the Princes themselves, in authority, power, wisdom, providence,[81] and righteousness in government of people and countries committed to their charge, should resemble his heavenly governance, as the majesty of heavenly things may by the baseness of earthly things be shadowed and resembled.

. . .

What shall subjects do then? Shall they obey valiant, stout, wise, and good princes, and contemn, disobey, and rebel against children being their princes, or against undiscreet[82] and evil governors? God forbid: For first what a perilous thing were it to commit unto the Subjects the judgment, which Prince is wise and godly and his government good, and which is otherwise: as though the foot must judge the head: an enterprise very heinous, and must needs breed rebellion. For who else be they that are most inclined to rebellion, but such haughty spirits? From whom springeth such foul ruin of Realms? Is not rebellion the greatest of all mischiefs? And who are most ready to the greatest mischiefs, but the worst men? Rebels therefore, the worst of all subjects, are most ready to rebellion, as being the worst of all vices, and furthest from the duty of a good Subject; as, on the contrary part the best subjects are most firm and constant in obedience, as in the special and peculiar virtue of good Subjects. What an unworthy matter were it then to make the naughtiest[83] Subjects, and most inclined to rebellion and all evil, judges over their Princes, over their government, and over their counsellors, to determine which of them be good or tolerable, and which be evil, and so intolerable, that they must needs be removed by rebels; being ever ready as the naughtiest subjects, soonest to rebel against the best Princes, specially if they be young in age, women in sex, or gentle and courteous in government, as trusting by their wicked boldness easily to overthrow their weakness and gentleness, or at the least so to fear the minds of such Princes, that they may have impunity[84] of their mischievous doings.

But whereas indeed a rebel is worse than the worst prince, and rebellion worse than the worst government of the worst prince, that hitherto hath been: both rebels are unmeet[85] ministers, and rebellion an unfit and unwholesome medicine, to reform any small lacks in a prince, or to cure any little griefs in government, such lewd[86] remedies being far worse than any other maladies and disorders that can be in the body of a commonwealth.

Some historians maintain that the Elizabethan era was actually characterized by increased social polarization, i.e. the gap between the rich and the poor grew wider. While this might have been the case, social mobility or the ability to move up the status and wealth ladder was greater than ever before though perhaps still limited from our modern perspective. Merchants became very wealthy; farmers who managed to acquire respectable amounts of land called themselves 'gentlemen'; the new humanist education, described in Chapter Four, brought many men into professions like law and medicine and gave them some claim to 'gentility'. Harrison wrote that whoever is educated, 'can live without manual labour, and thereto is able and will bear the port, charge, and countenance of a gentleman, he shall for money have a coat and arms bestowed upon him by heralds ... be called "master", which is the title that men give to esquires and gentlemen, and be reputed a gentleman ever after.[87]

Harrison has described the four social 'estates' in some detail. The first consisted of 'gentlemen' or the royalty and noblemen, the second, of 'citizens' or wealthy city merchants, the third, of 'yeomen' or farmers owning their own land and the fourth, of 'artificers' or landless labourers, artisans and manual workers. The aristocracy felt itself as not only superior to other classes but also as distinct from them both in blood and manners. Many aristocrats were also better educated than in the past. They were not just 'knights' carrying arms but 'courtiers' who could conduct themselves gracefully, display good taste and who could claim to be intellectually accomplished. While most of the nobility lived off their estates, many of them took on important positions in the government, were important players in politics and even invested in and profited from the new joint-stock companies.

Merchants and traders who had become rich through trade and enterprise were the new non-landed elites. They were shrewd, diligent and thrifty and increasingly competed with the gentry for power and money. Within the boundaries of London, the mercantile class enjoyed unprecedented power and privilege. Playwrights realized that the lives of this dynamic new class held plenty of potential for dramatic narrative. The new genre of 'city comedy' emerged from this.

From William Harrison, *The Description of England* (1577). (Courtesy of The Folger Shakespeare Library and Dover Publications)

***The Description of England* (1577) by William Harrison is a commentary of Elizabethan English society. Harrison drew his description from books and other documents as well as from his own observations. The following extract is from the chapter titled 'Of Degrees of People in the Commonwealth of England' and describes the merchant class, the yeomen and the labouring class.**

Citizens and burgesses[88] have next place to gentleman, who be those that are free within the cities and are of some likely substance to bear office in the same. But these citizens or burgesses are to serve the commonwealth in their cities and boroughs, or in corporate towns where they dwell. And in the common assembly of the realm, wherein our laws are made (for in the counties they bear but little sway), which assembly is called the High Court of Parliament, the ancient cities appoint four and the boroughs two burgesses to have voices in it give their consent or dissent unto such things as pass or stay there, in the name of the city or borough for which they are appointed.

In this place also are our merchants to be installed, as amongst the citizens (although they often change estate with gentlemen, as gentlemen do with them, by a mutual conversion of the one into the other), whose number is so increased in these our days that their only maintenance is the cause of the exceeding prices of foreign wares, which otherwise, when every nation was permitted to bring in her own commodities, were far better cheap and more plentifully to be had. . . . The wares that they carry out of the realm are for the most part broadcloths and kerseys[89] of all colors, likewise cottons, friezes,[90] rugs, tin, wool, our best beer, baize,[91] bustian,[92] mockadoes tufted and plain,[93] rash,[94] lead, fells,[95] etc., which, being shipped at sundry ports of our coasts, are borne from thence into all quarters of the world and there either exchanged for other wares or ready money, to the great gain and commodity of our merchants. And whereas in times past their chief trade was into Spain, Portingale [Portugal], France, Flanders, Dansk [Denmark], Norway, Scotland, and Iceland only, now in these days, as men not contended with these journeys, they have sought out the East and West Indies and made now and then suspicious [promising] voyages, not only unto the Canaries and New Spain, but likewise into Cathay,[96] Moscovia,[97] Tartary,[98] and the regions thereabout, from whence (as they say) they bring home great commodities. But alas! I see not by all their travel that the prices of things are any whit abated. . . . This only I know, that every function and several vocation striveth with other which of them should have all the water of commodity run into their own cistern.

Yeomen are those which by our law are called *legales homines*, freemen born English, and may dispend of their own free land in yearly revenue to the sum of 40s. sterling, or £6 as money goeth in our times. Some are of the opinion, by *cap. 2*, Rich. II, *an.* 20, that they are the same which the Frenchman call varlets, but, as that phrase is used in my time, it is far unlikely to be so. The truth is that the word is derived from the Saxon term . . . *geoman*, which signifieth (as I have read) a settled or staid man, such I mean as, being married and of some years, betaketh himself to stay in the place of his abode for the better maintenance of himself and his family, whereof the single sort have no regard but are likely to be still fleeting, now hither, now thither, which argueth want of stability in determination and resolution of judgment for the execution of things of any importance. This sort of people have a certain pre-eminance and more estimation than labourers and the common sort of artificers, and these commonly live wealthily, keep good houses, and travail to get riches. They are also for the most part farmers to gentlemen ... or at the leastwise artificers[99]; and with grazing, frequenting of markets, and keeping of servants (not idle servants as the gentlemen do, but such as get both their own and part of their master's living) do come to great wealth, insomuch that many of them are able and do buy the lands of unthrifty gentlemen, and often, setting their sons to the schools, to the universities, and to the Inns of the Court, or otherwise leaving them sufficient lands whereupon they may live without labour, do make them by those means to become gentlemen; these were they that in times past made all France afraid. And albeit they be not called master as gentlemen are, or sir, as to knights appertaineth,[100] but only John and Thomas, etc., yet have they been found to have done very good service; and the Kings of England in foughten[101] battles were wont to[102] remain among them (who were their footmen) as the French kings did amongst their horsemen, the prince thereby showing where his chief strength did consist.

The fourth and last sort of people in England are day labourers, poor husbandmen,[103] and some retailers (which have no free land), copyholders,[104] and all artificers, as tailors, shoemakers, carpenters, brickmakers, masons, etc. As for slaves and bondmen, we have none; nay, such is the privilege of our country by the especial grace of God and bounty of our princes that if any come hither from other realms, so soon as they set foot on land they become so free of condition as their masters, whereby all note of servile bondage is utterly removed from them, wherein we resemble (not the Germans, who had slaves also, though such as in respect of the slaves of other countries might well be reputed free, but) the old Indians and the Taprobaens [Ceylonese], who supposed it a great injury to Nature to make or suffer them to be bond whom she in her wanted course doth product and bring forth free. This fourth and last sort of people, therefore, have neither voice nor authority in the commonwealth, but are to be ruled and not to rule other; yet they are not altogether neglected, for in cities and corporate towns, for default of yeomen, they are fain to[105] make up their inquests[106] of such manner of people. And in villages they are commonly made churchwardens, sidemen,[107] aleconners,[108] now and then constables, and many times enjoy the name of headboroughs.[109]

In rural areas yeomen were prosperous farmers who cultivated their own land. The yeoman became an almost mythical figure – hearty, honest and generous – representing the best of all that was English. Harrison even contrasted yeomen favourably to profligate gentlemen. In addition to the prosperous yeomen were the wage labourers, artisans, craftsmen, servants and landless labourers, both men and women, who constituted the vast majority of the population. They engaged in physical labour and such work in the period was 'tough, monotonous, dirty, at times brutalizing, and affected by the whims of the weather.'[110] Wages were low and the danger of unemployment always loomed high. In rural areas, enclosure acts that prohibited the landless from growing crops or taking their animals to graze on what were formerly common lands owned by the entire community intensified poverty. Enclosure acts led to local rioting, but there was always the fear of large-scale rebellion by the lower orders. It is true that the Elizabethan government established a system of 'Poor Relief' to help the poor, which was paid for by compulsory taxes, but rural and urban poverty led to a large class of homeless people described as 'vagrants' or 'masterless men' who roamed the countryside and who were perceived as criminals and threats to the public peace.

Overall, it was a period of transition as far as social class was concerned. There was deference to one's social superiors but also rising tension between the social groups. While some scholars argue that drama reproduced and even celebrated the prevalent social order, others claim that it challenged and critiqued it. It would be hard to resolve this particular debate. Malvolio, the ambitious steward in *Twelfth Night* who wants to marry his aristocratic mistress, is humiliated at the end of the play, but the protagonist of *Tamburlaine* is a lowborn shepherd who becomes a king. Francisco in Webster's *The White Devil* (1612) contemplates the real meaning of rank: 'What difference is between the Duke and I?', he wonders, and asserts that only 'mere chance' placed one of them in a position of privilege and power over the other (5.1.103, 106).[111] In *Philaster* (1612–13) by Francis Beaumont and John Fletcher, countrymen, citizens and nobles live together in harmony, but the anonymous plays *Woodstock* (1590s) and *The Life and Death of Jack Straw* (1587–91) and Shakespeare's *Henry VI Part 2* (1591) depict rebellion. The rebel in *Jack Straw* is simply a malicious rogue and the play clearly defends the prevailing social hierarchy. Jack Cade, the rebel in *Henry VI Part 2*, is also a cross between a clown and a trouble-maker, but the play is more complex in its depiction of class relations. The aristocrats in *Henry VI Part 2* are also corrupt and ineffective leaders who actually provoke the poor in order to serve their own political ends.

Actors themselves occupied an interesting class position. Originally branded as 'vagabonds', some actors, including Richard Burbage, Edward Alleyn and Shakespeare, made enough money to attain respectability. Consequently, players became a symbol of the new social mobility, something that anti-theatrical writers found particularly troubling. Actors 'desire to walk gentleman-like in satin and velvet,' complained Stephen Gosson, and 'proportion is so broken, unity dissolved, harmony confounded'.[112] The fact that even lowly actors could play kings and noblemen was even more troubling. Drama had the potential to reveal rank and social difference to be a construction, simply a matter of good play-acting.

Discussion points

1 As discussed in the section on 'Kingship', royal power was constructed through performance. The portraits of Queen Elizabeth are good examples of a monarch deliberately fashioning her image for the public. You can look at these portraits on these websites:
    http://www.npg.org.uk/collections/search/person/mp01452/queen-elizabeth-i
    http://www.luminarium.org/renlit/elizface.htm
    http://www.marileecody.com/eliz1-images.html
    Pay attention to the queen's costume, stance and the backdrop, gather what information you can about the paintings and consider what image/idea of the monarch the visual is trying to represent.

2 A 'presentist' scholar would argue that our understanding of the past is conditioned by the culture and ideologies of the present. Think about how your understanding and reception of the social and political

issues around religion discussed in this chapter and in any of the plays you are reading are shaped by your understanding of the social and political issues around religion and religious identity in our present-day world.

3 Consider the excerpt from Harrison's *The Description of England*. Examined in the context of the information provided in the section on 'Social Rank', how does Harrison's text help the modern reader:

    i. to better understand social rank – how it was constructed in Renaissance plays and how it is constructed today?

    ii. to better understand Renaissance drama (select any play that you are studying that draws attention to issues of rank and status)?

4 Carefully read the excerpt from the 'Homily on Disobedience' reproduced in this chapter. Consider any play that you are studying that seems to deal with issues of authority (What is rightful authority? How does one establish it? Can one challenge it?) and read the play and the historical document in relation to each other. Does the play reinforce and reproduce what the sermon states? On the other hand, does the literary text deal with issues of power and authority quite differently from the sermon?

2

Men and Women

The nineteenth-century historian Jacob Burckhardt's assertion that Renaissance 'women stood on a footing of perfect equality with men' has been met with some incredulity by most modern scholars.[1] Joan Kelly, for instance, would argue that women of the time period did not experience a 'Renaissance' at all: new restraints were in fact imposed on women and the relations of the sexes was restructured to one of male authority and female submission.[2] In any case, what is quite clear is that the 'Renaissance' experienced by women was certainly quite different from that experienced by men and any attempt to understand gender relations and gender identity in the time period must examine this difference.

The term 'crisis' is often used to describe the state of gender relations between 1560 and 1640 because of the notable increase in the number of women being prosecuted for 'disorderly' conduct. While, as Laura Gowing points out, gender is always in 'crisis' as 'gender relations are continually renegotiated around certain familiar points,'[3] the Renaissance did see an extensive discussion of gender roles. There was an outpouring of pamphlets such as Joseph Swetnam's *The Arraignment of Lewd, Idle, Forward, and Unconsistent Women* (1615) that described women as weak, lustful and vain. These attacks on women provoked responses from men and women alike that extolled women's virtues and strengths. Apart from these 'pamphlet wars', there were other writings on gender relations by way of advice manuals such as William Whately's *A Bride-bush* (1619) and William Gouge's *Of Domesticall Duties* (1622), conduct books and sermons. Interestingly, in these texts gender roles are simultaneously 'natural' and ordained by God, even as they need to be carefully and self-consciously maintained by individual effort and social regulation. It is important to remember, however, that both the pamphlets and the advice literature do not tell us about the reality of men and women's lives in the Renaissance. The former set of texts are infused with anxiety and prejudice, while the latter prescribe ideal behaviour. The reality was surely more messy, more complicated and perhaps more interesting.

What about the drama? Virginia Woolf rightly points out that women played a subservient role in real life but were hypervisible as characters on stage.[4] One certainly cannot imagine Renaissance drama without Portia or the Duchess of Malfi. While we cannot rely on the plays to give us an exact sense of gender roles in the time period, drama is important in understanding these roles, just as an understanding of gender is important to fully appreciate the dramatic literature. This is partly because it is in and through language that the genders were categorized and organized and partly because gender is a 'role' or a performance that men and women enact either consciously or unconsciously as they make their way through the world. Drama especially draws our attention to the performative nature of gender identity, further emphasized on the Renaissance stage by cross-dressed actors and characters. Some of the dramatic representations of women in particular were certainly chauvinistic and limited, while others were more nuanced. The tensions of gender relations and family life were often the focal point of plays and the best drama explored the limitations of prescribed gender roles and imagined the excitement – and the danger – of challenging them.

Sex, sexuality, marriage

Renaissance physicians were fascinated by the physiological factors that determined a person's sex. One model of sexual difference was the one-sex model proposed by the Roman physician Galen. Galen argued that there was no essential difference between men and women. Women essentially had male organs that were retained inside the body. Hence the ovaries were the woman's testicles, her uterus was a scrotum and her cervix was the penis. In certain cases excess body heat could thrust the genitals out of a female body – and the woman could become a man. Renaissance medical textbooks gravely recount such stories of sexual transformation. The French surgeon Ambrose Paré, for instance, provided an account of a girl whose inner 'testicles' protruded as a result of strenuous physical action and who consequently transformed into and stayed a man. As Stephen Orgel writes, 'for Renaissance physiology, even the distinction between the sexes could be blurred, sometimes frighteningly so'.[5]

Although the 'one-sex' model of conceptualizing gender has fascinated modern critics who study cross-dressing in the theatre, we should remember that not all Renaissance physicians subscribed to it. Another doctor, Helkiah Crooke, in his book *Microcosmographia* (1615) described the Galenic model but then posited that men and women are absolutely different anatomically speaking. This difference between men and women preoccupied these thinkers. So men's 'seed' was 'active' in the reproductive process and women's were 'passive'; men's 'humours' were better balanced, while the 'colder' 'humours' of women were associated with lack of judgement and concentration. Generally speaking, women's bodies were less 'contained' and 'leakier' than men's – constantly expelling blood, urine, milk and other fluids.[6] Plays such as Jonson's *Bartholomew Fair* and Middleton's *A Chaste Maid in Cheapside* (c. 1613) connect this 'leakiness' to women's lack of emotional and moral self-control.

In real life too gender roles were structured around the difference between the sexes rather than the similarity. This is certainly at odds with the one-sex model though, of course, one could argue that the physiological possibility of the lines between female and male getting blurred made it all the more important to insist on absolutely different socio-cultural roles. In spite of the debates and disagreements between the doctors and anatomists, when ordinary people talked about gender it was in terms of difference. Men and women had different capacities and so had quite different roles to play.

It was in the institution of marriage that gender relations and differences where most defined and it was within marriage that the problems attendant on these definitions were most intensely experienced. Protestantism defined marriage as essential to the pious life. Marriage transformed young men into husbands and householders, and girls into wives and housekeepers. It was a serious affair, not to be taken lightly. But before marriage came courtship – the theme of so many Renaissance comedies. Young people, especially of the middle and lower classes, had considerable freedom when it came to choosing their spouses. Parental consent was desirable, but the choice itself was generally free of compulsion. This lends force to Hermia's desires in Shakespeare's *A Midsummer Night's Dream* (1590–96), her father Egeus's wishes notwithstanding, and makes young Sebastian of Thomas Dekker and Thomas Middleton's *The Roaring Girl* (c. 1611), who wishes to marry his Mary in spite of his father's disapproval, a romantic hero. Even among the social elite, where marriage involved property settlements and power transactions, marriage was probably not an entirely unemotional affair. In Shakespeare's *Henry V*, the king's marriage to the French princess is certainly a political one, but the courtship is marked by flirtation and professions of 'love'. Among all social classes many marriage decisions probably balanced affection and good sense.

Courtship involved visits, letters and gift exchange, but there was no fixed script. This was what allowed dramatists to give their imaginations free rein as they depicted it as an intricate yet enchanting dance where young people discover each other and themselves. Interestingly, in the comedies women too flirt with their suitors by engaging in witty and vibrant verbal exchange. Following comedy's roots in fertility ritual, stage courtships usually culminated in betrothal and marriage. This was the case in real life too though there is evidence of many cases of broken contracts and pregnant women abandoned by lovers (there was a high rate of pre-marital sex in the time period and one out of every five brides was pregnant at the time of marriage).[7] By law girls could be legally married at twelve and boys at fourteen, but among most non-aristocrats the average age of marriage was the mid-twenties.

Marriage licensed sexual activity and was for procreation, but it was also for companionship and friendship. It was during the Reformation that this model of 'companionate' marriage came into play. The emotional bond between husband and wife was important and to be celebrated, in contrast to the Catholic ideal of celibacy and chastity which considered marriage between a man and a woman as a necessary evil. In spite of this shift, the idea of companionship between husband and wife never fully replaced the hierarchical model in which the husband was the authority and superior. In fact, the Reformation actually strengthened traditional patriarchal authority. Both the church and the state reinforced the idea of the husband as 'the family despot, benevolent or malign according to temperament and inclination, lording it over his wife and children'.[8] The family was itself a metaphor for the state and familial and socio-political order served as models for each other. As Gouge stated, 'A family ... is a little Commonwealth ... a school wherein the first principles of government and subjection are learned'.[9] It is important to recognize that although this model of the man as authoritarian patriarch as well as cherishing husband and father might seem contradictory to modern readers, it was probably not seen as such in the time period. In fact, the wife's subjection was actually seen as necessary for her welfare. As Whately advised the young bride: 'If ever thou purpose to be a good wife, and to live comfortably, set down this with thyself, mine husband is my superior, my better; he hath authority and rule over me; nature hath given it to him.'[10] The wife was the 'weaker vessel', physically, emotionally and intellectually, and she needed the husband's guidance as well as his control. Thus in a play like Shakespeare's *The Taming of the Shrew* (1590–92) Petruchio claims to love Katherine even as he tames her so that she becomes a happy, respected wife. Upon marriage a woman legally became a 'femme covert', i.e. her legal entity was subsumed under that of her husband. By the law of coverture, a husband had full rights over his wife's property after marriage. As the author of *The Law's Resolution for Women's Rights* put it, 'If anything when he is married be given him, he taketh it by himself, distinctly to himself.' Besides, marital violence was commonplace, with wife-beating considered 'lawful and reasonable correction' by the husband,[11] even as preachers called on husbands to rule by reasoning rather than by violence. Many women did go to court with complaints, but they had to prove that the violence was longstanding and had put them in mortal danger.

The tension between the companionate and authoritarian models of marriage doubtless posed a challenge for many couples. In many cases it led to open conflict. Divorce in the modern sense was not recognized. The courts could grant 'separation from bed and board' on certain grounds, but this was not viewed with approval and remarriage was generally not possible. Stage tragedies recognized marriage and the domestic realm as spaces where high tragic drama could be enacted. Happy marriages did doubtless exist in real life, but they did not provide fodder for the tragedians. Intense marital conflict and the destructive emotions of doubt, jealousy and discord made for better ingredients for tragic drama

The remarrying widow is something of the comic stereotype in plays such as *Ralph Roister Doister* (c. 1553) and Philip Massinger's *A New Way to Pay Old Debts* (1625). Later conduct books perceived the remarrying widow as a threat to female decorum and chastity – an idea reflected in *The Duchess of Malfi* in which the widowed Duchess's brothers object to her remarrying. There were also single women, some of whom never married. Indeed, nearly all heroines of comedies are single women at first. But they usually marry by the play's end, perhaps not unexpectedly in the context of a society where, according to *The Law's Resolution* ..., 'all women are understood either married or to be married; and their desires are subject to their husbands ...'.[12]

From 'A Homily on the State of Matrimony' (1563).

'A Homily on Matrimony' is one of the sermons in the two-volume collection of sermons in the *Book of Homilies* issued in several editions (1547, 1563, 1571) by Queen Elizabeth's government. The homily urges the importance of marriage, acknowledges the challenges a couple can face, lays out the prescribed roles of husband and wife and takes up the issue of domestic violence.

The word of almighty GOD doth testify and declare, whence the original beginning of matrimony cometh, and why it is ordained. It is instituted of GOD to the intent that man and woman should live lawfully in a perpetual friendly fellowship, to bring forth fruit, and to avoid fornication.[13] By which means a good conscience might be preserved on both parties, in bridling[14] the corrupt inclinations of the flesh, within the limits of honesty. For GOD hath straightly forbidden all whoredom and uncleanness, and hath from time to time taken grievous punishments of this inordinate[15] lust, as all stories and ages hath declared. Furthermore, it is also ordained, that the Church of GOD and his kingdom might by this kind of life be conserved and enlarged, not only in that God giveth children by his blessing, but also in that they be brought up by the parents godly in the knowledge of GOD'S word, that thus, the knowledge of GOD and true religion, might be delivered by succession from one to another, that finally many might enjoy that everlasting immortality.

. . .

Learn thou therefore, if thou desirest to be void of all these miseries, if thou desirest to live peaceably and comfortably in wedlock, how to make thy earnest prayer to GOD, that he would govern both your heartes by the holy Spirit, to restrain the Devil's power, whereby your concord may remaine perpetually. But to this prayer must be joined a singular diligence, whereof St. Peter giveth his precept, saying. 'you husbands deal with your wives according to knowledge, giving honour to the wife, as unto the weaker vessel, and as unto them that their heirs also of the grace of life that your prayers be not hindered.' This precept doth particularly pertain to the husband: for he ought to be the leader and author of love, in cherishing and increasing concord,[16] which then shall take place if he will use moderation and not tyranny, and if he yield some things to the woman. For the woman is a weak creature, not endued[17] with like strength and constancy of mind, therefore they be the sooner disquieted,[18] and they be the more prone to all weak affections and dispositions of mind more than men be, and lighter they be, and more vain in their fantasies and opinions. These things must be considered of the man, he be not too stiff,[19] so that he ought to wink at some things,[20] and must gently expound[21] all things, and to forbear. Howbeit the common sort of men doeth judge, that's such moderation should not become a man: for they say that it is a token of womanish cowardness,[22] and therefore they think that it is a man's part to fume in anger, to fight with fist and staff. Howbeit, howsoever they imagine, undoubtedly Saint Peter doth better judge what should be seeming to a man, and what he should most reasonably perform. For he saith, reasoning should be used, and not fighting.

. . .

Now as concerning the wife's duty. What shall become her? Shall she abuse the gentleness and humanity of her husband and, at her pleasure, turn all things upside down? No surely, for that is far repugnant against GOD's commandment. For thus doth St. Peter preach to them, 'You wives, be you in subjection to obey your own husband.' To obey, is another thing to control or command, which yet they may do, to their children and to their family: But as for their husbands, them must they obey, and cease from commanding, and perform subjection. For this surely doth nourish concord very much, when the wife is ready at hand at her husband's commandment, when she will apply herself to his will, when she endevoreth herself to seek his contentation[23] and to do him pleasure, when she will eschew[24] all things that might offend him: For thus will most truly be verified the saying of the Poet. 'A good wife, by obeying her husband, shall bear the rule,' so that he shall have a delight and a gladness the sooner at all times to return home to her. But on the contrary part, when the wives be stubborn, froward[25] and malapert,[26] their husbands are compelled thereby to abhor and flee from their own houses, even as they should have battle with their enemies.

Howbeit, it can scantly[27] be, but that some offense shall sometime chance betwixt them: For no man doth live without fault, specially for that the woman is the more frail part. Therefore let them beware that they stand not in their faults and willfulness: but rather let them acknowledge their follies, and say: 'My husband, so it is that by my anger I was compelled to do this or that forgive it me, and hereafter I will take better heed.' Thus ought women the more readily to do, the more they be ready to offend. And they shall not do this only to avoid strife and debate: but rather in the respect of the commandment of GOD as Saint Paul expresseth it in this form of words, 'Let women be subject to their husbands, as to the Lord; for the husband is the head of the woman, as Christ is the head of the Church.'

. . .

Let not therefore the woman be too busy to call for the duty of her husband, where she should be ready to perform her own, for that is not worthy any great commendation.[28] And even so again let not the man only consider what [be] longeth to the woman, and to stand so earnestly gazing thereon, for that is not his part or duty. But as I have said, let either parties be ready and willing to perform that which belongeth especially to themselves. For, if we be bound to hold out our left cheek to strangers which will smite[29] us on the right cheek, how much more ought we to suffer an extreme and unkind husband?

But yet I mean not that a man should beat his wife. GOD forbid that, for that is the greatest shame that can be, not so much to her that is beaten, as to him that doth the deed. But, if by such fortune thou chancest upon such an husband, take it not too heavily, but suppose thou, that thereby is laid up no small reward hereafter and in this lifetime no small commendation to thee if thou canst be quiet. But yet to you that be men, thus I speak, Let there be none so grievous fault to compel you to beat your wives. But what, say I, your wives? No, it is not to be borne with, that an honest man should lay hands on his maidservant to beat her. Wherefore if it be a great shame for a man to beat his bondservant, much more rebuke it is to lay violent hands upon his free woman. And this thing may we well understand by the laws which the paynims[30] have made, which doth discharge her any longer to dwell with such an husband, as unworthy to have any further company with her that doth smite her. For it is an extreme point, thus so vilely to entreat[31] her like a slave that is fellow to thee of thy life and so enjoined unto thee beforetime[32] in the necessary matters of thy living.

. . .

But peradventure[33] thou wilt object that the woman proveketh thee to this point. But consider thou again that the woman is a frail vessel, and thou art therefore made the ruler and head over her, to bear the weakness of her in this her subjection. And therefore study thou to declare the honest commendation of thine authority, which thou canst no way better do, than to forbear to urge her in her weakness and subjection. For even as the King appeareth so much the more noble, the more excellent and noble he maketh his officers and lieutenants, whom if he should dishonour and despise the authority of their dignity, he should deprive himself of a great part of his own honour. Even so, if thou dost despise her that is set in the next room beside thee, thou dost must derogate[34] and decay the excellency and virtue of thine own authority. Recount all these things in thy mind, and be gentle and quiet. Understand that GOD hath given thee children with her and are made a father, and by such reason appease thyself.

This discussion of gender in the context of heterosexual relations and marriage would seem to imply that there was no same-sex sexual activity in Renaissance England. This simply could not have been true. Indeed, there are scattered references to male–male sexual activity in the period. King James I might have been bisexual, though he described sodomy as 'one of the horrible crimes that ye are bound in conscience never to forgive'.[35] What was 'different' about the Renaissance was not the absence of homosexual practice but the way it was understood, defined, the meanings attached to it and the anxieties it generated. 'Homosexuality' was not a category of self-definition at the time. In other words, no man would describe himself as 'homosexual' even though he might engage in sex with other men. Further, though sodomy was considered a 'sin' in moral and legal writings, it was more or less accepted in daily practice and probably not severely punished too often either, unless it was non-consensual. The 'crime' of sodomy became problematic only when associated with other dangerous and socially disruptive behaviours such as treason, atheism and 'papistry'.[36] So the playwright Christopher Marlowe's reputation for 'homosexuality' was part and parcel of his image as rebel, spy and atheist. The language of male–male friendship was intense and passionate.[37] It is hard to tell if this meant that the relationships in question were erotic. Shakespeare's plays have several instances of men whose attachment to other men is intense and profound. Antonio's feelings for Sebastian in Shakespeare's *Twelfth Night* (1601–02) and Antonio's for Bassanio in Shakespeare's *The Merchant of Venice* (1596–98) come to mind. The younger men do end up marrying women, and the plays' conclusions are oddly and somewhat poignantly silent about the older men, their desires and the future course their lives will take. Dekker's reference to the treatment of male–male desire is more playful in *The Roaring Girl*: when Sebastian embraces his beloved Mary, who happens to be disguised as a boy, he says that he actually prefers her in male garb ('I'd kiss such men to choose [by choice] … / Methinks a woman's lip tastes well in a doublet' [4.1.46–47]).[38] Christopher Marlowe's *Edward II* is possibly the most explicit dramatic treatment of same-sex desire. King Edward is infatuated with the young Gaveston, but the play is surprisingly neutral or amoral when it comes to the possibly homoerotic relationship. The relationship between the king and Gaveston is problematic only because it prevents Edward from being a good king and a good husband. In fact, the possibility of homosexuality lingers beneath all romantic encounters on the Renaissance stage as cross-dressed boy actors playing female roles courted male actors in male roles. This provoked the ire of Puritan critics of the stage, who believed that theatre actually encouraged homosexuality. In the words of Philip Stubbes, 'these goodly pageants being done, every mate sorts to his mate … and in their secret enclaves covertly play the sodomites, or worse'.[39]

Female homosexuality, though it probably did exist, goes almost completely unmentioned in Renaissance England and even the statutes against sodomy do not consider sexual relations between women. There is no evidence or documentation of female homoerotic activity partly because such activities were confined to the private space of the home, partly because these women did not set up social networks or create subcultures and largely because female homosexual activity did not threaten the social order in any obvious way. As Valerie Traub points out, lesbian desire in the period (unlike adultery) was not as problematic or subject to public discussion because it did not cast doubt on the paternity of children or 'threaten the basis of the social contract'.[40] Some female–female relations in drama, though not explicitly homoerotic as such, are rich and fulfilling. Olivia falls in love with Viola (albeit disguised as a boy) in *Twelfth Night* and the speeches between Helena and Hermia in *A Midsummer Night's Dream* and Celia and Rosalind in Shakespeare's *As You Like It* (1599) are, in spite of the conventional heterosexual closure of these plays, 'as erotically compelling as anything spoken in heterosexual moments in these comedies'.[41]

Disorder

The prescriptive literature insisted that women be restrained and submissive because it was feared that they were actually not so. Indeed, in many popular texts women were depicted as disruptive and as posing a threat to the social order.

The woman who spoke 'excessively' was seen as particularly problematic. Silence was perceived as a sign of ideal femininity. As Thomas Becon advised women, 'be not full of tongue and of much babbling ... For there is nothing that doth commend, advance, set forth, adorn, deck, trim and garnish a maid as silence.'[42] The female gossip was accused of wasting time and neglecting household work but was also considered potentially dangerous. Worse than the gossip was the 'shrew' – the woman with the unruly tongue who scolded and nagged her husband. 'Scold' was a term first used to describe any quarrelsome or brawling person but was eventually applied only to women. A woman accused of being a scold, if found guilty, could be punished either by ducking her in water or by collaring her with a 'scold's bridle', which was an iron collar with a metal bit in the mouth to prevent talking. In parts of England the accusation of being a scold was nearly a quarter of all offences brought against women.[43] The increased anxiety about scolds and shrews does not imply that a large number of women were quite suddenly engaging in what was considered disruptive behaviour. The percentage that was actually doing so was probably very small, but enough to create the threat of female rebellion.

The decades between 1560 and 1640 also saw many people persecuted as 'witches'. While it is important to remember that men too were accused of witchcraft, a large percentage, if not the majority, of victims of witch-hunting were women. Women were more likely to be victimized because they were seen as morally weak and susceptible to temptation. As King James wrote, women became witches because 'that sex is frailer than man is, so is it easier to be entrapped in these gross snares of the Devil, as was over well proved true, by the Serpents' deceiving of Eve at the beginning'.[44] In fact, many female 'witches' were simply women who rejected the traditional model of femininity. Some of them were just poor women who lived by themselves. When they begged for food and money and were turned away their disgruntled mumblings were interpreted as 'curses'. When a woman was accused of being a witch her accusers looked for the 'devil's mark' on her genitals to prove that she had had sex with the Devil. Male witches were rarely, if ever, accused of this, indicating that there was a 'much more sexualized understanding of female witchcraft'.[45] Clearly, in an age where conformity was expected, any woman who transgressed or even lived a somewhat unconventional life was subject to censure.

The transgressive woman was often portrayed in drama. Katherine the 'shrew' in Shakespeare's *The Taming of the Shrew* is remarkably 'curst and shrewd' (1.1.183). Ben Jonson's *Epicoene* (1609) contrasts the ideal 'silent women' with the 'collegiate' women who behave 'with most masculine, or rather hermaphroditical authority' (1.1.76–77) and are therefore both absurd and threatening.[46] This is much like how much of the cast of characters in *The Roaring Girl* perceives Moll who cross-dresses and wanders freely through the city. Interestingly, however, the play itself does not condemn Moll. The disorderly women of tragedies usually suffer. Desdemona of Shakespeare's *Othello* (*c*. 1604) asserts her autonomy even as she speaks the language of feminine duty. She says that she must stay with the man she has secretly married because 'so much duty as my mother showed / To you, preferring you before her father, / So much I challenge that I may profess / Due to the Moor my lord' (1.3.186–89). However, her husband, Othello, eventually begins to wonder if a girl who disobeyed her father would stay faithful to her husband. In several other tragedies the 'disorderly' women used their traditional positions as wives and lovers to influence men – Shakespeare's Lady Macbeth and Cleopatra, John Webster's Duchess of Malfi and Alice of *Arden of Faversham* (1592), a play recently attributed to Shakespeare, come to mind.[47]

Women's disorderliness was most associated with sexual misconduct. There were 'a staggering number of prosecutions in Church courts for sexual offenses in the Elizabethan period'.[48] In most of these cases the defendant was a woman. Women were considered to have a powerful and often uncontrolled sexual drive. According to Crooke, this was because women were of weaker intelligence and akin to animals ('lustful women', he wrote, 'are like the imagination of rude beasts which have no repugnancy or contradiction of reason to restrain them'[49]). This idea is echoed in the drama. In *Everyman in His Humour* (1598) by Ben Jonson, Cob tells his wife, Tib, 'you are a woman; you have flesh and blood enough in you; therefore be not tempted; keep the door shut upon all comers' (3.5.27–29).[50] In his turn, Hamlet in Shakespeare's *Hamlet* (1599–1602) rages against his mother's sexual appetite and declares, 'Frailty, thy name is woman' (1.2.146). Female chastity was linked to honour in the upper classes and what was termed 'honesty' in the poor. A man's sexual reputation on the other hand had little to do with the regard he was held in by family and community. In most affairs (whether adulterous or pre-marital), the woman was somehow more blameworthy than the man. As Laura Gowing points out, insults of women ('whore', 'jade', 'strumpet', 'bawd' and 'harlot', for example) usually attacked their sexuality, while insults of men rarely did. 'The language of slander', writes Gowing, made it clear that 'women remained the focus of sexual guilt and responsibility'.[51]

A woman who committed adultery threw the legitimacy of the family's heirs into question. She also subverted the family hierarchy and humiliated the man, who could be mocked for being a 'cuckold' who could not control his wife. While many sermons and marriage manuals did condemn men who committed adultery, it is quite apparent that in reality male adulterers were never as culpable as female ones. If women sued men for violence, men usually sued women for adultery (and were more likely to get a favourable sentence). The punishments for adultery became harsher with the passing decades and women who strayed from their marriage vows had almost everything to lose. In the domestic tragedy *Arden of Faversham*, Alice has an adulterous affair and even murders her unfortunate husband – an act considered equivalent to treason. In *A Woman Killed with Kindness*, Anne Franford, 'once an ornament to womanhood' (13.97, 98),[52] becomes its 'shame' after she commits adultery. She starves herself to death in penitence.

Manhood

Ideal manhood was nearly as rigidly defined as ideal femininity and was often challenging for men to achieve and retain. Men had a range of responsibilities as heads of households – they'd have to be good 'providers', adept, brave, as well as spiritual leaders of the family flock. Thomas Elyot wrote that 'A man in his natural perfection is fierce, hardy, strong in opinion and covetous of glory, desirous of knowledge'.[53] Gentry masculinity was linked to lineage, honour and responsibility for and control over servants and subordinates. The ideal model of aristocratic masculinity was the courtier. The Italian author Baldassare Castiglione's book *The Courtier* (1528) had been translated into English and outlined the skills every courtier ought to possess: he had to be a soldier and horseman and also had to cultivate the 'gentler skills', including the ability to make good conversation, play and appreciate music, write poetry and dress well. Every young man must strive hard to master these skills and must also carry them with a certain unselfconscious ease. However, even as this new model of masculinity was becoming popular among the nobility, there was the accompanying fear that these men who emphasized fashion and artistic skills would become vain, self-indulgent and effeminate. Indeed, the 'Homily against Excess of Apparel' expressed the concern that many young men were becoming effeminate because 'they care not what they spend in disguising themselves ever desiring new toys and inventing new fashions'.[54] Love, it was felt, could also effeminize a man. In *The Anatomy of Melancholy* (1621) Richard Burton stated that love is 'full of fear, anxiety, doubt, care, peevishness, it turns a man into a woman'.[55] Romeo, in Shakespeare's *Romeo and Juliet* (*c.* 1591–95), too worries that Juliet's 'beauty hath made me effeminate / And in my temper softn'd valour's steel' (3.1.115–16). Romeo has little chance when even warriors like Antony in Shakespeare's *Antony and Cleopatra* (*c.* 1607) and Tamburlaine are softened by love. The latter recognizes that his adoration of Zenocrate is 'unseemly … for my sex' and makes him 'effeminate and faint' (Part 1, 5.2.111, 114).

There were others fears attended on manhood. The man accused of being a cuckold (while not harshly punished like the adulteress was) was subject to humiliation. That is why the very word provokes the protagonist of *Othello*. The cuckold is treated with humour in comedies, but there is an undercurrent of anxiety in these plays too. Indeed, anxiety and insecurity possibly characterized manhood in the time period. Mark Breitenberg argues that in a society that conferred power and status on men it was inevitable that they lived in fear of losing this very same power and status. Masculine anxiety revealed the fears as well as the fissures and contradictions underlying patriarchy. However, it was that same anxiety that led to the maintenance and perpetuation of patriarchy because men were so disturbed at the prospect of losing their status that they were extra vigilant about defending it.[56]

The plays often pit different kinds of manhood against each other. In the city comedies *The Roaring Girl* and Thomas Middleton's *A Chaste Maid in Cheapside* (1613), the preying young 'gallants' or smart young city gentlemen are pitted against the solid middle-class citizens; in *Romeo and Juliet* the lovelorn Romeo is contrasted to the other men of Verona who are aggressive and belligerent. In many of the tragedies of the period, men struggled to live up to standards of masculinity or carried them to the extreme and so destroyed themselves and others, as in the case of Tamburlaine or Macbeth. Most plays had a man at the centre of the action and manhood was often portrayed as a complicated affair – insecure, fragile, extreme, but also admirable. The complexities of masculinity informed the characterization of the Renaissance tragic hero.

Staging gender

Sumptuary laws dictated the clothing one could or could not wear based on one's class and gender status and partly stemmed from the belief that clothing could signal class status and gender identity. However, several men and women apparently dressed in clothing of the opposite gender. This could have been 'for fashion, for pleasure, as a stratagem that facilitated theft or other crime, or as a cultural sign of their position, high or low'.[57] Women, especially working-class women, often cross-dressed simply because there were more job opportunities for men – there are, for instance, a few recorded cases of women disguised as men joining the army. Viola of *Twelfth Night* too dresses as a man to secure employment in the Duke's court. However, for critics of cross-dressing the practice was heinous and unnatural; cross-dressers were considered to have violated God-given rules that dictate that men wear men's clothing and women women's.

From *Hic Mulier* and *Haec-Vir* (1620).
(Courtesy of The Huntingdon Library)

***Hic Mulier* and *Haec-Vir* (both 1620) were among the most important documents in the controversy about gender in general and gender and clothing in particular. Public pronouncements by King James on the evils of cross-dressing and sermons on the same issue possibly motivated these two texts. *Hic Mulier* attacks women who wear men's clothing and *Haec Vir* criticizes male foppishness.**

From *Hic Mulier*.
For since the days of Adam women were never so Masculine; Masculine in their genders and whole generations, from the Mother, to the youngest daughter; Masculine in Number, from one to multitudes; Masculine in Case, even from the head to the foot; Masculine in Mood, from bold speech, to impudent action; and Masculine in Tense: for (without redress) they were, are, and will be still most Masculine, most mankind, and most monstrous.[58] . . .

Come then, you Masculine-women, for you are my Subject, you that have made Admiration and Ass, and fool'd him with a deformity never before dream'd of, that have made your self stranger things than ever *Noah's* Ark unladed, or *Nile* engendered[59]; whom to name, he that named all things, might study an Age to give you a right attribute, whose like are not found in any Antiquary's[60] study, in any Sea-man's travel, nor in any Painter's cunning[61]; you that are stranger than strangeness itself, whom Wisemen wonder at; Boys shout at, and Goblins themselves start at; You that are the Gilt dirt which Embroiders Play-houses, the painted Statues which adorn Caroches,[62] and the perfumed Carrion that bad men feed on in Brothels. 'Tis of you, I entreat, and of your monstrous deformity; You that have made your bodies like antique Boscage[63] or Crotesco work,[64] not half man, half woman; half fish, half flesh; half beast, half Monster: but all Odious, all Devil, that have cast off the ornament of your sexes, to put on the garments of Shame; that have laid by the bashfulness of your natures, to gather the impudence of Harlots[65]; that have buried silence, to revive slander; that are all things but that which you should be, and nothing less than friends to virtue and goodness; . . . you have taken the monstrousness of your deformity in apparel, exchanging the modest attire of the comely Hood, Cawl,[66] Coif,[67] handsome Dress or Kerchief, to the cloudy Ruffianly broad-brim'd Hat, and wanton Feather, the modest upper parts of a concealing straight gown, to the loose, lascivious civil embracement of a French doublet,[68] being all unbutton'd to entice, all of one shape to hide deformity, and extreme short waisted to give a most easy way to every luxurious action: the glory of a fair large hair, to the shame of most ruffianly short locks; the side, thick gather'd, and closeguarding safeguards,[69] to the short, weak, thin, loose, and every hand entertaining short bases;[70] for Needles, Swords; for Prayer books, bawdy jigs; for modest gestures, giant-like behaviours, and for women's modesty, all Mimic and apish[71] incivility: These are your founders, from these you took your copies, and (without amendment) with these you shall come to perdition.[72]

. . .

It is an infection that emulates the plague, and throws itself among women of all degrees, all deserts,[73] and all ages; from the Capital to the Cottage, are some spots of dwelling or this disease, yet evermore the greater the person is, the greater is the rage of this sickness, and the more they have to support the eminence of their Fortunes, the more they bestow in the augmentation of their deformities. Not only such as will not work to get bread, will find time to weave herself points[74] to truss[75] her loose Breeches. And she that hath pawned her credit to get a Hat, will sell her Smock[76] to buy a Feather: She that hath given kisses to have her hair shorn, will give her honesty to have her upper parts put into a French doublet. To conclude, she that will give her body to have her body deformed, will not stick to give her soul to have her mind satisfied.

But such that are able to buy all at their own charges, they swim in the excess of these vanities, and will be man-like not only from the head to the waist, but to the very foot, & in every condition: man in body by attire, man in behavior by rude complement, man in nature by aptness to anger, man in action by pursuing revenge, man in wearing weapons, man in using weapons: And in brief, so much man in all things, that they are neither men, nor women, but just good for nothing.

. . .

Remember how your Maker made for our first Parents coats, not one coat, but a coat for the man, and a coat for the woman; coats of several fashions, several forms, and for several uses: the man's coat fit for his labour, the woman's fit for her modesty: and will lose the model left by this great Work-master of Heaven?

The long hair of a woman is the ornament of her sex, and bashful shamefulness her chief honour: the long hair of a man, the vizard[77] for a thievish or murderous disposition: and will you cut off that beauty, to wear the others villainy? The Vestals[78] in *Rome* wore comely[79] garments of one piece from the neck to the heel; and the Swordplayers[80] motley[81] doublets, with gaudy points: the first begot reverence; the latter laughter; and will you lose that honour, for the other's scorn? The weapon of a virtuous woman was her tears, which every good man pitied, and every valiant man honoured. The weapon of a cruel man is his sword, which neither Law allows, nor reason defends: and will you leave the excellent shield of innocence for this deformed instrument of disgrace?

. . .

The fairest face covered with a foul vizard begets nothing but affright or scorn, and the noblest person, in an ignoble disguise, attains to nothing but reproach, and scandal. Away then with these disguises, and foul vizards; these unnatural paintings, and immodest discoveries; keep those parts concealed from the eyes, that may not be touched with the hands. Let not a wandering and lascivious thought read in an enticing Index the contents of an unchaste volume. Imitate nature; and she hath placed on the surface and superfices[82] of the earth, all things needful for man's sustenance, and necessary use; as Herbs, Plants, Fruits, Corn and such like, but locked up close in the hidden caverns of the earth, all things which appertain to his delight and pleasure: as gold, silver, rich Minerals and precious Stones. So do you discover unto men all things that are fit for them to understand from you: as bashfulness in your cheeks, chastity in your eyes, wisdom in your words, sweetness in your conversation, pity in your hearts, and a general and severe modesty in the whole structure or frame of your universal composition. But for those things which belong to this wanton and lascivious delight and pleasure: as eyes wandering, lips billing, tongue enticing, bared breasts seducing, and naked arms embracing. O hide them, for shame hide them in the closest prisons of your strictest government: shield them with modest and comely garments, such as are warm and wholesome, having every window closed with a strong Casement,[83] and every Loop-hole furnished with such strong Ordinance,[84] that no unchaste eye may come near to assail them, no lascivious tongue woo a forbidden passage, nor no profane hands touch relics[85] so pure and religious, Guard them about with counter-scarfes[86] of Innocence, Trenches of humane Reason and impregnable walls of sacred Divinity[87]: not with Antic[88] disguise, and Mimic fantasticness[89] where every window stands open like the *Sabura*[90], and every window a Courtesan with an instrument, like so many *Sirens*,[91] to enchant the weak passenger to shipwreck and destruction. Thus shall you be your selves again, and live the most excellentest creatures upon earth, things past example, past all imitation.

From *Haec Vir*:

Therefore to take your proportion[92] in a few lines (my dear Feminine Masculine) tell me what Charter,[93] prescription[94] or right of claim you have to those things you make our absolute inheritance? why do you curl, frizzle[95] and powder your hairs, bestowing more hours and time in dividing lock from lock, and hair from hair, in giving every thread his posture, and every curl his true fence and circumference than ever *Caesar* did in marshalling his Army . . . why do you rob us off our Ruffs,[96] of our Earrings, Carcanets,[97] and Mamillions,[98] of our Fans and Feathers, our busks and French bodice, nay, of our Masks, Hoods, Shadows[99] and Shapinas[100] not so much as the very Art of Painting,[101] but you have so greedily engrossed it, that were it not for that little fantastical sharp pointed dagger that hangs at your chins, & the cross hilt which guards your upper lip, hardly would there be any difference between the fair Mistress & the foolish Servant. But is this theft the uttermost of our Spoil? Fie, you have gone a world further, and even ravished[102] from us our speech, our actions, sports and recreations. Goodness leave me, if I have not heard a Man court his Mistress with the same words that *Venus* did *Adonis*, or as near as the Book could instruct him[103]; where are the Tilts and Tournies,[104] and lofty Galliards[105] that were danced in the days of old, when men capered in the air like wanton kids[106] on the tops of Mountains, and turned above ground as if they had been compact of[107] Fire or a purer element? Tut all's forsaken, all's vanished, . . . Lastly, poor shuttle-cock[108] that was only a female invention, how have you taken it out of our hands, and made yourselves such Lords and Rulers over it, that though it be a very Emblem of us, and our lighter despised fortunes, yet it dare now hardly come near us; nay, you keep it so imprisoned within your Bed-Chambers and dining rooms, amongst your Pages and Panders[109] . . . For this you have demolished the noble schools of Horse-manship (of which many were in this City) hung up your Arms to rust, glued up those swords in their scabbards that would shake all Christendom with the brandish, and entertained into your minds such softness, dullness and effeminate niceness,[110] that it would even make *Heraclitus*[111] himself laugh against his nature to see how pulingly[112] you languish in this weak entertained sin of womanish softness: To see one of your gender either show himself (in the midst of his pride or riches) at a Play house, or public assembly; how (before he dare enter) with the Jacob's Staff [113] of his own eyes and his Pages, he takes a full survey of himself, from the highest sprig in his feather to the lowest spangle that shines in his Shoe-string: how he prunes and picks himself like a Hawk set aweathering, calls every several garment to Auricular confession,[114] making them utter both their mortal great stains, and their venial and less blemishes, though the moat[115] be much less than a Atom. Then to see him pluck and tug everything into the form of the newest received fashion; and by *Durer's* rules[116] make his leg answerable to his neck; his thigh proportionable with his middle, his foot with his hand, and a world of such idle disdained foppery. To see him thus patched up with Symmetry, make himself complete, and even as a circle: and lastly, cast himself amongst the eyes of the people (as an object of wonder) with more niceness,[117] than a Virgin goes to the sheets of her first Lover, would make patience herself mad with anger . . .

Cast then from you our ornaments, and put on your own armours: Be men in shape, men in show, men in words, men in action, men in council, men in example: then will we love and serve you; then will we hear and obey you; then will we like rich Jewels hang at your ears to take our Instructions, like true friends follow you through all dangers, and like careful leeches[118] pour oil into your wounds. Then shall you find delight in our words; pleasure in our faces; faith in our

hearts; chastity in our thoughts, and sweetness both in our inward &
outward inclinations. Comeliness[119] then shall be our study; fear our
Armour, and modesty our practice. Then shall we be all your most
excellent thoughts can desire, and have nothing in us less than[120]
impudence and deformity.

Cross-dressing on stage is particularly interesting. Unlike in Italy, Spain and
France, female actors were not allowed on the English stage. Women did play
roles in local village festivities and in masques or court entertainments, so
the problem was apparently not women acting as such but women acting
before public audiences. For Puritans such as William Prynne, women actors
could only be 'notorious, impudent, prostituted strumpets'.[121] So, in spite of
the complex, interesting female characters in the drama, the fact remains
that women could not represent themselves. However, the boys or young
men who played women on stage were also subject to criticism. As discussed
earlier, they were accused of stirring up homoerotic desires in the male
spectator. The actor might also be provoked into lust because 'the putting
[on] of women's attire on men may kindle unclean affections ... because a
woman's garment put on a man doth vehemently touch and move him with
the remembrance and imagination of a woman; and the imagination of a
thing desirable doth stir up the desire'.[122] Stubbes wrote, 'our apparel was
given us as a sign distinctive to discern betwixt sex and sex, and therefore
one to wear the Apparell of another sex is to participate with the same, and
to adulterate the verity of his own kind'.[123] Further, anti-theatrical writers
also worried that the role and costumes of the boy actor would render him
female or effeminate. So a boy actor cross-dressing is 'immoral' because he is
projecting a mistruth, but there is also the danger that the lie could possibly
become the truth – the boy might turn into a woman. Playwrights defended
themselves against these charges. Heywood, in his *An Apology for Actors*,
argued that cross-dressed boy actors averted the possibility of the male
audience misbehaving with female actors and Jonson, in *Bartholomew Fair*,
has the actors cheekily raise their skirts, supposedly to reveal their real sex,
so mocking those who worried that cross-dressing confuses gender
identities. Jonson implies that most viewers have common sense enough to
tell male and female apart from each other, both on and off stage.

This 'transvestite theatre' complicates our understanding of gender on
the Renaissance stage in interesting ways. The audience was faced with the

Figure 2.1 Title page from *Hic Mulier, or, The Man-Woman: Being a Medicine to cure the Coltish Disease of the Staggers in the Masculine-Feminines of our Times: Exprest in a briefe Declamation*, 1620 (courtesy of The Folger Shakespeare Library).

challenge of imagining femininity even as women were absent from stage. Besides, the cross-dressing practice as well as the plots that involve cross-dressing blurred gender identity. The difference between the sexes became superficial, simply a matter of clothing and role play. The plots of the plays seemed to reinforce this idea. In *Gallathea* (1585) by John Lyly, two women dressed as men fall in love. Fortunately, the gods intervene and changes one of them to a man. The play interestingly validates both women's transgender identity and the marriage itself.[124] In *As You Like It* when Rosalind becomes Ganymede she becomes a 'man' in that she is self-controlled and protective of the weaker Celia. In *Twelfth Night* Viola recognizes that her identity is now plural, that ' I am not what I am' (3.1.142). Ultimately *Twelfth Night*'s take on gender might be quite conventional in that Viola (like other cross-dressed heroines) does shed her disguise, but it is also quite significant that the actual change back to women's clothing is not staged. In one sense Viola remains Cesario right up to the play's end. But perhaps the most radical of the cross-dressed heroines is Moll of *The Roaring Girl* who does not get into female clothing even at the play's conclusion. The original Moll is also supposed to have played the lute on stage at the Fortune theatre (according to the play's epilogue), a rare instance, and perhaps the only recorded one, of a woman treading the boards of a public stage.

But women still made up a substantial portion of the audience. Samuel Rowlands in his poem 'The Bride' asserted that a respectable married woman 'at public plays ... will never be known'[125] and women playgoers might have been accused of wasting time and subjecting themselves to attention from men, but women from all social classes did attend plays. Foreign writers in fact commented on the unusual freedom that Englishwomen enjoyed when they went to the theatre – their faces were uncovered and they sometimes went without male escort. Richard Levin also argues that the occasional sympathetic treatment of women one sometimes sees on stage and the fact that some plots takes sides with the women characters in battle-between-the-sexes stories was partially to please female spectators.[126] Women were also consumers of printed playbooks and some of them were patrons of the theatre or even share-holders, while others had the job of collecting money from the spectators. So women were engaged in a range of activities both in the theatre and out of it. Their status in Renaissance England is, as Dympna Callaghan puts it, 'paradoxically, that of excluded participants'.[127]

Rulers, readers, writers

The fact that England was ruled by a woman, Elizabeth I, complicates any discussion of gender in the era. How could a woman be at the head of a patriarchal society? Women's rule certainly did not go unchallenged. During the reign of Elizabeth's sister Mary, clergyman John Knox wrote that a woman ruler 'is repugnant to nature, contumely [a reproach] to God . . . and finally it [female rule] is the subversion of good order, of all equity and justice'.[128] Appointing a woman ruler, according to Knox, was as unnatural and foolish as charging the blind to lead the sighted; the sick, the whole; or the mad, the sane. After Elizabeth ascended the throne Knox hastily retracted his stand and stated that she was an exception to the rule and had God-given authority to reign. Other writers such as John Aylmer defended the Queen's rule. A woman who was legal heir to a king could legally rule, a fact 'established by law, confirmed by custom and ratified by common consent of all orders in the realm'.[129] Aylmer also felt that it was somehow possible for a woman to rule as a monarch but remain subservient as a wife.

As we saw in Chapter One, Elizabeth recognized that kingship was partly a well-orchestrated performance. The performance was all the more important because she was a woman. She had to perform a certain kind of feminine identity, describing herself as one married to England, mother to her people and mistress to her courtiers. Most famously, she was one 'who lived and died a virgin'.[130] In this and other ways she played up her femininity even as she rendered it mystical and mysterious. In her speeches she very deliberately acknowledged commonplace attitudes to women. For example, in an oration before Parliament she said that she was aware that she was 'a woman wanting wit and memory, some fear to speak and bashfulness besides, a thing appropriate to my sex'.[131] Yet, she continued, 'the princely seat and kingly throne' on which God had chosen to place her gave her the right to speak. In her appearance at Tilbury just before the battle with the Spanish Armada, she wore a silver breastplate over her dress and held a commander's baton as she proclaimed, 'I know I have the body but of a weak and feeble woman, but I have the heart and stomach of a king, and a king of England too,' words that were inscribed and distributed throughout the country and that caught the imagination of the public.[132]

In spite of Elizabeth's success, it is important to realize that other women had few or no political rights and no political representation. Elizabeth's rule did not immediately improve the status of women. However, she still was an

Figure 2.2 The Plimpton 'Sieve' portrait of Queen Elizabeth I, George Gower, 1579 (courtesy of The Folger Shakespeare Library).

indication that women could potentially be successful in the public realm. The figure of Elizabeth certainly influenced those strong, outspoken female characters in positions of power who appear in the drama (for example, Portia in *The Merchant of Venice* and Titania in *A Midsummer Night's Dream*). The maiden Bess, protagonist of Heywood's *The Fair Maid of the West*, is clearly a tribute to the Queen – fearless and spirited even as she is still maidenly and romantic.

Elizabeth was also exceptional in that she was a highly educated woman. The humanist system described in Chapter Four was mainly aimed at creating young gentlemen. While both boys and girls probably received similar education until they were around ten years old, girls stopped going to grammar school at that age, so many of them learned to read but not to write. The young ladies who belonged to the gentry had home tutors. Several humanist treatises on women's education were produced in the time period and there was a brief surge in the quality of women's education with eminent men such as Thomas More insisting on imparting a full-fledged humanist training to their daughters. But most women (even from the upper classes) did not benefit from humanist education. Whatever program of study was in place was often very limited and many books and subjects that were not seen as directly contributing to religious virtue were excluded. Sometime after 1560 women's education declined further and focused on imparting the 'social graces', including music, dancing, painting and a sprinkling of classical texts. That is perhaps why, with the exclusion of Portia, there are few learned heroines in Renaissance drama.

What of women dramatists? Writing was a 'manly' task and those few women who did write were challenging the dictum that women stay silent. Much of women's writing in the period was in the form of private letters, journals, recipe books, and household and medical manuals. Women, notably Rachel Speght, Esther Sowernam and Constantia Munda (the last two being pseudonyms), also became participants in the pamphlet wars over gender, writing back to the men who so bitterly attacked 'misbehaviour' in women. These writings are clearly products of their times but still prefigure modern feminist ideas. Other women such as Queen Elizabeth, Aemilia Lanyer and Isabella Whitney wrote poetry, while Mary Wroth is best known for her prose romance *Urania* (published 1621). However, in an age when the female author was still quite a scandalous figure it was almost inconceivable for women to write for the public theatre. Virginia Woolf imagines the fate of Shakespeare's imaginary 'wonderfully gifted sister' – she would probably have had an inadequate education, urged to focus on housework by well-meaning parents, fled to London to escape marriage, tried to gain a foothold in the theatre, but would have died broken-hearted and a failure. 'It would have been impossible, completely and entirely, for any woman to have written the plays of Shakespeare in the age of Shakespeare', concludes Woolf sorrowfully.[133] However, we do now treasure 'closet plays' (plays that were never performed) such as *Love's Victory* (*c*. 1620) by Mary Wroth, which was the first comedy by a woman, and Elizabeth Cary's *Mariam, Fair Queen of Jewry* (published *c*. 1613), the first tragedy. These plays were never staged, but their authors might have imagined their performance on a real stage, perhaps even with real women actors.

Discussion points

1 Closet plays and other literary writings by Renaissance women have been briefly discussed in this chapter. Feminist scholarship has vastly expanded the canon to include such work. What kind of non-literary writing do you think Renaissance women did? Think of different genres and different contexts that would allow or even provoke women to write. What do you think reading these kind of works could tell us about women's experiences during the time?

2 Imagine you are interested in understanding and interpreting a 'non-literary' document, the 'Sermon on Matrimony' for instance, rather than a play. How does your knowledge of any particular play further your understanding of the sermon? In other words, think of Renaissance plays as the 'contextual backdrop' to the sermon.

3 Our picture of the past is necessarily incomplete and imperfect. For instance, we briefly looked at how there are few (if any) records of the lesbian experience in the Renaissance. Are there other aspects of the experience of gender and sexuality that you think we will never be able to understand through the reading of documents, literary or otherwise? Do you think other non-linguistic artifacts will tell us something that written texts cannot?

4 Early practitioners of feminist criticism were accused of being ahistorical because neither the word 'feminism' nor the ideology or movement existed in the Renaissance. Based on your reading of this chapter and works of drama, do you think a feminist approach is valid at all? If yes, what form would it take and how exactly would it

contribute to our understanding and appreciation of Renaissance drama?

5 Feminist approaches to reading literature that focus on issues of gender and sexuality originated in and are associated with the modern political movement of feminism. What relevance do you think applying such an approach to Renaissance drama has to the movement towards gender equality in our own world?

3

Travel and Trade

For Thomas Coryat, the adventurous Englishman who voyaged through much of Europe and Asia, travel was among 'the sweetest and most delightful' of pursuits. 'For what can be more pleasant,' he wrote, 'than to see passing variety of beautiful Cities, kings and Princes Courts, gorgeous Palaces, impregnable Castles and Fortresses'.[1] Beyond the courts, castles and cities that so delighted Coryat were the oceans filled with mermaids and monsters, and on the other side of the waters was the wilderness populated by strange humans and beasts. This is where men went to experience new wonders and where they went to become heroes.

The Renaissance was the age of travel – men travelled for adventure, for trade and in quest of wealth and land. Many of the accomplishments of the age came about because of the commercial and cultural exchange brought about by travel. This was also, perhaps quite naturally, the age of mapmaking. Abraham Ortelius created the first world atlas, *Theatrum Orbus Terrarum*, in 1570, the cover of which depicted a crowned 'Europa' seated on top, with Asia (in the garb of an oriental princess), Africa (depicted as a half-naked, dark-skinned person) and America (also half-naked bearing a spear and arrows) arrayed below. In this symbolic representation of the continents, Europe was clearly imagined to be at the top and centre of the world. After 1570 England too became increasingly involved in the emerging 'global economy'. English joint-stock companies – trading corporations started by enterprising shareholder-merchants – were set up to trade globally and London shipping trebled between 1582 and 1629.[2] In London, pageants depicting ships laden with spices, silk and other foreign goods were regularly staged, with actors dressed as 'India' or the 'Queen of Merchandise' paying tribute to the English monarch. Apart from the consumer goods, travellers brought home exotic objects such as foreign artifacts, clothing and animal parts, all of which became part of the collections of Englishmen who proudly displayed these objects in 'wonder cabinets'. Travellers also sent home letters, official reports, journals and other narratives. English travel writing was first compiled by Richard Hakluyt in a multi-volume collection titled *The Principle Navigations, Voyages and Discoveries of the English Nation* (1589), a work that has been described as the 'prose epic of the modern English nation.'[3] Hakluyt collected and organized these narratives in order to celebrate the adventures of English travellers and to save their narratives 'from the greedy and devouring jaws of oblivion.'[4]

Dramatists' imaginations too were moved by these voyages to far-flung places and it is interesting that the best-known theatre of the time was called the Globe. The world, in all its variety, could be reproduced on stage. Drama could, to quote Marlowe in *The Jew of Malta*, 'enclose / Infinite riches in a little room' (I.i.36–37). Just like the foreign goods that were eagerly sought after by English consumers, plays too staged the foreign and the exotic for curious playgoers. While these plays did not always accurately reflect these other cultures, they do tell us something about the complexities of European attitudes to the new and the different. Very importantly, at a time when most Englishmen had little interaction with foreigners and people of different races, drama's representations of foreign lands and peoples helped shape attitudes towards cultural and racial 'others'.

Barabas of *The Jew of Malta* trades in Spanish oils, Grecian wines and Indian metals and Antonio in Shakespeare's *The Merchant of Venice* (1596–98) has ships bound to Tripolis, the Indies and Mexico. Both plays invoke the perils and promises of these distant worlds. Foreign characters were, however, also often the source of humour. So Portia in *The Merchant of Venice* makes fun of her international cast of lovers each with their own peculiar national trait. Other stage foreigners are more fearsome than comic (Aaron the Moor in Shakespeare's *Titus Andronicus* [1588–93] comes to mind), while still others were richly complex (like Shakespeare's black hero, Othello). Plays also increasingly depicted English or European 'venturing heroes' who went abroad and engaged in exciting exploits – these include Captain Stukely of *Battle of Alcazar* (1590) by George Peele, Bess of *The Fair Maid of the West* and the Shirley brothers in *The Travels of the Three English Brothers* (1607) by John Day, William Rowley and George Wilkins. Some heroes like Prospero of Shakespeare's *The Tempest* (1610–11) find themselves exiled in distant foreign lands, haunted all along by memories of home.

Old worlds

Humanist education encouraged travel and young Englishmen often went to Europe, usually accompanied by tutors. Protestant countries like Germany and Switzerland were usually praised in travel writing, while Catholic nations were viewed less favourably. The French were considered dandified and vain, the Spanish ambitious and treacherous and Italians were perceived as being duplicitous and overly sexualized even as their country was viewed with envy and grudging admiration for its vibrant commerce and high culture. This ambivalent attitude to Italy made that country a fit setting for dozens of Renaissance plays – high drama and intrigue of the kind that playwrights delighted in were conceivable only in an Italian setting.

European characters appeared regularly in many plays. In spite of the general admiration for European Protestant cultures in the travel literature, the fat, drunk Dutchman who speaks 'broken' English is the source of genial humour in many English comedies including Thomas Dekker and John Webster's *Northward Ho* (c. 1607), John Marston's *The Dutch Courtesan* (1604) and Thomas Dekker's *The Shoemaker's Holiday* (1599). Spanish characters are depicted unfavourably: Portia's suitor the Duke of Aragon is a prototype of the arrogant Spaniard and the Spanish characters in *The Three Ladies of London* (1584) by Robert Wilson are associated with treachery and evil. Similar anti-Spanish feeling is detectable in *The Spanish Tragedy*. Although Jews were expelled from England in 1290, the Jewish merchant was another favourite of the dramatists; Shylock in *The Merchant of Venice* and Barabas of *The Jew of Malta* are probably the most famous. These figures are represented as crafty, fraudulent and as perpetual outcasts and outsiders. The Jews, however, also exemplified the spirit of the new mercantile system – dynamic, flexible and ambitious, even as it was feared to be aggressive and self-serving.

Ireland was perceived to be savage and superstitious. Although the fact that the Irish were Christian could not be ignored, English commentators emphasized that that they were Catholics and that their version of Christianity was almost pagan. In the words of Edmund Spenser in his well-known book *A View of The Present State of Ireland* (1596), the Irish were 'so blindly and brutishly informed for the most part as that you would rather think them atheists or infidels'.[5] The English also criticized the Irish legal system (known as the law of tanistry) and Irish mantles, glibs[6] and other traditional styles of dress; the Irish language was dismissed as wild 'babbling' and their bards, whose music entertained and also heightened Irish political consciousness, were described as dangerous rabble-rousers. The English settlers saw it as their responsibility to civilize the Irish and bring them from a state of 'licentious barbarism, unto the love of goodness and civility'.[7]

From Fynes Moryson, *Of Ireland*.
(Courtesy of the Irish Manuscripts Commission)

Fynes Moryson was a widely-travelled English Protestant gentleman who visited and wrote about a number of countries in Europe and the Middle East. He worked in Ireland as secretary to the Lord Deputy, a representative of the English crown, and this particular extract is from the Irish Sections of the unpublished portions of his longer travelogue *An Itinerary* (1617).

But as horses Cows and sheep transported out of England into Ireland, do each race and breeding decline worse and worse, till in few years they nothing differ from the races and breeds of the Irish horses and Cattle. So the posterities[8] of the English planted in Ireland, do each descent grow more and more Irish, in nature manners and customs, so as we found in the last Rebellion diverse of the most ancient English Families planted of old in Ireland, to be turned as rude and barbarous as any of the meere[9] Irish lords. Partly because the manners and Customs of the meere Irish give great liberty to all men's lives, and absolute power to great men over the inferiors, both which men naturally affect. Partly because the meere Irish of old overtopped the English Irish in number . . . and nothing is more natural yea necessary, than for the less to accommodate itself to the greater. And especially because the English are naturally inclined to apply themselves to the manners and Customs of any foreign nations with whom they live and Converse, whereas the meere Irish by nature have singular and obstinate pertinacity[10] in retaining their old manners and Customs, so as they could never be drawn, by the laws, gentle government, and free conversation of the English, to any Civility in manners, or reformation in Religion.

Now to return to the meere Irish. The lords or rather chiefs of Countries (for most of them are not lords from any grants of our kings, which English titles indeed they despise), prefix O or Mac before their names, in token of greatness, being absolute Tyrants over their people, themselves eating upon them and making them feed their kern[11] or footmen, and their horsemen. Also they, and gentlemen under them, before their names put nicknames, given them from the Colour of their hair, from lameness, stuttering, diseases, or villainous inclinations, which they disdain not, being otherwise most impatient of Reproach,[12] though indeed they take it rather for a grace to be reputed active in any Villainy, especially Cruelty and theft. But it is strange how Contrary they are to themselves, for in apparel, meat, Fashions, and Customs, they are most base and abject, yet are they by nature proud and disdainful of reproach. In fighting they will run away and turn again to fight, because they think it no shame to run away, and to make use of the advantage they have in swift running, yet have they great Courage infighting, and I have seen many of them suffer death with as constant resolution as ever Romans did.

. . .

They are by nature extremely given to Idlenes. The Sea Coasts and harbors abound with fish, but the fishermen must be beaten out, before they will go to their Boats. Theft is not infamous[13] but rather commendable among them so as the greatest men affect to have the best thieves to attend upon them, and if any man reprove them, they Answer that they do as their fathers did, and it is infamy for gentlemen and swordmen to live by labour and manual trades. yea they will not be persuaded that theft displeaseth God, because he gives the prey into their hands and if he be displeased, they say yet he is merciful and will pardon them for using means to live. This Idleness makes them also slovenly and sluttish[14] in their houses and apparel, so as upon every hill they lie lousing themselves. . . . I have remembered four verses, of four beasts that plague Ireland namely, lice upon their bodies, Rats in their houses, Wolves in their fields and swarms of Romish[15] Priests tyrannizing over their Consciences. This Idleness, also makes them to love liberty above all things, and likewise naturally to delight in music, so as the Irish Harpers are excellent, and their solemn music is much liked of strangers, and the women of some parts of Munster, as they wear Turkish heads[16] and are thought to have come first out of those parts, so they have pleasant tunes of Moresco Dances.[17]

They are by nature very Clamorous,[18] upon every small occasion raising the hobou (that is a doleful outcry) which they take one from another's mouth till they put the whole town in tumult.

. . .

The women generally are not much commended for Chastity, but the Common voice was that generally, as kissing goes by favor, so they would rather offend with an Irish horseboy then with the English of better rank. And the foresaid author saith that Ireland abounded with Priests' bastards, known by their names as Mac Decan, Mac Phersan, that is the son of the Dean, or of the Church, and like names to that purpose, and that these men were the most notorious thieves & Rebels of Ireland.

. . .

. . . among meere Irish dwelling in the fields, marriage was rare, and when they were married divorces were most frequent, and because they were given to Incest many divorces were made upon pretense of Conscience. In our experience, till the end of the last Rebellion, these divorces Continued frequent among them, nothing being more ordinary than to take a wife with a Certain number of Cows (their Common Portion) and to send her back to her friends at the years end with some small increase of them, which Divorces the Brehounes or barbarous Judges among them easily admitted,[19] upon a bribe of Cows, and that upon trifling causes. And it was likewise a common Custom for a woman lying at the point of death, to name the true Father of each of her Children, and for the Children to leave their Father reputed by the law, and with the stain of Bastardy (which they regard not) to Follow the Father named by the dying mother, and this Custom caused many times disorders, for if the man child had a lord or gentleman named to be his Father, he would presently be a swordman, living by rapine[20] or Rebellion, holding nothing more infamous then to live by his labour . . . Touching Childbearing, women within two hours after they are delivered many times leave their beds to gossip and drinke with women coming to visit them, and in our experience a Soldiers wife delivered in the Camp, did the same day and within few hours after her delivery march six miles on Foot with the Army to the next Camping place. Some say that commonly the women have little or no pain in Childbearing, and attribute the same to a bone broken when they are tender Children, but whatsoever the cause be, no doubt they have easy deliverance, and commonly such strong ability of body presently after it, as I never heard any women in the world to have the like, . . .

. . .

In Christenings and like Rites of Religion, they use generally the Rites of the Roman Church in which they persist with obstinacy, little care having been taken to instruct them in the Reformed Doctrine. But in all things they intermix barbarous Customs, as when the Child is carried to be baptized, they tie a little piece of silver in the Corner of the Cloth wherein the Child is wrapped, to be given to the Priest, and likewise Salt to be put in the Child's mouth. And at Christenings they have plenty of drink, and of flesh meats to entertain the friends invited. Yea among the very English Irish remaining Papists, the Father entertains the guests, though he be a Bachelor and have disvirgined[21] the mother, for it is no shame to be or beget a Bastard.

The Irish were thus perceived as a contradictory mix: practically next door to England yet rendered distant and alien by their 'otherness', Christian yet not respectably or even recognizably so. Further afield, the peoples of North Africa and what we today describe as the 'Middle East' posed a somewhat similar problem. The Mediterranean was a vibrant cultural and commercial crossroads. The Muslim cultures that lay to the south and east of the Mediterranean especially fascinated Europeans. They visited the great cosmopolitan cities of Cairo and Istanbul for trade, diplomacy or pleasure, or went on pilgrimage to the Holy Land, which was part of Ottoman territory. As Nabil Matar writes, 'no other non-Christian people interacted more widely with Britons than the Muslims of the Ottoman Empire, the Eastern Mediterranean, and the North African regencies of Tunisia, Algeria and Libya along with Morocco'.[22] European sailors and traders were also sometimes captured by pirates in the Mediterranean and wrote 'captivity narratives' which described their imprisonment, sufferings and, in certain cases, their final release.

'The East' or the 'Orient' is often considered the West's 'cultural contestant', the great 'other' against which the 'West' defined itself.[23] However, Renaissance attitudes to Eastern, specifically Muslim, cultures were characterized by contradiction. These cultures could not easily be dismissed as primitive, but they were still depicted as decadent, despotic and cruel. Islam itself was largely understood to be a monotheistic religion like Christianity but was also seen as a mixture of fable, superstition and sensuality. Even captives who became servants or slaves in Muslim households had contradictory reports: for instance, the author of the *Famous and Wonderful Recovery of a Ship of Bristol ... from the Turkish Pirates of Algiers* (1622) wrote of 'the cruelty and inhumanity of Turks and moors ... who from a native barbarousness do hate all Christians and Christianity',[24] while another captive, 'TS', described Arabs in Africa as 'People very polite and well read ... they are affable, hospitable, courteous, kind, and very liberal.'[25] The Ottoman Empire was especially viewed with fear and awe. From their centre in Constantinople (modern-day Istanbul), the Ottomans had conquered the Arab peninsula, much of North Africa, Greece and the Balkans as far as Budapest. The English author Richard Knolles, who wrote the *History of the Turks* (1603), simply described the Ottomans as 'the present terror of the world'.[26] European travellers admired the Turks' military accomplishments, imperial ambitions and their disciplined armies. Henry Blount described them as 'the only modern people, great in action, and whose empire that suddenly so invaded the World, and fixed itself such firm foundations as no other ever did'.[27] In spite of the fact that the Christian clergy denounced the Turks as infidel non-Christians, merchants and politicians were more pragmatic. Realizing the economic promise held by trade with the Ottomans (a trade that involved spices, drugs, silks, cotton, carpets and other luxury goods), Queen Elizabeth appointed ambassadors to negotiate commercial agreements with Turkey and in 1582 supported the establishment of the Levant Company, a joint-stock company to trade with Turkey.

Reformation politics did impact anti-Muslim feeling, though in complex and contradictory ways. Elizabeth's advisor, Francis Walsingham, described the Turks as one of the 'two limbs of the devil' (with Catholicism being the other).[28] On the contrary, the Queen's representative to Morocco attempted to emphasize similarities between English Protestantism and Islam. Both religions, he said, forbade idol-worship and hence the Moroccan king 'beareth a greater affection to our Nation'.[29] However, the victory of joint Christian forces over the Turks at Malta was still celebrated all over Europe.

Irrefutably different from Christians yet neighbours to Europe, Muslim characters and settings fascinated English dramatists as seen in plays such as *Tamburlaine I* and *II*, Thomas Kyd's *Solymon and Persida* (1588), Philip Massinger's *The Renegado* (1624) and Massinger, John Fletcher and Nathan Field's *The Knight of Malta* (c. 1616–19). The plays set in Turkey or featuring Turkish characters are referred to as 'Turk plays' by many modern scholars. One detects certain common themes and motifs running through them, originating in real-life fears and fantasies. One is the figure of the Eastern monarch or the 'Great Turk' as depicted in Robert Greene's *Selimus* (1594), *The Raging Turk* (1613–18) by Thomas Goffe, Kyd's *Solyman and Perseda* and Lord Fulke Greville's *Mustapha*. Despotic and blustering, these fictional kings make interesting stage figures. The plays themselves tend to be melodramatic and extreme but do raise questions regarding the ethical aspects of political power. In all these plays ambitious monarchs brutally murder their siblings in order to attain the throne. Hence King Henry's reference to the Turkish emperor in Shakespeare's *Henry IV Part 2* (1596–99) when he says: 'This is the English, not the Turkish court; / Not Amurath an Amurath succeeds, / but Harry Harry' (5.2.47–49). English politics is made out to be just and orderly in contrast to the brutality of the Turkish court. Many of these Turkish tyrants are also depicted as lusting for Christian women. The Turkish Viceroy, Asambeg, desires the virtuous Paulina in *The Renegado* and Solyman's love for Perseda in *Solyman and Perseda* is irrational and excessive. At a time when many European travellers venturing to Muslim lands were converting to Islam or 'turning Turk', either for convenience, for profit, because they were forced to or perhaps simply wanted to, stage plays repeatedly turned to the theme of conversion or 'turning Turk'. In Robert Daborne's *A Christian Turn'd Turk* (1612) the pirate John Ward falls in love with a Turkish woman and converts. His act is depicted as one of betrayal of religion and country. In *The Renegado* the hero Vitelli almost converts for love of a Turkish princess. Most often the plays ended with the convert becoming penitent and the near-convert changing his mind.

Apart from the Ottomans, Europeans were well acquainted with other Muslim cultures. The attempts of three English brothers collectively known as the 'Shirley brothers' to establish diplomatic ties with Persia inspired the *Travels of Three English Brothers* and the Egyptian setting of Shakespeare's *Antony and Cleopatra* (1607) was influenced by perceptions of classical Egypt as well as the Islamic Egypt of the sixteenth and seventeenth centuries. Most of these old civilizations were considered advanced and sophisticated, although some writers saw them as 'degenerating' or beginning to lose their old prestige and grandeur, while European powers forged ahead and progressed. England had close trading ties with Morocco. The arrival of Abd al-Malik, the Moroccan ambassador to London in 1600, might have inspired Shakespeare to make a 'Moor' a protagonist of his play *Othello*. About a decade earlier (*c.* 1591), George Peele had presented Moorish characters in his *Battle of Alcazar*. In spite of the trade and diplomatic exchange, most plays reproduced stereotypes of the 'Moor' as cruel, oversexed, vengeful and emotionally excessive. In *All's Lost by Lust* (1619–20) by William Rowley and Thomas Middleton, a play set against the backdrop of wars with Moors and with the Spanish as the antagonists, 'Moorishness' becomes a trope, a way of describing barbarism and lust.

In fact, 'Moor' became a catch-all term both in and outside the drama. It was used with reference to lighter-skinned North Africans, relatively dark-skinned 'sub-Saharan' Africans, natives of India and even Native Americans. It signified multiple racial and religious identities and soon simply served to signify 'otherness' in the most generalized sense. So Portia's 'tawny' suitor, the Prince of Morocco, is a Moor, as are Muly Hamet and Abdelmelec of the *Battle of Alcazar*, Aaron of *Titus Andronicus*, Othello of Shakespeare's play *Othello* and Eleazer of Thomas Dekker's *Lust's Dominion* (1600). These Moors are of varying or indeterminate skin tone but are clearly meant to signify the alien and the outsider. Eleazer, 'That damned Moor, that Devil, that Lucifer' (2.1), murders and dissembles his way through the plot;[30] Muly

Hamet ('Black in his look, and bloody in his deeds' [Scene 1.16]) is a traitor to his uncle, Abdelmelec, who is a 'white moor' (clearly indicating the 'black moors' were considered to be lower on the moral scale than 'white moors');[31] and in *The Fair Maid of the West*, the Moorish Sultan Mullisheg lusts after the virginal English maiden Bess. While a few Moors are cast in good light (the brief list includes Selim Calymath in *The Jew of Malta* and Abdelmelec), perhaps the most complex of the moors is the 'Moor of Venice', Othello. Possibly inspired by the Moroccan ambassador mentioned earlier and also by Leo Africanus, a North African moor who converted to Christianity and settled down in Europe and who wrote *The Geographical History of Africa*, Othello is the 'noble moor' as well as a brutal killer consumed by jealousy. Othello's skin tone has been a topic of some debate. Is he a 'blackmoor' or a lighter-skinned 'tawny moor' with origins in North Africa? It is virtually impossible to know for certain, but attitudes towards both kinds of moors inform the creation and the reception of Shakespeare's tragic hero.

**From Nicholas de Nicolay, *The navigations, peregrinations and voyages, made into Turkie* (1585).
Trans. T. Washington (courtesy of the Huntingdon Library)**

Nicholas de Nicolay was French ambassador to Turkey in the early 1550s. He wrote a fairly detailed account of Turkish and North African societies, *The navigations, peregrinations and voyages, made into Turkie* (1576, translated into English 1585). The following extract touches on Turks, the inhabitants of Persia, Turkey's neighbour to the east, as well as on the Jewish traders in the Ottoman Empire.[32]

The most part of the Turks of Algier, whether they be of the king's household or the gallies,[33] are Christians renied,[34] or Mahumetised,[35] of all nations, but most of them, Spaniards, Italians, and of Provence, of the islands and coasts of the Sea Mediterranean, given all to whoredome, sodometry,[36] theft, and all other most detestable vices, living only of rovings,[37] spoils, and pill[ag]ing at the seas, and the island, being about them: and with their practical art bring daily to Algiers a number of poor Christians, which they sell unto the Moores, and other merchants of Barbary for slaves, who afterward transport them and sell them where they think good, or else beating them miserably with staves, do employ and constrain them[38] to work in the fields, and in all other vile and abject[39] occupations and servitude almost intolerable: . . . [A]ll along the river and the shore the Moorish women and maiden slaves of Alger do go to wash their linen, being commonly whole naked, saving that they wear a piece of cotton cloth of some strange colour to cover their secret parts, (which notwithstanding for a little piece of money they will willingly uncover). . . . But as for the wives of the Turks or Moors, they are not seen [to] go uncovered, for they wear a great bernuche made of a blanket of white, black, or violet colour, which covereth their whole body and the head. . . .

There is moreover within the midst of [Constantinople], the old Sarail,[40] which first was builded and inhabited by Mehmet the Second . . . within which do dwell the wives and concubines of the great Turk, which in number are above 200 being the most part daughters of Christians, some being taken by courses on the seas or by land . . . some of the other are bought of merchants, and afterwards . . . presented unto the great Turk, who keepeth them within this Sarail, well appareled, nourished and entertained under straight keeping of . . . an eunuch of the late Barbarousse. . . .

The Turk's wives . . . do delight at all times to haunt the baths, as well for the continuance of their health, as beautifying of their persons. . . . [T]he other and principalest reason is, to have good occasion and honest excuse to go abroad out of their houses, within the which they are continually closed up for the great jealously of their husbands . . . and oftentimes under colour of going to baths, they resort to other places where they think good to accomplish their pleasures. . . . [They] do familiarly wash one another, whereby it cometh to pass. . . sometimes [they] become so fervently in love the one of the other as if it were with men, in such sort that perceiving some maiden, or woman of excellent beauty, they will not cease until they have found means to bathe with them, and to handle and grope them everywhere at their pleasures, so full they are of luxuriousness and feminine wantonness . . .

. . .

Persians nowadays, contrary to their ancient customs, are much given to all pleasure and voluptuousness,[41] appareling themselves very sumptuously[42] . . . using singular perfumes, and taking pleasure and delight in all jewels and precious stones. By their law it is permitted unto them to have many wives which because they are very jealous of them, they keep shut up under the keeping of the eunuchs, and nevertheless like unto the Turks and other nations of the East part, they are so given unto the detestable sin against nature, that they take it for no shame, but have places appointed and ordained for the same. . . . [B]ut to say truth, I do find them without comparison, more noble, more civil, more liberal, and of better spirit and judgment than the Turks are, unto whom (what countenance soever they do show) they are mortal enemies . . .

. . .

The number of the Jews dwelling throughout all the cities of Turkey and Grecia, and principally at Constantinople is so great, that it is a thing marvelous and incredible, for the number of these, using trade and traffic of merchandise, like of money at usury, doth there multiply so from day to day . . . that it may be said with good reason that at this present day they have in their hands the most and greatest traffic[43] of merchandise and ready money, that is in all Levant. And likewise their shops and warehouses the best furnished of all rich sorts of merchandises, which are in Constantinople are those of the Jews. Likewise they have amongst them workmen of all arts and handicrafts most excellent; and specially of the Maranes[44] of late banished and driven out of Spain and Portugal, who to the great detriment and damage of Christianity, have taught the Turks diverse inventions, crafts and engines of war, as to make artillery, harquebuses,[45] gunpowder, shot and other munitions. . . . [T]hey have also the commodity and usage to speak and understand all other sorts of languages used in Levant, which serveth them greatly for the communication and traffic, which they have with other strange nations, to whom oftentimes they serve for dragomans, or interpreters. Besides, this detestable nation of the Jews, are men full of all malice, fraud, deceit, and subtle[46] dealing, exercising execrable[47] usuries amongst the Christians and other nation without any consciences or reprehension. . . . [S]ince their extermination and the vengeance upon Jerusalem into this present day, they had at no time any certain dwelling place upon the face of the earth, but have always gone straying dispersed and driven away from country to country.

Indeed, both kinds of 'moors' were often conflated in the drama though travellers distinguished between the two (and more) races of Africans as they became better acquainted with that continent. Several of the major routes to America were through African waters. The Portuguese were already trading in the interiors and the English too got involved in the African trade. The Company of London Adventurers Trading into Parts of Africa (also known as the Guinea Company) was created in 1618. Voyagers, including the medieval traveller John Mandeville, came back with a picture of Africa as filled with strange grotesque people – one-eyed men, headless, lipless men and men with animal faces. Some of these legends are repeated in *Othello* when Othello describes his birthplace as the land populated by 'the cannibals that each other eat, / The Anthropophagi, and men whose heads / Do grow beneath their shoulders' (1.3.144–46). A North African himself, Leo Africanus claimed that northern moors are superior to southern ones who 'are not only ignorant of all good learning and liberal sciences, but are likewise careless and destitute of virtue'.[48] This sentiment was echoed by one Captain John Lock in *Hakluyt's Voyages*, where sub-Saharan Africans were described as a 'beastly people without a God, law, religion or commonwealth'.[49] They were also accused of cannibalism and were overall considered as not too different from the strange, fearful animals that roamed that fecund continent. The Africans' perceived lack of human status perhaps served to eventually justify slavery. Portugal had held monopoly over the African slave trade, but England got involved in the 1550s. In 1562 English slave trader John Hawkins took 300 Africans as slaves to the Caribbean. The tragic history of transatlantic slavery had clearly begun.

The English had a limited presence in the further reaches of Asia, including China and Japan, but perceived them as wealthy, sophisticated and somewhat mysterious cultures. There was conflict between the European powers (mainly the Dutch, the Portuguese and to an extent the English) over trade in the 'spice islands' (the present-day Moluccas) with their treasures of pepper, clove, nutmeg and mace. It is in these islands that John Fletcher's play *The Island Princess* (1619–21) is set. The English East India Company (established in 1600) worked hard to secure rights to trade with India. English representative Thomas Roe tried to impress the 'Grand Moghul' (who ruled much of India) with gifts from England in return for the opportunity to bargain for trading privileges. Roe's accounts described how the coach, paintings and silverware sent by the Company from England 'are extremely despised' in the Moghul court as 'here are nothing esteemed but the best sorts'.[50]

'India' did not always refer to the Indian sub-continent as such but became a trope that stood for all that was distant and wonderful. The poet John Donne in his poem 'The Sun Rising' writes of 'both the Indias of spice and mine' (line 17) as symbols of all that is fantastic and desirable. The treasure troves of spice lay to the east. Westwards were the gold and silver mines and also the home of those other 'Indians' named in error, the natives of the Americas.

New worlds

Tamburlaine announces that once he completes his conquest of the known world he will conquer another world with wealth 'More worth than Asia and the world beside ...' (Part 2, 5.3.153). The wonders of this other world, the Americas, were first communicated to Europeans through Peter Martyr's *Decades of the New World* (1511), translated into English by Richard Eden in 1555. Martyr and other writers told fabulous stories of dangerous ocean crossings, fearful hurricanes and a New World inhabited by dog-headed men and flesh-eating cannibals. Once in America one left behind the world one knew. Besides, voyagers felt that they had done more than merely travel to a new place; they had somehow 'discovered' it, uncovered it for the world and brought it into history – this, in spite of the visible presence of natives. America was a 'tabula rasa', a blank slate that Europeans could write on and shape as they saw fit.

Spain had already gained a foothold in America and it was the rivalry with Spain that prompted England to join the race for the Americas. But in comparison to other European powers, England's interest in America was quite delayed. John Cabot sailed to Newfoundland in 1497 and Martin Frobisher attempted to find a north-west passage to the East Indies in the 1570s but never succeeded (returning instead with two Eskimos and a ship full of pyrite or 'fool's gold'). There was very little English expansion into the Americas until the colony of Virginia was set up by adventurers associated with the Virginia Company. The Virginia experiment went wrong at first – the colonists found it hard to grow food, the natives turned hostile and the colony was evacuated after an early attempt in 1586. It was only in 1607 that a relatively secure settlement was established in Jamestown. Much of the writing from Virginia settlers was deeply pessimistic (John Smith wrote that Virginia was 'a misery, a ruin, a death, a hell'[51]) although others wrote determinedly upbeat reports, hoping to motivate other settlers to join the enterprise. Over a decade after Jamestown, the Pilgrims settled Cape Cod, Massachusetts in 1620. For these Puritans, America was God's destiny for them as well as His gift. However, Anglo–Spanish rivalry in the Americas continued and the writings of the Jesuit priest Bartolome Las Casas – who

Figure 3.1 Map of Raleigh's colony in Virginia, 1585 (© The Trustees of the British Museum).

wrote about the Spanish colonizers' 'torture, rape and mutilation of the natives and cruelties never neither seen, nor read, nor heard of' – drew much attention in England.[52] This came to be known as the 'Black Legend of Spain' and was used by the English to project their own presence in America as benign and just in contrast.

Most accounts of the natives of America represented a wild people whose lack of civilization was manifest in their nakedness and barbaric lifestyle. Samuel Purchas, another famous compiler of travel narratives best-known for his four-volume collection of travel writing, *Hakluytus Posthumus, or Purchas his Pilgrimes* (1625), wrote that they were a 'bad people, having little of Humanity but shape, ignorant of civility, of arts, of religion; more brutish than the beasts they hunt'.[53] This picture of the wild and uncouth Indian makes its way into the drama in the form of Caliban in Shakespeare's *The Tempest* (1610–11) whose name might be an anagram for 'cannibal' (the cannibals, devourers of human flesh, in fact, stood for everything that was fearful and alien about America). While the location of the play's island setting is indeterminate (it could well be a Mediterranean island), the references to the 'Bermoothes' (the Bermudas) and the Native American deity 'Setebos' have prompted many readers to describe *The Tempest* as the Renaissance's 'New World' play that was possibly inspired by the wreck of a ship called the *Sea Venture* off the coast of Bermuda in 1609. Caliban, the 'savage and deformed slave', first welcomes Prospero, the European visitor to the island, but later turns hostile – just like the native Virginians did towards the English. Half-animal who 'wouldst gabble like / A thing most brutish' (1.2.357–58) until taught language by Prospero, and persistently rebellious, lecherous and drunk, Caliban certainly brings European attitudes to the natives to mind.[54] However, there was quite another view of America and its natives. According to some writers, Americans were not a savage people but innocent and child-like, 'most gentle, loving and faithful, void of guile and treason, and such as live after the manner of the golden age'.[55] Indeed, from this perspective the New World was an Eden-like paradise. This idea of the new world as utopic space is most famously expressed by the French writer Michel de Montaigne in his essay 'Of the Cannibals' (1580). 'It is a nation', he writes, 'that hath no kind of traffic, no knowledge of letters, no intelligence of numbers, no name of magistrate . . . no use of service, of riches or of poverty',[56] lines that are repeated almost verbatim in *The Tempest*. For some writers such as Las Casas, the goodness and wild nature of the Indians made them 'teachable and capable of good learning' and hence open to being converted to Christianity.[57] A few Native Americans were transported to England. Apart from the two Inuits brought back by Frobisher, later colonists brought home native Virginians, and the colonist John Rolfe presented the native princess Pocahontas, whom he had married, at the royal English court. These American natives were objects of wonder and curiosity, but they all died premature and tragic deaths.

It wasn't only the desire for adventure that drew all Europeans, including the English, to the Americas. The land was vast and astoundingly rich. The English courtier and explorer Walter Raleigh's title to his travel narrative 'Discovery of the large, rich and beautiful Empire of Guiana' (1596) indicated the promise held by the mysterious land. Because the natives did not enclose the land and have the concept of 'private property', Europeans saw the land as 'vacuum domicilium' or vacant land to be taken at will. As John Cotton wrote in 1620, 'where there is a vacant place, there is liberty for the son of Adam or Noah to come and inhabit'.[58] The land was also, of course, additionally attractive because of the promise of gold. 'I will show you a Region', wrote Eden, 'flowing with gold, where you might satisfy your ravening appetites.'[59]

Virginia did not have gold but had another money-spinner, tobacco. The promise of the money to be made from this commodity was dangled before many prospective colonizers.

From Thomas Harriot, *A Brief and true Report of the New Found Land of Virginia* (1588).
(Courtesy of The Huntingdon Library)

Thomas Harriot was a scientist, mathematician and colonizer who first reached Virginia in 1584. He was interested in carefully noting the details of the lives of the Algonquin tribe that was native to that part of America. *A Brief and true Report of the New Found Land of Virginia* (1588, 1590) was a record of his observations and was also meant to function as an advertisement for Virginia in order to tempt other English colonizers to settle there.

I thought also good to note this unto you, that you which shall inhabit and plant there, maye know how specially that country corn is there to be preferred before ours: Besides the manifold ways in applying it to victuall,[60] the increase is so much that small labour and pains is needful in respect that must be used for ours. For this I can assure you that according to the rate we have made proof of, one man may prepare and husband[61] so much ground (having once borne corn before) with less than four and twenty hours labour, as shall yield him victual in a large proportion for a twelve month, if he have nothing else, but that which the same ground will yield, and of that kind only which I have before spoken of: the said ground being also but of five and twenty yards square . . .

. . .

There is an herb which is sowed a part by itself & is called by the inhabitants Uppowoc: In the West Indies it hath divers names, according to the severall places & countries where it growth and is used: The Spaniards generally call it Tobacco. The leaves thereof being dried and brought into powder: they use to take the fume or smoke thereof by sucking it through pipes made of clay into their stomach and head; from whence it purgeth[62] superfluous phlegm & other gross humors,[63] openeth all the pores & passages of the body: by which meanes the use thereof, not only preserveth the body from obstructions; but also if any be, so that they have not beene of too long continuance, in short time breaketh them: whereby their bodies are notably preserved in health, & know not many greevous[64] diseases wherewithal we in England are oftentimes afflicted.

This Uppowoc is of so precious estimation amongst them, that they think their gods are marvelously delighted therwith. Whereupon sometime they make hallowed[65] fires & cast some of the powder therein for a sacrifice: being in a storm upon the waters, to pacify their gods, they cast some up into the air and into the water: so a wear for fish being newly set up, they cast some therein and into the air: also after an escape of danger, they cast some into the air likewise: but all done with strange gestures, stamping, sometime dancing, clapping of hands, holding up of hands, & staring up into the heavens, uttering therewithal and chattering strange words & noises

We ourselves during the time we were there used to suck it after their manner, as also since our return, & have found many rare and wonderful experiments of the virtues thereof; of which the relation would require a volume by itself. The use of it by many of late, men & women of great calling as else, and some learned Physicians also, is sufficient witness.

. . .

It resteth I speak a word or two of the natural inhabitants, their natures and manners . . ., as that you may know, how that they in respect of troubling our inhabiting and planting, are not to be feared; but that they shall have cause both to fear and love us, that shall inhabit with them.

They are a people clothed with loose mantles made of Deer skins, & aprons of the same round about their middles; all else naked; of such a difference of statures only as we in England; having no edge tools or weapons of iron or steel to offend us withal, neither know they how to make any: those weapons that they have, are only bows made of Witch hazel, & arrows of reeds; flat edged truncheons also of wood about a yard long, neither have they any thing to defend themselves but targets made of barks; and some armours made of sticks wickered together with thread. . . .

If there fall out any wars between us & them, what their fight is likely to be, we having advantages against them so many manner of ways, as by our discipline, our strange weapons and devises[66] else; especially by ordinance great and small, it may be easily imagined; by the experience we have had in some places, the turning up of their heels against us in running away was their best defense.

In respect of us they are a people poor, and for want of skill and judgement in the knowledge and use of our things, do esteem our trifles before things of greater value. Notwithstanding in their proper manner considering the want of such means as we have, they seem very ingenious; For although they have no such tools, nor any such crafts, sciences and arts as we; yet in those things they do, they show excellency of wit.[67] And by how much they upon due consideration shall find our manner of knowledges and crafts to exceed theirs in perfection, and speed for doing or execution, by so much the more is it probable that they should desire our friendships & love, and have the greater respect for pleasing and obeying us. Whereby may be hoped if means of good government be used, that they may in short time be brought to civility, and the embracing of true religion.

Some religion they have already, which although it be far from the truth, yet being as it is, there is hope it may be the easier and sooner reformed. They believe that there are many Gods which they call *Mantóac*, but of different sorts and degrees; one only chief and great God, which hath been from all eternity. Who as they affirm when he purposed to make the world, made first other goddess of a principal order to be as means and instruments to be used in the creation and government to follow; and after the Sun, Moon, and Stars, as petty gods and the instruments of the other order more principal. First they say were made waters, out of which by the gods was made all diversity of creatures that are visible or invisible . . .

. . .

Most things they saw with us, as Mathematical instruments, sea compasses, the virtue of the loadstone[68] in drawing iron, a perspective glass[69] whereby was showed many strange sights, burning glasses, wildfire works, guns, books, writing and reading, spring clocks that seem to go of themselves, and many other things that we had, were so strange unto them, and so far exceeded their capacities to comprehend the reason and means how they should be made and done, that they thought they were rather the works of gods than of men, or at the leastwise they had been given and taught us of the gods. Which made many of them to have such opinion of us, as that if they knew not the truth of god and religion already, it was rather to be had from us, whom God so specially loved then from a people that were so simple, as they found themselves to be in comparison of us. Whereupon greater credit was given unto that we spoke of concerning such matters.

Many times and in every town where I came, according as I was able, I made declaration of the contents of the Bible; that therein was set foorth the true and only GOD, and his mighty works, that therein was contained the true doctrine of salvation through Christ, with many particularities[70] of Miracles and chief points of religion, as I was able then to utter, and thought fit for the time. And although I told them the book materially & of itself was not of any such virtue, as I thought they did conceive, but only the doctrine therein contained; yet would many be glad to touch it, to embrace it, to kiss it, to hold it to their breasts and heads, and stroke over all their body with it; to show their hungry desire of that knowledge which was spoken of.

. . .

One other rare and strange accident, leaving others, will I mention before I end, which moved the whole country that either knew or heard of us, to have us in wonderful admiration. There was no town where we had any subtle devise practiced against us, we leaving it unpunished or not revenged (because wee sought by all means possible to win them by gentleness) but that within a few days after our departure from every such town, the people began to die very fast, and many in short space; in some towns about twenty, in some forty, in some sixty, & in one six score, which in truth was very many in respect of their numbers.

This happened in no place that we could learn but where we had been, where they used some practice against us, and after such time; The disease also so strange, that they neither knew what is was, nor how to cure it; the like by report of the oldest men in the country never happened before, time out of mind. A thing specially observed by us as also by the natural inhabitants themselves. Insomuch that when some of the inhabitants which were our friends & especially the *Wiroans Wingina*[71] had observed such effects in four or five towns to follow their wicked practices, they were persuaded that it was the work of our God through our means, and that we by him might kill and slay whom wee would without weapons and not come near them.

Race and racism

Did increasing contact with different cultures heighten consciousness of 'race'? And was there 'racism' in the Renaissance? There are several accounts of what appear to be 'racist' thinking. 'Aliens' or foreigners, including Scots, Irish, Welsh, Dutch and a small number of Africans, most of them either traders or workers, constituted about 5 per cent of England's population. There were a number of anti-alien riots, and in 1593 a bill was introduced in Parliament to control 'merchant strangers' as they were supposedly doing the native English out of jobs. Elizabeth's doctor, a converted Portuguese Jew named Dr Lopez, was accused of trying to poison her and was executed. His 'Jewishness' was part of the argument raised against him (Dekker's play *The Whore of Babylon* depicts Roppus a 'doctor of physic' conspiring against the 'Fairy Queen', and Shakespeare's *The Merchant of Venice* might also have been prompted by this incident). A law was passed to expel 'Egyptians' or gypsies from the nation. Similarly, 'blackmoors' were also expelled from the realm on the basis that they were 'infidels' who consumed public relief in times of scarcity and that they were 'of great annoyance' to the natives.[72]

There was great interest in the reason for differences amongst human beings. One reason given for the dark skin of Africans was the Biblical story in which Noah cursed his disobedient son Ham with dark-skinned progeny. Another theory often put forward was based on humours.[73] Southerners, for instance, had more 'black bile' and were therefore more emotional and uncontrollable. These traits conferred by the humours made for distinct differences that were difficult to change. Another theory was that climate resulted in human difference: so, for example, the Irish were supposedly 'intemperate' because of the damp air and soil of Ireland. Such thinking is reflected in *Henry V* when King Henry says that the 'air of France / Hath blown vice in me' (3.6.152–53). Similarly, for a long time dark skin was seen to be an effect of heat. However, the travel writer George Best wrote that the fact that white people do not turn black when living in hot climates indicates that dark skin had little to do with heat and sun. Best recounted the story of an Ethiopian 'black as coal' who lived in England and married a white woman. Their child was as dark as the father, pointed out Best, proving that blackness had little to do with climate but was a 'natural infection'.[74] If this was the case, miscegenation or the mixing of different groups through sexual contact was a worrying prospect since it could change the appearance of people. In *Titus Andronicus* the child born of the black Aaron and the white Tamora is dark and described as 'A joyless, dismal, black and sorrowful issue' (4.2.68).

The term 'race' was first used in John Florio's 1598 Italian–English dictionary and was defined as 'a brood, a stock, a descent, a lineage, a pedigree'.

It therefore implied lineage or descent as 'in 'race of Abraham'. The English, in fact, liked to see themselves as a distinct race. Much later, in the nineteenth century, a person's race was linked to his skin colour and physical appearance and racist thinking made generalized assumptions about an individual's moral character, intellectual and other abilities based on his physical appearance. According to some modern scholars, one cannot talk of this kind of racism in the Renaissance. Renaissance notions of race, argue these scholars, were not based in biology but on religion and culture. So, for instance, when James I described Muslims as 'circumcised turbaned Turks' in contrast to the 'baptiz'd race' of Christians in his 1591 poem *Lepanto,* he emphasized religious identity.[75] Similarly, attitudes to Jews and the Irish too are a good example of racism based on cultural rather than biological difference. In fact, it was not quite understood whether Jews were a distinct 'race' though they were also often referred to as a 'nation'. But stereotypes abounded: Jews smelled bad because of their diet, they abducted Christian children, circumcised Christian men, were timid and incapable of war, devious, malicious and engaged in exploitative lending practices. Barabas in the *Jew of Malta* gloatingly confesses to killing 'sick people groaning under walls' (2.3.174) and driving men to suicide or madness with his 'extorting, cozening and forgery' (2.3.194). Shakespeare's Shylock is a greedy money-lender and blood-thirsty avenger. In John Webster's *The Devil's Law Case* (*c.* 1617) Romelio, a Christian doctor disguised as a Jew, is associated with similar crimes. The evil in these characters is represented as emerging from their Jewishness. It has been said that the Renaissance inherited these cultural understandings of race from the Middle Ages. While medieval texts portray non-Christians as converting to Christianity and transforming their cultural and consequently their 'racial identity', cultural racism – both in the Middle Ages and the Renaissance – was not necessarily benign. As Ania Loomba and Jonathan Burton point out, it was still accompanied by prejudice and fear of the worst kind.[76]

Does this mean that biological notions of race – race as an inherited characteristic that was immutable and constant – were unknown in the Renaissance? The 'Spanish Blood Laws' created in the sixteenth century, which declared that descendants of Muslim and Jews continued to be Muslim or Jewish even though they might have converted to Christianity, indicate that an understanding of race as biology too existed. As the Geneva Bible stated, the leopard could not change his spots, nor could a black-moor be washed white. While this is technically true of course, the point being made was that – like physical features – moral, psychological and intellectual attributes were also unchangeable. So Caliban can be described as 'Abhorred slave, / Which any print of goodness will not take' (1.2.352–53). Attitudes to African people showed that biological factors, notably skin colour, did matter in the Renaissance as much as cultural factors did. Blackness was sometimes spectacular and exotic (King James had 'blackmoors' dance naked in the snow at his wedding – they died a few days later of pneumonia) and black skin served to show up white skin by contrast (Kim Hall has discussed how black people were increasingly incorporated in portraits of aristocratic Europeans for precisely this reason[77]). While Cleopatra, with her 'tawny front' (1.1.6) and skin made dark by 'Phoebus' amorous pinches' (1.5.29), is dangerously seductive, most often darkness was a short-cut term for all that was unattractive (for example, Lysander in *A Midsummer Night's Dream* rejects Hermia saying 'Away, you Ethiop' and 'Out, tawny Tartar' [3.2.257, 263]). Further, black and white were produced as exclusive and opposing categories and it was through this binary that the English began to formulate the notion of 'self' and 'other'. Besides, as typical in racist thinking, blackness was associated with negative attributes – stupidity, immorality and hypersexuality. This association of blackness with evil certainly had its roots in Christian symbolism of darkness and light but was further intensified and complicated by Renaissance Europeans' interactions with real Africans. Shakespeare's Aaron and his Othello are his most famous dark-skinned characters. In a sketch of a scene from *Titus Andronicus* by Henry Peacham, Aaron, standing to the side, is startlingly black, clearly distinguished from the others by his skin colour. Aaron's terrible capacity for evil is connected with his dark skin: he 'will have his soul black like his face' (3.1.206). Even Othello, the noble general of the Venetian army, descends into the violence and irrationality associated with blackness and by the end of the play he is 'the blacker devil!' (5.2.131). This account of cultural understandings of race and of notions of race as rooted in bodily differences indicates that we cannot make any simple distinctions between the two understandings of race in the Renaissance. Both were interconnected and coexisted, and 'race' was not defined in a coherent manner (as it continues not to be), nor was one understanding of race more flexible or somehow more tolerant than the other.

Gendering difference

The ways in which a society ordered gender relations and sexual behaviour was often seen as a mark of civilization. 'Disorderly' gender relations and 'unruly' sexuality were often seen as characteristic of other cultures. As Loomba writes, 'gender and sexuality provided a language for expressing and developing ideas about religious, geographic, and ultimately racial difference'.[78] So Native American and Muslim men were accused of having sex with other men; Jewish men were said to menstruate and to cross-dress; Egyptian women to urinate standing up. Almost every foreigner was said to be to be 'lecherous'. The Moorish king in *The Fair Maid of the West*, who commands his men to 'Find us concubines, / The fairest Christian Damsels you can hire, / Or buy for gold: the loveliest of the Moors / We can command, and Negroes everywhere: / Italians, French, and Dutch, choice Turkish girls' (Part 1, 4.1.28–34), is just one instance of a foreigner with a ravenous sexual appetite.[79] This image of the lustful Muslim ruler with the large international harem was a recurring one in drama and was described with horror, fascination and perhaps a little envy.

Foreign lands were also described as women and vice versa. Both the woman and the land were objects of desire. For example, Ireland was described by English commentator Luke Gernon as a 'Nymph' who 'is at all points like a young wench that hath the green sickness for want of occupying. She is very fair of visage, and hath a smooth skin of tender grass . . . Her flesh is of a soft and delicate mound of earth, and her blue veins travelling through every part of her like rivulets'.[80] Similarly, a famous engraving by Stradanus depicting Vespucci discovering America showed America as a naked woman reclining on a hammock when the male explorer encountered her. Guiana in South America is described by Walter Raleigh as a country that is still virgin: she 'hath her maidenhead, never sacked, turned, nor wrought . . . it hath never been entered by any army and never conquered or possessed by any Christian prince'.[81] Consequently, European voyages of exploration and discovery became endeavours that involved possessing, husbanding and/or raping – in short making the foreign land/woman one's own. This discourse made its way into drama. In *Twelfth Night* Sir Toby calls Maria 'my metal of India' (2.5.13), and in Shakespeare's *The Comedy of Errors* (c. 1594) Luce's body is 'spherical, like a globe' so Dromio 'could find out countries in her' (3.2.114, 115). Foreign lands were, however, also associated with 'unruly' women who did not conform to accepted notions of femininity. South America and Africa were associated with the mythical female tribe, the Amazons, who sacrificed men. Irishwomen were considered lustful, loud and chaotic, and 'vile and abominable witches' were said to live in Africa.[82] By implication these 'disorderly' women needed to be domesticated and brought under control. Drama reproduced these legends of wild femininity in the form of Sycorax the evil, witch from Algiers in *The Tempest*, and Zanthia, the black maid in *The Knight of Malta*, who plots to kill her own mistress and who has a 'black shape, and blacker actions', making her 'hell's perfect character' (4.2).[83]

Zanthia also has an affair with one of the European knights in the play. Trade and international contact inevitably led to relationships between people of different races. Fear of sexual contact with foreign women permeated European travel narratives. Spenser, for example, condemned English–Irish sexual relationships as they could only 'bring forth an evil race'.[84] These relationships when represented in drama lend tension to the plays and are often depicted as destroying an individual's identity (Antony notably forgets his Roman-ness due to his obsession with the Egyptian Cleopatra) or even endangering a European character's Christian soul (Jack Ward in *A Christian Turn'd Turk* becomes a Muslim for love of a Turkish woman). Other plays set in the Muslim world counter this horrifying possibility of conversion by having the (usually beautiful and fair-skinned) Muslim woman convert to Christianity. This theme is seen in *The Island Princess* and *The Renegado*. This motif of the 'convertible' non-Christian

Figure 3.2 *Discovery of America: Vespucci Landing in America.* Jan van der Straet, called Stradanus, *c.* 1587–89 (The Metropolitan Museum of Art, Gift of Estate of James Hazen Hyde, 1959 / www.metmuseum.org).

woman is also discernible in two plays featuring Jewish women: both Abigail in *The Jew of Malta* and Jessica in *The Merchant of Venice* are eager converts to Christianity. In a world where sumptuous goods moved between countries and cultures, the convertible, beautiful body of the woman is another example of such movement. In Loomba's words, women constituted the 'delicious traffic' between races and cultures.[85] Christian women, however, are depicted in drama as unwaveringly faithful to their religion and to Christian men. So Paulina in *The Renegado* will have nothing to do with the Turkish viceroy or his religion and Bess in *The Fair Maid of the West* will not yield to the Moorish king's attempts at seduction and remains, right to the end, the 'girl worth gold'.

Transforming identities

While racial identity was described as rooted and unchangeable on the one hand, the notion of transforming and converting the 'other' was an appealing one on the other. For example, the English felt that they could eventually civilize the Irish and make them shed their Irish identity (signified in Jonson's 1613 *Irish Masque* by the Irish characters shedding their Irish glibs and mantles). Similarly, Christian preachers had long voiced a desire to convert the Jewish people. This fantasy was sometimes enacted in drama – Shylock has to convert to Christianity at the end of *The Merchant of Venice*.

Intercultural contact, however, also raised the possibility that *all* identity was unstable. Ascham worried that Englishmen changed too easily under foreign influence. He particularly dwelt on how Englishmen get 'Italianated' after travelling to Italy. This, for Ascham, meant that they are drawn to Catholicism, became quarrelsome, and picked up all 'variety of vanities and … filthy living.[86] This sentiment is echoed in *The Merchant of Venice* when Portia says that her English suitor got his 'doublet in Italy, his round hose in France, his bonnet in Germany, and his behaviour everywhere' (1.2.72–74). Besides, it was feared that the greed for profits in trade led to the loss of a distinct identity. In Robert Wilson's *The Three Ladies of London*, Lady Love and Lady Conscience bemoan the rise of Lady Lucar (Lucre or money). For her sake men 'forsake mother, prince, country, religion, kith, and kin / Nay, men care not what they forsake, so Lady Lucre they win' (Act 1).[87] The fear that identity is not stable and that the self is dangerously flexible especially manifested itself in the 'Turk plays' in which, as discussed earlier, Christian characters converted or are tempted to convert to Islam. However, the best travel writing as well as the best drama explored the subtleties of hybrid or multiple identities rather than simply condemn them. Othello is 'an extravagant and wheeling stranger / Of here and everywhere' (1.1.134–35), and although he falls at the end of the play, he persists in drawing attention to his complex identity right until his death – he is both Venetian and 'Turk' at once, both insider and alien.

The marketplace of the world

Merchants were regular figures on the English stage and trade itself became a force that impacted the lives and destinies of characters. It involved complex transactions, economic as well as moral and cultural, that made it an attractive subject for dramatists. The play *Four Prentices of London* (*c.* 1592) by Thomas Heywood actually substitutes the questing knights of older romances with tradespeople who go to the Holy land to fight for the Christian cause.

Samuel Purchas saw trade and religion as intertwined: many nations conducting 'commerce and intercourse of amity' to unite the world 'in one band of humanity' and ultimately under 'one Church, truly catholic, one Pastor and one sheepfold'.[88] But the general attitude to trade was ambivalent. Trading companies were accused of pursuing profit rather than national prestige and emerging capitalism was viewed with suspicion as being unethical and cold-blooded. Consequently, stage merchants were depicted as crafty and fraudulent tricksters. Mercantilism is the foundation of all relationships in *The Jew of Malta* and for Barabas anything is acceptable as long as his business interests are protected. He does not care if Muslims or Christians triumph in Malta for 'loving neither, will I live with both, / Making a profit of my policy' (5.3.111–12).

While anxieties about the immorality of trade are deflected to Malta in Marlowe's play, it is Venice, the great trading centre of Europe, that became the symbol of the glamour as well as the anxieties attendant on the new economic system. International trade inevitably made Venice cosmopolitan. As *The Merchant of Venice* states, 'the trade and profit of the city / Consisteth of all nations' (3.3.30–31). Profit, loss and risk dominate the dramatic landscape of *The Merchant of Venice* and Shylock and Antonio's rivalry has an economic as well as a religious basis. In Ben Jonson's *Volpone* (1606), which is also set in Venice, the characters are predatory and distorted by greed. Writers were worried that London too was becoming like Venice, a city in which profit overruled all other considerations. Global trade also brought luxury goods to England and encouraged excessive and conspicuous consumption. In *The Roaring Girl* and Jonson's *Everyman out of His Humour* (1599) London's shops are filled with goods eagerly sought after by customers and the protagonist of *The Shoemaker's Holiday* becomes rich by involving himself in the trade of luxury foreign goods like sugar, almonds and cambric. Some of these foreign goods could also, it was feared, alter personalities and identities. Tobacco could make one like the American heathen who grew it in the first place, and coffee could possibly 'blacken' Christian men's personalities. Trade clearly generated anxiety; it led to moral degeneration, the loss of bullion, the influx of foreign goods and foreign people – but it was also exciting and filled lives with new things, new experiences and new possibilities.

Early colonialism

'Give me a map,' orders Tamburlaine, 'then let me see how much / Is left for me to conquer all the world' (Part 2, 5.2.123–24). Is it possible to think of the Renaissance English as world conquerors and of their travels as instances of early colonialism? After all, England was to become the world's most powerful imperial power in a couple of centuries. In the sixteenth and seventeenth centuries Spain already had colonies in the Americas, the Portuguese and Dutch controlled trading outposts in the East Indies and the Ottoman Turks had a vast empire. England was very aware of its own 'belatedness' in this regard, but this 'imperial envy' motivated the English and prepared the way for a real empire – though that reality was still in the future.

Ireland is often been described as England's first colony and as a testing ground for England's imperial dreams. Small colonies of English had settled throughout Ireland, established 'plantations' and instituted policies by which they got Irish feudal chiefs to surrender their lands. The language of conquest was often couched in the language of the 'civilizing mission' – the true purpose of the English presence in Ireland was to make that 'rude' and savage people less barbaric, even if it involved the use of force. In the words of Captain Thomas Lee who served Elizabeth in Ireland, 'martial law is very necessary and ... ought to be granted to all governors of remote and savage places where your majesty's laws are not received ... until such time as the people shall become civil, and embrace the laws, and peacable living'.[89] Europeans also appropriated land in the Americas and deemed it legal ownership obtained by virtue of 'discovery'. Hakluyt's influential 'Discourse of Western Planting' (1584), which laid out the reasons for colonizing America, emphasized the economic and trade benefits. Not only would the colonies yield raw materials and provide markets for English goods, they would also offer jobs to the poor and curb idleness and rebellion back home. It is important to realize that neither the colonialism of the Americas nor the colonialism of Ireland is a story of unalloyed victory – colonists faced hostility from the natives, natural disasters and financial setbacks, but they persisted for the most part.

What one can conclude is that England was definitely not a full-blown colonial power during the Renaissance. Rather, it was an era of 'protocolonialism' when the foundations of what was to become an empire were just being laid and certain assumptions and beliefs characteristic of imperialism were coming into play. Even if the English did not feel economically or politically superior to all cultures, they represented themselves as morally and culturally superior. Ideologies of race were also used to justify plunder and exploitation and later become central to colonial ideology. Drama did not stay untouched: *The Island Princess* is a projection of English colonial ambition in the East Indies and *The Tempest* is today regarded as the Renaissance's foremost 'colonial play'. Though it is often read as set in America, it could also easily be about the English settlement of Ireland, as Dympna Callaghan points out.[90] Caliban can be read as the native deprived of his land by the European settler. He is constructed as uncivilized and immoral but is also sensitive and articulate in expressing his resentment. The play, consciously or otherwise, raises questions about the ethics of taking possession of another person's land. Similarly, *Tamburlaine* makes its protagonist a symbol of the ambition and energy that inspired English merchants and colonists. But Tamburlaine is also terrible in his cruelty and brutality and will let nothing come in the way of his political ambitions. Both Shakespeare's play and Marlowe's, in different ways, move readers to reflect on the moral and human cost of empires.

Discussion points

1 Think about whether there are any 'outsiders' or marginal figures in the plays you are studying who are depicted in ways that indicate some attempt to understand or even sympathize with their experiences. Do you think we can truly understand marginal identities and experiences through canonical English Renaissance plays?

2 Consider a play that figures foreigners or characters marked as outsiders in some way. If you had access only to the play (and no knowledge of historical context or other texts) what might you think about these foreigners and the ethnic/racial groups they belong to?

3 Is it possible to balance our interest in attitudes to and representations of foreigners and 'outsiders' in the plays we study with the exploration of form and aesthetics? Another way of thinking about this: can texts that seem particularly, even embarrassingly, 'racist' or prejudiced from our perspective be aesthetically pleasing and/or entertaining to us modern-day readers of Renaissance drama?

4 Compare the three excerpts on the natives of three diverse parts of the world reproduced in this chapter. While they obviously communicate different details about the cultural groups that the authors describe, are the texts similar (or different) as far as tone, style and structure are concerned? Also think about what other details you wish the writer had included that would tell you more about Renaissance attitudes to these foreigners.

4

Humanism

Even as Renaissance voyagers set out in search of new lands, there was another group of explorers engaged on their own travels of discovery. Scholars from across Europe, these travellers ventured into the nearly lost worlds of classical Greece and Rome by studying the writings of these ancient civilizations. These people came to be known as the 'humanists' and their cultural and social legacy has proved to be widespread and enduring. Like Renaissance travellers, they too experienced encounters with mysterious and exciting worlds that they attempted to make their own. The intellectual pursuits of the humanists remind us that that the Renaissance thinkers felt a tremendous sense of continuity with the past, even as they perceived themselves as living in an exciting age of renewal and growth.

Humanism is often associated with many things including the rise of secularism and individualism, but it is best understood as a programme of study. While it is hard to define humanism or set its limits, broadly speaking it involved the revival of the study of the classics in order to appreciate and to imitate them. The Latin term *studia humanitas* meant the study of language, philosophy and history; the fifteenth-century Italian word to describe the teacher of this learning was *umanista*. The English term 'humanist' appeared in the late sixteenth century. Ideas on what exactly constituted the *studia humanitas* varied, but most modern scholars would agree with Paul Kristeller that the humanities 'came to stand for a clearly defined cycle of scholarly disciplines namely grammar, rhetoric, history, poetry and moral philosophy'.[1] The study of Latin grammar, an emphasis on rhetoric and focused attention on written texts were all central to humanism, and the humanists went on to become prolific writers of speeches, letters, treatises and poetry. The humanist approach also came to pervade political thought, ethics, the study of history, theology, the creative arts and even medicine.

Humanists liked to say that they were more concerned with the study of humans than with abstract metaphysical speculation. They defined 'wisdom' as self-knowledge and rational thinking although they nearly always added that these attributes were God-given. It was this that differentiated humans from beasts and made it possible for humans to become 'civilized'. Eventually, knowledge acquired social prestige and was connected to social status. As Fritz Caspari writes, 'the aristocracy of the pen began to invade and even to displace that of the sword'.[2] While it is difficult to say whether humanism was a formal movement, a coherent 'ism' or simply an intellectual practice that was propagated through social networks across Europe and whether the typical humanist was a professional scholar or was more likely to be an amateur or even a dabbler in the classics, it is important to realize that humanism was not a simple unified system. Humanists never fully agreed among themselves as to what constituted the best programme of study and there were conflicts between the scholarly version of humanism and the kind of humanist learning pursued by fashionable young courtiers.

The 'Renaissance' is itself a humanist creation in one sense – the humanists felt that they were living in a bright, new age characterized by a vibrant new energy. This, they liked to say, was in contrast to the 'dark ages' which preceded them and which separated them from the glorious classical era. Humanism – pursued in universities, courts and homes of noblemen – was set up in opposition to 'scholasticism', the intellectual system that dominated the Middle Ages in which the study of church law and logic dominated and where monasteries were the primary centres of learning. However, most modern scholars would agree that the Middle Ages were certainly not a morass of gloom and ignorance and that, in fact, humanism has its roots in medieval scholasticism. Kristeller explains that the medieval Italian tradition of rhetoric and the study of classical poetry in the Middle Ages were the roots of humanism, while other scholars have pointed out that humanism was also influenced by the twelfth-century Italian art of letter writing, *ars dictaminis*, and the medieval codification of Roman law.[3] These medieval pursuits took on new form and shape in the Renaissance with the rise of city states in Italy and the corresponding need to train gentlemen for careers in civic administration and commerce. The professionalization of these young men became inseparable from the new learning.

'The courts of ancient men': The study of the classics

The study of Greek and Roman texts was central to the humanist project. The Italian poet Petrarch, one of the pioneering figures of Italian humanism, expressed his admiration for Cicero, Virgil and other Latin authors, and the political thinker Niccolò Machiavelli noted that studying the classics was a way of conversing with the past. Whenever he reads these texts, wrote Machiavelli, 'I enter the courts of ancient men, where, received by them with affection, I feed on that food which only is mine and which I was born for, where I am not ashamed to speak with them and to ask them the reason for their actions; and they in their kindness answer me; and for four hours of time I do not feel boredom, I forget every trouble, I do not dread poverty, I am not frightened by death, entirely I give myself over to them.'[4] Renaissance Italians liked to emphasize that they were the descendants of the ancient Romans, while the writers of Tudor England saw ancient Athens and Augustan Rome as its cultural predecessors and also often described London as 'Troynovant' or the new Troy. As Gabriel Harvey wrote, 'pure Italy, and fine Greece planted themselves in rich England.'[5] The humanists perceived antiquity as the basis of culture and as holding up an ideal they strove to attain. They themselves, they felt, were mediators between their own age and a vanished era. The study of the classical tongues and classical literature became prestigious and served to attract the attention and interest of patrons and employers.

While the study of Latin and Latin works first dominated humanist scholarship, by the early fifteenth century Greek was also added to the humanist repertoire. The translation of Greek texts into Latin was an important part of humanist achievement and, if it were not for the humanists, the works of Homer, Sophocles, Herodotus and Plutarch would have remained unknown. Scholars roamed Europe searching for, copying and studying both Greek and Latin classics with extraordinary perseverance. Apart from translating the classics (eventually into the vernacular languages of Europe), naming, compiling and commenting on ancient manuscripts and 'cleansing' Latin of what they saw as medieval 'contaminations' were other important aspects of humanists' intellectual work. Greek and Latin grammar became central to the curriculum with the works of Aristophanes, Homer, Euripides, Demosthenes, Terence, Virgil, Horace and, most importantly, Cicero used to teach it. Classical authors furnished school and university students with moral examples and precepts (humanists somehow succeeded in producing moralistic readings of even the bawdy comedies of the Roman dramatist Terence), but what is possibly most interesting is the fact that Renaissance writers drew upon these ancient models to attain much sought after 'eloquence'. Imitation was the dominant method of teaching the skills of rhetoric to young writers. It was not seen as slavish copying; instead it was understood to be a way of adding authority to one's own thoughts and eventually a way to project one's own voice. As Joanna Martindale writes, 'Imitation should not be viewed as a restrictive doctrine; writers may respond to the same model in different ways and classical authors offered inspiration for more than one kind of poetry.'[6]

The humanists' admiration for the classical pagan world was viewed with suspicion by the clergy, who worried that Christian readers could be contaminated by pagan texts. The humanists in their turn insisted that theirs was not an anti-Christian project. For Petrarch the knowledge of man was linked to understanding the Divine, and Erasmus maintained that the wisdom of the ancients was in harmony with Christianity. In fact, Erasmus insisted that the best way to read scripture was as a good humanist would read a classical text – one should keep audiences and contexts in view, 'for it is from a comprehensive examination of these things that one learns the meaning of a given utterance'.[7]

From Erasmus of Rotterdam, *The Antibarbarians* (first printed in 1520).
Trans. Robert Parker.

Erasmus of Rotterdam was a Dutch scholar and classicist, and among the foremost humanist thinkers and writers of his time. *The Antibarbarians* is a defence of humanist learning. It is cast in the form of a dialogue where the speakers are engaged in a discussion on the decline of learning. This passage is spoken by one of the participants who defends classical learning from the attacks of those who felt that the ancients were 'pagans' and that no good Christian should read their works.

On the absurdity of faulting something merely because it was discovered by pagans 'When we pour this vinegar over them, it's remarkable what a shout they raise as they charge against us; they say we aren't Christians but pagans, idolaters, more pernicious[8] than the pagans themselves. 'Can one really', they say, 'count as a Christian anyone who takes so much trouble over profane[9] disciplines, devised by impious men to serve their pride, and so relishes them? – who finds all his relaxation in them, consecrates[10] all his leisure, all his activity to them, relies on them for all his comfort? Isn't it obvious what a sacrilege it is for a man who's once enlisted in Christian service, who's been initiated and enrolled in the name of Christ the general, to desert to the devils, the enemy, and have dealings with the worshippers of idols? Can you deny that a man is having dealings with them if he likes being called a Ciceronian in oratory, a Virgilian or a Horatian in poetry, an Aristotelian, an Academic, a Stoic, an Epicurean in philosophy?'[11] You've heard of the Chrysippean enthymeme?[12] You've heard of the horned syllogism?[13] You can see what tricky snares they're trying to net you simple folk in.' I can see that we need some of Carneades' hellebore.[14] What are you saying, you anti-Chrysippeans? That anything deriving from pagans is automatically evil and banned to Christians? Does this mean that we can't make use of any of the inventions of the gentiles[15] without immediately ceasing to be Christians? Well, I do suggest then that a public warning ought to be issued to your carpenters not to venture to use their saws, axes, adzes, bores, in future, nor their wedges, rules, plumb-lines and levels. Why so? It was a pagan, Daedalus,[16] who thought up both of the craft of carpentry and its tools. Blacksmiths had better stop working; iron-working was invented by those monstrous men, the Cyclopes.[17] No one must fashion things in bronze; tradition says that the Chalybes[18] revealed this technique. Pottery is Coroebus' work[19]; potters will have a holiday. One Boethus is responsible for cobbling; let no Christian stitch a shoe. Niceas discovered fulling,[20] no one must wash dirty clothes. The Egyptians gave us weaving; let's go back to wearing the skins of wild animals. . . . If we're forbidden to use the inventions of the gentiles, what on earth will be left in fields, towns, churches, houses, workshops, in civic life, in warfare, in private or in public? We Christians just don't have anything that we haven't inherited from pagans. We received from the pagans the practice of writing, and of speaking Latin; they discovered the alphabet and the use of formal speech. 'Am I', they say, 'to hold in my hands the books of damned men, am I to press them to my heart, read them repeatedly, reverence them? Virgil burns in hell, and does a Christian recite his poems?' As if there weren't lots of Christians burning there too, but if good writings by them survive, no one thinks they ought to be rejected for that reason. Who can bear this arbitrariness of judgement that allows them, with Mercury's rod,[21] as it were, to banish anyone they choose to the underworld and bring up anyone they choose from the shades?[22] I'm not going to embark here on that quarrelsome controversy, not fit even for women, about pagans; it's not our job to argue whether the pagans who lived before our Faith are damned. If we wanted to indulge in guessing I could easily show that either the pagans I'm talking about are saved or none at all are; but what matters to us is how good their teachings were, not how well they lived. A magistrate orders actors to be given a hearing, even though he condemns their lives from his own knowledge of them. The Christian Church reads the works of Origen[23] to benefit from his learning, even though they stand condemned of heresy on many points; but we shun the sacred writings of others on whose morals it would be most presumptuous to pass judgement. Indeed, to be more accurate, these are men whom it would be creditable to judge favourably and a great fault to condemn. 'Away with you', they say, 'Am I to put up with being called a Ciceronian or a Platonist after I've made my decision to be called a Christian?' Why not, you monster of a man? If we're right to call you a Sardanapalian[24] because you imitate the cursed luxury of Sardanapalus, or a Gnathonian[25] because you're a flatterer, or rather, given your thick-headed conceit, a Thrasonian,[26] why should someone else who imitates Cicero's language be ashamed to be called a Ciceronian, or I a Virgilian if I can emulate some of his qualities? You can go on adopting barbarian titles, and delighting in being called an Albertist or Thomist or Scotist or Occamist or Durandist,[27] just as long as you're named after a Christian; I'm happy to be named after any pagan, just as long as he's very learned and very eloquent. I won't be ashamed of this title provided the pagan teaches me something more worthwhile than a Christian. To bring the matter to a conclusion at last, if our opponents weren't made blinder than moles by their own envy, they'd certainly see what's obvious even to the blind, that there are differences among the discoveries of the pagans: some are useless, doubtful, pernicious,[28] while others are thoroughly useful, wholesome, indeed indispensable. Let's leave them the evil, but why shouldn't we appropriate the good for ourselves? That's what's proper for a Christian, a man of sense and a lover of knowledge. But in fact, incredible though it seems, we act all the wrong way round: we

> imitate the vices of the ancients everywhere, their lust, ambition, superstition – indeed we outdo them – but their learning, perhaps the only thing we ought to imitate, is the one thing we spurn; whether that shows more folly in us or pride I'm not yet sure. If we've adopted from them things that are only moderately useful and no blame attaches to us for that, what stops us from doing the same with their arts, than which, if we believe Jerome,[29] there's nothing more useful or more excellent in human affairs?

In time the Bible, like the classical texts, was subject to humanist scholarly and philological[30] treatment by the so-called 'Christian humanists' of the late fifteenth and early sixteenth centuries. Erasmus's *Enchiridion Militis Christiani* (*The Handbook of the Christian Soldier*) was published in 1501 (the English translation was published in 1533). In this work, Erasmus formulated a 'philosophy of Christ' in which he asserted that the Bible contained the only moral values men needed to observe, even as he moved for an allegorical (as opposed to a literal) interpretation of the Bible. Because humanists' celebration of the past implied a criticism of the prevailing order and because they often questioned the ideological basis of the Catholic Church, church hierarchy and monasticism,[31] their work lent itself to the Protestant cause and many Protestant reformers were prominent humanists themselves. Martin Luther and John Calvin felt that humanist learning could be put in the service of the reformed religion. Luther, however, had his reservations about the study of the classics and was of the opinion that pagan wisdom, however useful, should not be enjoyed.

Vernacular humanism

Humanist scholars travelled across Europe and influenced each other's work. In spite of their shared commitment to the classics, it was a matter of time before humanist intellectual cross-pollination influenced the vernacular or regional languages of Europe. French romances based on classical materials came to be popular, and by the 1530s and 1540s several major vernaculars became increasingly influential and even rivalled Latin in prestige and status. For instance, Italian writers such as Dante, Petrarch, Tasso and Ariosto came to constitute a new canon. Along with French and

English poets, these regional writers showed that 'one could imitate, emulate and satirize the ancients in their languages as well'.[32] Not only were classical texts translated into the vernacular tongues, works were also translated from one vernacular to another.

Humanism became influential in England by the end of the fifteenth century. Modern scholar Michael Pincombe writes that English humanism was never well regulated or organized but 'was a more or less loose set of associations with the words "humanity" and "*humanitas*" acting as a semantic and ideological centre of gravity'.[33] But Englishmen were clearly inspired by the new humane arts and travelled to Italy to study with the prominent humanists of the day. In their turn, Continental humanists came to England. Erasmus's visits to England were particularly notable. His meetings with John Colet, who started St Paul's, the first English school based on humanist principles, and with the young lawyer Thomas More, who collaborated with Erasmus to translate the Greek author Lucian and who went on to write the great English humanist work *Utopia*, gave impetus to English humanism. Erasmus's writings were recommended in English schools by educators such as Thomas Elyot and Roger Ascham. Other prominent English humanists included William Latimer, Thomas Linacre, William Grocyn, Edmund Spenser, Gabriel Harvey, Philip Sidney, George Puttenham and Mary Sidney. Harvey was the first Englishman to describe himself as a 'humanitarian of the old world'.[34] The English humanists were convinced that the glories of the ancient world could be recreated in their own northern island. There was a flurry of translation activity – Arthur Golding translated the Roman poet Ovid's *Metamorphoses* (8 AD) into English in 1567 and Thomas North translated Plutarch's *Lives* in 1579. The best-known of modern European works were also being made available in England – Thomas Hoby translated Castiglione's *The Courtier* in 1561 and the French essayist Michel de Montaigne's *Essays* were translated into English by the scholar-diplomat John Florio in 1603. English education was transformed by the new learning.

Humanism and English education

English humanists, like their European counterparts, saw themselves as radical educators and wrote extensively about the purpose and meaning of teaching and learning. Thomas Elyot wrote a part-pedagogical treatise titled *His Boke named the Governour* (1531) in which he presented a humanist programme based on 'the learning and study whereby noble men may attain to be worthy to have authority in public weal.'[35] Roger Ascham also wrote *The Scholemaster* (1570) in which he outlined his own ideas of a good humanist education and Richard Mulcaster wrote *Positions Concerning the Training of Children* (1581) and *Elementarie* (1582). The humanist beliefs that humans could 'fashion' themselves, shape their own identities and destinies to a large extent and that education can better what was endowed by nature provided the philosophical basis of the new educational system. A number of 'grammar schools' were established in England, Wales and Scotland. The schoolmaster replaced the local priest as teacher and the dissemination of the new learning was further assisted by the widespread use of printing. By the fifteenth century, humanism was enshrined in the universities as well. It was no longer simply the intellectual pursuits of individual scholars – humanism had become an institutionalized curriculum. The grammar schools offered a largely 'secular' education. The study of classical grammar and rhetoric was central to the learning programme, and history, mythology and textual criticism were taught alongside these disciplines. The educators' greatest admiration was reserved for Cicero, whose rhetorical works provided the theory behind fine writing and speech. His orations, letters and dialogues served as models of the same. The English humanists too taught grammar by observing and copying. As Ascham wrote, grammar 'is sooner and surer learned by examples of good authors, than by naked rules of grammarians'.[36] The classical authors provided examples that young students strove to imitate.

The emphasis was on rhetorical prowess – elegance, clarity of style, the neat organization of thought and the apt use of allusions and quotes. While students were trained in executing these skills in Latin, they were expected to carry them over into written and spoken English as well. Eloquence was certainly about writing and speaking to an audience, but, as Tony Davies points out, it was connected to the individual's very sense of self: 'The human being is fashioned and defined in language, and belongs inseparably, in its public and private aspects alike, to the medium of discourse.'[37] Identity was defined and created through language. In addition to verbal agility, students were also taught textual criticism and trained to see texts as functioning in certain contexts. This rhetorical training culminated in 'declamation' and 'disputation' – the former was an exercise in which students were expected to produce orations in response to very specific situations; in the latter they engaged in debates that called on them to organize and present their ideas and points of view. The humanists engaged in other pedagogical experiments – they encouraged travel as a mode of education (beginning in the late sixteenth

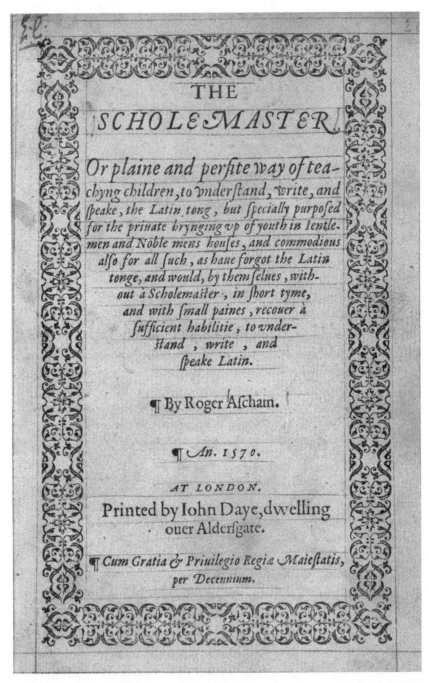

Figure 4.1 Title page from *The Scholemaster*, Roger Ascham, 1570 (courtesy of The Folger Shakespeare Library).

century, young noblemen, accompanied by their tutors, were sent on the Grand Tour, an educational journey to the major learning centres of Europe) and they produced the first anthologies or *de copia* – rich and usable collections of excerpts from the best in the classics. Like modern teachers, they disagreed on what constituted best classroom practice – should a child be chastised or subject to corporeal punishment? To what extent should students be given freedom to direct their own learning? Like any practice in the making, the humanists never quite agreed on the answers to these questions.[38]

From Roger Ascham, *The Scholemaster* (1570).

Roger Ascham was among the best known of humanist educational reformers in England. In 1548 he became tutor to Queen (then Princess) Elizabeth and after her accession he became Greek expert at the royal court. His book *The Schoolmaster* (1570) is a classic of English humanism. In this famous passage from the book he makes an argument for the connection between words and ideas, form and content.

Imitation, is a faculty to express lively and perfectly that example: which ye go about to follow. And, of itself, it is large and wide: for all the works of nature, in a manner, be examples for art to follow.

But, to our purpose, all languages, both learned and mother tongues, be gotten, and gotten only, by Imitation. For as ye use to hear, so ye learn to speak: if ye hear no other, ye speak not yourself: and whom ye only hear, of them ye only learn.

And therefore, if ye would speak as the best and wisest do, ye must be conversant[39] where the best and wisest are: but if you be born or brought up in a rude country, ye shall not choose but speak rudely[40]: the rudest man of all knoweth this to be true.

Yet nevertheless, the rudeness of common and mother tongues, is no bar for wise speaking. For in the rudest country and most barbarous mother language, many be found can speak very wisely; but in the Greek and Latin tongue, the two only learned tongues, which be kept not in common talk, but in private books, we find always wisdom and eloquence, good matter and good utterance, never or seldom asunder. For all such Authors, as be fullest of good matter and right judgment in doctrine,[41] be likewise always, most proper in words, most apt in sentence, most plain and pure in uttering the same.

And contrariwise, in those two tongues, all writers, either in Religion, or any sect of Philosophy, whosoever be found fond[42] in judgement of matter, be commonly found as rude in uttering their mind. For Stoics, Anabaptists[43] and Friars: with Epicures, Libertines[44] and Monks, being most like in learning and life, are no fonder and pernicious in their opinions, than they be rude and barbarous in their writings. They be not wise, therefore that say, what care I for a man's words and utterance, if his matter and reasons be good. Such men say so, not so much of ignorance, as either of some singular pride in themselves, or some special malice of other, or for some private and partial matter, either in Religion or other kind of learning. For good and choice meats, be no more requisite for healthy bodies, than proper and apt words be for good matters, and also plain and sensible utterance for the best and deepest reasons: in which two points standeth perfect eloquence, one of the fairest, and rarest gifts that God doth give to man.

Ye know not, what hurt ye do to learning, that care not for words but for matter, and so make a divorce betwixt the tongue and the heart. For mark all ages: look upon the whole course of both the Greek and Latin tongue, and ye shall surely find that, when apt and good words began to be neglected, and properties of those two tongues to be confounded, then also began ill deeds to spring: strange manners to oppress good orders, new and fond opinions to strive with old and true doctrine, first in Philosophy: and after in Religion: right judgment of all things to be perverted, and so virtue with learning is contemned, and study left off: of ill thoughts cometh perverse judgment: of ill deeds springeth lewd[45] talk. Which four misorders,[46] as they mar man's life, so destroy they good learning withal.

Courtly humanism

Humanist education's lofty aim was to create philosopher-kings, wise and benign rulers modelled after the likes of Alexander the Great and Julius Caesar. Indeed, many of the best-known humanist educators were teachers in royal households. More commonly, humanism trained effective civic servants and diplomats. In many cases it simply produced 'gentlemen'. The schoolroom was not the only training ground for these well-born humanist scholars. They were also trained in and flourished in royal courts. This brand of humanism, often described as 'courtly humanism', sometimes came into conflict with the scholarly strain of humanism. Ascham, for example, expressed reservations about the court as a fit school for the humanities although Castiglione's *The Courtier* made an explicit link between the courtier and the humanities. The ideal courtier, wrote Castiglione, has to be 'more than indifferently well seen [in learning], at the least in those studies, which they call Humanities, and to have not only the understanding of the Latin tongue, but also of the Greek, because of the many and sundry things that with great excellency are written in it. Let him exercise himself in poets, and no less in Orators and Historiographers, and also in writing both rime and prose, and especially in this our vulgar tongue.'[47] For Castiglione, these skills made young men fit for fashionable society, appealing to ladies and, most importantly, gave the young noblemen themselves a profound and enduring sense of fulfilment. So, in this conception, the courtier became the new masculine ideal – the man who knew the classical and several modern tongues and who could write poetry, dance, dress elegantly and handle himself with unselfconscious grace and dignity. However, courtiers were commonly perceived as lightweight versions of the true scholars and even as triflers and dilettantes despite the fact that in many cases it was the elite who had the wealth and leisure to develop intellectual skills and social graces. The coexistence of (and conflict between) scholarly and courtly humanism indicates that Elizabethan humanism occupied a range of social and intellectual positions.

Humanism has been subject to some criticism from modern scholars. It is accused of having created a cultural elite and stamped them with 'an indelible seal of superiority'.[48] For C.S. Lewis the very aspirations of the humanists were 'vulgar' and indicate that they were unsophisticated and insecure.[49] According to some critics, the humanists did not create any real positive social change. On the other hand they fostered a 'docile attitude towards authority'.[50] Their educational system was impressive in theory perhaps, argue some modern scholars, but in reality it trained students in little but empty copying and rote learning and engaged them in a variety of unimaginative and dull verbal compositions. There is certainly some truth to these criticisms – humanism, like any other programme or practice, most likely had its shortcomings and drawbacks, but new studies in marginalia (comments made by readers on the margins of texts) indicate that scholars critiqued and challenged accepted ideas. In fact, humanism's admirers would contend that humanism was characterized by the questioning of authority and the challenging of established truths.[51] Besides, humanism has left its imprint on our own educational system and even its fiercest critics would agree that to the humanists we owe the recovery of the lost classics of the ancient world. Humanism, in spite of its drawbacks, was also still, in Rebecca Bushnell's words, 'committed to tolerance … shaped by a cheerful acceptance of ambivalence and contradiction; and informed by an almost painful historical consciousness, which sees the past as estranged yet able to illuminate present concerns'.[52] The modern world has been shaped by this legacy.

A humanist philosophy

While humanism is not primarily a philosophical movement, there are certain common philosophical ideas running through the writings of humanist thinkers. Humanists were especially interested in exploring human nature in relation to both the divine and to animals or 'brutes'. Man was not entirely different from the beasts, but it was considered important to distance oneself from one's brutish nature. The most unique aspect of human nature was the soul. This made humans superior to beasts and even somewhat god-like. Cultivating this immortal, divine element of the self in order to attain perfection was the primary duty and function of human life. Learning was an important element of this self-cultivation. This emphasis on the privileged place of humans in the universe was, like many other aspects of humanist thought, of classical origin. In Greek myth Prometheus rebelled against the gods to accord humans a unique place in the cosmic scheme, and the Greek philosopher Socrates rejected purely abstract speculation in favour of investigating questions of everyday human life. Humanist philosophy subsequently emphasized individualism, the dignity and freedom of human beings and the importance of intellectual curiosity, and also expressed impatience with the constraints of orthodox religion.

Humanism also insisted that rather than seeing life only as a preparation for the hereafter, humans need to value their earthly existence, live life to the fullest and strive to understand themselves. Kristeller recounts an anecdote about Petrarch in which the poet visits Mount Ventoux and was overwhelmed by its beauty. He subsequently read a book by St Augustine who bemoaned the fact that humans admire natural landscapes but rarely contemplate themselves. Following this Petrarch realized that 'nothing is admirable but the soul in comparison to which … nothing is great'.[53] A number of treatises on the dignity of man were produced by the mid-fifteenth century.

Florentine humanist Giannozzo Manetti wrote an essay countering Pope Innocent III's treatise on the miserable state of mankind, and Pico della Mirandola wrote his famous *Oration on the Dignity of Man* in 1486. This perception of the individual as a free agent is central to modern Western thinking.

From Pico della Mirandola, *Oration on the Dignity of Man* (1486). Trans. Richard Hooker.

Described as the 'manifesto of the Renaissance' and 'Epiphany of the modern spirit', the *Oration on the Dignity of Man* (1486) by the Italian philosopher Pico della Mirandola celebrates the excellence of the human self that was positioned between God and the beasts and elaborates on the tremendous potential of such a position.

I once read that Abdala the Muslim,[54] when asked what was most worthy of awe and wonder in this theatre of the world, answered, 'There is nothing to see more wonderful than man!' Hermes Trismegistus[55] concurs with this opinion: 'A great miracle . . . is man!' However, when I began to consider the reasons for these opinions, all these reasons given for the magnificence of human nature failed to convince me: that man is the intermediary between creatures, close to the gods, master of all the lower creatures, with the sharpness of his senses, the acuity of his reason, and the brilliance of his intelligence the interpreter of nature, the nodal point[56] between eternity and time, and, as the Persians say, the intimate bond or marriage song of the world, just a little lower than angels as David[57] tells us. I concede these are magnificent reasons, but they do not seem to go to the heart of the matter, that is, those reasons which truly claim admiration. For, if these are all the reasons we can come up with, why should we not admire angels more than we do ourselves? After thinking a long time, I have figured out why man is the most fortunate of all creatures and as a result worthy of the highest admiration and earning his rank on the chain of being, a rank to be envied not merely by the beasts but by the stars themselves and by the spiritual natures beyond and above this world. This miracle goes past faith and wonder. And why not? It is for this reason that man is rightfully named a magnificent miracle and a wondrous creation.

What is this rank on the chain of being? God the Father, Supreme Architect of the Universe, built this home, this universe we see all around us, a venerable temple of his godhead, through the sublime laws of his ineffable[58] Mind. The expanse above the heavens he decorated with Intelligences, the spheres of heaven with living, eternal souls. The scabrous[59] and dirty lower worlds he filled with animals of every kind. However, when the work was finished, the Great Artisan desired that there be some creature to think on the plan of his great work, and love its infinite beauty, and stand in awe at its immenseness. Therefore, when all was finished, as Moses and Timaeus[60] tell us, He began to think about the creation of man. But he had no Archetype[61] from which to fashion some new child, nor could he find in his vast treasure-houses anything which He might give to His new son, nor did the universe contain a single place from which the whole of creation might be surveyed. All was perfected, all created things stood in their proper place, the highest things in the highest places, the midmost things in the midmost places, and the lowest things in the lowest places. But God the Father would not fail, exhausted and defeated, in this last creative act. God's wisdom would not falter for lack of counsel in this need. God's love would not permit that he whose duty it was to praise God's creation should be forced to condemn himself as a creation of God.

Finally, the Great Artisan mandated that this creature who would receive nothing proper to himself shall have joint possession of whatever nature had been given to any other creature. He made man a creature of indeterminate and indifferent nature, and, placing him in the middle of the world, said to him 'Adam, we give you no fixed place to live, no form that is peculiar to you, nor any function that is yours alone. According to your desires and judgement, you will have and possess whatever place to live, whatever form, and whatever functions you yourself choose. All other things have a limited and fixed nature prescribed and bounded by Our laws. You, with no limit or no bound, may choose for yourself the limits and bounds of your nature. We have placed you at the world's centre so that you may survey everything else in the world. We have made you neither of heavenly nor of earthly stuff, neither mortal nor immortal, so that with free choice and dignity, you may fashion yourself into whatever form you choose. To you is granted the power of degrading yourself into the lower forms of life, the beasts, and to you is granted the power, contained in your intellect and judgement, to be reborn into the higher forms, the divine.'

> Imagine! The great generosity of God! The happiness of man! To man it is allowed to be whatever he chooses to be! As soon as an animal is born, it brings out of its mother's womb all that it will ever possess. Spiritual beings from the beginning become what they are to be for all eternity. Man, when he entered life, the Father gave the seeds of every kind and every way of life possible. Whatever seeds each man sows and cultivates will grow and bear him their proper fruit. If these seeds are vegetative, he will be like a plant. If these seeds are sensitive, he will be like an animal. If these seeds are intellectual, he will be an angel and the son of God. And if, satisfied with no created thing, he removes himself to the centre of his own unity, his spiritual soul, united with God, alone in the darkness of God, who is above all things, he will surpass every created thing. Who could not help but admire this great shape-shifter? In fact, how could one admire anything else?

God, wrote Mirandola in his treatise, made man because He desired a creation that would wonder at and take delight in the universe. Mirandola wondered what sets humans apart from the rest of creation. He was unconvinced by the arguments that humans are unique because they are between the animal and the divine or that they are masters of other animals. The distinctiveness of humans is their unique ability to shape their own destinies 'with free choice and dignity'. This idea that humans have control over their lives and are not merely puppets of an inscrutable fate or under full control of an imperious God was a new one. This privileging of human thought and action lead to another characteristic feature of the humanist philosophy of man, which was, in Kristeller's words, the 'tendency to express, and to consider worth expressing the concrete uniqueness of one's feelings, opinions, experiences and surroundings'.[62] The French essayist Montaigne, for example, claimed that his own self was the main subject of his philosophy. This celebration and exploration of the self has been described by Jacob Burckhardt as 'individualism' and he describes this as most characteristic of the brave new age. Kristeller writes, 'we cannot escape the impression that after the beginnings of Renaissance humanism, the emphasis on man and his dignity becomes even more persistent, more exclusive, and ultimately more systematic than it ever had been during the preceding centuries and even during classical antiquity'.[63] Pincombe, however, cautions us that the Renaissance idea of man was a subtle philosophy – it did not simply emphasize a Faustian rebelliousness (humans straining against the limits imposed by heaven), nor did it insist, at the other extreme, that human learning should be in the service of the state or the church and that the individual self should be subservient to larger forces. Instead, it recognized the complex position of humans and the ambiguities and tensions that informed human existence.

There were other aspects to 'philosophical humanism' – thinkers emphasized the solidarity of all human beings and the need to hold one's fellow humans in esteem and respect; humanists such as Montaigne even suggested early forms of what we would call 'cultural relativism' – the notion that 'right' and 'wrong', 'good' and 'evil' are not universal or 'natural' but vary depending on cultural context. The Italian poet Dante projected a cosmopolitan identity that transcended local borders when he wrote that 'My country is the whole world. Can I not everywhere behold the light of the sun and the stars; everywhere meditate on the noblest truths …?'[64] Humanists, through their eternal questioning and interrogation of accepted truths and the prevailing order, inspired many later currents of 'free thought'. Humanist thinking for the most part was not essentialist or authoritarian but informed by scepticism and ambivalence. It explored the tensions between free will and fate, individual and community, the human and the Divine – tensions that also structure the literary writings of the period.

Humanism and English drama

Literature was fundamental to the humanist curriculum. Students studied the Roman writers Virgil, Horace, Juvenal, Ovid and Seneca and learnt to compose in classical metres. Good prose writing, it was believed, came from knowing how to compose poetry. Literature and learning were clearly linked. In his *De Oratore* (55 BC) Cicero wrote that the truly accomplished orator should also be able to master a variety of rhetorical forms including poetry ('For, indeed, there is no man able to be an orator worthy to be loaded with all praise, without he must have pursued the knowledge of all Arts'[65]). This kind of education led to the development of a common literary and aesthetic ideal and a burst of literary activity – diplomats, courtiers and rulers were all writing poetry. Arthur Kinney argues for the existence of a rich and vibrant tradition of 'humanistic poetics' that is grounded in rhetorical training and characterized by wit, energy and the immediacy that humanists strove for in their compositions.[66] The students' training in classical, French and Italian texts meant that they could invoke a wide range of references extending over history, mythology and philosophy. The sonnet, an Italian poetic form which was imported into England and which a number of English courtier-scholars tried their hand at, is an example of a trans-European humanist poetic tradition, even as the rising prestige and popularity of literary writing in English was a consequence of vernacular humanism and the English aspiration to reach the heights scaled by their classical predecessors. Even the Renaissance treatises on poetry were humanist-influenced – Sidney's idea of poetry, expressed in his *The Defence of Poesy* (published 1595; also published in the same year entitled *An Apology for Poetry*), as yielding both pleasure and delight is an adaptation of Cicero's ideas; Puttenham's detailed exposition on English poetic form and technique is an example of a humanist *arsi*, a manual that teaches a specific skill; even anti-theatrical critique by Stephen Gosson and others often evoked classical thinkers like Plato and Cicero.

Erasmus and other humanist teachers recommended that classical drama be used to teach students both eloquence and morality. Hence the works of Seneca, Terence and Plautus were staples in the schoolboy's curriculum and were doubtless studied by Shakespeare and other writers who had a grammar school education. Plays were also regularly performed in schools. Humanist training made classical drama seem universal and timeless. But schoolroom activities apart, can one really talk of an English humanist theatre? Greek and Roman plays were staged in private theatres by university students or elite amateur players, but no professional playwright who wrote for the Renaissance public stage (even those who prided themselves on their knowledge of the classics) ever billed their plays as adaptations of Greek or Roman ones. C.S. Lewis sees little connection between humanism and English theatre (or English literature in any form, for that matter). 'The great literature of the fifteen-eighties and nineties was something which humanism, with its unities[67] and Gorboducs[68] and hexameters,[69] would have prevented if it could,' writes Lewis, 'but failed to prevent because the high tide of native talent was then too strong for it.'[70] It was the 'native' English impulse – earthy, spontaneous and relatable – that was the creative force behind Renaissance English literature. Other critics such as David Bevington and Robert Weimann have also insisted that 'popular' and 'native' traditions of drama, notably medieval morality drama, along with 'plebian taste' primarily influenced Renaissance public theatre.[71] The indigenous drama had humour, vitality and a freedom that humanist drama with its insistence on form and decorum and its weighty philosophical concerns could never match.

While native English traditions doubtless had a major influence on Renaissance drama, it is also true that humanism did have an impact on the public theatre. Playwrights such as Jonson made clear their veneration for classical learning, never flouted the unities or indulged in the anachronisms his contemporaries were notorious for. His two tragedies *Sejanus* and *Catiline* (1611) were based on the idea that public plays could be also be finished works of art in the classical sense. The two plays were admittedly unsuccessful at the time and most other professional playwrights quite blithely flouted the unities and other structural requirements of humanist theatre. But humanist drama was not simply dry and rule-bound. In fact, as Kent Cartwright argues, the lines between 'humanist' and 'popular' theatre was not as clear-cut as made out. Vernacular humanist plays, including the fifteenth-century *Gammer Gurton's Needle*, began as school plays but managed to achieve wide appeal. Humanist writing in general wasn't just about fine figures of speech and learned allusions – it was ultimately a very pragmatic mode that attempted to express the realities of contemporary life and personal experience and emotion through the medium of classical rhetoric. Tudor drama too combined the joy of experimenting with language, the presentation of concrete events and experiences, and the expression of sensations, feelings and memories with the exploration of complex themes. In Cartwright's words, 'The excitement of the Tudor stage derives partly from a humanist dramaturgy that embroils feelings and emotions in the creation of meaning.'[72]

While dramatists might not have ever directly proclaimed their plays as classical adaptations, they did ransack classical sources for plots. Shakespeare's Roman plays (most famously *Anthony and Cleopatra* and *Julius Caesar*) are examples of such borrowings and Thomas Heywood turned repeatedly to Plautus for plot, character and even dialogue. Shakespeare's *Titus Andronicus* has a Roman subject but also includes several references to Seneca and Greek myth. Its theme of the virtuous Roman warrior is also a classical one. Playwrights did not see classicism as adhering to the 'purity' of the original and rewrote classical plots quite liberally and adapted classical styles and themes to suit their own social situation and artistic needs. More significantly perhaps, the classics opened up new possibilities for English dramatists. Classical tragedy in particular posed awkward ethical questions, often in tension with Christian dogma. It figured larger-than-life heroes living in a world governed by an indecipherable fate. Misfortune was not brought about by choices that were immoral or sinful from a Christian perspective but by unconscious erroneous acts committed by protagonists. These stories inspired, moved and challenged public playwrights and the tension between pagan and Christian world-views lent Renaissance theatre, specifically tragedy, its unique power. A play like Christopher Marlowe's *Doctor Faustus* is doubtless influenced by the morality tradition, but the rhetorical force, the depth of its protagonist and the sheer intensity of the emotions expressed in the play are surely influenced by classical drama. *King Lear*, in which a hapless protagonist battles the outer darkness of an indifferent universe, is also reminiscent of the ancient worlds of Sophocles, Euripides and other Greek tragedies. The confluence of classical and native traditions led to a rich and unique theatre. As Bruce Smith puts it, 'out of the dynamic between ancient scripts and modern experience emerged plays that fascinate still'.[73]

The humanist classroom trained its students in argumentative speech by getting them to put themselves in the place of different characters, each of whom would have had a different perspective on the issue at hand. 'Students were required, again and again, to play opposing roles, to simulate varying personalities, to create characters'.[74] It is not difficult to see how such training would have prepared the budding playwright to create fictional characters for the stage. Dialogues were also a popular form of humanist writing. Two or more characters were depicted as engaging in conversation to arrive at a truth through discussion and repartee. Renaissance dialogues were complex, open-ended and entertaining forms, with writers using humour and irony to make serious points. Renaissance drama, with its witty or intense verbal exchanges that moved plot, created character and explored the most complex of themes, was clearly shaped by this emphasis on humanist dialogue writing. Besides, the study of classical rhetoric also helped playwrights look at plays as rhetorical events, i.e. as forms of address and as human interactions taking place in a certain context. The actor is the orator who uses devices of persuasion to convince his audience of moral or political arguments. In fact, in its grandeur and intensity, the language of Renaissance drama is, in T.S. Eliot's words, 'as near to oratory as to ordinary speech'.[75]

Ben Jonson is a playwright whose debt to this rhetorical tradition is very self-conscious. The introduction to *Sejanus*, for example, indicates how closely his view of tragedy allied to academic precepts. Jonson writes that he aims at 'truth of argument, dignity of persons, gravity and height of elocution, fullness and frequency of sentence'.[76] All of these were celebrated traits of classical writing. Moreover, Aristotle's treatise on drama, *Poetics* (*c.* 335 BC), arrived in Europe by the middle of the fifteenth century. Aristotle reminded playwrights that the play was an art object with a beginning, middle and end. In other words, it had, or ought to have, a specific and well-thought out structure. The ways in which the action was arranged was crucial to the effect it had on the audience. Besides, the purpose of the play was neither to convince (as in rhetoric) nor to teach a moral lesson (as in morality drama) but to elicit an emotional response, specifically pity and fear, in the audience. The tension between the rhetorical approach that emphasized the use of language and the Aristotelian one that emphasized dramatic structure and emotional effect proved to be a creative one and impacted the drama of the period.

Grammar school exercises made their way onto the stage in other ways. Since imitation was the dominant method of study, students were required to copy the style of classical passages. Niobe's lament for her children as written in Homer's *Iliad* was used often as an example of emotionally charged first-person speech. This makes its way into *Hamlet* in the 'O that this too too sullied flesh' speech (1.2.129–59), which is a deliberately overdramatic lamentation.[77] Shakespeare did not hesitate to poke fun at his grammar school training either. For example, Holofernes, the dull pedant of *Love's Labour's Lost* (mid-1590s), indulges in a trick of speech students were taught in school where the speaker produces strings of related terms to illustrate the same concept (as Holofernes says, 'The deer was, as you know, *sanguis*, in blood; ripe as pomewater, who now hangeth like a jewel in the ear of *caelo*, the sky, the welkin, the heaven, and anon falleth like a crab on the face of *terra*, the soil, the land, the earth' [4.2.5–9]). The playwright uses a similar trick of variation to more serious effect in *Hamlet* when the prince describes this 'sullied flesh' that will 'melt / Thaw and resolve itself into a dew' (1.2.129–30).

Scattering one's original compositions with references to other texts was also considered a hallmark of elegant writing and Renaissance plays do not lack such allusions (for example, the reference to the 'sea of troubles' in Hamlet's 'To be, or not to be' soliloquy has echoes of Erasmus, and Jonson's epistle dedication to *Volpone* also draws from Erasmus). Very often intertextuality went beyond allusion. The Latin poet Ovid (whose *Metamorphoses* was read by every school boy) had a profound influence on Shakespeare. Ovid's idea that the universe is characterized by flux, that 'there is not that that standeth at a stay',[78] impacted a number of his plays including *The Tempest* and *A Midsummer Night's Dream*, with their themes of change and transformation, and also influenced Thomas Kyd's *The Spanish Tragedy*.

Playwrights customarily borrowed liberally from earlier writers (very few Renaissance play plots are absolutely original) – this was also perhaps influenced by the humanist tradition of synthesizing ideas from varied sources. This was not seen as 'plagiarism' but rather as a way of demonstrating learning. Shakespeare, for example, borrowed from sources as varied as the ancient Roman writer Plutarch and the Italian writer Boccaccio, travel writing and the humanistic histories of Edward Hall and Ralph Holinshed. The modern poet T.S. Eliot has insisted that the individual talent of the writer only operates with a full awareness of tradition and a 'historical sense' that 'compels a man to write not merely with his own generation in his bones, but with a feeling that the whole of the literature of Europe from Homer and within it the whole of the literature of his own country has a simultaneous existence and composes a simultaneous order'.[79] Renaissance writers were already convinced of this and drew on the works of their predecessors to fulfil their own artistic ends and to make their moral and political points. The best of them also realized, to turn to T. S. Eliot once more, that 'Immature poets imitate; mature poets steal; bad poets deface what they take, and good poets make it into something better, or at least something different.'[80]

The Roman tragedian Seneca has often been described as the single greatest influence on Renaissance drama. All ten of Seneca's plays were translated into English during the Elizabethan age and while the best Elizabethan drama is clearly very far removed from the flat characterization and bombast of much Senecan tragedy, it was Seneca who gave the drama its five-act structure as well its proclivity for melodrama and sensationalism. Seneca's most discernible influence is on the revenge tragedies (Thomas Kyd's *The Spanish Tragedy* and Thomas Middleton's *The Revenger's Tragedy*, for example) that enact stories of bloodthirsty and violent acts of revenge. Seneca's penchant for the horrid and macabre is seen in John Webster's *The Duchess of Malfi*, a 'magnificent nightmare' of a play,[81] with its typical Senecan motifs of ghosts and insanity. Seneca also influenced the language of Renaissance drama. Long-winded sententious speeches that characterize, for example, Marlowe's thunderous style are very Senecan though, as Eliot reminds us, the forcefulness and concision of Elizabethan dramatic language is also Senecan-inspired. The soul-searching and self-revealing soliloquy came from Seneca, and Eliot argues that blank verse emerged as a vehicle for Elizabethan drama rather than the heroic couplet or even prose because it was 'the nearest equivalent to the solemnity and weight of the Seneca iambic'. Even Senecan bombast is appropriated by Shakespeare; and 'Without bombast we would not have had *King Lear*'.[82]

Any study of literary influence should, however, acknowledge that it operates in complex ways. Writers can imitate or reproduce a style or literary mode but also be inspired enough by it to attempt a departure from it. So in Marlowe's hands Senecan horror becomes dark farce (as in *Jew of Malta*) and in Shakespeare's *Hamlet*, revenge tragedy is rewritten as a story of a young prince who simply cannot push himself to take revenge. Playwrights also took stock types from Roman drama and rewrote characters, often to brilliant effect. Falstaff in *Henry IV Part 1* (c. 1597), for example, is something of the *miles gloriosus* or braggart warrior, and *Hamlet* is populated by characters who are inspired by humanism. Polonius, with his pedantic zeal for classification of types of drama and his laboured commentary on Hamlet's recital of Aeneas's speech, is once again Shakespeare's gentle mockery of the humanist scholar; Osric, also in *Hamlet*, is a satire on the dilettante-courtier, and Hamlet himself is the archetypal serious humanist student who attempts to use language and learning to understand his experiences. The relationship and conflict between language and experience was a topic of humanist discourse and is examined in this play.[83] Claudius, on the other hand, reflects the dangers of eloquence. He is the smooth talker whose interest in presentation often hides the truth (a critique often levelled against humanism). A play like *Hamlet* has a complex relationship with humanism. It emerges from humanist thought but also problematizes and challenges it, so reflecting the tensions informing humanism itself, tensions that were often productive.

The link to humanism of Marlowe's *Doctor Faustus* is also interesting. For Pincombe, it is hard to see the play as a humanist one since the conflict between theology and human-centred learning is not central to the play. Besides, Faustus's learning is not always lofty in intent. His magic, in fact, degenerates into rather self-indulgent and foolish trickery. But the play does reflect the tensions inherent in the humanist 'philosophy of man'. Faustus represents human aspiration, the desire for 'a world of profit and delight, / Of power, of honour, of omnipotence, / . . . . promised to the studious artisan!' (1, 53–55).[84] The human self is as large as the universe itself and is ever-seeking and ever-restless. Faustus strives after knowledge and in doing so interrogates religion and God. The humanist awareness of the limitless possibilities of human knowledge along with its inherent dangers is central to the play. *Doctor Faustus* is a wondrous outcome of the coming together of morality tradition and humanist rhetoric and themes. Renaissance drama at its best is a result of this confluence.

Discussion points

1   Trace the classical references in any Renaissance play you are reading (you could begin by simply looking at the footnotes provided in your

book and then research further by turning to sources in your library or online). Does knowing any of them change or enhance your understanding of the play?

2   As we saw in this chapter, the chief aim of classical rhetoric was to persuade an audience/listener and Renaissance playwrights were influenced by this rhetorical training. Select any monologue from a play you are studying and consider how it operates as a piece of rhetoric. In other words, how does it use language to inform, delight and also to persuade both the listener in the story as well as the audience?

3   Humanist training was geared towards men. Do any of the women in the plays you are reading appear to display learning to any degree? Do any of them use language with rhetorical force?

4   In the excerpt from *Oration on the Dignity of Man* reproduced in this chapter, Pico writes that 'man is the most fortunate of all creatures and as a result worthy of the highest admiration and earning his rank on the chain of being, a rank to be envied not merely by the beasts but by the stars themselves and by the spiritual natures beyond and above this world'. Consider this quote, review the entire excerpt and think about whether this view on humans and human freedom is borne out in any Renaissance play you are reading. Also think about how a play conveys philosophical ideas somewhat differently from the way a philosophical treatise does.

5

The Stage

'London is the Metropolis and Glory of the Kingdom. . .' wrote John Stow in his *Survey of London* (first published 1598). It was this city, 'the fairest built of any in the world', that was home to the theatre of the English Renaissance.[1] Drama is a performance art – scripts come to completion on stage and in the minds and hearts of audiences – and the English theatre as a form of public entertainment was an urban phenomenon. London was becoming increasingly important as a centre of trade and commerce, and its population doubled from 100,000 to 200,00 between 1580 and 1600 and again doubled to 400,00 by 1650.[2] It was 'quite literally the biggest market in the world for playing'.[3] The public flocked to see plays and thirsted for new productions.

While the theatre was a medium of self-expression and a form of entertainment, it was also a professional and financial institution. Philip Henslowe, manager of the playing company the Lord Admiral's Men, maintained painstaking accounts of the company's expenses and income. His figures indicate that the average takings per day were six to seven pounds. To this can be added the tickets paid for by those who sat in galleries, doubling the total daily collection to twelve to fourteen pounds.[4] Theatres are thus 'best understood in terms of commerce, as centres for the production and consumption of an aesthetic product'.[5] Plays were also commodities subject to the rules of supply and demand and although playing companies had their patrons, they were more like modern joint-stock companies. In fact, it is no coincidence that the theatre grew in popularity and reputation at the same time as the economy was being structured along the lines of what we would today call capitalism and that many of the entrepreneurs who built the theatres were tradesmen or partnered with tradesmen. These men were financially shrewd and wanted good returns on their investments. Writers too recognized this commercial aspect of the theatre, usually with mixed feelings. In *Bartholomew Fair*, Jonson writes of signing 'Articles of Agreement' similar to a commercial contract with

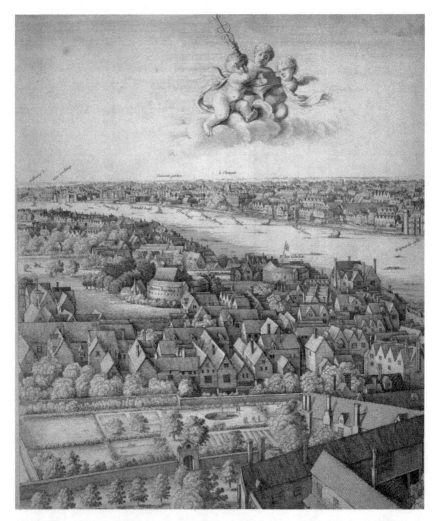

Figure 5.1 *Long View of London from Bankside,* a panorama of London by Wenceslaus Hollar, 1647.

his audience. Spectators, he satirically states, could criticize plays only in proportion to the ticket prices they paid (Induction 58–65).[6]

The playhouses

Plays had been performed in inn yards and taverns until the Privy Council, backed by the Lord Mayor of London, ordered them closed in 1594. Oddly enough, it was this attempt to control plays that led to the flowering of the public theatre. Permanent playhouses were built in the Liberties or suburbs of London that were free of the jurisdiction of the city authorities. They were also built near alehouses, brothels and other arenas of public entertainment, including bear-baiting, wrestling, fencing and juggling. This was a world apart from the courts, palaces and colleges of the main city.

Between 1567 and 1642 twenty-three professional theatres (seventeen of them public and six private[7]) were built in London. The first of the public playhouses was the Red Lion, constructed in 1567, after which came the Theatre, built by the actor-entrepreneur James Burbage in 1576. These two were followed by the Curtain (c. 1577), the Rose (1587), the Swan (1595), the Globe (1599), the Fortune (1600) and the Hope (1614). The Globe burnt down in 1613 but was rebuilt on the same site in 1614 and was perhaps the most iconic of these playhouses. The permanent playhouses not only ensured that the plays attracted more clientele and hence larger profits, they also assured the actors security and stability. Not all permanent playhouses were 'public' theatres. There were also 'private theatres' that were indoors and roofed (in contrast to the open-air public theatres). The best known of these private playhouses was the Blackfriars theatre, which was actually located within city limits. Blackfriars was an old monastery that was first leased out as a playhouse for boy actors in 1576. The lease passed from hand to hand and the space continued to be used by companies of boy actors until it was eventually used by adult companies as their playing house during winters. The private playhouses were certainly more comfortable – they had cushioned seats and the enclosed structure surely made a difference during the wet and cold seasons of the year. They also had performances only once or twice a week for smaller, possibly more selective audiences. But there is no obvious reason why they were designated as 'private' playhouses unless it was only to distinguish them from the larger 'public' theatres or because they grew out of the tradition of playing in private houses. These private theatres were still open to the general public and did charge a price for admission.

The insides of the public theatres had galleried seats surrounding the raised stage which jutted out into the yard. The main acting area was large. The jutting 'apron stage' made it possible for actors to be intimate with the audience, but they could also, if they so wished, create a distance from the spectators by moving back. The physical proximity gave the audience the impression of participating in an event that was just unfolding before them.

The stage had a trapdoor through which demons, witches and other 'underworld' creatures could emerge. On either side were two pillars holding up a canopy called the 'heavens' (a tradition inherited from miracle plays and performances at court[8]). The 'heavens' was a cloth painted with stars and other celestial bodies to signify the sky; sometimes gods and other divine creatures descended from it using cord-and-pulley arrangements (indeed many actors were semi-acrobats and could quite easily fly up and down and across stage using ropes and other such devices). The two pillars that held up the heavens were also used by actors to conceal themselves in scenes that involved spying (Polonius, for instance, would have hidden behind a pillar as he eavesdropped on his daughter in *Hamlet*). Balconies that were set higher up and back were also a regular feature (the most famous balcony scene being the one in *Romeo and Juliet*) and there were also alcoves or 'discovery spaces' set further back from the 'outer stage' where scenes set in bedchambers and other private interior spaces might have been enacted. There were multiple exits on both sides of stage, and exits and entrances were carefully orchestrated with one group of characters typically entering from one side and another group from the opposite one. The audience closest to the stage stood under the open sky and on the ground (and were hence called the 'groundlings') while the others sat in tiered galleries. The theatres generally got more comfortable with time: the seating area for the 'gentlemen' was plastered and even public theatres got cushioned seats. Private theatres also allowed about a dozen ticket holders (notably the gallants who paid higher fares) to actually sit on stage.

Outside, eager audiences would have waited for performances to start. The public playhouses advertised their fare through playbills posted around the streets and with flags conspicuously flown on playhouse roofs, while private ones announced their offerings either through word of mouth or smaller handbills that were distributed amongst the public. There were no programmes as we are accustomed to find in modern productions. In public playhouses a trumpeter attired in a black velvet coat played three 'soundings' on his instrument before the play began. The audience paid anything from one pence to six pence for their tickets, with the groundlings paying the least and those who wished to occupy the 'lords' rooms' at the back paying the highest. A charge for sitting in the gallery was usually two pence. Blackfriars and other private playhouses charged a minimum of three to six pence with the highest price of thirty pence or half a crown being charged for a box alongside the stage. Playgoers could book tickets in advance in these private theatres. Whatever one paid, the experience likely involved much spectacle and noise with loud oratory from the stage and vocal audiences. While all plays had music of some kind, the Blackfriars had an elaborate orchestra with lutes, violins, flutes and an early version of banjos. Plays such *The Tempest* that involved lots of music and processional masques were clearly designed for the indoor private theatre

Players performed pretty much through the year with the playing season being divided into three: Autumn – from August to October, Winter – from All Hallows (late October) to Lent, and Spring – from Eastertide to summer. There were no performances during Lent and many performances during Christmas. Public theatres had performances through the week including Sunday. Performances began at two o'clock in the afternoon (three or four o'clock in private theatres). *Romeo and Juliet* refers to the 'two hours' traffic of our stage' (Prologue, 12) and in *The Alchemist* Jonson writes that his play will last 'two short hours' (Prologue, 1).[9] We can infer from this that the average performance lasted for about that period of time. In the winter months the darkness would have descended before the end of the performance. While the private playhouses lit up the stage with candlelight (the five-act structure might have partly originated in breaks being needed to cut back the wicks and relight the candles[10]), the public amphitheatres relied entirely on natural light or had to deal with the lack of it. In fact, the author John Webster complained that his play *The White Devil* was a failure because the play was unfortunately enacted 'in so dull a time of winter, presented in so open and black a theatre, that it wanted ... a full and understanding Auditory' ('To the Reader', 4–6). It must have been quite the surreal experience – watching *The Jew of Malta* or *Macbeth* or even the light sunny comedies as the darkness fell thick and fast. But the players strove to lighten the mood before the audience left – jigs and improvised comic verse often followed the main performance. In fact, according to one observer, a jig followed even a sombre play like *Julius Caesar*!

The players occasionally left London and went on tour. Indeed, they had to do so when the London theatres were shut down due to plague (the notable closures due to plague were in 1603 and 1604 and again in 1608). Some companies travelled quite regularly and kept two groups of actors – one to play in London and the other for travel. Scholars differ in their opinion on how profitable touring was to the companies. According to Andrew Gurr, touring was cumbersome and yielded low profits at best, while Arthur Kinney argues that touring increased the stature of players and gave them the opportunity to perform in noble houses across the country (as the players do in Hamlet).[11] In any case, when on tour the companies probably travelled with fewer actors and a smaller stock of costumes and props. The covered wagons in which they stored their goods must have been a welcome sight in the English countryside.

Costumes and props

Costume is an important part of Renaissance drama. What, for instance, would Ariel of *The Tempest* be without his fantastical and varied shapes? Or Tamburlaine, who changes his clothing from white to black to scarlet? While there was some interest in costumes being authentic and accurate when the plays had a contemporary setting, this was less the case with plays set in the past. So in Peacham's 1595 sketch of a staging of *Titus Andronicus*, some characters are dressed in Roman tunics in accordance with the play's Roman setting, while others are clad in Elizabethan armour – an instance of an unselfconscious collapsing of the centuries. Costumes were spectacular in their own right. They also helped to identity a character's class status, and indeed, the companies put much effort into keeping up with the latest fashion when it designed the costumes of gallants and fashionable young ladies. Clothing became a marker of personality, social identity, difference and similarity. So the twin brothers in Shakespeare's *The Comedy of Errors* were projected as twins, not necessarily because they looked alike, but because they dressed identically. Clothing became all the more significant with disguise and role play being important themes in the plays. The listing of the inventory owned by the Admiral's Men in *Henslowe's Diary* includes more than three hundred separate garments owned by the company including a 'friar's gown' a 'little doublet for a boy', a 'suit for Neptune', a 'fool's coat' and a 'gown of Calico for the Queen'. Some costumes are associated with particular characters – so we have 'Tamburlaine's breeches of velvet', 'Robin Hood's suit' and 'Faust's jerkin'. There is also the assortment of wigs and beards and one 'ass's head' (probably used in *A Midsummer Night's Dream*). Costumes were a major investment for playing companies and hence a valuable part of their capital. So Henslowe paid a tailor the kingly sum of twenty-two shillings for a velvet and satin gown for Thomas Heywood's play *A Woman Killed With Kindness*. In the summer of 1598 he paid out a total of forty-five pounds for costumes and thirty-seven pounds for eight new plays – indicating that costumes cost more than the play scripts. Because so much money was invested in costumes, they were used in multiple productions and companies hired 'tiring men' or wardrobe keepers to maintain the costumes, as well as tailors, milliners and lace makers. A small industry developed around theatrical costume. Some of the costumes were purchased second hand from dealers or pawnbrokers (Henslowe himself ran a pawn-broking business alongside the playing company). It was also customary to use clothing discarded by the nobility. As Swiss traveller Thomas Platter wrote, 'it is the English usage for eminent lords or knights at their disease to bequeath and leave almost the best of their clothes to their serving men, which it is unseemly for the latter to wear, so they offer them for sale for a small sum to the actors'.[12] Because actors donned the clothing of nobility on stage, they were breaking the sumptuary laws that regulated clothing mainly along class lines. Stephen Gosson, a vehement critic of the theatre, complained that one of the problems of the theatre was the fact that 'the very hireling of some of our players ... jet under gentlemen's noses in suits of silk'.[13]

Stage props were also among a company's valuable possessions and were a crucial part of a play's performance: *Hamlet* would be unimaginable without Yorick's skull, *Friar Bacon and Friar Bungay* without the brass head and Moll of *The Roaring Girl* without her viol. Like clothing, props too served to identify social status – so kings wore crowns and carried sceptres, while tradesmen carried tools. Indeed props (like costumes) made the important point that material goods were crucial to the formation of social identities. As Margaret De Grazia writes, 'what one is depends on what one owns'.[14] Props were often symbolic: in the preface of *A Warning for Fair Women* (1599), History carries a drum and martial banner, Tragedy a knife and Comedy a fiddle.

Stage props are poorly documented for the most part except for, once again, Henslowe's list of the properties belonging to the Rose (although this list too is most likely incomplete). Henslowe spent £1,317 on props between 1597 and 1603, a small fortune at that time. Playbooks accounted for only half this amount.[15] Henslowe's list includes such curious objects as a 'hell's mouth', a 'tree of golden apples', a 'cauldron for the Jew' and even the 'city of Rome'! Modern criticism, which tends to privilege the language of the plays, sees props as rather silly add-ons, and even some Renaissance playwrights despised them or saw them as distractions from their own literary art. So Dekker complained that plays are reliant more on carpenters and craftsmen than writers[16] and Jonson was annoyed by the 'creaking throne comes down, the boys to please',[17] a reference to the common practice of lowering deities on a throne. But audiences went to see as well as to hear plays and the props helped create the spectacles the ticketholders longed for. Consequently, handkerchiefs, letters, books and more blood-curdling props like 'raw flesh', 'dead men's heads and bones' and 'vials of blood' (all used in *The Battle of Alcazar*) were part of performances. Besides, props were created by numerous craftsmen, provided work to people outside the immediate world of the theatre and indicate the complex ties that linked the playing companies to the world around them. As Jonathan Gil Harris and Natasha Korda point out, they were nodes 'in the network of social relations that are the stuff of drama and society alike.'[18] In fact, some props made their way onto the stage from monasteries that were dissolved after the Reformation.

From *Henslowe's Diary* (1591–1609).

Philip Henslowe was an entrepreneur who built both the Rose and Fortune theatres and was the manager of the Lord Admiral's Men playing company. Between 1591 and 1609 he kept a detailed account of the activities, expenses and profits of the company in his *Diary*, a text that is very important to modern theatre historians. The excerpt below is a list of the stage props owned by the playing company in 1598.
(See the Appendix for a modern spelling transcript of this document.)

The Enventary tacken of all the properties for my Lord Admeralles men, *the* 10 *of Marche 1598.*
    Item, j rock, j cage, j tomb, j Hell mought.
    Item, j tome of Guido, j tome of Dido, j bedstead.
    Item, viij lances, j payer of stayers for Fayeton.
    Item, ij stepells, & j chyme of belles, & j beacon.
    Item, j hecfor for the playe of Faeton, the limes dead.
    Item, j globe, & j golden scepter; iij clobes.
    Item, ij marchepanes, & the sittie of Rome.
    Item, j gowlden flece; ij rackets; j baye tree.
    Item, j wooden hatchett; j lether hatchete.
    Item, j wooden canepie; owld Mahemetes head.
    Item, j lyone skin; j beares skyne; & Faetones lymes, & Faeton
      charete; & Argosse heade.
    Item, Neptun forcke & garland.
    Item, j crosers stafe; Kentes woden leage.
    Item, lerosses head, & raynbowe; j littell alter.
    Item, viij viserdes; Tamberlyne brydell; j wooden matook.
    Item, Cupedes bowe, & quiver; the clothe of the Sone & Mone.
    Item, j bores heade & Serberosse iij heades.
    Item, j Cadeseus; ij mose banckes, & j snake.
    Item, ij fanes of feathers; Belendon stable; j tree of gowlden
      apelles; Tantelouse tre; jx eyorn targates.

Item, j copper targate, & xvij foyles.
Item, iiij wooden targates; j greve armer.
Item, j syne for Mother Readcap; j buckler.
Item, Mercures wings; Tasso picter; j helmet with a dragon;
  j shelde, with iij lyones; j eleme bowle.
Item, j chayne of dragons; j gylte speare.
Item, ij coffenes; j bulles head; and j vylter.
Item, iij tymbrells, j dragon in fostes.
Item, j lyone; ij lyon heades; j great horse with his leages; j sack-bute.
Item, j whell and frame in the Sege of London.
Item, j paire of rowghte gloves.
Item, j poopes miter.
Item, iij Imperial crownes; j playne crowne.
Item, j gostes crown; j crown with a sone.
Item, j frame for the heading in Black Jone.
Item, j black dogge.
Item, j cauderm for the Jewe.

Backdrops ranged from simple ones (black hangings for tragedies) to fairly elaborate ones (the shopping complex in *The Roaring Girl*). This, along with the extensive use of props, indicates that the Renaissance stage was not completely 'bare'. Plays were also for the audience's visual pleasure though we should remember that the theatre was 'non-illusionistic' – the players did not try to or even want to recreate reality on stage as we might do in realistic theatre or film. Props and backdrops were obviously artificial and scenes were shifted and props changed in full view of the audience. In fact, the play's awareness that it was a play rather than reality is reflected in prologues, choruses, plays within plays and jokes to the audience. So *Henry V* starts with an apology for the limitations of 'this wooden O' (Prologue, 13) in which mighty battles would be staged, and Cleopatra's reference to a 'squeaking Cleopatra' who will 'boy my greatness' (5.2.218) is a wry joke about boy actors playing female roles.

The players and their audience

The players organized themselves into 'companies' or well-organized professional groups. The theatrical company was an important unit that shaped all theatrical activity in the time period. It was fundamentally an economic cooperative, loosely modelled on the guilds of the day. Each member of the company was called a 'sharer' and typically the sharers together held stock in the company, jointly owned costumes, props and playbooks, incurred other expenses as a group, acted together and then divided the profits amongst themselves. Shakespeare, for instance, made most of his wealth from the shares he held in the Lord Chamberlain's Men and the King's Men. Managing and running these companies was a shared effort and the companies came close to operating as non-authoritarian organizations in what was a very authoritarian and hierarchical society. The ten to twelve sharers of a company accepted or rejected scripts, decided how much to pay the scriptwriter, took casting decisions, decided on the weekly performance schedule and took care of the publicity. There might have been someone like a stage manager who had a supervisory role though he was not in any sense the 'boss'. The companies worked very hard. Plays were mounted at rapid speed and there were usually only two or three weeks between reading and accepting a script and the first performance. Rehearsal, casting, licensing and costuming all took place in that short time. Apart from the actor-sharers, there were hired workers who were musicians, the tiring men and those used to 'swell a scene' or to make up the numbers when a crowd was needed for a battle scene or procession. There was a bookkeeper who might have been a prompter who also inserted stage directions into scripts; there were also hired scribes to make 'fair copies' from the 'foul papers' or rough manuscript. The playwrights themselves worked for the companies and were not always well-paid. However, companies tried to acquire all the scripts of a successful playwright. So, for example, the King's Men company owned all of Shakespeare's scripts, nearly all of Beaumont and Fletcher's and most of Massinger's, Middleton's and Jonson's.[19] Indeed, companies were known by and owed their success to the plays they owned and staged (their 'repertory') as suggested by the titles on some of the quarto editions of the plays: '*Tamburlaine the Great . . . shewed upon the Stages in the City of London. By the Right Honourable Lord Admiral, his servants*' and '*The Troublesome Reign of John king of England . . . (sundry times) publicly acted by the Queen's Majesties players*'. Even as the companies were professional units, there were close relationships between the members. They certainly quarrelled with each other on occasion but were bound together by ties of friendship and trust and often left each other legacies, as seen in their wills.

The 'Vagabond Act' of 1574 had designated actors as wandering rogues. Securing the patronage of a nobleman protected the companies from this act, added to their stability and enhanced their status. The best known and most successful companies were the Lord Admiral's Men (later Prince Henry's Men) and the Lord Chamberlain's Men (who secured the patronage of the king and became the King's Men). The Earl of Worcester's Men was another large company that was subsequently designated as Queen Anne's Men. The companies operated under licences awarded by the patrons and received their protection. Technically, they were in the service of the sponsor and their performances were meant to add to the magnificence of the patron's household. Nearly all of these patrons were very high ranking men who belonged to the monarch's first circle of advisors or the Privy Council. As a result of this the players had the protection of the court. In fact, Sir Edmund Tilney, Queen Elizabeth's 'Master of the Revels' who was in charge of organizing court entertainments, found that it was expensive to stage private entertainments or masques at court and started hiring actors to stage plays for the monarch. While Queen Elizabeth herself did not officially patronize any company, she enjoyed plays. Under her, the players were summoned to court four to eight times a year. When James became king he immediately became the official patron of a company and had as many as twenty plays staged at court every year by the public players.[20] It is important to remember that with time the companies became less and less dependent on patrons and more reliant on public ticket sales for their success; but patronage continued to serve them in many ways and the system persisted.

After 1594 the playing companies had to be licensed and get approval for a play script before they staged it. After 1610 licences had to be obtained to print plays. The state-appointed office with the authority to do this was the Revels Office. The Master of the Revels most likely 'perused' or read the script and insisted on changes he saw as necessary. He then added his 'allowance' or gave permission to the corrected version, which was then called the 'allowed copy'. The permission or licence was given to the theatrical company that had bought the script rather than to the author. The companies paid the Revels Office a fee of about seven shillings to licence a play. Some playwrights, including Jonson, complained of being harassed and summoned by authorities several times. In fact, Jonson was accused of treason after the staging of his play *Sejanus* in 1603. But scholars agree that the Revels Office generally cooperated with players.

The companies were in intense competition with each other, especially because there were usually about four to five companies playing simultaneously in London.[21] They also competed with the private theatres, especially the companies made up entirely of young boys who performed there. In *Hamlet* Shakespeare expresses resentment towards 'the little eyases that cry out on the top of question, and are most tyrannically clapped for't'[22] (2.2.341–42). These companies preferred to perform modern plays such as satiric comedies, while more traditional fare was performed by the adult companies. In fact, the boy companies often poked fun at the 'old fashioned' plays performed in the public theatres. After 1613 the fortunes of these boys' companies declined – partly because they performed plays on politically sensitive topics – and they soon became absorbed into adult companies.

But who were the players? These men who were artists, professional entertainers and businessmen? Today we tend to focus so much on the playwrights and the play scripts that we often forget that the success of a play depended on the men who brought it to life on stage. Ben Jonson openly acknowledged the contribution of the actors by printing their names in the first complete edition of his works (1616). Subsequently, Shakespeare's first folio (the complete edition of his works that came out in 1623) included the names of the twenty-six principal actors who performed his plays. There were possibly only about eight or nine regular actors for every company and about six boy actors. This meant that the doubling of parts was frequent and even expected. Doubling added to the sense of intrigue as actors entered, exited and re-entered in a different role. Sometimes seemingly irrelevant scenes – including comic scenes – were inserted to give an actor time to change his costume before returning in a different role. The very fact that actors could play multiple roles in a single production indicates that they were very versatile and that the audience's imaginations were flexible enough to accept them in different roles. By the seventeenth century there was less of a taste for doubling and more 'literalist' casting where the actor came to play one unique part became more of the norm.

Some of the actors (including Alleyn, Burbage and Shakespeare) made fortunes, but most of them did not. However, they were all remarkably hard-working and skilled artists who often performed before the public after only one complete rehearsal. It is hard for us to say what the dominant style of acting was, but it is unlikely to have been the 'realistic 'style we tend to prefer in modern times. The actors did not attempt to become a character but to represent one.[23] This practice was known as 'counterfeiting'. They were clearly playing roles, not pretending to be the 'real thing'.

There were stars among the actors: Richard Tarlton, described as 'the wonder of his age',[24] was known for his comic repartees, dances and impromptu speeches; William Kempe, member of the Lord Chamberlain's Men, was also known for comic roles including Falstaff, Bottom and Launcelot Gobbo; Richard Burbage played famous tragic roles including Romeo, Richard II,

Hamlet, Othello and Ferdinand (in *The Duchess of Malfi*); and Edward Alleyn played Tamburlaine, Faustus and Barabas. Roles were often written with specific actors in mind. When Kempe was acting for the Lord Chamberlain's Men, Shakespeare created a certain kind of clown: the comic fool who entertained with slapstick humour (Bottom and Dogberry come to mind). After Kempe left the company in 1599, the fool became more the wise, singing fool, like Feste of *Twelfth Night*.[25] Plays with prominent female roles were probably written keeping specific outstanding boy actors in mind. Andrew Gurr speculates that certain pairings of heroines with contrasting looks and personalities (Hermia and Helena, Rosalind and Celia) also came about because of certain boy actors available to the company.[26] Indeed, one of the most interesting features of the stage was the use of boy actors. The tradition of boy players was a fairly old one dating back to the thirteenth century and there is evidence of juvenile singers and actors in medieval pageants and processions. So when players became professionalized it was not so novel to include boys among the cast. The lives of these boys must have been very unusual from our modern perspective. They were usually apprentices to adult actors though legally apprentices had to be at least seventeen years of age and the companies needed younger children; consequently, the companies did not follow the structures laid out by apprentice laws. The boys were usually procured from one of the other trading guilds or from parents. They were trained in acting and music as well as rhetoric and grammar by the master who paid them in food and lodging rather than money. Any fees owing to them went to the master. While there were doubtless cases of exploitation and unhappiness, there is also plenty of evidence of affection between the masters and their young apprentices. Some of them went on to become little stars in their own right.

According to Harbage, about 15,000 people went to all the theatres combined each week in the year 1595.[27] This number, of course, varied over the years and even by day and season, but it does give us some sense of the popularity of plays. The most interesting feature of the Renaissance audience was that it was very mixed in terms of social class. Dekker famously wrote that 'the theatre is your Poet's Royal Exchange ... your Gallant, your Courtier, and your Captain had wont to be the soundest playmasters'.[28] So apprentices, artisans, sailors, tradesmen, housewives and noblemen patronized plays. Unlike almost any other social space in Renaissance England, anyone could go to a playhouse. While there was a hierarchy of viewing places in the playhouses, it was money rather than social status that determined where one sat (or stood). The theatre became a space of social intercourse where different social groups could potentially mix with each other. So the 'stinkards', as the groundlings were known, 'has the selfsame liberty to be there in his Tobacco-fumes as your sweet Courtier hath'.[29] While one has to be cautious about describing the theatre as a utopic egalitarian space, it was certainly an unusual institution for its time as far as the heterogeneous audience was concerned. Consequently, in order to be truly successful a play had to cater simultaneously to different sections of the audience. The intellectual references in a play such as *Doctor Faustus* would have appealed to the well-read portion of the audience, the slapstick humour to the less scholarly and, we can assume, the psychological and moral conflicts to all. So there was a unique 'unity of taste' tying the audience together. In the words of Robert Weimann, 'It was a multiple unity based on contradictions, and as such allowed the dramatist a flexible frame of reference that was more complex and more vital to the experience of living and feeling within the social organism than the achievement of any other theatre before or since.'[30] In this way the drama of the period achieved what no drama had achieved before.

Those hostile to the theatre often commented on the fact that it attracted vagrants and other undesirables. What was worse, said some critics, was that respectable ladies in the audience interacted with 'the light women' or prostitutes who apparently frequented the theatre hoping to pick up customers. The crowd was loud and rowdy at times, smoked plentifully and ate and drank of the refreshments being offered on sale. Their responses to the play were loud and very physical, involving clapping and cheering as well as hissing, mewing and throwing ammunition by way of nuts and apples onto stage. Fights sometime broke out often between different factions of the groundlings such as the serving men (servants) and apprentices. Unseemly behaviour was not confined to the 'penny patrons' alone. The gallants arrived late, played cards during performances, affected boredom at everything, laughed loudly at tragic episodes and often stood up and left noisily at the play's climactic moments. Playwrights often complained about audience behaviour. Dekker wrote of 'the Greasy-apron' audience'[31] and Shakespeare's Hamlet expresses his disdain for the groundlings who 'for the most part are capable of nothing but inexplicable dumb-shows and noise' (3.2.11–13). Dekker also satirized 'the insolent, over-weening Coxcombe' who sat conspicuously on stage and Jonson complained about the 'capricious gallant' who mocked the players and loudly derided their efforts.[32] The complaints about an ignorant, unappreciative and insensitive audience were particularly loud when a play failed – for instance, Webster railed at the audience after the failure of *The White Devil* and Fletcher after that of *The Faithful Shepherdess*. The ideal audience, writes Jonson wistfully in *Everyman out of His Humour*, was appreciative, attentive and came to be entertained, moved and educated. They would be 'attentive auditors, / Such as will join their profit with their pleasure, / And come to feed their understanding parts' (Induction, 201–03).[33] In Jonson one can see the conflict between scorn for the 'dullards' who came to watch his plays and his reliance on them. Shakespeare was generally more willing to embrace the audience in all its diversity and often addresses them genially.

Andrew Harbage has proposed that the audiences which patronized private theatres were more privileged than those which came to the public theatres.[34] Consequently, the plays that were performed in these two types of venues were also quite different. More recently, other scholars have refuted this and said the fare at both kinds of stages was quite mixed, as was the audience. Even members of the so-called privileged audiences at the private theatres ranged from gentry to impoverished students from the local universities. So Francis Beaumont's *The Knight of the Burning Pestle* (1607), a play first performed at the Blackfriars which makes fun of the citizen class, was a failure possibly because there were a significant number of citizens in this theatre (supposedly frequented only by the high-born) who did not quite appreciate the play's satire. It is true, however, that later on, in the era of King James, court culture became more exclusive, and later theatres like the Cockpit (which opened in 1616) attracted slightly less mixed audiences.[35]

While the word 'audience' emphasizes the aspect of hearing ('audio' – sound), the word 'spectator' emphasizes the element of seeing. As Andrew Gurr points out, 'There is no English term which acknowledges the full experience of hearing and seeing the complete "action" of a play'.[36] The success of the play depended on the collaboration of the audience. 'For 'tis your thoughts that now must deck our kings', writes Shakespeare in *Henry V* (Prologue, 29). It is not easy for us to imagine how the audience of the time responded to those aspects of the text that move, inspire, trouble and puzzle us. We have nothing approaching reviews or elaborate commentary that would allow us to access a Renaissance audience's response. The few playgoers who actually recorded responses usually restricted themselves to brief plot summaries. What we do know is the audience liked novelty and fresh theatrical fare every day. Fashions and tastes changed rapidly; a particular genre might be in style for one season and quite outmoded the next. As Thomas Middleton writes in his preface to *The Roaring Girl*, 'the fashion of play-making I can properly compare to nothing so naturally as the alteration in apparel' ('To the Comic Play-readers', 1–2). New plays were introduced at a rapid rate. For example, the Admiral's Men staged seventeen new plays (roughly one new one every fortnight) in the first nine months of its operations.[37] Gurr writes that the total number of play scripts written between 1560 and 1642 was probably at least three times the thousand or so titles that we know of (of which we have only about five hundred or so texts).[38] Popular plays such as *Tamburlaine* and *Dr. Faustus* were revived and other plays were rewritten for revival (for example, Jonson rewrote Kyd's *The Spanish Tragedy* in 1592 and Fletcher wrote a sequence to Shakespeare's *The Taming of the Shrew* in the 1620s). Writers realized the importance of pleasing their audiences. As Feste's refrain in *Twelfth Night* goes: 'And we'll strive to please you everyday' (5.1.400).

Anti-theatrical writing

In spite of its growing popularity and success – or because of it – the theatre was constantly the subject of debate and attacked from a number of quarters. The Lord Mayor of London, the alderman and other civic authorities were worried that plays would keep apprentices from work and encourage idleness. They were also concerned that the crowds coming to the theatres could create traffic congestion on the streets and even turn disorderly and cause riots. Besides, the tightly packed crowds could possibly lead to the spread of the plague. In fact, it was even felt that the 'sinfulness' of the theatre would bring down plague upon the populace! The most vociferous and virulent criticism of the stage, however, came from the growing Puritan sect. Writers such Stephen Gosson in his *The School of Abuse* (1579) and *Plays Confuted in Five Actions* (1582), Philip Stubbes in *Anatomie of Abuse* (1583) and William Prynne in *Histrio-mastix* (1633) were most vocal in their critique. Prynne described theatres as 'shops of all wickedness', and Stubbes wrote of plays as propagating 'heathenrie idolatry and sin'.[39] They considered plays unsavoury because of the ribald songs and music and accused them of stimulating dangerous passions and glamorizing evil. The theatre was also described as excessive, wasteful and gaudy. These critics often condemned the theatre in the same terms they did heathen religions and festivities. They associated plays, with their emphasis on the spectacular, with Catholic ritual. The plays reminded them of idolatry, the worship of the material form rather than the inner essence. Plays, most troublingly, also drew crowds away from church, especially since they were performed even on Sundays and holidays. Stubbes asks, 'Do they not draw the people from hearing the word of God, from godly lectures and sermons? For you shall have them flock thither, thick and threefold, when the church of God shall be bare and empty.'[40]

From Stephen Gosson, *Plays Confuted in Five Actions* (1582). (Courtesy of The Huntingdon Library)

Stephen Gosson had already lamented the evils of plays in *The School of Abuse* (1579). This work provoked quite a few responses in defence of the theatre. In response, Gosson wrote yet another essay, *Plays Confuted in Five Actions* (1582), in which he replied to his critics and restated his condemnation of plays. The excerpt below is from the latter work.

From The Second Action:
The argument of Tragedies is wrath, cruelty, incest, injury, murder either violent by sword, or voluntary by poison. The persons, Gods, Goddesses, furies, fiends, kings, queens, and mighty men. The ground work of Comedies, is love, cozenage,[41] flattery, bawdry . . . The persons, cooks, queens, knaves, bawds, parasites, courtesans, lecherous old men, amorous young men. . . . The best play you can pick out, is but a mixture of good and evil, how can it be then the schoolmistress of life? The beholding of troubles and miserable slaughters that are in Tragedies, drive us to immoderate sorrow, heaviness, womanish weeping and mourning, . . . Comedies so tickle our senses with a pleasanter vein, that they make us lovers of laughter, and pleasure, without any mean, both foes to temperance,[42] what schooling is this? Sometime you shall see nothing but the adventures of an amorous[43] knight, passing from country to country for the love of his lady, encountering many a terrible monster made of brown paper, & at his return, is so wonderfully change, that he cannot be known but by some posy in his tablet,[44] or by a broken ring, or a handkerchief, or a piece of a cockle shell, what learn you by that? When the soul of your plays is either mere trifles, or Italian bawdry, or wooing of gentlewomen, what are we taught?

From The Third Action:
. . . Whatsoever he be that looketh narrowly into our Stage Plays, or considereth how, and which ways they are represented, shall find more filthiness in them, the Players dream off. The Law of God very straightly forbids men to put on women's garments, garments are set down for signs distinctive between sex & sex, to take unto us those garments that are manifest signs of another sex, is to falsify, forge, and adulterate, contrary to the express rule of the word of God. Which forbiddeth it by threatening a curse unto the same. . . . which way I

beseech you shall they be excused, that put on, not the apparel only, but the gait, the gestures, the voice, the passions of a woman? . . . The proof is evident, the consequence is necessary, that in Stage Plays for a boy to put on the attire, the gesture, the passions of a woman; or a mean person to take upon him the title of a Prince with counterfeit port, and train,[45] is by outward signs to show themselves otherwise than they are, and so within the compass of a lie . . .

From The Fifth Action:
As at the first, so now, Theatres are snares unto fair women . . . our Theatres, & playhouses in London, are as full of secret adultery as they were in Rome. In Rome it was the fashion of wanton young men, to place themselves as nigh as they could to the courtesans, to present them pomegranates, to play with their garments, and wait on them home, when the sport was done. In the playhouses at London, it is the fashion of youths to go first into the parade, and to carry their eye through every gallery, the like unto ravens where they spy the carrion thither they eye,[46] and press as near to the fairest as they can. Instead of pomegranates they give the pippins,[47] they dally with their garments to pass the time, they minister talk upon all occasions,[48] & either bring them home to their houses on small acquaintance, or slip into taverns when the plays are done . . . This open corruption is a prick in the eyes of them that see it, and a thorn in the sides of the godly, when they hear it. This is a poison to beholders, and a nursery of idleness to the Players. Most of the Players have been either men of occupations, which they have forsaken to live by playing, or common minstrels, or trained up from their childhood to this abominable exercise & have now no other way to get their living. A commonweal[49] is likened to the body, whose head is the prince, in the body: if any part be idle, by participation the damage redoundeth[50] to the whole, if any refuse to do their duty, though they be base, as the guts, the gall, the bladder, how dangerous it is both to the body, and to the head, every man is able to conjecture. . . .

Plays are the inventions of the devil, the offerings of Idolatry, the pomp of worldlings,[51] the blossoms of vanity, the root of Apostasy,[52] the food of iniquity,[53] riot, and adultery. Detest them. Players are masters of vice, teachers of wantonness, spurs of impurity, the Sons of idleness, so long as they live in this order, loath them. God is merciful, his wings are spread to receive you if you come betimes, God is just, his bow is bent & his arrow drawn, to send you a plague, if you stay too long.

Besides these complaints, opponents of the theatre were particularly troubled by male actors playing female roles. As discussed in Chapter Two, these men and boys were accused of violating the laws of nature and God. Apart from projecting a false sexual identity, actors were generally associated with deception. They played other selves and so were reminiscent of the Devil, who could pretend to be what he was not. As Gosson wrote in *Plays Confuted in Five Actions* (1582), 'in Stage plays for a boy to put on the attire, the gesture, the passions of a woman; for a mean person to take upon him the title of a Prince with counterfeit port and train, is by outward signs to show themselves to be otherwise than they are, and so within the compass of a lie'.[54] This performative aspect that was inherent to drama, which was duplicity as far as the Puritans were concerned, implied that drama was essentially corrupt and could never be truly reformed.

Anti-theatrical writers very often worried that the stage would disturb carefully constructed social hierarchies. As we saw in Chapter One, actors could potentially demystify political power by playing kings and rulers on stage. The theatre was also the cause of 'confusing the degrees' in other ways: the mixed audience led to different social classes consorting with each other and actors in their resplendent costume broke the dictum that people dress according to their class status, suggesting the possibility of a world in which social hierarchies are subverted.

From Philip Stubbes, *Anatomie of Abuses* (1583).
(Courtesy of Early English Books Online)

Philip Stubbes was among the best known of the Puritan social reformers. His *Anatomie of Abuses* was printed in 1583 and went through four editions in three years. Stubbes condemns several kinds of sinful behaviour, including gambling, sports, extravagant costume and stage plays. He expressly addresses the topic of stage plays in this excerpt.

Besides this, there is no mischief which these Playes maintain not. For, do they not nourish Idleness? . . . Do they not draw the people from hearing the word of God, from godly Lectures and Sermons: For you shall have them flock thither thick and three fold, when the Church of God shall be bare and empty. And those that will never come at Sermons will flowe thither apace. . . . Do they not maintain

Bawdry, insinuate foolery, & renew the remembrance of Heathen Idolatry? Do they not induce to whoredome and uncleanness: Nay, are they not rather plain devourers of maidenly Virginity and chastity: For proof whereof, but mark the flocking and running to Theatres and Curtains, daily & hourly, night and day, time and tide, to see Plays and Interludes,[55] where such wanton gestures, such bawdy speeches, such laughing and fleering, such kissing and bussing,[56] such clipping and culling,[57] such winking and glancing of wanton eyes, and the like is used, as is wonderful to behold. Then these goodly Pageants being ended, every mate sorts to his mate, every one brings another homeward of their way very friendly, and in their secret conclaves[58] (covertly) they play the Sodomites, or worse.[59] And these be the fruits of plays and Interludes for the most part. And whereas you say, there are good examples to be learned in them: truly so there are: if you will learn falsehood: if you will learn cosonage[60]: if you will learn to deceive: if you will learn to play the hypocrite: to cog,[61] to lie and falsify, if you will learn to jest, laugh and fleer,[62] to grin, to nod, and maw[63]: if you will earn to play the Vice, to swear, tear and blaspheme both heaven and earth: If you will learn to become a Bawd, unclean, and to divirginate Maids, to deflower honest Wives: If you will learn to murder slay, kill, pick, steal, rob, and roué[64]: If you will learn to rebel against Princes, to commit Treason, to consume treasure, to practice idleness, to sing and talk of bawdy love and Venerie[65]: If you will learn to deride, scoff, mock and flout, to flatter and smooth: If you will learn to play the Whoremaster, the Glutton, Drunkard or incestuous person: If you will learn to become proud, haughty and arrogant: and finally, if you will learn to condemn God and all his laws, to care neither for heaven nor Hell, and to commit all kind of sinne & mischief, you need to go to no other school, for all these good examples may you see painted before your eyes in Interludes & Plays.

. . .

Therefore, I beseech all Players, Founders and maintainers of Plays and Interludes in the bowels of Jesus Christ, as they tender the salvation of their souls, & others, to leave off that cursed kind of life, and give themselves to such honest exercises, and godly mysteries, as God hath commanded them in this word to get their livings withal: For who will call him a wise man that playeth the part of a fool and a Vice: Who can call him a Christian, who playeth the part of a Devil, the sworn enemy of Christ: Who can call him a just man, that playeth the part of a dissembling Hypocrite: And to be brief, who can call him a straight dealing man, who playeth a Cosoners[66] part: And so of all the rest. Away therefore with this so infamous an Art: for, go they never so brave, yet are they counted and taken but for beggars. And is it not true? Live they not upon begging of every one that comes? And are they not taken by the Laws of the realm, for Rogues & Vagabonds: (I speak of such that travel the Countries, with Plays and Interludes making an occupation of it) and ought to be punished if they had their deserts.[67]

These attacks on the theatre by the likes of Stubbes and Gosson did not go undefended. Jonson's *Bartholomew Fair* satirizes one Justice Overdo, who makes it his business to visit the fair and pry into the lives and doings of the people who work there with the aim of reforming them. This character was probably inspired by the Lord Mayor of London who was reported to visit 'lewd houses' in disguise to catch those who frequented them. Heywood in his *An Apology for Actors* wrote that plays were the 'ornament of the city' that added to its culture and grandeur. They contributed to social harmony and taught moral and political lessons.

From Thomas Heywood, *An Apology for Actors* (1612). (Courtesy of The Folger Shakespeare Library)

The playwright Thomas Heywood wrote *An Apology for Actors* in 1612 in defence of the stage. He was responding to the attacks of the Puritans and other anti-theatrical writers.

From *The First Book*:
To turn to our domestic histories, what English blood seeing the person of any bold English man presented and doth not hug his fame, and hunnye[68] at his valor,[69] pursuing him in his enterprise with his best wishes, and as being wrapped in contemplation, offers to him in his heart all prosperous performance, as if the Personater were the man Personated,[70] so bewitching a thing is lively and well spirited action, that it hath power to new mold[71] the hearts of the spectators and fashion them to the shape of any noble and notable attempt. What coward to see his countryman valiant would not be ashamed of his own cowardice? What English Prince should he

behold the true portraiture of that famous King *Edward* the third, foraging[72] France, taking so great a King captive in his own country, quartering the English Lyons with the French Flower-delyce,[73] and would not be suddenly Inflam'd with so royal a spectacle, being made apt and fit for the like achievement.

From *The Third Book*:

To proceed to the matter: First, playing is an ornament to the City, which strangers of all Nations, repairing hither, report of in their Countries, beholding them here with some admiration: for what variety of entertainment can there be in any City of Christendom, more than in *London*? But some will say, this dish might be very well spared out of the banquet: to him I answer, *Diogenes*,[74] that used to feed on roots, cannot relish a March-pane.[75] Secondly, our *English* tongue, which hath been the most harsh, uneven, and broken language of the world, part *Dutch*, part *Irish*, *Saxon*, *Scots*, *Welsh*, and indeed a gallimaffry[76] of many, but perfect in none, is now by this secondary means of playing, continually refined, every writer striving in himself to add a new flourish unto it; so that in process, from the most rude and unpolished tongue, it is grown to a most perfect and composed[77] language, and many excellent works, and elaborate Poems writ in the same, that many Nations grow enamored of our tongue (before despised.) . . . Thirdly, plays have made the ignorant more apprehensive, taught the unlearned the knowledge of many famous histories, instructed such as cannot read in the discovery of all our *English* Chronicles: & what man have you now of that weak capacity, that cannot discourse of any notable thing recorded even from *William* the *Conqueror*, may from the landing of *Brute*,[78] until this day, being possessed of their true use, for, or because Plays are writ with this aim, and carried with this method, to teach the subjects obedience to their King, to show the people the untimely ends of such as have moved tumults, commotions, and insurrections,[79] to present them with the flourishing state of such as live in obedience, exhorting them to allegiance, dehorting[80] them from all traitorous and felonious stratagems.

. . .

If we present a Tragedy, we include the fatal and abortive ends of such as commit notorious murders, which is aggravated and acted with all the Art that may be, to terrify men from the like abhorred practices. If we present a foreign History, the subject is so intended, that in the lives of *Romans*, *Grecians*, or others, either the virtues of our Country-men are extolled, or their vices reproved, as thus, by the example of *Cesar*[81] to stir soldiers to valor, & magnanimity: by the fall of *Pompey*, that no man trust in his own strength[82]: we present *Alexander* killing his friend in rage, to reprove rashness[83]: *Mydas*, choked with his gold, to tax covetousness[84]: *Nero* against tyranny[85]: *Sardanapalus*, against luxury[86]: Nynus, against ambition[87]: with infinite others, by sundry[88] instances either animating men to noble attempts, or attaching the consciences of the spectators, finding themselves touched in presenting the vices of others. If a moral, it is to persuade men to humanity and good life, to instruct them in civility and good manners, showing them the fruits of honesty, and the ends of villainy.

. . .

If a Comedy, it is pleasantly contrived with merry accidents, and intermixed with apt and witty jests, to present before the Prince at certain times of solemnity, or else merrily fitted to the stage. And what is then the subject of this harmless mirth? Either in the shape of a Clown, to show others their slovenly[89] and unhandsome behavior, that they may reform that simplicity in themselves, which others make their sport, lest they happen to become the like subject of general scorn to an auditory, else it intreats[90] of love, deriding foolish inamorates,[91] who spend their ages, their spirits, nay themselves, in the servile and ridiculous employments of their Mistresses: and these are mingled with sportfull accidents, to recreate such as of themselves are wholly devoted to Melancholy, which corrupts the blood: or to refresh such weary spirits as are tired with labour, or study, to moderate the cares and heaviness of the mind, that they may return to their trades and faculties with more zeal and earnestness, after some small soft and pleasant retirement. Sometimes they discourse of Pantaloons,[92] Usurers that have unthrifty sons, which both the father and sons may behold to their instructions: sometimes of Courtesans, to divulge their subtleties and snares in which young men may be entangled, showing them the means to avoid them. If we present a Pastoral,[93] we show the harmless love of Shepherds, diversely moralized, distinguishing betwixt the craft of the City, and the innocence of the sheep-coat. Briefly, there is neither Tragedy, History, Comedy, Moral or Pastoral, from which an infinite use cannot be gathered.

. . .

To end in a word. Art thou addicted to prodigality[94]? envy? cruelty? perjury[95]? flatter? or rage? our Scenes afford thee store of men to

> shape your lives by, who be frugal, loving, gentle, trusty, without soothing, and in all things temperate. Wouldst thou be honourable? Just, friendly, moderate, devout, merciful, and loving concord? Thou mayest see many of their fates and ruins, who have been dishonourable, unjust, false, gluttonous, sacrilegious, bloody-minded, and brochers of dissention.[96] Women likewise that are chaste, are by us extolled, and encouraged in their virtues. The unchaste are by us showed their errors . . . What can sooner print modesty in the souls of the wanton, than by discovering unto them the monstrousness of their sin? It follows that we prove these exercises[97] to have been the discoverers of many notorious murders, long concealed form the eyes of the world.

Heywood's listing of the virtues of theatre was as intense and passionate in tone as that of the critics of playing. The very fact that these debates between the anti-theatrical faction and supporters of the theatres raged on indicates that drama was recognized by both detractors and defenders alike to be a powerful and influential medium of expression.

The stage as political space

As we saw in Chapter One, plays engaged directly or indirectly with social and political questions of the day. They were, in the words of Hamlet, 'the abstract and brief chronicles of the time' (2.2.524–25). Sometimes the players got more directly involved with politics. For example, when the Earl of Essex was planning a coup in 1601 his faction approached the Lord Chamberlain's Men and asked them to stage Shakespeare's *Richard II* (a play that involves the deposition of a king) the day before the attempted coup. The coup subsequently failed, but this incident is supposed to have provoked Elizabeth's famous statement: 'I am Richard II'. Similarly, the Spanish ambassador put pressure on the government to have Middleton's *A Game of Chess* withdrawn because it showed Spain in very poor light. Scholars have wondered whether the stage served as an instrument for those in power or whether it was a social force that challenged and questioned political authority. According to Stephen Greenblatt, the authorities allowed the stage to question and challenge the dominant order, to stage subversion as it were, but only to eventually control or contain it.[98] This is much like festivities and carnivals being allowed in traditional societies as an outlet for the masses. Disorderliness was temporarily allowed in a carnival setting, but at the end of the festivities order was restored and life went back to normal.

However, other scholars have argued that public playhouses emerged at a time when traditional hierarchies were breaking down and could not easily be contained. Steven Mullaney emphasizes the fact that the theatres were built in the Liberties. This put them outside the reach of city authorities and gave them the freedom to ask questions, challenge the dominant ideologies and look at issues from multiple perspectives. Both acting and playing were, in a sense, 'time out' out from traditional rules and structures. The stage was always a part of – yet outside – the social order. It could thus look upon and comment on it from that unique perspective. It became an alternative site of authority, very different from either the church or the court.[99]

Further reasons have been proposed for why the theatre challenged the dominant order. Drama by nature relies on tension and the postponement of resolution to produce a dramatic effect.[100] This meant that plays tend not to offer simple and obvious answers to political and moral questions. Besides, plays were authored by multiple writers and it was inevitable that different ideologies and viewpoints were reflected in the final product. Even if the messages of plays were conservative, the unusual staging practices (cross-dressing, the breaking of sumptuary laws by actors) were ways of questioning the accepted norm. The socially mixed audience was another way order was suspended, and since that audience had bought tickets and come to the play of their own choice (unlike, say, the congregation at a church service), they felt they had the right to ask questions and judge things for themselves.

Plays also raised social issues in more subtle ways. For instance, Renaissance drama was very self-reflexive – it repeatedly reflected on the nature and meaning of performance itself. This is seen in the number of plays that stage 'plays within plays': 'The Mousetrap' in *Hamlet*, the final play in *The Spanish Tragedy* and the masque of madmen in *The Duchess of Malfi*. The fairgrounds in *Bartholomew Fair* are also reminiscent of the theatre – big, noisy, vulgar and yet somehow magical. Shakespeare famously wrote in *As You like It* that 'all the world's a stage, / And all the men and women merely players' (2.2.139–40). This was a recognition that all social roles are precisely roles and that we are all playing to a certain script. So social rank itself was a performance. But one could, if one so wished, manipulate and alter that script. Identity was thus theatrical and performative. This must have provoked a thoughtful audience into thinking about whether they wanted to follow socially given scripts or challenge and refashion them.

For the players, acting was a way of life. All the world was a stage and the stage was a world unto itself. Sometimes this sense of living in the borderland between role and reality was disturbing – it is hard to know for certain whether *The Tempest*'s vision of the 'baseless fabric of this vision' and 'the great globe itself' (4.1.151, 153) dissolving and fading implies disillusionment with theatrical life or a sense of fulfilment as the actor-playwright looks back on his theatrical career. Heywood is, however, more straightforwardly enthusiastic in his *An Apology for Actors*. The world in all its variety and brilliance is a theatre, he writes, and 'He that denies then theatres should be, / He may as well deny a world to me.'[101]

Discussion points

1 Of late some directors have been applying what are called 'original practices' (OP) to contemporary productions of Renaissance plays. For example, they would have the setup on stage mimic that of a Renaissance stage. Select any play you have read and, based on what you have gathered in this chapter, think about what 'original practices' you could bring to the production of the play. What exactly would the director, actors and audience get out of such a production? In other words, what possibilities does historical knowledge of past productions offer for future productions?

2 You have read two pieces of anti-theatrical discourse (the texts by Stephen Gosson and Philip Stubbes) in this chapter. Imagine you are an actor on the Renaissance stage and compose your own defence of the theatre in response to the critics of the theatre.

3 Look carefully at the list of stage props reproduced in Henslowe's Diary. Select any play you have read and think about which of these props would enhance the production. Explain why.

4 Try to watch a contemporary production of a play you are studying. Discuss the potential effects and meanings of choices made by the directors, actors and others involved in the production.

6

Authors, Books and Readers

Even before they were staged, Renaissance plays were manuscripts produced by authors associated with the playing companies. Indeed, William Shakespeare, Christopher Marlowe and some of their peers are not only icons of literary culture but have come to represent writing as a creative act of mystical and inexplicable genius. Who were these men who wrote stage plays for a living and what were the conditions under which they authored their works? In other words, what did authorship mean in the Renaissance and how was it different from authorship today?

Many Renaissance plays also had an afterlife in print. Indeed, in large measure these works were preserved and went on to become central to English literary tradition because they became printed books that could be easily and widely circulated. The printing press was the most important technological innovation of the Renaissance and revolutionized life and learning in many ways. Although movable type as well as paper first appeared in China, the German printer Johannes Gutenberg mechanized the transfer of ink from movable type to paper in 1439, so making the printing process more efficient. By 1455 he had produced the first printed book of the Western world, the majestic Gutenberg Bible. Some twenty years after that William Caxton established a press in England. Manuscript (hand-written texts) and print continued to coexist for centuries, but Europe was now undergoing a media revolution.[1] Printing technology made it possible for works to be standardized, produced more cheaply and efficiently and preserved longer, not because printing paper was more durable than the vellum[2] or parchment on which scribes had written, but because printed works could not be rewritten or altered. Print also had far-reaching social effects though these were not immediately discernible. The written word was available to more people; ideas and stories could be more easily transmitted across cultures. The transforming power of print troubled those in power although they did not hesitate to use it for their own purposes. By the mid-sixteenth century, English authorities denounced the printing as well as the staging of plays as socially disruptive, an attitude evident in a 1553 proclamation 'prohibiting Religious Controversy, Unlicensed Plays and Printing'. But plays continued to be staged and also to be printed, and eventually enjoyed a long history of print production that continues to this day.

It is this history that 'book history' (the scholarly study of how books as material objects were conceptualized, produced, marketed and consumed) is most concerned with. While many of us tend to see 'works of literature' as independent of the physical books in which we encounter them, a book historian would argue that the content and the material form of a book are closely connected. The specific forms and contexts in which we encounter a play and the ways in which it is transmitted, writes David Kastan, 'exert influence over our judgments and interpretations' as much as language and genre do.[3] Studying book history is also a way of acknowledging the other kinds of labour that go into making a book – the work of printers, proof readers and editors. It also means paying attention to the consumer of the book, the reader, and the contexts in which he or she received and interpreted it. Reading, like authorship, is not universal and varies with time and culture.

Authors

Many educated young men and some young women enjoyed writing poems, essays and romances. In fact, some contemporaries felt that there was far too much mediocre writing in circulation in what they disapprovingly described as 'this scribbling age'. But playwriting was, for the most part, professional work rather than a leisure pursuit. In *Henry V* Shakespeare briefly mentions the 'bending author' (Epilogue, 2), conjuring up images of a solitary writer at work, focusing his creative powers on the production of a great literary work. However, the truth is that many plays were written by more than one author. During the first decade of the seventeenth century, for instance, about 20 per cent of printed plays were attributed to multiple authors.[4] For example, Shakespeare and Fletcher wrote *The Two Noble Kinsmen* (1613–14); Day, Rowley and Wilkins wrote *The Travels of Three English Brothers*; Dekker and Webster wrote *Northward Ho*; Chapman and Jonson, *Eastward Ho* (1605) and Massinger and Dekker, *The Virgin Martyr* (1622). Collaboration generally involved teams of up to four writers. After the storyline was drawn up by the chief collaborator, the work was divided up with writers working on individual acts and scenes. The completed text was then delivered to the sharers of the company for their approval and acceptance. Writers also 'mended' or rewrote plays that were revived years after the original production, adding new prologues, epilogues, songs and scenes and adapting the play to suit the taste of new audiences. So the witches' songs in Shakespeare's *Macbeth* were probably written by Thomas Middleton and the 'Hecate scene' in the same play was also added later by someone not involved in the original writing. Similarly, the comic scenes in *Doctor Faustus* might have been added by someone other than Christopher Marlowe, while Jonson revised Kyd's *The Spanish Tragedy*. The play that was performed and read was thus a complex whole made up of a number of disparate parts. It is usually difficult (and often quite pointless) to determine who wrote what section of a play and to separate it out into sections using stylistic or other criteria (as 'attribution studies' try to do). Collaborative writing was certainly very different from modern authorship. It disrupts modern notions of creativity, talent and originality, all of which are valued today in the creative arts, and challenges the 'author–text–reader continuum assumed in later methodologies of interpretation'.[5] But it was the most natural and effective mode of writing in the context of the Renaissance theatre where efficiency and speed were called for. It might also have been quite natural in the context of humanist pedagogy that emphasized imitation of the masters rather than originality of style. Collaborative writing might also be the outcome of a social system where 'individuality' and 'individualism' in the modern sense did not exist because a person's identity was continuous with the identity of the larger social group – that of the playing company in this case.

A number of men took up the writing of plays as a profession. Some of them were scholars, some hacks, some of them had university degrees and are described as the 'university wits' (Marlowe, Greene and Peele are among them), while others (most famously Shakespeare) did not. Many writers were sharers and some writers had interests in particular companies (Shakespeare, Marlowe), while others wrote freelance for more than one company (Massinger, Middleton, Fletcher, Dekker). Many of them were also actors (notably Shakespeare), while others were not. But they were nearly all professionals who wrote as a career. Each professional dramatist wrote about thirty-seventy plays in his career, either alone or in collaboration. In the preface to his 1633 play *The English Traveller*, Thomas Heywood claims to have had 'an entire hand, or at least a main finger' in no less than 220 plays.[6] Companies could produce four to five plays per week, so writers wrote quickly to meet the incessant demand for new manuscripts. Some of them possibly had contracts with the companies to provide a minimum number of plays per year. Each play took about six weeks to write. It was written in the secretary hand, which was the most commonly used handwriting style in the period. This first draft of the plays in which edits and revisions were visible were known as the 'foul papers', and a few of these are still extant in the archives of some libraries.

Writers might have been the moving force behind theatre, but they were not paid much. We know that Henslowe paid each of his writers three to six pounds for a play. Overall, Henslowe's company's investment in play scripts was only half of the amount spent on costumes. If someone like Shakespeare was a wealthy man at the end of his career it was because of the money he made as a sharer, not because of what he earned as a writer. Low pay apart, there was very little glory. Dramatists (much like modern screenwriters) were known to insiders in the playing company but largely invisible to the public. Plays are catalogued by titles rather than by the names of authors. When plays went into print it was not uncommon (especially before 1600) for the names of the dramatist to go unmentioned – as we see on the title-page of Marlowe's *Tamburlaine*: *Tamburlaine the Great – Divided into two tragicall Discourses, as they were sundrie times shewed upon Stages in the citie of London By the honourable the Lord Admiral, his servants.* Obviously, the performance of the play was considered more important than the author. The 1604 quarto edition of *Doctor Faustus* indicates the name of the author (Christopher Marlowe) as 'Ch. Marl' on the title page and he is listed as 'Ch. Markin' in the 1616 quarto. The author was thus a 'curiously imprecise intermittent and shifting figure'.[7] Since the first copyright laws were not passed until 1710, the author had no rights over his own creation. It became the property of the playing company that paid for it.

Other hands also played a part in the production of the script. The Revels Office that censored plays read the script and insisted on changes. Usually criticism of the government, negative representations of friendly foreign powers, commentaries on religious controversies, unfavourable portraits of living important personages and profanity were forbidden.[8] The Revels Office insisted that the opening scenes of the collaboratively written play *Sir Thomas More* (1591–93) be deleted since it depicted riots against aliens, and a play by Philip Massinger was not licensed because it depicted the deposing of King Sebastian of Portugal and was hence considered hostile to England's foreign policy. As discussed in Chapter Five, some writers got into trouble for disregarding the censor (apparently the only attention the author or authors got was when a play script was considered offensive!). But the censor's office was quite lenient for the most part. In the words of Trevor Howard-Hill, the

Revels Office's 'relation with the players although ultimately authoritarian was more collegial than adversarial'.[9] In fact, the possibility of censorship motivated writers to exploit language for its ambiguity and slipperiness so that they could convey meaning without getting into trouble. This did not go unrecognized by the Revels Office but was usually let go. Even though the Massinger play mentioned earlier was rejected, a play by the same author titled *Believe As You List* was licensed five months later though it was only a slight reworking of the original play. The playwright had simply transposed the setting to classical antiquity so that it appeared not to comment directly on contemporary affairs.[10] Once the censor approved of a text it was considered an 'allowed' script and returned to the company with permission to stage it.

Other members of the playing company also had a hand in the script. The scribe who copied the first draft not only removed all traces of editing but cleaned up inconsistencies, spelling and punctuation and sometimes even changed the metre as he produced the 'fair copy' of the script. The book-keepers, in their turn, added stage directions and act-scene notations, essentially getting the script ready for performance. Actors also improvised lines and shortened speeches they considered too long, usually without the author's permission. Some writers objected to these changes and even Shakespeare has Hamlet tell the actors to 'speak no more than is set down' (3.2.40), though Hamlet himself decides to 'set down' and insert 'some dozen or sixteen lines' in the players' script (2.2.542, 541). However, for the most part, writers understood that a number of people left their mark on a play script and that texts were inevitably 'polyvocal', or the product of multiple voices and minds.

Consequently, we cannot determine a single author's original intended meaning. Given that plays went through so many versions, we cannot settle upon a definite date of composition either. Attempts to recover an 'authentic' or truly original version are also misguided. Since the author might not have produced a definitive text to begin with, we cannot talk of texts being 'corrupted'. Rather than looking at texts as 'corrupted' and 'uncorrupted' or 'authentic' (or 'bad' and 'good' versions as they were called by earlier editors), it is more useful and accurate to see each version of a play as the product of specific historical circumstances.

Books

The printing revolution accelerated through the sixteenth and seventeenth centuries and all kinds of books including bibles, sermons, law books, almanacs, grammars and dictionaries were printed in England. On an average about 136 books were published every year in the 1570s. This number rose to 202 books in the 1580s.[11] Plays were admittedly a small percentage of this number – between 1583 and 1602 an average of 4.8 new plays were printed every year, about 5.75 between 1603 and 1622 and 8.00 between 1623 and 1642.[12] In all only about 20 to 30 per cent of all performed plays made their way into print.[13] For a long time scholars assumed that players were reluctant to print plays because they did not want to share their repertory or because they worried that reading a play would lower demand for its performance. However, both these theories have been rejected of late. While the number of plays that came into print is certainly not high and while some writers expressed the need to distance themselves from print (for instance, Heywood writes that while some writers 'have pursued a double sale of their labours, first to the Stage, and after to the press,' he himself stayed 'ever faithful to the first, and never guilty to the last'[14]), it is quite clear that plays eventually began to exist both on stage and on page and were sold to printing companies either to promote playgoing, to include material that couldn't be staged, or quite simply to make money. In fact, the plays would probably not have continued to exist nor eventually become part of the literary tradition if they had not come into print. As David Kastan writes, 'without print there is no Shakespeare for all time'.[15]

At first printed plays were linked to performance. Titles emphasized the playing company and venue that the play was staged in ('As it was played by the Admiral's Men . . ', 'As it hath been lately acted before his Royal Majesty . . .'), indicating that the printed text was only meant to supplement the performance and was directed at those who especially admired the staging or who might have missed it. There is no evidence that Shakespeare sought out publication, but eighteen of his thirty-seven plays were still printed in his lifetime in forty-five surviving editions. Even writers such as Heywood and Marston, for all their seeming reluctance to print, had their works published in book form. Heywood writes that his play *The Rape of Lucrece* (1608) was printed even though it had not been 'my custom . . . to commit my plays to the press' because the copies that were already in print were in such 'corrupt and mangled form' that a corrected version was needed.[16] Some writers, notably Jonson, went out of their way to seek publication.

Many of these early plays were published in quarto format. A quarto was a book printed by folding a sheet of paper twice to create four leaves and was roughly 6.75 × 8.5 inches in size. These were cheaply put together editions (the publisher's investment was about 2.7 pence per copy) that could be sold for the relatively low price of six pence and were certainly not considered 'literature' or 'high culture' in any sense. Quarto play texts were quite plentiful and some scholars argue that the supply probably exceeded the demand for them because there was no large reliable market for play texts. According to Peter Blayney, about 48 per cent of plays published between 1583 and 1602 went into reprint; the number was 50 per cent for 1603–22 and less than 29 per cent for 1623–42.[17] Other scholars, however, disagree with this argument and claim that publishers made reliable profits from playbooks (judging by profits, reprints and market shares), and while they might not have become rich from selling printed plays, they could count on making modest profits.[18] The fact remains that the output of plays increased as the decades rolled by, and by the first decade of the seventeenth century an average of thirteen plays were printed every year, about eight of them being new.[19] Several of them went on to become best sellers include Shakespeare's *Richard II* and *Henry IV Part 1*, Kyd's *The Spanish Tragedy* and Marlowe's *Doctor Faustus*. Indeed, by 1633 the Puritan William Prynne was complaining that play books are 'now more vendible[20] than the choicest sermons'.[21]

Plays reached the publisher from a variety of sources. They could be brought in by the author but also by a scribe, actor or someone else associated with the playing company, often without the writer's knowledge or permission. Some of these manuscripts were the 'foul papers' or first drafts, while others were 'fair copies'. Traditional scholarship divided printed plays into 'good quartos' or those that were supposedly based on 'original' texts that came from 'legitimate' sources and 'bad quartos' that were based on revised or corrupted texts that were essentially pirated by the publisher. However, modern scholars are wary of this distinction. In a pre-copyright age the publisher did not have to obtain a manuscript through fair means, the only thing that mattered was that he did not violate another printer's claim to the text. Besides, as discussed earlier, there were many versions of a text, making it difficult and even unnecessary to determine the original and reliable version. So a variation of the famous line in *Hamlet*, 'To be, or not to be, that is the question' (3.1.56), appears in the first quarto of the play as 'To be or not to be, ay there's the point.' This version would not have struck the quarto's publisher as particularly 'corrupted' or incorrect because that is what the script he worked from said. It is important to remember that 'A published play text … was not a priceless literary relic but a cheap pamphlet; it represented not the immortal words of a great writer but the work of professional actors whose skill involved improvisation as much as recall.'[22] So multiple printed versions of several plays continue to exist. There are three versions of *Hamlet* – the Q1 of 1603, the Q2 of 1604 and the folio of 1623 (a folio is a large-sized book, approximately thirteen inches high and nine inches wide, made of sheets folded once along the longer side to make two leaves or four pages; usually important books of law and theology were printed in this format). We have no idea which one these versions Shakespeare intended to be the 'correct' version though they read quite differently. In Q1 Hamlet's mother is more innocent and as much a victim of Claudius as Hamlet is and the play as a whole is less meditative and philosophical. Similarly, the quarto version of *King Lear* (1608), called the *Chronicle History of King Lear*, represents Cordelia differently. For example, in this edition she works alongside her husband to help Lear, while she works alone in the folio version. Besides, the quarto includes the 'mad trial' scenes and is generally paced slower than the folio version. The 1616 quarto edition of *Doctor Faustus* (the 'A text') is also different from the 1604 quarto edition. The former includes many 'low' comic scenes and the Good and Bad Angel scenes. The A text has been interpreted as an ultra-Protestant text with sin being depicted as inborn and inevitable, while the 'B text' depicts sinful behaviour as a result of the machinations of evil agents outside the self.[23] Both versions of the play were probably performed depending on the audience and date of performance (with the A text being more popular in the 1590s and the B text in the early 1600s). These examples should indicate how different versions of a play could be distinct enough to yield varied interpretations. Editors today often abstain from cleaning up or meshing the two versions and instead place them alongside each other in modern editions.

It is also important to recognize all of the other labour that went into the making of books. Rag-pickers collected the cloth from which paper was made; paper-makers, compositors, ink-makers, pressmen, proof readers and binders also played their part. Publishing was a fairly advanced and large industry with about two dozen printing houses in London with a total of fifty presses. The publishers were regulated by the Stationers' Company, which was established in 1557. The original function of the Company was to control works that were considered seditious or intending to incite revolt against authority, but eventually it came to oversee apprenticeship, regulate the number of master printers, maintain a list of licensed books (known as the 'Stationers' Register') and regulate book sales. Publishers also had to obtain a licence from the Company that gave them the exclusive right to print a work. The publisher himself was often also the printer – a master artisan who owned presses and movable type. A bookseller was the retailer who actually sold books and 'stationer' was a generic term for all those involved in the book trade. Indeed, printers, booksellers and stationers were often one and the same. Printing itself had to be done speedily, so it was not uncommon for errors to creep into a work. Since printing materials were expensive, printers were often reluctant to destroy sheets with errors, instead simply including an apology. Apart from errors that were a result of accident or carelessness, compositors or typesetters often used different spellings simply because spellings were not yet standardized in the era (scholars have determined that two different compositors with different spelling habits probably worked on the version of *Othello* in the 1623 folio[24]). They also used variable spellings or extra space between words to justify or spell out lines. So 'composing' was quite a creative task and compositors too played their part in the creation of the printed play.

From plays to literary works

For the most part, the cheap printed play texts had no particular cultural value or prestige. Their reputation was more like that of cheap comics or penny thrillers in our own time rather than that of fine works of literature. As Kastan puts it, 'the plays that did find their way into print for the most part did so as the ephemera of an emerging entertainment industry rather than as valued artifacts of a high culture.'[25] Neither publishers nor readers were impressed by the fact that a play might have been by 'greats' such as Shakespeare or Marlowe and, as discussed earlier, editions routinely left out the author's name from the title page. The first time Shakespeare's name is mentioned is on the 1598 quarto of *Love's Labour's Lost* and even then as something of an afterthought ('Newly corrected and augmented by W. Shakespeare'). Quarto playbooks also lacked dedications, epistles and other such prefatory material, and the pages were often sold simply stitched together and unbound.

Gradually, however, some later quartos did attempt to distance plays from their theatrical origins by omitting the company name. So we have title pages that read: '*The Alchemist* – Written by Ben Jonson' (1612) or quite simply: '*The Knight of the Burning Pestle*' (1613). Books were prefaced by addresses to readers, dedicatory letters and character lists indicating that they were primarily meant to be read. Some plays were published even if they were flops on stage: the preface to Webster's *The White Devil* indicates that the author handed it to the printer to compensate for the play's failure in the box office and the prefatory material to *The Knight of the Burning Pestle* (1613) implies that the play was rejected by an audience supposedly lacking taste and judgement and so needed to be printed to rescue it from 'perpetual oblivion.[26] Editions began to mention the name of the author with increasing frequency. So the 1597 edition of *Richard II* did not mention Shakespeare's name, but the very next edition in 1598 did so; the 1594 edition of *Tamburlaine* included the author's name, unlike the 1590 edition. By the 1620s, 80 per cent or more titles were attributed to specific authors.[27]

So playbooks began to be gradually marketed as literary works created by a single author whose name was celebrated and drawn attention to. Ben Jonson was among the first writers who self-consciously projected his authorship of texts. Even his quartos indicate that he was interested in validating his plays as 'dramatic poetry' rather than as simply stage entertainment. The title page of the 1600 quarto of *Everyman Out of His Humour* claims to present the play '*As it was First Composed by the author B.J. Containing more than hath been Publickly Spoken or Acted*' and the prefatory material to the 1605 quarto of *Sejanus* states that the printed text is 'not the same with that which has been acted on the public stage', and that while 'a second pen had a good share' in writing the stage version, he, Jonson, has removed and rewritten the contributions of the collaborator ('To the Reader', 43–45). Here Jonson is clearly detaching the play from the performance and declaring the printed text a new and improved version of the stage play. Jonson is the first example of 'possessive authorship' where a writer claims exclusive ownership and credit for a play.[28] For Jonson print was a way of distancing himself from the stage. In the year 1616, Ben Jonson's plays along with his other writing were printed in a handsome folio edition titled *The Workes of Ben Jonson*. Jonson's folio was clearly a text for reading. The title page bore engraved figures, classical columns and an arch of royal arms specifically designed for this book. Stage directions were either removed or elaborated on so that they didn't sound simply like instructions to an actor. The folio included Latin inscriptions and scholarly annotations and the plays were clearly meant to be accorded the status of 'classics'. Unlike other playwrights who cared little about the quality of the printed versions of their plays, Jonson might have involved himself with the proofreading and preparation of the text for publication. *The Workes of Ben Jonson* included nine plays, not printed as they were performed or even first composed, but as Jonson wanted them remembered by future generations of readers. Jonson was mocked for his ambitions, which were seen as overly lofty. As a contemporary sardonically wrote: 'Pray tell me Ben, where does the mystery lurk, / What others call a play you call a work.'[29] But Jonson's folio remains an important work and 'probably no other publication ... did so much to raise the contemporary existence of the generally belittled form of plays'.[30]

Ben Jonson, Preface, *Sejanus* (1605; printed 1616).

Ben Jonson was among the first playwrights to consciously and actively seek to establish a literary reputation. For this he turned to print. Although his play *Sejanus* failed on stage, Jonson hoped it would endure in book form. The preface to the 1605 quarto edition of Ben Jonson's *Sejanus* tells us something about the author's literary ambitions.

SEJANUS: HIS FALL
TO THE NO LESS NOBLE BY VIRTUE THAN BLOOD
ESME LORD AUBIGNY

My LORD, If ever any ruin were so great, as to survive; I think this be one I send you: the *Fall of Sejanus*. It is a poem, that (if I well remember) in your lordship's sight, suffered no less violence from our people here, than the subject of it did from the rage of the people of Rome; but with a different fate, as (I hope) merit: for this hath outlived their malice, and begot itself a greater favour than he lost, the love of good men.[31] Amongst whom, if I make your Lordship the first it thanks, it is not without a just confession of the bond your benefits have, and ever shall hold upon me,
Your lordship's most faithful honourer.
BEN JONSON.

TO THE READERS
THE following and voluntary labours of my friends, prefixed to my book, have relieved me in much whereat, without them, I should necessarily have touched. Now I will only use three or four short and needful notes, and so rest.
First, if it be objected, that what I publish is no true poem, in the strict laws of time, I confess it: as also in the want of a proper chorus; whose habit and moods are such and so difficult, as not any, whom I have seen, since the ancients, no, not they who have most presently affected laws, have yet come in the way of. Nor is it needful, or almost possible in these our times, and to such auditors as commonly things are presented, to observe the old state and splendour of dramatic poems, with preservation of any popular delight. But of this I shall take more seasonable cause to speak, in my observations upon Horace his Art of Poetry, which, with the text translated, I intend

shortly to publish. In the mean time, if in truth of argument, dignity of persons, gravity and height of elocution, fulness and frequency of sentence, I have discharged the other offices of a tragic writer, let not the absence of these forms be imputed[32] to me, wherein I shall give you occasion hereafter, and without my boast, to think I could better prescribe, than omit the due use for want of a convenient knowledge.[33]

. . .

Lastly, I would inform you, that this book, in all numbers, is not the same with that which was acted on the public stage; wherein a second pen had good share: in place of which, I have rather chosen to put weaker, and no doubt, less pleasing, of mine own, than to defraud so happy a genius of his right by my loathed usurpation.

BEN JONSON

The next major publication that also is testimony to the increasing status of plays was the 1623 folio that includes thirty-six of Shakespeare's plays. *Mr. William Shakespeare's Comedies, Histories and Tragedies* is an impressive volume of approximately 900 pages, about thirteen by eight inches in size, and the first book consisting entirely of plays designed to be the complete plays of a single author. By emphasizing Shakespeare's name and including a large (and now iconic) portrait of him on the title page, the folio in some sense created Shakespeare's reputation as sole author of outstanding works and eventually as a literary genius. The plays also became entities unto themselves independent of performance (there is no mention of where the plays were staged and no attempt to name the acting companies though the names of the principal players are included). The plays were put together by John Heminge and Henry Condell, Shakespeare's friends and fellow actors. They should have known better than anyone else that the manuscripts or print editions that the folio was printed from were most likely not Shakespeare's own, but the title page claims that the plays are published according to the 'True Original Copies.' The preface also indicates that the folio presents the plays as they flowed from the author's pen and as untouched by the contaminations of the playing house or by the earlier versions 'maimed and deformed by the frauds and stealths of injurious imposters'.[34] The folio was an expensive venture and the 750 copies that were printed were priced accordingly. The book cost fifteen shillings without binding and one pound sterling for a bound edition. We should remember the commercial context of the folio's publication. 'Read him again and again', the preface urges its readers, and also adds: 'whatever you do buy'. The publishers certainly took a risk with this book, but it must have paid off since work started on a second folio edition of Shakespeare's plays in 1632, less than a decade after the first one. The next folio playbook after Shakespeare's second folio was the 1647 edition of the plays of Beaumont and Fletcher titled *Comedies and Tragedies written by Francis Beaumont and John Fletcher Gentlemen*. The publisher insists that the writers are 'poets' and not mere playwrights and that drama is 'most absolute' of the poetic arts with 'composers' like Beaumont and Fletcher displaying 'transcendental abilities'.[35] The prefatory material also insists that versions printed in the book were authentic, original and error-free.[36]

Preface, *Mr. William Shakespeare's Comedies, Histories & Tragedies* (the 'First Folio' – 1623).
(Courtesy of the Bodleian Library)

The first folio edition of Shakespeare's plays published in 1623 is a hallmark publication in more ways than one. The publishers, Henry Condell and John Heminge, address potential readers in the preface, urging them to buy the book and assuring them that the versions of the plays reproduced in it are original and authentic.

To the Great Variety of Readers.
FROM the most able, to him that can but spell: There you are numbered. We had rather you were weighed; especially, when the fate of all Books depends upon your capacities: and not of your heads alone, but of your purses. Well! it is now public, & you will stand for your privileges we know: to read, and censure. Do so, but buy it first. That doth best commend a Book, the Stationer says. Then, how odd soever your brains be, or your wisdoms, make your license the same, and spare not. Judge your sixe-pen'orth, your shillings worth, your five shillings worth at a time, or higher, so you rise to the just rates, and welcome. But, what ever you do, Buy. Censure will not drive a Trade, or make the Jack go. And though you be a Magistrate of wit, and sit on the Stage at *Black-Friars*, or the *Cock-pit*, to arraign[37] Plays daily, know, these Plays have had their trial already, and stood out all Appeals; and do now come forth quitted rather by a Decree of Court, then any purchased Letters of commendation.[38]

It had been a thing, we confess, worthy to have been wished, that the Author himself had lived to have set forth, and overseen his own writings; But since it hath been ordained otherwise, and he by death departed from that right, we pray you do not envy his Friends, the office of their care, and pain, to have collected & published them; and so to have published them, as where (before) you were abused with diverse stolen, and surreptitious[39] copies, maimed, and deformed by the frauds and stealths[40] of injurious imposters, that exposed them: even those, are now offered to your view cured, and perfect of their limbs; and all the rest, absolute in their numbers, as he conceived them. Who, as he was a happy imitator of Nature, was a most gentle expresser of it. His mind and hand went together: and what he thought, he uttered with that easiness, that we have scarse received from him a blot in his papers.[41] But it is not our province, who only gather his works, and give them you, to praise him. It is yours that read him. And there we hope, to your diverse capacities, you will find enough, both to draw, and hold you: for his wit can no more lie hid, then it could be lost. Read him, therefore; and again, and again: and if then you do not like him, surely you are in some manifest danger, not to understand him. And so we leave you to other of his Friends, whom if you need, can be your guides: if you need them not, you can lead your selves, and others.
And such Readers we wish him.

John Heminge
Henrie Condell

These folios and some quartos are important in that they made a move towards creating dramatic authorship in the modern sense. Publishers found that attributing play texts to single writers made them more marketable. As Kastan writes, 'the English author in a recognizable modern form came into being with print and [was] at least as much a function of the ambitions of the book trade as of the ambitions of English writers.'[42] Print also helped dissociate plays from the disreputable playhouses and consequently attracted a more literary and culturally sophisticated readership to the playbooks. Renaissance plays were gradually becoming literary works and some of them went on to become part of the English literary canon.

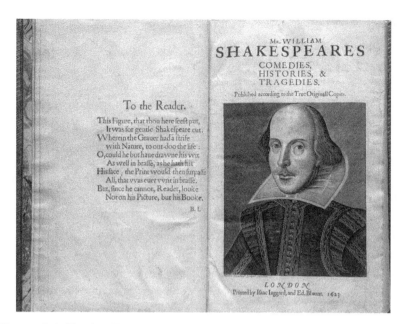

Figure 6.1 'To the Reader'. Title page from *Mr. William Shakespeares comedies, histories, & tragedies: published according to the true originall copies*, 1623 (courtesy of The Folger Shakespeare Library: http://www. folger.edu/publishing-shakespeare).

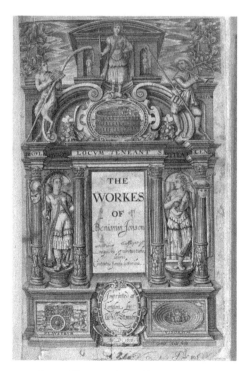

Figure 6.2 Title page from *The workes of Beniamin Ionson*, 1616 (courtesy of The Folger Shakespeare Library).

Readers

The history of reading is an important aspect of cultural history. How and why do people read? What were the consequences of reading? And has the practice of reading altered with time? These are interesting questions to ponder. Book buyers in London would have most likely come to St Paul's, the centre of the book trade where bookshops were clustered together with title pages displayed in shop windows to tempt readers. Books were part of the new consumer economy, being bought and sold in large numbers. While the printing press had increased the *supply* of books, rising literacy rates had increased the *demand*. David Cressy estimates that about 30 per cent of men and 10 per cent of women could read by the 1640s, and while these figures might seem very low to us, they were considerably higher than they had been before the Reformation.[43] Literacy rates also varied by the province and might have been substantially higher in bigger cities. Besides, historians determine literacy rates by whether people could sign their names in parish registers and other public records. This is not an indication of the ability to read and it is very likely that more people could read than write. In any case, the burgeoning book trade catered to a wide variety of readers from the learned to the barely literate. Aristocrats, schoolmasters, curates, students, tutors, clerks, domestic staff and women all constituted the new reading public. They read works of philosophy, religious texts, letters, pamphlets, sonnets, almanacs, travel writing, poems and stories. Just like today, reading was both 'heavy' and 'light', or, as Francis Bacon put it, 'some books are to be tasted, others to be swallowed, and some few to be chewed and digested; that is, some to be read only in parts: others to be read but not too curiously; and some few to be read wholly and with diligence and attention'.[44]

Renaissance readers took reading seriously. Humanist education emphasized reading as an art to be mastered. Students were trained to pay attention to grammar, rhetoric, style and the morals imparted by a text. Reading was intellectual work as well as a pleasurable pastime and a means of improving oneself and society. It was a way of conversing with the world and also with the past. Through books, readers could engage in a nourishing relationship with those who read and wrote before them. More and more people were also reading 'silently' (i.e. not reading aloud) and reading in solitude. Reading alone meant that one could interpret a work for oneself without mediating figures like teachers and priests shaping interpretation. Renaissance readers were also 'active' readers – they were encouraged in school to write on books and so wrote with pen in hand, correcting errors, underlining words they did not understand, glossing terms, marking memorable passages, commenting and often just doodling. Readers customized books to suit their individual tastes – so references to the Virgin Mary and other Catholic saints were erased from several post-Reformation prayer books and one mid-seventeenth-century reader deleted what he deemed unacceptable passages from Shakespeare's folio. So, just as books shaped readers, 'we must acknowledge that early modern readers shaped the books they read and used'.[45]

What we would call 'literature' was also part of reading fare. There was great interest in reading classical legends, poems, plays and medieval tales of chivalry as well as in reading contemporary poetry and stories. One certainly read this kind of work in appreciation and for pleasure, but delight was always linked to 'profit' or learning and self-improvement. As discussed earlier, there is a debate about how popular the printed plays were among the reading public. The collector Sir Thomas Bodley dismissed plays as 'riff-raff and baggage books' that could not be included in his library though he did purchase a bound edition of Shakespeare's 1623 folio.[46] While the early quartos indicate that readers saw the play text as a way of catching up on a missed performance or as a way of recalling a good one, the publication of the expensive folios indicates that publishers were interested in distinguishing readers from a theatrical audience and, further, in marketing plays to a more educated readership which, it was hoped, had good taste and judgement. To this end, readers were routinely addressed in prefaces as 'learned readers', 'courteous readers', 'gentle readers' and 'discreet readers' – a tradition Dekker made fun of in *The Wonderful Year* (1603) when he wrote that modern custom insisted that the reader 'be honeyed, and come-over with *Gentle Reader, Courteous Reader* and *Learned Reader*, though he have no more *Gentilitie* in him than *Adam* had (that was but a gardener) no more *Civilitie* than a Tartar,[47] and no more *Learning* than the most errand *Stinkard*, that (except his own name) could never find anything in the Horn-book'.[48] Even typeface was a way of appealing to a more educated readership. Later playbooks were published in roman type rather than the black letter type used to print cheap ballads and jestbooks. Prefaces, title pages and addresses to the reader were a way of attracting certain kinds of readers and also of shaping their response in specific ways by preparing them for a certain kind of book. Jonson's annotations to his *Sejanus* where he cites the text's sources also direct the reader in specific ways. Even the play's genre, as mentioned in the title, also shaped reader response, as we will see in the next chapter.

We don't know who exactly bought these plays since very few texts survive with names of the owners inscribed on them. They probably came from a range of social backgrounds and truly constituted the 'great variety of readers' that are addressed in the preface to Shakespeare's folio. Through these nameless readers Renaissance playbooks travelled far and wide. Some of them even stood the test of time and are available today in rare book archives. They might have been cheap little 'riff-raff' books in their day, but are today mementos from the past, as valuable as those magical books Prospero of *The Tempest* prized 'above my dukedom' (1.2.168). These books have become makers and preservers of the tradition of English literature – much like the modern editions of Renaissance plays we have on our own bookshelves.

Discussion points

1 You have read the preface to Shakespeare's First Folio excerpted in this chapter. What does it attempt to accomplish? Does it succeed in doing so? What would you say if you had to write a piece of text marketing a particular Renaissance play?

2 As we saw above, Renaissance plays often existed in more than one version. First think about why the idea of a single, stable text has been so appealing. Then look carefully at the edition of any play you are reading, paying particular attention to the editors' note on the text they consulted when putting this edition together. Do you agree with the approach the editors have taken in cases where more than one 'original' version exists?

3 Editors serve as mediators between the play and the reader in many ways. Pay attention to footnotes and other material the editors of the edition that you are reading have provided and think about how they influence your engagement with the play.

4 If you are reading an online or e-book version of a play, discuss how that experience is different from (or similar to) reading a printed text.

7

Genre

Even as the Renaissance theatre appeared to be a modern phenomenon rooted in the life of the big city, the plays had their roots in older forms of entertainment. Mystery and morality plays based on religious and biblical themes constituted the major dramatic mode of the Middle Ages. Morality plays in particular were allegorical in nature with 'characters' (Pride, Sloth, Patience and so forth) representing numerous abstract qualities. The intent was essentially didactic. By the early sixteenth century the moralities gave way to a new kind of drama that used personalities rather than abstractions to teach moral lessons and also to 'interludes', short comic pieces that were neither didactic nor religious performed by strolling players.

The early Tudor writers adapted these popular conventions. So even as the new drama lost the ceremonial and ritual aspect of church drama, the abstract Vice (representing evil) of morality drama became a flesh and blood character in the new drama, personified in figures such as Volpone or Iago. *Doctor Faustus*, for example, clearly reproduces morality themes and conventions with the parade of the 'Seven Deadly Sins', the conflict between the Good and Bad Angels, and Mephastophilis as a version of the Vice. The figure of the 'fool', the scenes of farcical humour, the occasionally episodic nature of Renaissance drama (the play *Tamburlaine*, for instance, is a series of carefully crafted episodes in the tradition of morality drama, each of which illustrates one of the qualities of the protagonist[1]), the general tendency to ignore the classical unities of time, place and action, the inclination to allow noble-born and lower-class characters to mingle and the introduction of folkloric elements such as fairies and witches into stories, all indicate the popular origins of English drama of the period. Indeed, the festive atmosphere that pervaded folk rituals across the English countryside made its way into the arena of the public theatre. Robert Weimann contrasts this earthy drama of everyday life to the intellectual humanist or academic drama being played in schools and universities. Writers for the public stage expressed the reality of life through 'a concrete idiom that was reflected in the physicality of verbal expression and communication, as well as in the capacity for sensuous action and spectacle that the purely literary drama [of the humanist tradition] could never achieve'.[2] While the legacy of the native English tradition was certainly very important to the drama of the English Renaissance, one cannot ignore the contribution of humanist education as well, as we saw in Chapter Four. Many young playwrights were trained in rhetoric and brought that training to bear in their writing for the theatre. They borrowed plots and references from classical literature and engaged in a certain self-conscious artistry that surely had something to do with their knowledge of classical drama. Overall, Renaissance drama was a happy synthesis of morality and mystery plays, interludes, classical drama, courtly masques and pageants. This is why in plays such as *A Midsummer Night's Dream*, figures like Puck and the fairies from native English folklore that wander through wood and dale coexist with classical figures such as Hippolyta and Theseus, and together they make one complex, magical whole.

While classical literature had distinct generic divisions, the medieval drama's idea of genre was more flexible. Broadly defined, a literary genre is a category of literary composition. Plays, as well as other literary texts, are classified as certain genres ('tragedy', 'comedy', 'romance', 'thriller' and so forth) depending on technique, tone and content. Genre is admittedly a loose, perhaps even somewhat arbitrary, system of describing and classifying a literary text. But Renaissance writers' consciousness of it had some impact on their language and other narrative choices, just as genre set up a framework of expectation within which audiences and readers responded to the work. Printed editions of plays certainly drew attention to genre. The title page of Ben Jonson's *Works* (1616), for instance, depicts the personified figures of Tragedy and Comedy. Tragedy wears an embroidered gown and the high buskin shoes of the ancient Greek actor, while Comedy is dressed in a plain gown and socks and carries a rustic staff. The editors of Shakespeare's first folio also divided his works into 'Comedies', 'Tragedies' and 'Histories'.

Aristotle's *Poetics* defined tragedy and comedy as the two major genres in drama and described them as formal categories with each having its own specific type of plot, structure and characterization. Aristotle's works, however, did not become well known until the mid-sixteenth century and much of Renaissance thinking about genre came from the Latin writer Horace and his *The Art of Poetry* (19 BC). Horace's work emphasized the idea of 'decorum': certain styles were appropriate to particular subjects;

consequently, some subjects lent themselves to tragedy and others to comedy. Professional drama writing was, however, removed from these theorizations. Genres were constantly subverted, revised and renewed. The boundaries between genres were unclear, resulting in all kinds of hybrids as gently satirized by Shakespeare in *Hamlet* where Polonius talks of 'tragedy, comedy, history, pastoral, pastoral-comical, historical-pastoral, tragical-historical, tragical-comical-historical-pastoral' (2.2.398–400). In spite of this tendency to mix and mingle, we cannot entirely dismiss genre when we study a play. Because genres are categorized by style as well as by theme and content, genre is the space where the literary text as a self-contained artifact meets forces outside of itself, where 'purely' literary or formal aspects of a text encounter the historical and the contextual; or, as Mikhail Bakhtin writes, generic classifications are 'the drive belts from the history of society to the history of language'.[3] Further, every literary text, by virtue of its generic affiliation is characterized by tension between the individual style and vision of the artist and the demands of a literary tradition that call for conformity and compliance. This tension resulted in some of the most remarkable of Renaissance plays.

Comedy

Renaissance readers of the classics would have been familiar with the Latin writer Cicero's famous statement that comedy is an 'imitation of life, the mirror of custom, the image of truth'. They would also have read another Latin writer, Donatus, who said that comedy was the product of advanced civilizations that knew how to enjoy life and leisure. But comedy as a genre predated the classics. It had its roots in the festivities of agrarian communities where the common folk participated in rituals involving celebration and laughter. The ritualistic element of comedy in which the event itself becomes more important than any meanings that can be ascribed to it lingered through the ages. The comic play too was imbued with the spirit of holiday, mirth and freedom from the everyday.

We can discern multiple influences on Renaissance comedy. The works of the Roman playwrights Plautus and Terence were studied widely in grammar schools and made young writers aware of the possibilities of the comic mode. The delight in error and confusion and the multiple plots and sub-plots that needed to be juggled deftly was a legacy of these writers. Plays such as George Chapman's *All Fools* (1599–1601) and Shakespeare's *The*

Comedy of Errors were actually based on comic plays by Plautus and Terence. The native roots of comedy lay in the comic interludes of the Middle Ages that tended to farce and included absurd situations and slapstick humour – all of which are discernible in Renaissance comedy. There were other influences as well: medieval romances, Italian comedy and, of course, the jests of streets and taverns. The best Renaissance comedy came of the artful mingling of these diverse traditions. Very early English comedies included *Ralph Roister Doister*, written by a schoolmaster, Nicholas Udall, for performance by his students, and the anonymous *Gammer Gurton's Needle*. The first comic dramatists for the public stage were George Peele and Robert Greene. The latter's *Friar Bacon and Friar Bungay* brings together romance, clowning, disguise, magic and a nationalist theme, all to entertaining effect.

Comedy was a versatile mode and characterized by great variety. However, the typical comic plot moved from error and confusion to resolution. In the tradition of Roman comedy, Renaissance writers sometimes created comic character types. So we have the *miles gloriosus* or braggart warrior type (Sir John Falstaff in *Henry IV Part 1*), the greedy and sensual older man (Volpone in *Volpone*, Sir Epicure Mammon in *The Alchemist*) and the rogue who lives by his wits (Subtle and Face in *The Alchemist*). The Fool was a staple figure and could be either a straightforward comic figure who engaged in physical and verbal humour or elegant, witty and musical (like Feste of *Twelfth Night*). The language of comedy ranged from lyrical blank verse to crude prose with the free use of songs and doggerel rhyme.

The general air of confusion, misunderstanding and folly showed up humans as ridiculous and foolish but not as evil. As George Chapman wrote in his prologue to Jonson's *Every Man in His Humour*, comedy represented 'an Image of the times, / And sport with human follies, not with crimes' (Prologue, 23–24). Other writers also highlighted this element of the ridiculous. Philip Sidney wrote that 'comedy is an imitation of the common errors of our life, which he [the writer] representeth in the most ridiculous and scornful sort that may be, so it is impossible than any beholder can be content to be such a one'.[4] Sidney emphasized the satirical element of comedy: one ridicules to reform society and people. While this reformative impulse is true of many Renaissance plays, others laughed at human folly but still accepted and embraced it. To this end comedy has been categorized into 'realistic' satirical comedy, which highlighted the grossness and folly of human nature, and 'romantic' comedy, which displayed human weakness as well as human longings and human dreams.

Romance was at the centre of romantic comedy. The lovers were young and beautiful, and multiple couples were often involved, as in Shakespeare's *As You Like It* or John Fletcher's *The Wild Goose Chase* (1621–22). Courtship was playful and happy with the lovers often matching each other in verbal agility and rapidly exchanging witty, clever lines in a 'set of wit well played' (*Love's Labour's Lost*, 5.2.29). The women of romantic comedies were among the most interesting in Renaissance literature, often asserting their right to marry for love. For these women, and also for men, romance was a quest for identity, completion and fulfilment. The dramatic conflict involved overcoming obstacles coming in the way of true love. These obstacles could take on the form of objecting parents as in *The Roaring Girl* or *A Midsummer Night's Dream*, or be a result of confusion and error of other kinds. In any case, the comic plot moved towards harmony and reconciliation. The conclusion of these plays followed the tradition of the ancient fertility rituals that comedy originated in. Marriage and the implied sexual union defined the comic ending, indicating that the cyclical patterns of marriage and birth continued. Marriage bonds also brought communities and families together. Overall, these plays offered a positive understanding of human experience: life was delightful and wondrous and human folly was viewed with generosity and kindness.

The satirically conceived plays by Ben Jonson and other writers were, on the other hand, less forgiving. Human greed and weaknesses were caricatured and satirized, often with the intent to correct and inform. This tradition of comedy has often been described as 'realist' comedy. Jonson's *Everyman Out of His Humour* describes this comedy as 'a mirror, / As large as is the stage, whereon we act: / Where they shall see the time's deformity / Anatomiz'd in every nerve, and sinew, / With constant courage and contempt of fear' (Induction, 118–22). The writer's job was to starkly expose human nature, especially its 'deformities' or 'weaknesses'. Satire ranged from the gently mocking to the aggressive and even malevolent. As Jonson writes, 'I'll strip the ragged follies of the time, / Naked as their birth . . . / . . . and with a whip of steel, / Print wounding lashes on their iron ribs' in order to 'unmask a public vice' (Induction, 17–20, 22). Unlike in romantic comedies, realist comedies such as *The Dutch Courtesan* by John Marston or Thomas Middleton's *A Trick to Catch the Old One* (*c.* 1605) treat sexual desire as a weakness or vice rather than an experience to delight in. In Middleton's *A Chaste Maid in Cheapside* erotic desire is linked to financial concerns and sex is a commodity that people trade in. Jonson's *Epicoene* (1609) is also deliberately 'anti-romantic' with a marriage between an old man and a woman, who turns out to be a boy, ending in separation.

Many of these 'realist' comedies were set in the city of London and are described as 'city comedies'. City comedy became very popular in the early seventeenth century as the rising middle class, proud of its new success, wanted to see its lives and concerns portrayed on stage. The city was the vibrant backdrop to these plays which portrayed the complexities of the urban swirl and people competing under the newly emerging capitalist system. Some city comedies, notably Thomas Dekker's *The Shoemaker's Holiday* (1599), depicted the 'citizen' or middle-class merchant as a heroic figure. In Dekker's play the tradesman Simon Eyre rises up to become Lord Mayor, and aristocrats and citizens live together in unity and harmony. In Thomas Heywood's *The Four Prentices of London* (1594), four young apprentices go to the holy land and fight a range of foreign enemies. In most other city comedies, however, the city was a predatory space where self-interest and aggressive individualism ruled. Inter-class rivalry also dominated, with middle-class citizens and courtiers or 'gallants' in competition. The plays by Jonson, Marston and Middleton are populated by a gallery of greedy merchants, idle gentry, hypocritical puritans, credulous gulls or fools, and wily rogues. In Jonson's *Volpone* and *The Alchemist*, the protagonists con a series of people whose greed makes them vulnerable to deception. Philip Massinger's *The City Madam* (1632) also deals with similar themes of selfishness, greed and stupidity. In these plays dramatists expressed a mix of admiration and contempt for knaves and rogues and this was what perhaps make the plays entertaining comedies rather than simply satirical or didactic pieces intended to reform. Similarly, in all city comedy the city is both repulsive and fascinating, confusing and delightful, as seen in Jonson's *Bartholomew Fair* (1614) where the fair, a venue of entertainment and trickery, becomes a mirror of the city itself. However, one must be careful about making absolute distinctions between 'romantic' and 'realist' comedy. Jonson and other writers of satirical drama did borrow romantic elements, and romantic comedies also commented on social issues. What is appealing about the best Renaissance comic plays is that the comic tone ranges from raucous laughter to biting satire to lyrical sentiment.

Comedy has been viewed as an essentially conservative form. Authority might be overturned for a while, but by the end of the plays the prevailing order was re-established: men regained authority; women took on traditional female roles; the topsy-turvy world righted itself; and everything was in place once more. The festivity of comedy, it has been said, was actually licensed or allowed by the socio-political authorities. After a brief period during which chaos and misrule prevailed, participants simply went home and renewed their ordinary lives. This is certainly a valid reading of Renaissance comedy. However, comedies were also complex narratives that challenged authority, often in productive ways. In fact, authority figures in comedy were often ridiculous (Justice Overdo in *Bartholomew Fair*) or were conflicted (Prospero in *The Tempest*). Besides, comedies with their themes of disguise and deception destabilized identity and questioned the very nature of truth. The best example of this would be the cross-dressed heroines of so many Renaissance comic plays who assumed male roles and often proved more 'manly' than the men. Since comedy has its roots in folk carnival, when disorder and misrule were given licence – albeit temporarily – we are at least allowed to imagine a world where the normal is set aside and traditional hierarchies and social structures are turned upside down, conservative ending notwithstanding. Laughter is a form of imaginative and social freedom.

Tragedy

'For God's sake let us sit upon the ground / And tell sad stores of the death of kings', writes Shakespeare in *Richard II* (3.2.155–56). The convention of Renaissance tragedy did require that the plays end in the death of the usually high-born protagonist. The narratives by John Lydgate in *The Fall of Princes* (1430s) and the multi-authored *A Mirror for Magistrates* (early sixteenth century) that told the stories of royal crime and retribution and the abuses and insecurities of earthly power come closest to being the native precedents for English tragedy. The influence of the Roman playwright Seneca, introduced through humanist education, is also very discernible in Renaissance tragedy. The tales of extreme passion and revenge, the self-conscious rhetoric, often bordering on bombast and the taste for melodrama that we see so often in Renaissance tragedy were Senecan in origin. However, just as in the case of medieval morality plays that included comic interludes, English writers generally did not hesitate to embed comic scenes and low-born characters in their tragic narratives and so created a new, entirely unique form. The first English tragic play is generally considered to be *Gorboduc* (1561) by Thomas Norton and Thomas Sackville, which tells the story of an ancient king of Britain who divides his kingdom amongst his sons and the civil war that follows. *Gorboduc* was admired by Sidney for its 'stately speeches' and 'notable morality', but it was never performed on a public stage.[5] The first great writers of tragedy for the public theatre were

Thomas Kyd and Christopher Marlowe, followed by William Shakespeare, John Webster and others.

Tragedies dealt with the theme of human suffering and tragic dramatists explored ways of expressing suffering that was often so extreme that it was beyond expression. The structure of tragedies was the reverse of comedy. As Thomas Heywood wrote (translating Donatus), 'Comedies begin in trouble and end in peace; tragedies begin in calms and end in tempest.'[6] However, the final vision of disorder and turbulence is detectable early in the plays – the feud in Verona bodes the tragedy to come in *Romeo and Juliet* (1591–95) and the poisonous court atmosphere does not promise a happy ending for the Duchess in *The Duchess of Malfi*. The world of tragedy was a world of storms and hostile landscapes, evil spirits, witches, devils and ghosts. It was also a world littered with human bodies, dead or maimed. Skulls, severed tongues, hands, heads and gouged-out eyes were displayed on stage, reminding one of the frailty of the body and the vulnerability of all humans. As Sidney wrote, tragedy exposed the truth of the human condition; it 'openeth the wounds, and showeth forth the ulcers that are covered with tissue, that maketh kings fear to be tyrants ... that ... teacheth the uncertainty of this world, and upon how weak foundations gilden roofs are builded'.[7]

Tragedy was characterized by conflict. This conflict could be between individuals, between the individual and society, within the individual torn apart by contradictory impulses and desires or between opposing values, ideologies and interests within the social and political order. Although, as mentioned earlier, Aristotle's *Poetics* was probably not widely known to Renaissance playwrights, it informs our modern understanding of all literary tragedy. For Aristotle tragedy involved a plot that narrated 'peripety' or the reversal of fortune of a great man due to an error of judgement. So Macbeth and Faustus, both men of great potential, fall due to misjudgement provoked by ambition. The structure of the tragic plot was essential to the tragic effect – a well-constructed plot primarily aroused the responses of pity and fear. Pity came from connecting to the protagonist, feeling for his suffering and seeing it as undeserved and unjust. One felt fear because tragedy reminded one of the vulnerability of all humans. For instance, Hieronimo in *The Spanish Tragedy* is a good man who was an agent of justice; but his son is murdered and he himself, after vainly pursuing justice, ends his life in misery. Similarly, while one might think that King Lear of Shakespeare's play is short-sighted and foolish and perhaps even deserves what happens to him, one cannot but feel pity for the unhappy old man who is 'More sinned against than sinning' (3.2.60). Further, the famous scene where Lear wanders in the storm-swept plain is a reminder of the defencelessness of all humans in the face of familiar and primal but hostile forces larger than ourselves. This evokes fear in the reader or spectator. Lear, in that scene, is not only a king, but also everyman – what has happened to him could well happen to us, and as his follower Kent puts it, 'Man's nature cannot carry / Th'affliction, nor the fear' (3.2.48–49). At the end of the tragic play, according to Aristotle, one felt 'catharsis'. This term implies a purging or cleansing of intense emotion although it is hard to say what exactly Aristotle meant by the cathartic effect of tragedy. In Renaissance tragic drama narration, catharsis takes many forms: the tragic narrative moved some characters to face up to guilt (as in the case of the play within *Hamlet* that moves Claudius to confront his wrongdoing) and had a therapeutic effect on other characters (after all the upheaval Hamlet realizes that in the face of sorrow and death 'The readiness is all' [5.2.221], and in *King Lear* Gloucester resolves to 'bear / Affliction till it do cry out itself / "Enough, enough" and die' [4.6.75–77]). One can also speculate that the aesthetics of literary tragedy, its pleasing form and structure, control and shape the human experience of suffering, helps us, readers/spectators, make sense of and perhaps even transcend pain. The combination of tragic events along with the formal structure and aesthetic appeal of the play means that we are not only saddened but also derive pleasure and satisfaction from what would simply depress or devastate us in real life. In spite of Hieronimo's despair and though he might believe that his words are 'unfruitful' (3.7.67) and pointless, the superb symmetry of his mournful rhetoric makes Kyd's play an artful, even sublime, expression of human grief that fills readers with awe and wonder even as it makes us feel pity and fear.

From Aristotle, *Poetics* (c. 335 BC).
Trans. Gerards F. Else, 1967.
(© University of Michigan Press)

The Greek philosopher Aristotle's *Poetics* (c. 335 BC) is considered the first work of literary theory. It became available to Renaissance humanists through a Latin translation. While the section on comedy is lost, the following excerpt on tragedy informs modern understandings of that genre.

We have established, then, that tragedy is an imitation of an action which is complete and whole and has some magnitude (for there is also such a thing as a whole that has no magnitude). 'Whole' is that which has beginning, middle, and end. 'Beginning' is that which does not necessarily follow on something else, but after it something else naturally is or happens; 'end,' the other way around, is that which naturally follows on something else, either necessarily or for the most part, but nothing else after it; and 'middle' that which naturally follows on something else and something else on it. So, then, well constructed plots should neither begin nor end at any chance point but follow the guidelines just laid down.

Furthermore, since the beautiful, whether a living creature or anything that is composed of parts, should not only have these in a fixed order to one another but also possess a definite size which does not depend on chance – for beauty depends on size and order; hence neither can a very tiny creature turn out to be beautiful (since our perception of it grows blurred as it approaches the period of imperceptibility) nor an excessively huge one (for then it cannot all be perceived at once and so its unity and wholeness are lost), if for example there were a creature a thousand miles long—so, just as in the case of living creatures they must have some size, but one that can be taken in a single view, so with plots: they should have length, but such that they are easy to remember. As to a limit of the length, the one is determined by the tragic competitions[8] and the ordinary span of attention . . . But the limit fixed by the very nature of the case is: the longer the plot, up to the point of still being perspicuous[9] as a whole, the finer it is so far as size is concerned; or to put it in general terms, the length in which, with things happening in unbroken sequence, a shift takes place either probably or necessarily from bad to good fortune or from good to bad—that is an acceptable norm of length.

. . .

Furthermore, since the tragic imitation is not only of a complete action but also of events that are fearful and pathetic, and these come about best when they come about contrary to one's expectation yet logically, one following from the other; that way they will be more productive of wonder than if they happen merely at random, by chance – because even among chance occurrences the ones people consider most marvelous are those that seem to have come about as if on purpose: for example the way the statue of Mitys at Argos killed the man who had been the cause of Mitys' death, by falling on him while he was attending the festival[10]; it stands to reason, people think, that such things don't happen by chance – so plots of that sort cannot fail to be artistically superior.

Some plots are simple, others are complex; indeed the actions of which the plots are imitations already fall into these two categories. By 'simple' action I mean one the development of which being continuous and unified in the manner stated above, the reversal comes without peripety or recognition, and by 'complex' action one in which the reversal is continuous but with recognition or peripety or both. And these developments must grow out of the very structure of the plot itself, in such a way that, on the basis of what has happened previously, this particular outcome follows either by necessity or in accordance with probability; for there is a great difference in whether these events happen because of those or merely after them.

'Peripety' is a shift of what is being undertaken to the opposite in the way previously stated, and that in accordance with probability or necessity as we have just been saying; as for example in the *Oedipus*, the man who has come, thinking that he will reassure Oedipus, that is, relieve him of his fear with respect to his mother, by revealing who he once was, brings about the opposite[11]; and in the *Lynceus*, as he (Lynceus) is being led away with every prospect of being executed, and Danaus pursuing him with every prospect of doing the executing, it comes about as a result of the other things that have happened in the play that *he* is executed and Lynceus is saved.[12] And 'recognition' is, as indeed the name indicates, a shift from ignorance to awareness, pointing in the direction either of close blood ties or of hostility, of people who have previously been in a clearly marked state of happiness or unhappiness.

The finest recognition is one that happens at the same time as a peripety, as is the case with the one in the *Oedipus*. Naturally, there are also other kinds of recognition: it is possible for one to take place in the prescribed manner in relation to inanimate objects and chance occurrences, and it is possible to recognize whether a person has acted or not acted. But the form that is most integrally a part of the plot, the action, is the one aforesaid; for that kind of recognition combined with peripety will excite either pity or fear (and these are the kinds of action of which tragedy is an imitation according to our definition), because both good and bad fortune will also be most likely to follow that kind of event. . . .

These then are two elements of plot: peripety and recognition; third is the *pathos*. Of these, peripety and recognition have been discussed; a *pathos* is a destructive or painful act, such as deaths on stage, paroxysms of pain, woundings, and all that sort of thing.

Tragedies raised the difficult question of why bad things happen, often to good people. Some Renaissance tragedies indicated that human fortune is determined by God or fate or some force bigger than oneself. So the lovers are 'star-crossed' (Prologue, 6) in *Romeo and Juliet* and one can say that Faustus's fall is predetermined in *Doctor Faustus*. But Renaissance tragedies have been read as being essentially human-centred. Critics such as A.C. Bradley see suffering in these plays as self-authored – humans fell because of a personality flaw or an error of judgement.[13] However, 'materialist readings' of Renaissance tragedy reject readings of the plays as commentaries on human nature. Instead, they locate the tragedies of the period in the social structures and ideology of the time. Value systems were conflicting and incompatible. So even as ambition and individualism were celebrated, tragic heroes like Macbeth or Faustus are also punished for being ambitious. Renaissance tragedy, according to these critics, shed light on a flawed social order rather than on flawed individuals. It was also the product of a period of rapid change and transition when people were unsettled from traditional roles and hierarchies, propelled in new directions – and uncertain of what all this meant.

More often than not, Renaissance tragedy centred around a single figure, that of the tragic protagonist, usually male. The tragic hero was high born, a prince or nobleman. His high station and outstanding personality meant that his fall was all the more poignant and dramatic. However, and more interestingly perhaps, the hero was often a conflicted figure, caught between opposing social roles and identities. Hamlet's desire to be the vengeful hero is incompatible with his introspective, philosophical personality, Macbeth's ambition, with his political loyalty and Faustus's aspiration, with his Christian self. The Duchess of Malfi's personal desires are limited by familial and social constraints. Macbeth, Faustus and the Duchess are among those Renaissance tragic protagonists who are determined to assert themselves and shape the course of their own destinies. The struggle between individual autonomy and the limits placed on it was a common theme in Renaissance drama and tragic protagonists came into being through this struggle and were finally destroyed in spite of, or because of, their will to assert themselves. Faustus's desire for a 'world of profit and delight, / Of power, of honour, of omnipotence' (1.53–54) and the Duchess's pride and dignity as she asserts that 'I am Duchess of Malfi still' (4.2.130) are admirable, moving, as well as destructive. Faustus's and Tamburlaine's ambitions make them heroic but also evil, blurring the line between protagonist and antagonist. We are repulsed by them even as we sympathize with their dreams and their anguish. Nearly all tragic heroes were also extremely self-conscious and self-aware and often expressed their innermost thoughts and struggles through lengthy soliloquies.

Revenge tragedy, a form directly inherited from Seneca's plays and inaugurated by Thomas Kyd's *The Spanish Tragedy* was among the most popular modes of tragic drama. The plot of revenge tragedy, revolved around an embittered protagonist seeking revenge for a past wrongdoing. *The Spanish Tragedy* represents Hieronimo, a knight marshal in the Spanish court avenging the death of his son and *The Revenger's Tragedy* narrates the story of Vindici seeking vengeance on the duke who has poisoned his beloved. Scholars have argued that revenge tragedy became popular as old modes of personal retribution were replaced by legal systems where courts rather than individuals meted out justice. The impatience with what was perceived as flawed and prolonged judicial procedure made people yearn for an era where revenge was a matter of personal honour and speedy personal action. Revenge was also a fraught theme because the Bible stated that God was the sole executor of justice ('Vengeance is mine sayeth the Lord' – Romans 12.19) and that humans ought to turn the other cheek. However, in the tragic plays the revengers insisted on seeing their actions as moral and even divinely sanctioned: 'And all the saints do sit soliciting / For vengeance on these cursed murderers', cries Hieronimo in *The Spanish Tragedy* (4.1.33–34)[14] and in the play *Bussy D'Ambois* by George Chapman (1606–07) it is believed that 'Justice will soon distinguish murderous minds / From just revengers' (2.1.169–70).[15] Revenge also offers the avenger a sense of relief from anguish (perhaps also a form of catharsis). In the words of Hieronimo, 'in revenge my heart would find relief' (2.5.41).

Revenge tragedies involved certain typical motifs: the play was ushered in by a ghost who urged revenge and avengers often went mad, or at least seemed to be imbalanced because of the obsessive single-mindedness of their pursuit. Foreign settings, intrigue, lust, extreme violence and numerous deaths were also characteristic of the revenge plot. In spite of the sensationalism of revenge tragedy, the plays were fairly complex in the effect they had on audiences who sympathized with and rooted for the aggrieved revenger even as they realized that the revenge often exceeded the original crime and the man who was once the victim had become the predator. Revenge tragedy also took up serious issues like patricide, incest and the abuse of power. The plot of revenge tragedy often involved the staging of plays (for example, Vindici in *The Revenger's Tragedy* kills his enemies while performing a masque and Hieronimo in *The Spanish Tragedy* also murders Lorenzo while staging a play) and so commented on the purpose of drama itself.

While many tragedies involved family conflicts and tensions, the new sub-genre 'domestic tragedy' emerged in the late sixteenth and early seventeenth centuries. *Arden of Faversham* (1585–92), the anonymous *A Warning for Fair Women* (1599) and Thomas Heywood's *A Woman Killed with Kindness* (1603) are among the best-known examples of those plays that tell the stories of adulterous and murderous wives and treacherous servants. Unlike other tragedies, characters belonged to the middle classes or minor gentry and the plays were written in a more simple, less elevated literary style. These plays explored the breakdown of husband–wife relationships and made the household the locus of conflict. In *Arden of Faversham* Alice, the wife of Arden, has an affair with their servant Mosby and conspires with him to kill her husband. In *A Woman Killed with Kindness* Master Frankford exiles his wife to a lonely country home after she lets herself be seduced by his friend, while George Sanders in *A Warning for Fair Women* is killed by his wife's lover. Since the household was seen as a model of the kingdom with the husband as ruler, disobedience on the part of wives was likened to political treachery. Women in these dramatic works consistently departed from the role of the good wife though they often ended up repenting for their sins, making the plays an odd mixture of sensationalism and conventional morality tales.

There were several other traditions of tragedy besides revenge and domestic tragedy. Stories of tragic or forbidden love, such as *Romeo and Juliet, Antony and Cleopatra* and *'Tis A Pity She's a Whore* (1629–33) by John Ford, were popular, as was tragic heroic drama, like *Tamburlaine, Selimus* by Robert Greene and *Solymon and Perseda* by Kyd, all based on real-life figures and representing in hyperbolic terms the extravagance, pride and tyranny of power and its eventual downfall. In all these plays, like in other tragic drama, the narrative culminated in death.

Death was a reminder of mortality and it erased differences between high and low, victim and villain, revenger and wrongdoer. Another defining characteristic of the tragic hero was that he died with dignity and courage or by asserting himself in the very face of death. Many tragic heroes also staged the moment of death with long speeches, theatrical suicides and transformed dying into a performance of self-assertion. Cleopatra's suicide is one such example and Bussy D'Ambois makes himself a monument in his last speech saying, 'I am up; / Here like a Roman statue I will stand / Till death hath made me marble' (5.3.143–45). Tragedies had sad endings, but according to some critics, notably A.C. Bradley, the Renaissance tragic universe was still moral, there was a sense of goodness prevailing at the end, leaving the spectator with 'a sense of law and beauty . . . a consciousness of greatness in pain, and of solemnity in the mystery we cannot fathom.'[16] Others would disagree with this reading; tragic endings are often so brutal that ethical categories and life itself seem meaningless. But it is still true that many tragic heroes reach, or at least appear to reach, a place of understanding at the end of most plays. Hamlet, who had been thrashing out against his circumstances all along, accepts that 'There's a divinity that shapes our ends . . .' at the conclusion of the play (5.2.10). It is up to the audience to decide whether that lesson stands up to scrutiny in the light of the play's tragic events.

Mixed modes and histories

While comedy and tragedy are useful categories, we should realize that neither comedy nor tragedy existed in any pure, singular form on the stage. Philip Sidney might have written disapprovingly of 'mongrel tragi-comedies', plays that were 'neither right tragedies nor right comedies' and that mingled clowns and kings, tears and laughter, but most writers disregarded classical convention and mixed modes quite easily.[17] In fact, the mystery and morality plays of the native tradition had also conjoined the sublime and the everyday. So the most poignant of Renaissance tragedies included elements of the comic. *Hamlet* has its darkly comic grave-digger scene and the line between tragedy and farce is blurred in *The Jew of Malta* where the grotesque villain Barabas's actions are so extreme that they provoke laughter. *The Malcontent* (*c.* 1603) by John Marston takes the conventional formula of revenge tragedy and gives it comically extravagant language, verbal ingenuity and a final resolution. The so-called 'problem plays' of Shakespeare such as *Measure for Measure* (1609) and *All's Well That Ends Well* (1601–05) indicate how porous generic boundaries are by mingling a dark tone with the comic mode.

From Philip Sidney, *An Apology for Poetry* (1595).

Sir Philip Sidney (1554–86) was a knight, scholar and poet. His *An Apology for Poetry* (published 1595) is a well-known commentary on the value of 'poetry', or literature in general. The following extract deals specifically with stage plays' treatment of the unities of time, place and action.

Our Tragedies and Comedies (not without cause cried out against), observing rules neither of honest civility nor skillful Poetry, excepting

Gorboduc (again, I say, of those that I have seen), which notwithstanding, as it is full of stately speeches and well-sounding phrases, climbing to the height of Seneca's style, and as full of notable morality, which it doth most delightfully teach, and so obtain the very end of Poesy, yet in truth it is very defectious[18] in the circumstances, which grieveth me, because it might not remain as an exact model of all tragedies. For it is faulty both in place and time, the two necessary companions of all corporal actions. For where the stage should always represent but one place, and the uttermost time presupposed in it should be, both by Aristotle's precept and common reason, but one day, there is both many days, and many places, inartificially imagined.[19]

But if it be so in *Gorboduc*, how much more in all the rest? where you shall have Asia of one side, and Afric of the other, and so many other under-kingdoms, that the player, when he cometh in, must ever begin telling where he is, or else the tale will not be conceived.[20] Now ye shall have three ladies walk to gather flowers, and then we must believe the stage to be a garden. By and by we hear news of shipwreck in the same place, and then we are to blame if we accept it not for a rock. Upon the back of that comes out a hideous monster with fire and smoke, and then the miserable beholders are bound to take it for a cave. While in the meantime two armies fly in, represented with four swords and bucklers, and then what hard heart will not receive it for a pitched field?

Now of time they are much more liberal, for ordinary it is that two young princes[21] fall in love. After many traverses,[22] she is got with child, delivered of a fair boy, he is lost, groweth a man, falls in love, and is ready to get another child, and all this in two hours' space: which, how absurd it is in sense, even sense may imagine . . . But besides these gross absurdities, how all their plays be neither right tragedies, nor right comedies, mingling kings and clowns, not because the matter so carrieth it, but thrust in clowns by head and shoulders, to play a part in majestical matters, with neither decency nor discretion, so as neither the admiration and commiseration, nor the right sportfulness, is by their mongrel tragi-comedy obtained. . . . So falleth it out that, having indeed no right comedy, in that comical part of our tragedy, we have nothing but scurrility,[23] unworthy of any chaste ears, or some extreme show of doltishness,[24] indeed fit to lift up a loud laughter, and nothing else: where the whole tract of a comedy should be full of delight, as the tragedy should be still maintained in a well-raised admiration.

But our comedians think there is no delight without laughter; which is very wrong, for though laughter may come with delight, yet cometh it not of delight, as though delight should be the cause of laughter; but well may one thing breed both together. Nay, rather in themselves they have, as it were, a kind of contrariety: for delight we scarcely do but in things that have a conveniency[25] to ourselves or to the general nature; laughter almost ever cometh of things most disproportioned to ourselves and nature. Delight hath a joy in it, either permanent or present. Laughter hath only a scornful tickling. For example, we are ravished with delight to see a fair woman, and yet are far from being moved to laughter. We laugh at deformed creatures, wherein certainly we cannot delight. We delight in good chances, we laugh at mischances; . . .

But I speak to this purpose, that all the end of the comical part be not upon such scornful matters as stirreth laughter only, but, mixed with it, that delightful teaching which is the end of Poesy. And the great fault even in that point of laughter, and forbidden plainly by Aristotle, is that they stir laughter in sinful things, which are rather execrable[26] than ridiculous; or in miserable, which are rather to be pitied than scorned. For what is it to make folks gape at a wretched beggar, or a beggarly clown; or, against law of hospitality, to jest at strangers, because they speak not English so well as we do? . . . But rather a busy loving courtier[27]; a heartless threatening Thraso[28]; a self-wise-seeming schoolmaster[29]; an awry-transformed traveler[30]: these if we saw walk in stage names, which we play naturally, therein were delightful laughter, and teaching delightfulness . . .

By the seventeenth century, plays that were explicitly labelled as 'tragicomedies' began to appear. The Italian writer Giambattista Guarini's 1601 essay on tragicomedy was the first substantial analysis of this hybrid genre that also justified the mingling of comic and tragic conventions. In tragicomedy the obstacles in the protagonist's path to happiness were often more formidable than in 'pure' comedy. Loss and death were real possibilities but were averted, often quite suddenly and miraculously. Tragicomedy writers delighted in experimenting with and resisting classical forms, and spectators and readers were called upon to respond in new ways, either falling into sorrow or into laughter, or both. So *Philaster* (1608–10) by Francis Beaumont and John Fletcher places despairing and doubting lovers in a pastoral world and introduces the serious theme of political usurpation and *A King and No King*

(1609–10) by the same authors has an intense and disturbing storyline with King Arbaces's apparently incestuous love for his sister, Panthea, and his decision to rape her if he cannot marry her. The 'happy' comic end is ensured when he discovers that he is not really her brother. Other notable tragicomedies are *The Renegado* by Philip Massinger and *The Faithful Shepherdess* (1608) by Fletcher. The latter play easily mingles gods and shepherds and loss and farce.

From John Fletcher, Preface to *The Faithful Shepherdess* (1608).

The dramatist John Fletcher wrote many tragi-comedies. The preface to his play *The Faithful Shepherdess* (1608) includes a well-known defence of the mixed mode.

A tragicomedy is not so called in respect of mirth and killing, but in respect it wants[31] deaths, which is enough to make it no tragedy, yet brings some near it, which is enough to make it no comedy; which must be a representation of familiar people, with such kind of trouble as no life be questioned; so that a God is as lawful in this as in a tragedy, and mean people as in a comedy.

Some Renaissance plays are studied today as 'romances'. While very few plays were labelled as such at the time, *The Tempest*, *Pericles* (1607), *Cymbeline* (1611), *The Winter's Tale* (c. 1610) and *The Two Noble Kinsmen* (1613), all written or co-written by Shakespeare, were later described as romances, as were other plays, including Fletcher's *The Island Princess*. In these plays, as in tragicomedy, the protagonist's trials were harsh; death and evil were acknowledged as realities that cannot be expelled from this world. The romance had its origins in folk tales, in the classical epic – notably Virgil's *Aeneid* – and medieval narrative tradition recounting the adventures of wandering knights. It involved a journey both real and metaphorical, a quest for something outside and inside the self. Romances were often set in distant, exotic lands, magic islands, the spice islands of the east, ancient Britain and Rome, provoking Sidney to write sardonically of tales 'where you shall have Asia of the one side, and Afric of the other'.[32] The plays involved visual spectacle and had elements of the magical and miraculous – all of which culminate in a happy ending tempered by some lingering sadness and doubt.

Although Sidney wrote that history was inferior to poetry since history dealt with particular events whereas poetry dealt with higher and universal truths, 'history plays' that dramatized events from English history were immensely popular in the 1580s and 1590s. The material of the plays might have already been familiar to the original audience, and characters and events in individual plays were often continued into other plays. The upsurge of interest in history plays during the Elizabethan era might have happened because England was still recovering from the effects of decades of civil war and nation-building was an important preoccupation. History plays constructed narratives of a shared national past and contributed to this project. Besides, it was believed that the past was a living presence that could teach lessons. Shakespeare's history plays were doubtless the best known of the genre with the three parts of the *Henry VI* cycle proving box-office hits. But the history play was not invented by Shakespeare. It had its roots in the morality tradition with plays like John Bale's *King Johan* (1530s), the anonymous *The Troublesome Reign of John* (1580s) and the anonymous *The Famous Victories of Henry the Fifth* (1580s) laying the foundation of the genre and also serving as sources for Shakespeare. Marlowe's play *Edward II* (1593) and the anonymous *Woodstock* (1590) might also be considered history plays. But Shakespeare's contributions to the genre were unique and his plays have proved the most enduring, raising as they do complicated political questions on legitimacy, tyranny and the rights and responsibilities of both the ruler and the ruled. Shakespeare drew mainly on the non-dramatic English chronicles composed by historians Ralph Holinshed and Edward Hall, and he (and other dramatists) addressed themes of war, civil strife, kingship and nation in their plays. The dramatist was not a historian and there was no interest in absolute historical accuracy. For example, in *Henry IV Part 1* Prince Hal and Hotspur are depicted as being of the same age to enhance the sense of rivalry between the two men though Hotspur was in reality much older than the prince. Anachronism, or attributing customs and objects to periods to which they do not belong, also did not bother dramatists: so clocks existed in ancient Roman settings and pistols in medieval European ones. Shakespeare's histories in particular did not confine themselves to the happenings in the corridors of power alone – lower nobility, waiters at taverns, soldiers, grooms and women were among the colourful cast of characters. The plays had tragic as well as comic elements. Richard II is much like a character from tragedy, while Falstaff is a comic. The deaths in battle are tragic in *Henry V*, but the play has the conventional comic ending in marriage.

History plays have been read as being politically conservative. They served to show that the Tudor rulers were the legitimate kings of England; they promoted the monarchy, taught lessons of political obedience and warned of the evils of rebellion. Thomas Heywood defended theatre by claiming that history plays aim to teach 'subjects obedience to their King, to show people the untimely ends of such as have moved tumults, commotions and insurrections'.[33] It has been argued that these plays reflected and subscribed to the idea of social hierarchy and social order.[34] *Henry V*, with its theme of war, its celebration of the glories of England and fiery patriotic speeches, also prompted nationalist feeling and created a 'band of brothers' (4.3.60). More recently, however, scholars have pointed out that the plays, particularly Shakespeare's histories, were complex narratives because they demonstrated how history is marked by continuous dissent and discord, betrayal and injustice; kings too are frail and often simply evil. *Richard II* cleverly balances sympathy for the king and those who wish to supplant him, and Henry V is a charismatic, attractive figure even as he is a troubling one. The plays also raised questions about political legitimacy – who indeed has the right to rule – without really answering them. Even Henry V is haunted by his father's crime of killing Richard II, 'the fault / My father made in compassing the crown' (4.1.289–90). Unlike the official histories of the time, the plays juxtaposed contradictory ideas and ideologies and were, in the words of Phyllis Rackin, a 'cacophony of contending voices'.[35] They allowed characters (such as Falstaff) who were marginal figures in official histories to occupy centre-stage; they were played to a socially diverse audience by actors who actually donned the guise of kings, so calling into question the very reality of kingship itself. As a genre, history plays remind us that the past is made real to us only through retelling and it is the retelling that makes all the difference. A writer can alter perspectives through the manipulation of character, plot and language, making the truth about the past evasive.

The variety of genres in Renaissance drama have resulted in a multiplicity and abundance of literary riches. Genres certainly did not exist 'as unchanging essences' but more as 'sets of loose similarities amongst artworks'.[36] Plays can be clubbed together and categorized even as they resist categorization. The complexity of genre in Renaissance drama has led us to revise our ideas about comedy, tragedy and indeed, about the nature of genre itself. Like their own protagonists, dramatists challenged tradition and pushed boundaries as they produced these literary works.

Discussion points

1 We have discussed some of the prominent genres in Renaissance drama. Let us think about drama itself as a literary genre. What are the

difficulties of reading (as opposed to watching) drama? Can any of these difficulties be seen as positive challenges that actually help us better understand and appreciate the play?

2 It has been argued that the comic is even more culture-specific than the tragic (in other words, different cultures often find quite different things funny, while the same things usually make us *all* sad). Consider any Renaissance comedy you are reading and think about what makes it funny (or not funny) to you, the modern reader.

3 Most Renaissance tragedies end with death. Consider any Renaissance play that you are studying and think about how the play would need to be reworked to make it remain a tragedy even if there were no death at the end.

4 Anachronisms were briefly discussed above. Look for instances of anachronism in any Renaissance play you are studying. Are they simply evidence of carelessness or ignorance on the author's part? If not, is it possible to say anything about the place and function of anachronism in Renaissance plays? Also, consider modern productions of Renaissance plays that might be deliberately anachronistic (for example, they might be set in the modern world). Think about why the director might have made a deliberate artistic choice to be anachronistic in these cases.

8

Language and Style

One cannot but help be impressed by the sheer eloquence and the dazzling verbal display of Renaissance drama. The language informs, moves, conveys the plot and setting and complements physical action. Fictional characters exist in and through language, as motives and feelings are explored and expressed through words. For characters such as Marlowe's Tamburlaine, speech is an instrument and expression of power. The rhetoric of Jonson's Volpone is as agile and sharp as his intelligence, and language offers Hamlet solace even as it impedes action. Hamlet, like many other characters on the Renaissance stage, almost never runs out of words.

English, the 'vulgar tongue'

During the Renaissance the classical languages, Greek and Latin, were considered the most beautiful and eloquent. English fell short in comparison. It did not have the rich vocabulary or the ornate grammar of the ancient tongues. At best it was an honest, homespun language and at worst a 'crude', 'vile' and 'barbarous' one. Scholars preferred to write in Latin and those who did write in English were apologetic about their choice. For example, even though the humanist Thomas Elyot did write in English, he said authors who wrote in Latin 'do express them [good ideas] incomparably with more grace and dedication to the reader, than our English tongue may yet comprehend'.[1] Roger Ascham too wrote his treatise *Toxophilus* (1545) in English but went out of his way to explain that it would have been far better for his reputation to write it in Latin because 'everything is so excellently done in them [Greek and Latin], that none can do better: in the English tongue contrary, everything in a manner so meanly, both for the matter and handling, that no man can do worse'.[2]

This did not mean that English did not have its uses. Its very simplicity and the fact that it was understood by the common people made it the language of choice for post-Reformation religious and political instruction. That is why, wrote Ascham, he decided it was best to write *Toxophilus*, 'this English matter, in the English tongue, for English men' for 'the pleasure or profit of many'.[3]

It was felt that borrowing words from the classical tongues could improve and enrich English. So through the latter half of the sixteenth century a number of foreign loan words made their way into the language, resulting in more than one word for the same thing or experience (so, for example, the native word 'see' found a synonym in the newly coined Latin-origin word 'perceive', and while 'moon' had its origins in Old English, the word 'lunar' was from Latin). Some writers were cautious about adopting these foreign words, what they called 'inkhorn terms'; as Sidney complained, these foreign words 'must seem strangers to any poor Englishman'.[4] In spite of these protests, augmenting the language by borrowing from foreign languages was generally favoured and the practice continued, adding to the English language words such as 'absurdity', 'adapt', 'armada', 'critic', 'utopian', 'fact', 'chocolate', 'moustache', 'balcony', 'sonnet', 'lottery', 'cannibal', 'tobacco', 'coffee', 'mosquito' and 'yogurt', to name just a few.

Gradually, the homely, utilitarian language of English came to be considered a suitable language for poetry. Though early Renaissance thinkers had paid tribute to Chaucer and other English poets of the Middle Ages, they had not felt that English could embody the literary arts. It was up to Edmund Spenser and a few other English poets to declare that poetry could and should be written in English. Spenser, in a letter to his friend Gabriel Harvey, wondered 'why a god's name, may not we as else the Greeks, have the kingdom of our own language',[5] implying that an English literary tradition was possible and desirable. By the 1590s it was felt that English had been purged of its 'rudeness' and 'barbarism' and had been sufficiently embellished to develop its own native poetic tradition. The rhetorician George Puttenham wrote that 'there may be an art of our English poesy, as well there is of the Latin and Greek'.[6] Old attitudes to the language did linger, but the language's rhetorical and artistic potential was acknowledged. As Richard F. Jones wrote in 1953, 'the rude, gross, base, and barbarous mother tongue recedes into the past, and its place is taken by the eloquent language, confidence in which mounts higher and higher until it yields nothing even to Latin and Greece'.[7] Not only was English now considered a fit medium for poetry ('poetry' was the term used at the time for all imaginative and creative literature in general), it was also thought that one of the functions of poetry was to refine and adorn the language. For instance, even though the public drama had always been less relatively self-conscious about using English, the playwright Thomas Heywood felt that drama played a role in enriching the language:

> Our English tongue, which hath been the most harsh, uneven and broken language of the world … is now by this secondary means of playing, continually refined, every writer striving in himself to add a new flourish unto it; so that in process from the most rude and unpolished tongue, it is grown to a most perfect and composed language, and many excellent works and elaborate poems writ in the same: that many nations grow enamoured of our tongue (before despised).[8]

Apart from the change in status, the English language changed rapidly during the Renaissance. The neologisms and new compounds resulted in a rich language with a large vocabulary. Rising literacy rates and an increasing number of printed books also led to many transformations. The fact that no dictionaries existed before the seventeenth century allowed for a range of spellings. Nor were there any very rigid notions of grammatical correctness. The English of the age was a supple tongue whose grace and sheer loveliness delighted writers, readers and audiences.

Eloquence

'Above all things, the Renaissance is an age of eloquence', writes Madeline Doran.[9] In other words, Renaissance culture was a verbal one and 'eloquence', or the ability to speak and write elegantly and persuasively, to effectively do things with words, was considered both admirable and necessary. As Thomas Wilson put it in the preface to *Art of Rhetoric* (1553), 'the gift of utterance' was granted by God so that humans 'might with ease win folks at their will, and frame them by reason to all good order'.[10] Eloquence was therefore not only an art but a civilizing force that created social order and fellowship.

'Rhetoric' was fundamentally the art of persuading an audience and producing certain emotional effects through the manipulation of language. Humanist classrooms and textbooks emphasized Latin grammar and rhetoric and this eventually impacted literature. As Peter Mack put it, 'The humanist tradition of bringing together rhetoric, dialectic and grammar helped create the conditions in which the linguistic inventiveness of sixteenth-century writers could flourish.'[11]

The prolonged reading and writing of Latin in school provided a standard for clarity and lyricism. But this was perhaps less important than the fact that studying a second language was 'a means of perceiving more lucidly the nature of the first language'.[12] In other words, the study of Latin made students more aware of the structure of the English language and also led them to be more self-conscious and attentive in their use of it. Unlike our modern era, which is somewhat wary of rules and regulations when it comes to artistic creation, young writers were taught rules that would help them to write well. This was different from writing grammatically or correctly. As mentioned above, there were no rigid notions of correctness. In fact, as Richard F. Jones wrote, 'English was eloquent before it became grammatical.'[13] Several rhetorical discussions of the English language were published in the sixteenth century, the best-known of which are Thomas Wilson's *The Art of Rhetoric* and George Puttenham's *The Art of English Poesie* (1589). The chief end of classical rhetorical training was to create good orators or public speakers. Cicero had described the tri-fold aim of the orator as to 'teach, please, move'. These three aims were applied to poetry in the Renaissance. Sidney famously wrote that poets wrote 'to teach and delight'[14], and Jonson was conscious about merging poetry and oratory in order to persuade – 'The Poet', he wrote, 'is the nearest Borderer upon the Orator . . . . because in moving the minds of men, and stirring of affections (in which Oratory shows, and especially approves her eminence), he chiefly excels.'[15]

This kind of deliberate, patterned speech was heard from the pulpit and in parliament as well, but in drama it allied itself with plot and created a sense of suspense and pleasure. The language of drama was also not meant to be 'realistic' or 'natural' – stylization and artifice were desired and valued. A play or a lyrical poem was after all a work of art, and this suggested 'artifice' – a deliberate departure from the 'natural', which was often understood as being crude and unpolished. The language of literature was therefore beautified deliberately and adorned 'cunningly' (artfully) and 'curiously' (with care and attention to detail). Ornamentation was not an accessory or a superficial add-on – it was necessary to move and to delight. Jonson deliberately distanced his dramatic language from ordinary speech. 'That were a precept no less dangerous to language than to life,' he wrote, 'if we were to speak or live after the custom of the vulgar.'[16]

From George Puttenham, *The Art of English Poesy* (1589).

George Puttenham's *The Art of English Poesy* (1589) is a comprehensive treatment of 'poetry', as creative literature in general was called. Apart from providing a historical account of poetry, Puttenham analyses metrical forms and categorizes figures of speech. This excerpt is a consideration of the effect of stylistic devices used to enhance poetic language.

Of Ornament Poetical:

As no doubt the good proportion[17] of any thing doth greatly adorn and commend it, and right so our late-remembered proportions do to our vulgar poesy,[18] so is there yet requisite to the perfection of this art, another manner of exornation,[19] which resteth in the fashioning of our makers language and style to such purpose as it may delight and allure as well the mind as the ear of the hearers with a certain novelty and strange manner of conveyance, disguising it no little from the ordinary and accustomed, nevertheless making it nothing the more unseemly or misbecoming, but rather decenter and more agreeable to any civil ear and understanding. And as we see in these great Madams of honour, be they for personage or otherwise never so comely[20] and beautiful, yet if they want their courtly habiliments[21] or at leastwise such other apparel as custom and civility have ordained to cover their naked bodies, would be half-ashamed or greatly out of countenance[22] to be seen in that sort, and perchance[23] do then think themselves more amiable in every man's eye, when they be in their richest attire, suppose of silks or tissues and costly embroideries, then when they go in cloth or in any other plain and simple apparel. Even so cannot our vulgar poesy show itself either gallant or gorgeous, if any limb left naked and bare and not clad in his kindly clothes and colours, such as may convey them somewhat out of sight – that is from the common course of ordinary speech and capacity of the vulgar judgment – and yet being artificially handled, must needs yield it much more beauty and commendation.

This ornament we speak of is given to it by figures and figurative speeches, which be the flowers as it were and colours that a poet setteth upon his language by art, as the embroiderer doth his stone and pearl, or passements of gold upon the stuff of a Princely garment, or as the excellent painter bestoweth the rich orient colours upon his table of portrait. So, nevertheless as if the same colours in our arte of Poesie (as well as in those other mechanical arts) be not well-tempered, or not well-laid, or be used in excess, or never so little disordered or misplaced, they not only give it no manner of grace at all, but rather do disfigure the stuff and spill the whole workmanship taking away all beauty and good liking from it, no less than if the crimson taint, which should be laid upon a Ladies lips, or right in the centre of her cheeks, should by some oversight or mishap be applied to her forehead or chin, it would make (ye would say) but a very ridiculous beauty. Wherefore the chief praise and cunning[24] of our Poet is in the discreet using of his figures,[25] as the skillful painter's is in the good conveyance of his colours and shadowing traits of his pencil, with a delectable[26] variety, by all measure and just proportion, and in places most aptly to be bestowed.

Of course, there were a range of attitudes to ornamentation of language. Ornamentation (and eloquence in general) was viewed with suspicion by Puritans, who valued plainness and simplicity and believed that beautified language was a sign of vanity and quite simply deceitful. Gosson disapproved of eloquence because it 'dwelleth longest in those points, that profit least; and like a wanton whelp, leaveth the game to run riot'.[27] For others, eloquence was both a strength and a weakness. Even though Sidney himself revelled in ornamented language in his own poetry, he criticized the excessive use of it, and Wilson advocated a language that did not seek 'to be over-fine' even as it was not as 'over-careless' as ordinary speech was wont to be.

Dramatists obviously varied to the extent they dressed up their language – this is what led to a variety of styles and effects. Marlowe was known for his verbal display and bombastic style, what was described by Jonson as 'Marlowe's mighty line'.[28] As the prologue to *Tamburlaine* indicates, the author wants to create a drama far from 'the jiggling veins of rhyming mother wits'. His intent is to write of a hero who is not only known for 'scourging kingdoms with his conquering sword' but also for 'Threat'ning the world with high astounding terms' (Part 1, Prologue, 1.6, 5). Jonson poked fun at this style: he saw it as over-done and too sensational. A true poet's language, he wrote, must not 'fly from all humanity, with the Tamerlans and Tamer-Chains of the late Age, which had nothing in them but the scenical strutting and furious vociferation to warrant them to ignorant gapers'.[29] Shakespeare's style is usually more subtle than Marlowe's, and Middleton's, Dekker's and Heywood's styles are even plainer. These later playwrights appear to follow Gertrude's advice to Polonius that good speech is characterized by 'More matter, with less art' (2.2.95).

Shakespeare, in fact, sometimes made fun of characters such as Polonius and Osric, both in *Hamlet*, who use rhetorical figures excessively. But we should remember that the 'realistic' speech we look for and find in modern-day literature simply did not exist in Elizabethan drama. Characters did not speak 'naturally', nor were they expected to. So comedies such as Shakespeare's *Love's Labour's Lost* (*c.* 1595) with its sophisticated wit and clever use of words is a joyous celebration of the 'great feast of languages' (5.1.35). Even Sidney, for all his criticism of ornament, felt that *Gorboduc* was an excellent tragedy because of 'its stately speeches and well-sounding phrases climbing to the height of Seneca's style'.[30]

From Philip Sidney, *An Apology for Poetry* (1595).

In this excerpt from *An Apology for Poetry* (1595) Philip Sidney takes up the issue of 'eloquent' language and the extent to which it really enhances communication.

Now, for the outside of it, which is words, or (as I may term it) diction, it is even well worse. So is that honey-flowing matron eloquence appareled, or rather disguised, in a courtesan-like[31] painted affectation[32]: one time with so far-fetched words, that many seem monsters, but must seem strangers, to any poor Englishman; another time with coursing of a letter,[33] as if they were bound to follow the method of a dictionary; another time with figures and flowers[34] extremely winter-starved.[35] But I would this fault were only peculiar to versifiers, and had not as large possession among prose-printers, and (which is to be marveled) among many scholars, and (which is to be pitied) among some preachers. . . . Truly I could wish, . . . the diligent imitators of Tully[36] and Demosthenes[37] (most worthy to be imitated) did not so much keep Nizolean paper books [38] of their figures and phrases, as by attentive translation (as it were) devour them whole, and make them wholly theirs . . .

. . . For now they cast sugar and spice upon every dish that is served to the table, like those Indians, not content to wear ear-rings at the fit and natural place of the ears, but they will thrust jewels through their nose and lips, because they will be sure to be fine.

Tully, when he was to drive out Catiline,[39] as it were with a thunderbolt of eloquence, often used that figure of repetition, Vivit. Vivit? Imo vero etiam in senatum venit, &c.[40] Indeed, inflamed with a well-grounded rage, he would have his words (as it were) double out of his mouth; and so do that artificially which we see men in choler do naturally. And we, having noted the grace of those words, hale them in sometime to a familiar epistle, when it were too much choler to be choleric.[41] . . .

Now for similitudes[42] in certain printed discourses, I think all herbalists, all stories of beasts, fowls, and fishes are rifled up, that they may come in multitudes to wait upon any of our conceits; which certainly is as absurd a surfeit to the ears as is possible: for the force of a similitude not being to prove anything to a contrary disputer, but only to explain to a willing hearer; when that is done, the rest is a most tedious prattling, rather over-swaying the memory from the purpose whereto they were applied, then any whit informing the judgment, already either satisfied, or by similitudes not to be satisfied.[43] For my part, I do not doubt, when Antonius and Crassus,[44] the great forefathers of Cicero in eloquence, the one (as Cicero testifieth of them) pretended not to know art, the other not to set by it,[45] because with a plain sensibleness they might win credit of popular ears; which credit is the nearest step to persuasion; which persuasion is the chief mark of Oratory – I do not doubt (I say) but that they used these tracks[46] very sparingly . . .

Undoubtedly (at least to my opinion undoubtedly) I have found in divers[47] small-learned courtiers a more sound style than in some professors of learning; of which I can guess no other cause, but that the courtier, following that which by practice he findeth fittest to nature, therein (though he know it not) doth according to art, though not by art: where the other, using art to show art, and not to hide art (as in these cases he should do), flieth from nature,[48] and indeed abuseth art.

Patterned speech

Fluency and variety were key to good style. So writers heaped up detail, varied words and phrases, and used figures, allusions and illustrations plentifully. Of course, practising playwrights knew exactly what actors could deliver and what audiences wanted and could understand, and accordingly modified the scholastic forms of rhetoric for the theatre. Figures of speech were divided into 'tropes', which involved the transposing of meaning from one word to another (metaphors, similes and puns would be examples) and 'schemes', in which writers departed from normal grammatical usage (switching word order or using incomplete sentences would be examples). Drama was characterized by 'patterned speech' – the consistent and noticeable use of tropes and schemes. Kyd's *The Spanish Tragedy* is noted for putting the full art of Elizabethan rhetoric on display. Hieronimo is grief-stricken at his son's death and moved to make this speech:

> O eyes, no eyes, but fountains fraught with tears!
> O life, no life, but lively forms of death!
> O world, no world, but mass of public wrongs,
> Confused and filled with murder and misdeeds!
> O sacred heavens, if this unhallow'd deed,
> If this inhuman and barbarous attempt,
> If this incomparable murder thus
> Of mine but now no more my son,
> Shall unrevealed and unrevenged pass,
> How should we term your dealings to be just
> If you unjustly deal with those that in your justice trust?
> . . .
> Eyes, life, world, heavens, hell, night and day,
> See, search, show, send some man some mean that may
>
> (3.2.1–23)

The monologue is filled with balanced and antithetical words and phrases ('heavens' – 'hell'; 'night' – 'day'; 'life' – 'death'), repetitions, variations ('just' – 'justly' – 'justice'; 'life' – 'lively') and alliteration ('seek', 'search', 'send'). The strength of the passage lies in the contrast between the symmetrical formality of Hieronimo's speech and the wildness of his grief.

Hieronimo uses metaphor when he describes his eyes as 'fountains fraught with tears', indicating the fullness and spontaneity of his grief. Figurative language expresses one thing in terms of another, most often through the use of simile and metaphor. In doing so, it creates a rich network of meanings, some of which are easier to work out than others. Indeed, one of the pleasures of poetic language is its complexity and ambiguity, when meaning is obscured rather than fully disclosed. So when Macbeth says 'O! full of scorpions is my mind, dear wife!' (3.2.36), the metaphor conjures up connotations that the reader has to unpack in order to understand the character's state of mind. *Macbeth* is dense with other rich metaphors. Hope is 'drunk' (1.7.35), implying that it is often irrational and uncontrolled; ambition is 'vaulting' and so energetic and often excessive (1.7.27) and pity is 'a naked new-born babe, / Striding the blast . . .', making it an interesting combination of vulnerability and strength (1.7.21–22). Marlowe's *Edward II* uses a powerful simile coupled with mythical allusion to convey the character's state of mind: 'My heart is an anvil unto sorrow,' says the king, 'Which beats upon it like the Cyclops' hammers, / And with the noise turns up my giddy brain' (1.4.313–15). Of course, such figurative language is not restricted to tragedy. John Marston's *Antonio and Mellida* (1601) is filled with vivid and unexpected comparisons ('He is made like a tilting-staff, and looks / For all the world like an o'er roasted pig; / A great tobacco-taker too, that's flat; / For his eyes look as if they had been hung / in the smoke of his nose' [1.1.123–27] and 'Thy voice squeaks like a dry cork shoe' [5.2.16–17]), all of which create a tone that is sharply observant, clever and satirical.[49]

Hieronimo's speech quoted above is also a good example of amplification. 'Amplification' refers to a practice where the writer embellishes the sentences in order to emphasize meaning and heighten poetic effect. So, for instance, the world is not simply 'unjust' – the character's intense resentment provokes a stream of words, and the world is a 'mass of public wrongs, confus'd and fill'd with murder and misdeeds'. Even Falstaff in *Henry IV Part 1* uses amplification when he speaks of thieves as 'Diana's foresters, gentlemen of the shade, minions of the moon' (1.2.25–26) and Volpone uses it to brilliant effect when he heaps adjective upon adjective to describe 'these turdy-fasey-nasty-patey-lousy-fartical rogues' (2.2.59).[50] In another example from *Macbeth*, sleep is 'The death of each day's life, sore labour's bath / Balm of hurt minds, great Nature's second course, / Chief nourisher in life's feast' (2.2.37–39). Here each phrase that describes 'sleep' is a metaphor in itself, creating a dense web of meaning.

The pun was another way of enriching language. The extensive use of puns showed the variety and depth of Renaissance English, drew attention to the delights of human speech and made the speaker sound witty, clever, sarcastic and sometimes deceptive. Shakespeare especially delighted in puns. As Feste in *Twelfth Night* says in a celebration of the pliability of language, the ability to turn meaning inside-out: 'A sentence is but a chev'ril glove to a good wit – how quickly the wrong side may be turned outward!' (3.1.11–12). Hamlet bitterly puns that Claudius is to him 'A little more than kin, and less than kind' (1.2.65) and comments, when Claudius calls him 'son' a little too often, that he is 'too much in the sun' (1.2.67). Many of Shakespeare's puns had sexual meanings, as when Hamlet tells Ophelia that 'nothing' lies between a 'maid's legs' (3.2.120–21).

The language of the plays was also replete with imagery that appealed to multiple senses. Marston's combined strong imagery with alliteration and internal rhyme to convey the setting of *Antonio's Revenge* (1599–1600): 'The rawish dank of clumsy winter ramps / The fluent's summer's vein; and drizzling sleet / Chilleth the wan bleak cheek of the numbed earth, / Whilst snarling gusts nibble the juiceless leaves / From the nak'd shudd'ring branch' (Prologue, 1–5).[51] We may not fully be able to fully understand the details in Caliban's description of the island of *The Tempest* with its 'crabs', 'pignuts', 'clustering filberts' and 'young scamels', but the description is so thick and detailed that we get a sense of a lush space brimming with life. *Volpone* is also characterized by a series of description of objects: 'ropes of pearls' 'carbuncles' and 'diamonds' (amongst other things) suggest the sensual delights of wealth, even as the play satirizes greed.

Hieronimo's speech obviously uses repetition ('eyes' – 'eyes'; 'world' – 'world') and also utilizes parallelism (repetition of the structure of a sentence for poetic effect) in the first two lines. Both were common devices in dramatic speech. Earlier in the play, we are told that the Portuguese viceroy has been defeated in battle:

> His men are slain, a weakening to his realm;
> His colours seized, a blot unto his name;
> His son distressed, a corrosive[52] to his heart

> (1.2.142–44)

The parallel structures in these lines reinforce the finality of the defeat. They also link the defeat in battle to the loss of name or honour and finally, and worst of all, to the pain that the viceroy feels at his son's capture. Besides, since these lines are spoken by Balthazar, a representative of the losing side, the neat structure renders the act of conceding defeat a dignified and even elegant one, indicating that the loser is noble and honourable. Shakespeare's *Othello* also uses parallelism when the hero says 'I kissed thee ere I killed thee' (5.2.358). Here repetition as well as alliteration emphasize the ironic – and terrible – connection and contrast between love and murder, desire and death. Lear's simple repetition of the word 'never' in *King Lear* ('Never, never, never, never, never' [5.3.307]) seems less formalized and deliberate than the other examples presented here but is all the more startling, powerful and despairing for that.

Playwrights also manipulated grammar. They deliberately used verbs such as 'hath', 'doth', 'forgetteth', 'bringeth' and so forth that had already become old-fashioned in order to invest characters' speech with grandeur. They also moved between 'thou' and 'you'. The latter pronoun was used in formal contexts and was used for superiors and to indicate respect, while 'thou' indicated familiarity and intimacy (so it is noteworthy that Juliet uses 'you' with Romeo at their first meeting, but Romeo moves quickly to using 'thou'). They also used double comparisons as in 'the most unkindest cut of all' (3.2.181) in Shakespeare's *Julius Caesar* and 'the most perfectest man' in *A Woman Killed with Kindness* (6.19). In the extract from *The Spanish Tragedy* quoted above, Kyd also changes the usual order of the sentence when he writes: 'if this incomparable murder . . . Shall unreveal'd and unrevenged pass'. This kind of inversion or anastrophe was common in drama either to maintain metre or for emphasis. For example, Prospero says in *The Tempest*, 'Bravely the figure of this harpy hast thou / Performed, my Ariel' (3.3.83–84) and in *Hamlet* Laertes says of Ophelia, 'Thought and affliction, passion, hell itself, / She turns to favour and to prettiness' (4.5.185–86). In the first instance the inversion serves to highlight Prospero's appreciation (since the word 'Bravely' is placed first) and to add an interesting pause early in the line, while the placement of 'my Ariel' at the end allows the lines to culminate in a note of tenderness. In the example from *Hamlet*, the inverted syntax allows the sentence to begin and end with two sets of words that stand in startling contrast to each other ('thought and affliction, passion, hell' on the one hand, and 'favour and to prettiness' on the other), highlighting Laertes's tendency to aestheticize even Ophelia's darkest and most intense experiences. Another example of word-play at the level of grammar was the functional shift – this is when one part of speech takes on a new grammatical function. So when Cleopatra says that Caesar 'words me' (5.2.190), she uses a noun as a verb, just as Lear does when he says that Gloucester 'childed as I fathered' (3.6.108). In both cases the shift makes the lines more compact and dense with meaning.

Disputation or debate was an important aspect of humanist education, with students trained to take a stand on a chosen topic and argue for or against it. In stage tragedies, where conflict is the seed of the action, such debates are inevitable and often finely constructed. So Faustus repeatedly debates between temptation and fear in *Doctor Faustus*:

Now Faustus, must thou needs be damned,
And canst not now be saved.
What boots it then to think of God or heaven?
Away with such vain fancies and despair,
Despair in God, and trust in Beelzebub:
Now go not backward; no, Faustus, be resolute:
Why waverest thou? O, something soundeth in mine ears:
'Abjure this magic, turn to God again.'
Ay, and Faustus will turn to God again.
To God? He loves thee not:

The god thou servest is thine appetite,
Wherin is fix'd the love of Beelzebub.
To him I'll build an altar and a church,
And offer luke-warm blood of new-born babes.

(5.1–14)

The speech begins by reinforcing Faustus's inability to believe in God and his consequent faith in the Devil and his forces; the return to God is signalled by the primal sounds 'O' and 'Ay'. The passage deliberately juxtaposes abstract and traditionally Christian rhetoric ('saved', 'damned') with words connoting the bodily and sensual ('appetite', 'luke-warm', 'blood'). The latter set of words also offer a startling contrast to the 'altar' and 'church' of the previous line. The word 'love', which is so central to the Christian vision of God, is not associated with God (indeed Faustus thinks God does *not* love him) and is instead linked to the Devil's associate, Beelzebub. While the declarative clauses ('must thou needs be damned ..', 'He loves thee not ...' etc.) and the imperative ones ('despair in God ...' and 'abjure this magic ...') indicate Faustus's seeming certainty and control over his own thoughts and actions, the questions in the text ('What boots it then ...?', 'To God?') reinforce the mood of doubt and uncertainty. Throughout the speech Faustus refers to himself in the third person as if he embodies, in turns, both good and evil forces, urging him on one way first and then the other. Similarly, Hieronimo in *The Spanish Tragedy* wonders whether he should leave revenge to heaven or avenge his son's death himself. In the same play when Balthazar contemplates his chances of Bel-imperia's love he debates with, himself, conveying the turmoil of the lover's mind:

Yet might she love me for my valiancy;
Ay, but that's slandered by my captivity.
Yet might she love me to content her sire;
Ay, but her reason masters his desire.
Yet might she love me as her brother's friend;
Ay, but her hopes aim at some other end.

(2.1.19–24)

Here the series of parallel structures, the regular metre and rhyming couplets highlight the terms of the young man's argument as he feverishly speculates on the affections of the woman he loves. While such intense conflicts were not characteristic of comedy, witty arguments and verbal exchanges were features of comic dialogue. Renaissance stage lovers often court each other by engaging in 'a set of wit well play'd' (*Love's Labour's Lost*, 5.2.29) that involved rapid-fire, clever verbal exchanges (the courting of Petruchio and Katherine comes to mind, or the

Castabella and Rousard scenes even in a tragedy such as Cyril Tourneur's 1611 play *The Atheist's Tragedy*). Flyting or the quick exchange of insults makes for several witty scenes as seen in the opening of Jonson's *The Alchemist*:

> SUBTLE
>> Away, you trencher-rascal
>
> FACE
>> Out, you dog-leech,
>> The vomit of all prisons –
>
> . . .
>
> SUBTLE
>> Cheater!
>
> FACE
>> Bawd!
>
> SUBTLE
>> Cow-herd!
>
> FACE
>> Conjurer!
>
> SUBTLE
>> Cut-purse!
>
> FACE
>> Witch!

(1.1.103–04, 106)

The language here is startling in its hostility and aggression but also clever and amusing and prepares us for the razor-sharp dialogue that is to follow.

In modern drama we assume that characters always address each other rather than the audience. This was not the case in Renaissance drama where 'direct address' to the audience was common either in the form of the lines of the chorus or asides or soliloquies. This kind of direct address was possibly a legacy of morality drama where the audience was deliberately drawn into the story. Some asides were lengthy, while others were short and either explanatory or ironic. Othello engages in a number of bitter asides towards the end of the play as he grows increasingly suspicious of Desdemona. Villains too often delivered asides, so drawing the audience into the intrigue. So the speeches of Iago in *Othello*, Barabas in *The Jew of Malta*, Lorenzo in *The Spanish Tragedy* and Volpone and Mosca in *Volpone* are filled with asides. In fact, in the final scene of *Volpone* a fairly lengthy verbal exchange goes on between Volpone and Mosca entirely in asides.

The soliloquy is another form of direct address and is a feature of tragedy. By revealing the hero's thoughts and feelings, the soliloquy gives the impression of interiority and leads us into the dark, tangled internal landscape of the minds of tragic heroes. Some soliloquies are meditations, others are ethical arguments. Faustus's opening speech expresses doubt and desire and takes us through the protagonist's thoughts and experiences of many years. While Barabas's actions in *The Jew of Malta* might be comically crude, his soliloquies reveal a more complex self. The world of Jonson's *Sejanus* is one of dissimulation and disguise. It is in the soliloquy that the villainous Sejanus reveals his true self:

> Adultery? It is the lightest ill
> I will commit: a race of wicked acts
> Shall flow out of my anger and o'erspread
> The world's wide face ...
> On then, my soul, and start not in thy course
> Though heav'n drop thunder and hell belch out fire,
> Laugh at the idle terrors: tell proud Jove
> Between his power and thine there is no odds.
> 'Twas only fear, first, in the world made gods.

> (2.2.12–20)

Sejanus makes the audience his confidante as much as he addresses himself, sharing his resolve and plans to execute his evil intentions. Unlike Marlowe's villains, he suffers neither guilt nor fear. The speech adds to the mood of cynicism that pervades the play. However, Sejanus's arrogance, as exhibited in this soliloquy, and his conviction that his evil acts are grand and cosmic become ridiculous in light of his subsequent fall. Interestingly, soliloquies not only reveal the innermost thoughts of the speaker – characters such as Hamlet, Faustus and Tamburlaine actually shape their identity through the language of inner exploration and self-analysis.

The language of Renaissance drama is also poetic in that sound matters nearly as much as sense. Writers often used devices like alliteration (repetition of an initial sound) as in this sentence from *The Spanish Tragedy*: 'My woes whose weight hath wearied the earth' (3.7.2), assonance (repetition of identical or similar vowel sounds) as in this line from *The Tempest* where the repeated 'ai' enhances the obvious alliteration: 'Full fathom five thy father lies' (1.2.397) and consonance (repetition of consonant sounds in the middle of neighbouring words) as in 'All fled, fail'd, died, yea, all decayed with this' from *The Spanish Tragedy* (4.4.95) where the 'd' sound and the 'l' sound are repeated. All these devices enhanced the lyricism of the lines and served to suggest connections between words and ideas. Besides, Renaissance drama was largely written in iambic pentameter or unrhymed blank verse (a line in iambic pentameter consisted of five *iambs*; each iamb consisted of one unstressed syllable followed by a stressed one). The first English poet to use blank verse was the Earl of Surrey in his translation of Virgil's *Aeneid*. Surrey found the form more flexible and fluid than the rather monotonous fourteen-syllable lines of earlier English writing and felt it could better convey the grandeur of Latin syntax and diction. The first play to be written in iambic pentameter was *Gorboduc*, but it was Marlowe who brought blank verse to the public stage. These famous lines from *Doctor Faustus* where the beautiful Helen is being invoked are an example of the masterful use of iambic pentameter:

> Was this the face that launched a thousand ships,
> And burnt the topless towers of Ilium?
> Sweet Helen, make me immortal with a kiss:
>
> (12.89–91)

Here the blank verse is regular in that every line is end-stopped (i.e. a thought ends with each line, indicated by punctuation at the end of the line) though Marlowe renders it more flexible and varied by varying the metre slightly and adding a brief pause after 'Sweet Helen.' Blank verse became very popular after Marlowe and was soon the dominant vehicle of drama. Shakespeare brought it new levels of sophistication by turning it into a form that was even more varied, and hence less rigid and monotonous. For instance, he moved away from end-stopped lines and added enjambment (where the lines end without completing a sentence or a clause) as in these lines from *Hamlet*:

> To be, or not to be, that is the question: (1)
> Whether 'tis nobler in the mind to suffer (2)
> The slings and arrows of outrageous fortune, (3)
> Or to take arms against a sea of troubles (4)
> And by opposing end them. To die – to sleep, (5)
> No more; and by a sleep to say we end (6)
> The heart-ache, and the thousand natural shocks (7)
> That flesh is heir to: 'tis a consummation (8)
> Devoutly to be wish'd. (9)
>
> (3.1.56–64)

The number of enjambed or run-on lines in this excerpt (lines 2–3, 4–5, 6–7, 7–8 and 8–9) gives the lines a sense of urgency as Hamlet's thoughts are propelled swiftly from one line to the next. Besides, the first line can be scanned as the expected five iambs (with an additional syllable):

˘ ╱ / ˘ ╱ / ˘ ╱ / ˘ ╱ / ˘ ╱ / ˘
To be / or not / to be / that is / the ques / tion

or as :

˘ ⁄ | ˘ ⁄ | ˘ ⁄ | ⁄ ˘ | ˘ ⁄ | ˘
To be / or not / to be / that is / the ques / tion

In the first version, the foot 'that is' is an example of a regular iamb with the stress falling on the second syllable, while in the latter version, the stress is reversed in 'that is' with the stress falling on the first syllable, so placing emphasis on 'that' (indicating that Hamlet has been looking for and has, at last, found the right question). Shakespeare also varied iambic pentameter in this passage by adding an extra unstressed syllable to lines 1–3 (in line 1 the last syllable of 'question' is the extra one in the line), so giving the lines a 'feminine ending'. This variation on the pattern of iambic pentameter without a complete departure from the conventional scheme is a defining mark of the elegance and flexibility of Shakespeare's style.

About two-thirds of the lines in Shakespeare's plays are in iambic pentameter.[53] In the hands of Shakespeare and some of his contemporaries, blank verse could be made to sound like grand public oratory or to convey lyrical romantic moments, even as it could also sound colloquial and speech-like. As readers and listeners, we may not always be fully conscious of the effects of metre, but it is because of iambic pentameter that we get the sense of rhythm, grace and musicality as the lines of a play are delivered.

While blank verse is generally unrhymed, end rhyme was occasionally used. In Hieronimo's 'O eyes, no eyes' lament quoted above, Hieronimo's wild, unruly passions are abruptly checked as signalled by the sudden use of a rhymed couplet: 'How should we term your dealings to be just / If you unjustly deal with those that in your justice trust?' (3.2.10–11). In another example, Shakespeare (who often ended scenes with rhymed couplets) has Hamlet express his new-found confidence with the ringing couplet: 'The play's thing / Wherein I'll catch the conscience of the King' (2.2.606–607). Here the sheer unexpectedness of the rhyme catches the attention of the reader or listener.

Varieties of speech

The sheer variety of dramatic genres, storylines and characters demanded a variety of styles. One remembers characters such as the nurse in *Romeo and Juliet* for her non-stop chatter and unconscious sexual references, Ursula, the 'pig woman' in Jonson's *Bartholomew Fair*, for her cheerfully crude style, Othello for his lofty language and Volpone for his slick use of words.

The most obvious kind of variation was the movement between verse and prose. This choice often indicated social class: the nobility spoke in verse, while commoners delivered their lines in prose. The choice of verse was also dictated by other things: for example, decorum required that lovers speak in verse. This is notable in Thomas Dekker's *The Shoemaker's Holiday*, which is largely in prose except for the love scenes. The shift to verse also indicated the grandeur and enormity of a moment. In the opening of *King Lear*, the earls speak in prose, but Lear's first entrance is marked by his utterance in verse, signalling his status and the magnitude of his intended actions: 'Meantime we shall express our darker purpose. / Give me the map there. Know that we have divided / In three our kingdom' (1.1.35–37). Shakespeare, however, was not shy about breaking with convention and has Hamlet's lofty 'What a piece of work is a man' (2.2.295–312) speech delivered in prose, relying on diction and repetition rather than metre to achieve his intended effect.

Comedy especially required rhetorical variety. Not only did comic character types have their own style of speech, the plays themselves often moved between lyrical love scenes, verbal duels and raucous humour. Comic language was often coarse and filled with sexual innuendo, a source of great delight to the audience.[54] City comedy, which was often satirical, had its own cutting style of speech. Jonson's city comedies were particularly marked by their style: sophisticated, witty and stingingly satirical. Jonsonian comedy depended for its success on a learned audience that would recognize and appreciate irony, whether it be the mocking piety of Volpone's and Mosca's speeches in *Volpone*, or Volpone successfully imitating the language of a mountebank conning the public with his fake potions and cures. The trickery of the rogues in *The Alchemist* is nearly all verbal hocus-pocus. They are fluent in the language of alchemy, which they use to con their victim. Here is Face talking about the so-called 'Philosopher's Stone':

> 'Tis a stone, and not
> A stone; a spirit, a soul, and a body:
> Which, if you do dissolve, it is dissolved,
> If you coagulate, it is coagulated,
> If you make fly it flieth.

$$(2.5.40–44)$$

The language is obscure, impressive, pseudo-scientific and even poetic. The success of parody is reliant on an audience's ability to recognize it as poking fun at other serious styles of speech. The hero of *The Knight of the Burning Pestle* solemnly speaks of honour in these lines:

But heaven, methinks it were an easy leap
To pluck bright honour from the pale-faced moon,
Or dive into the bottom of the sea,
Where never fathom line touched any ground,
And pluck up drowned honour from the lake of hell.

(Induction, 77–81)

Here only those spectators and readers who recognize this as an echo of Hotspur's language of honour in Shakespeare's *Henry IV 1* will understand that the playwright was mocking the rhetoric of honour. Jonson especially enjoyed caricaturing Puritan speech. We see this in the exalted speech of the Anabaptist Brethren in *The Alchemist* and the language of Zeal-of-the-Land Busy in *Bartholomew Fair*, which is rife with biblical phrases and other Puritan turns of speech, all of which are rendered particularly ridiculous in the following passage since what the men are really talking about are the (delightful) 'evils' of eating roast pig:

Verily, for the disease of longing, it is a disease, a carnal disease, or appetite, incident to women; and as it is carnal, and incident, it is natural, very natural. Now Pig, it is a meat, and a meat that is nourishing, and may be longed for, and so consequently eaten; very exceeding well-eaten. But in the Fair, and as a Bartholmew-pig, it cannot be eaten, for the very calling it a Bartholmew-pig, and to eat it so, is a spice of Idolatry, and you make the Fair, no better than one of the high places.

(1.6.43–50)

The language of tragedy was, on the other hand, quite genuinely lofty, stately and grand. This heightened speech was needed to move the audience to the appropriate responses of pity and fear. Tragic heroes often used big words: Faustus dismisses law as too 'servile and illiberal' (1.36), Hamlet says that death is 'a consummation / Devoutly to be wish'd' (3.1.63–64) and Hieronimo speaks of the air being 'surcharged' with 'ceaseless plaints for my diseased son' (3.7.3, 4). This impressive manner of speaking indicated an intelligent and profound persona. The language of tragedy was also characterized by hyperbole or overstatement. Note Cleopatra's glorious hyperbole when she speaks of Anthony in Shakespeare's *Anthony and Cleopatra*: 'His face was as the heavens; and therein stuck / A sun and moon. ... His legs bestrid the ocean; his reared arm / Crested the world' (5.2.81–82). Hyperbole is especially characteristic of heroic drama as in this description of Tamburlaine in *Tamburlaine Part 1*:

As princely lions when they rouse themselves,
Stretching their paws, and threat'ning herds of beasts,
So in his armour looketh Tamburlaine.
Methinks I see kings kneeling at his feet
And he, with frowning brows and fiery looks,
Spurning their crowns from off their captive heads.

(Part 1, 1.2.52–57)

While you do have the rare example of the playing down of passion in tragic drama, the contrast between heightened speech and more earthy language is noticeable when the switch is abrupt. In *King Lear* Shakespeare deliberately moves between Lear's heightened passion and the fool's wry, down-to -earth comments, enhancing the effect of both styles:

KING LEAR
    O me, my heart! My rising heart! But down!
FOOL
    Cry to it, nuncle, as the cockney did to the eels when she put 'em i' the
    paste alive: she knapped 'em o' the coxcombs with a stick, and cried 'Down,
    wantons, down!'

(2.2.313–17)

However, even colloquial speech in drama, signalled by the use of oaths and simple sentence structure was stylized. There were other kinds of variations in speech style. Then, as now, English was not a monolithic language and had class and regional variations. In *King Lear* Shakespeare has Edgar, disguised as Poor Tom, use a rustic style:

Good Gentleman, go your gait and let poor volk pass. And 'ch'ud ha' bin
zwagger'd out of my life, 'twould not ha' been zo long as 'tis by a vortnight.
Nay, come not near th' old man; keep out, che vor ye, or I'se try whither your
costard or my baton be the harder. Ch'ill be plain with you.

(4.6.233–38)

The Welsh, Irish and Scots soldiers' accents in *Henry V* have marked regional accents. Many city comedies including *The Alchemist* and Dekker's *The Roaring Girl* enjoy displaying 'canting' or London street slang. A character named Trapdoor in *The Roaring Girl* says: 'Ben mort, shall you and I heave a booth, mill a ken, or nip a bung? … And then we'll couch a hogshead under the ruffmans, and there you shall wap with me, and I'll niggle with you.' This translates into 'Good wench, shall you and I steal a shop, rob a house, or cut a purse? And then we'll lie under a hedge and have sex' (5.1.177–80). Styles of speech like this would have seemed both exotic and amusing to more elite spectators. At the other extreme, a writer like Jonson liked to parade his classical learning with the use of Latin words. The speeches in *The Spanish Tragedy* also incorporate quotes from Latin for ornamentation. Other foreign languages were heard on stage. *Henry V* has much of one scene in French, and Hans the Dutch shoemaker in *The Shoemaker's Holiday* sometimes speaks a nonsensical language, supposedly Dutch, to the audience's puzzlement and delight.

The use of specific discourses or styles of speech enrich the plays and also affect our interpretation of them. Religious language permeates the plays, as we saw in Chapter One, but are these examples of moral sententiousness always sincere and serious? Following this, do we take the pious criticism of magic in *Friar Bacon and Friar Bungay* seriously? And do the homiletic lines in *Doctor Faustus* on the evils of ambition really constitute the play's lesson? Similarly, is the patriotic, even chauvinistic, language of *Henry V* or Heywood's two-part play *If You Know Not Me* (*c.* 1606) meant to be read as sincere or even honest? These are questions to ponder. Writers also experimented with the language of love – sometimes clichéd, sometimes original, and often aware of its own inadequacy in the face of deep emotion. Juliet, for one, is sceptical of her lover's oaths: 'Conceit more rich in matter than in words, / Brags of his substance, not of ornament' (2.6.30–31), she says. Language is unreliable, but it is all that the lovers have at the moment.

Language was the stuff of writing. It is no wonder that writers repeatedly contemplated its power as well its limitations. Some characters will not speak – Coriolanus refuses to put his heroic deeds into words, and at the very end of *The Spanish Tragedy* – that play that is a veritable feast of rhetoric – the protagonist tears his tongue out, signalling the failure of language. On the other hand, although both Hamlet and Hieronimo are surrounded by skilled but insincere rhetoricians such as Claudius and Lorenzo, they seek relief from their pain in words. Simon Eyre of *The Shoemaker's Holiday* too refuses to recognize verbal constraints and adheres to his eccentric style of speech even after becoming Lord Mayor, so claiming authority for himself through language. The speech of female characters – Shakespeare's Katherine in *The Taming of the Shrew*, Webster's Duchess in *The Duchess of Malfi* and Elizabeth Cary's Mariam in *The Tragedy of Mariam*, for example – is viewed with fear and disapproval, but they do make themselves heard. In *The Tempest* Caliban has learned his master's language and uses it to curse, to cry out for freedom and to share his dreams.

Discussion points

1 The excerpt from Puttenham's *The Art of English Poesy* argues for the need for ornamentation in poetic language, while the section from Sidney's *An Apology for Poetry* declares excessive ornamentation as 'vulgar' and unnecessary. Consider a monologue from a play you are reading. Identify the figures of speech, sound effects and other examples of 'ornamentation'. What purpose do they serve? Do they seem excessive or take away from the writing?

2 Pay attention to the movement from verse to prose in a play you are reading. What purpose does each form serve when it is used? Think about how the verse sections would sound if they were in prose and vice versa.

3 Rewrite a passage from a Renaissance play in modern English (you can use any variation or dialect of modern English). What did the exercise tell you about the way language works in Renaissance English drama? As far as you are concerned, is the modern version better than the original or is it lacking in some way?

4 The works of the Roman writer Cicero became a staple of Renaissance humanism. He believed that the tri-fold aim of the orator was to 'teach, please, move'. Select a passage or scene from any play you are studying and consider whether it fulfils all these intentions. Also think about whether it does all three – teach, please and move – equally well.

Part II

9

The Alchemist

Ben Jonson

The earliest recorded performance of *The Alchemist* was in 1610 although it might have premiered earlier. Among the best-known of Renaissance city-comedies, Jonson's play was first published in quarto in 1612 and included in the 1616 folio edition of Ben Jonson's *Works*. It is not possible to identify a single source for the play though *The Alchemist* is obviously indebted to classical drama for its plot structure: the action takes place within twenty-four hours, is set in one single site and revolves around a single story. Jonson makes the pseudoscience of alchemy the means by which three rogues trap gullible citizens. Subtle sets himself up as a skilled alchemist with Face as his assistant and Dol playing whatever female role the situation requires. Using Face's absent master Lovewit's house as their 'laboratory', the tricksters promise to convert whatever metal their victims bring into gold. In reality they simply keep and resell the stuff brought to them. Jonson chooses to make his scene London because 'No clime breeds better matter, for your whore, / Bawd, squire, imposter, many persons more' (Prologue, 7–8). The play is thus a satire on the greed and folly of London citizens that leaves them vulnerable to exploitation.

The rogues are among the most resourceful and lively of the tricksters who inhabit the Renaissance stage. They are artistic in their creativity. Subtle plays the wise alchemist, the 'rare physician' who has 'done / Strange cures with mineral physic' (2.3.230–31). He cons people into believing that he is the unworldly, dedicated man of science. Face is cool, predatory and witty as he moves between being 'Captain Face' and 'Lungs', Subtle's soot-stained assistant. The two men work effectively together even as their relationship is marked by hostility. Face constantly reminds Subtle that the trickery could not be carried out 'if I had not helped thee out' (4.7.94), while Subtle claims that he is the one indispensable to the project.

The scenes where the rogues work with their victims are examples of outstanding comic drama. The tricksters overwhelm and impress the gulls (or foolish victims) as well as the audience with their nonsense. For example, Subtle tells one dupe, in the manner of a physician, 'Sir, against one o'clock, prepare yourself. / Till when you must be fasting; only take / Three drops of vinegar, in, at your nose' (1.3.164–66). The action continues at a dazzling speed and the intrigue gets increasingly complicated as the dupes come in thick and fast. At one point the trio keep at least seven different comic plots running parallel to each other. But they survive crisis after crisis: when Sir Mammon arrives in the middle of Dapper's audience with the 'Fairy Queen', for instance, or when Surly appears in the guise of a Spanish lord and attempts to expose the rogues. As unethical as Subtle and Face are, they enjoy themselves and we too cannot help enjoying their energy, wit and resourcefulness. We laugh at the hilarious scenes they set up: when the poor Dapper is blindfolded and tricked into believing he is being pinched by fairies, when Dol plays Fairy Queen and when she startles Mammon with her rantings as a learned but mad noblewoman.

More than anything, the cheats are experts at reading people and manipulating their temperaments. 'You must have stuff, brought home to you, to work on' (1.3.104), Face tells Subtle. The rogues might claim to work on metal and other material things, but their 'stuff', or raw material, is really people. Subtle spins gold out of human follies. The gulls represent an interesting cross-section of London society and each knock on the door brings in someone different. All the dupes are greedy for wealth, an avarice the rogues can understand and identify with and so exploit. They are also lustful, hypocritical and obviously foolish, driven to believe in what we can see is hocus-pocus. But most interestingly, the gulls are a self-deluded lot, making up for their constrained lives with large fantasies. Dapper is a lawyer's clerk who wants to be a gambler and dashing rake. Face tells him that Subtle has divined that Dapper was 'born with a caul o' your head' (1.2.128). A caul (a membrane that can cover a newborn's head and face) was supposed to predict good luck and Dapper soon does believe that he is specially favoured by none other than the Fairy Queen. He ends up mistaking a whore (Dol) for the Fairy Queen and soon finds himself blindfolded, pinched by 'fairies' and eventually in a privy with gingerbread stuffed in his mouth. But he pathetically and ridiculously clings to his fantasy even in the stench of the privy, crying out, 'For God's sake, when will her Grace be at leisure?' (5.3.64). Drugger's ambitions are humbler; he wishes for good luck as he sets up his tobacco business. But his dreams are elevated by Face and Subtle and he starts dreaming of marrying a wealthy widow. Kastrill, a coarse and rather stupid young man, aspires to be a 'roaring boy', or loud quarrelsome rake about town, and is similarly duped. The two religious men, Ananias and Tribulation, are Anabaptists working for their exiled brethren but come to imagine themselves as temporal lords who will buy the King of France out of his realm and will dislodge Spain from the Indies. Significantly, they will only help those orphans whose parents were of their own sect. Ananias does wonder if alchemy is a 'work of darkness' (3.1.9), but Tribulation justifies it by saying that 'The children of perdition are, oft-times, / Made instruments even of the greatest works' (3.1.15–16). The rogues too convince them that making metal out of gold is not the same as coining money; it is, they say, the legitimate act of 'casting' (3.2.152) – a verbal sleight-of-hand that appears to satisfy.

Sir Epicure Mammon is among the most colourful of the gulls. Mammon is full of himself and appears to be proficient in the language of alchemy. He is self-dramatizing, projecting himself as poet, courtly lover and public benefactor. He first pretends that he will use the money he will make for public welfare ('Funding of colleges, and grammar schools, / Marrying young virgins, building hospitals, / And now, and then, a church' [2.3.50–53]), and comes to believe this image of himself. But for all the poetry and pretension, Mammon is simply greedy. He has claim over the Philosopher's Stone, which will bring him luck and fortune, not because he is morally pure (supposedly a prerequisite for possessing the stone), but simply because 'I buy it. / My venture brings it me' (2.2.100–101). He shamelessly engages in fantasies of unimaginable luxury and sensuality and becomes the embodiment of Renaissance aspiration and desire for wealth and grandeur. Even Mammon's companion Surly, who is sceptical of the alchemists and believes that alchemy is 'Somewhat like tricks o' the cards, to cheat a man, / With charming' (2.3.181–82), is finally gulled. Surly exposes himself to ridicule in his guise as a Spanish gallant and loses the widow because he is, ironically, too honest and gallant with her. As Lovewit tells him, he took all the trouble to dress up as an exotic lover but 'then did nothing. What an oversight, / And want of putting forward, sir, was this!' (5.5.54–55). So Surly is less resourceful and quick than the cheats and is also forced to recognize that people *want* to be deluded, that they prefer fantastic lies to simple and often dull truths.

Alchemy is based on transformation of base metal into gold. The motif of transformation informs the play. Subtle transformed Face: wasn't he the one, he asks, who 'Raised thee from brooms, and dust, and wat'ring-pots? /

Sublimed thee, and exalted thee, and fixed thee / I' the third region, called our state of grace?' (1.1.67–69). In other words, he changed his partner-in-crime from a household drudge into something bigger and grander. Similarly, Subtle was a rag-picker mired in poverty until Face gave him the means to exalt himself to the position of a recognized alchemist. The prostitute is transformed into the Fairy Queen, the city house into a site of magic and a place of hope, and all the gulls, at least temporarily, into the people they dream of being. In spite of the satire, there is something wondrous in this. As Face says, 'this is yet / A kind of modern happiness, to have / Dol Common for a great lady!' (4.1.22–24). Not only are Subtle and Face successful actors, and not only do the gulls play at being the fantasy person of their dreams, Jonson's own real-life theatre too is involved in creating and re-creating worlds. At the very end of the play we are reminded of what the house really looks like with its 'empty walls' and 'A few cracked pots, and glasses' (5.5.39, 40). But, for a while, we too have been taken in by the illusions and transformations wrought by the play.

Few Renaissance plays end in quite the way *The Alchemist* does. Lovewit returns unexpectedly and Face momentarily panics. 'What shall I do? I am catched' (5.3.75), he exclaims, and we do expect that he and his fellow-tricksters are to be 'catched' and punished. But Jonson will not offer us the conventional moral ending. Subtle and Dol lose their ill-gotten gains but escape. Face protests his innocence to his master, claims that nothing suspicious has taken place in the house in Lovewit's absence and gets away scot-free, saved once more by his quick intelligence. Lovewit prefers not to play the stern, punitive master simply because 'I love a teeming wit, as I love my nourishment' (5.1.16). Besides, he too benefits as Face facilitates his marriage to the rich widow. The unusual absence of a moral conclusion might be discomfiting to some readers but is nevertheless convincing. Besides, many of us, like Lovewit, appreciate the artistry of the tricksters and simply enjoy the play's 'feast of laughter' (1.1.166).

Discussion points

1 Chapter Seven ('Genre') describes the increasingly popular genre of 'city comedy'. Read the chapter and identify features of city comedy in *The Alchemist*. What does the play tell us about the risks and the excitements of life in a big city?

2　As we saw in Chapter Seven, comedy was meant to 'instruct' as well as 'delight' and satirical comedy had a reformative impulse. What particular vices does the play seek to reform? How do we reconcile the satirical imperative and our enjoyment of the trickery?

3　Jonson sets *The Alchemist* in the actual time and play of its first staging (London, early seventeenth century). Imagine you are directing *The Alchemist*. Would you set the play in Jonson's London, or would you relocate it to some other time and place? If you do decide to set the play in modern times, what would the setting be and what kind of tricksters would the alchemists of the original play become?

4　When Lovewit's house is claimed by its rightful owner in Act 5 a piece of graffiti is found on the walls: '**MADAM**, with a dildo, writ o' the walls (5.5.66)'. Apart from being the first recorded written mention of 'dildo', the bold lettering is a typographical joke. As we saw in Chapter Six, Jonson saw his plays not only as pieces to be performed but also as works to be read. Find other instances in the play where the writer is aware of the interplay between language in print and spoken language.

5　One editor of *The Alchemist* wonders if there are 'any really "minor" characters in this play? Can a director of it afford to cast any but thoroughly accomplished actors in any of the roles?'[1] Imagine you are casting director for a TV or film production of *The Alchemist* and are required to assemble a cast of outstanding comic actors. Think about which actor you would cast in each of the roles the play offers. Explain why the role is particularly suited to this actor and what he or she would bring to it.

10

Arden of Faversham

Arden of Faversham has long been considered a play written by an author or authors unknown. Quite recently, however, some scholars have made the case that Shakespeare is wholly or largely responsible for its central scenes.[1] The play was performed for the first time *c.* 1591 and printed in quarto form in 1592. It is an example of the genre of 'domestic tragedy'. *Arden of Faversham* is based on a real-life incident recorded in the second edition of Ralph Holinshed's *Chronicles of England, Scotland, and Ireland* (1587). On 15 February 1551, Thomas Arden, mayor of the small market town of Faversham in Kent and the town's largest landowner, was murdered by his wife, her lover, two neighbours and two hired killers. The domestic crime appealed to a sensation-craving audience and had already been the subject of numerous pamphlets before the play was written. The private nature of the event and the sheer ordinariness of Arden's world that was the setting for the killing was a reminder of the darkness lurking in the corners of family life and the fact that the home too could be the centre of conflict; even the seemingly ordinary could indeed be quite extraordinary. The play itself does not have a place in the canon of Renaissance literature but is of interest to modern readers as the earliest 'crime story' in English drama and as an example of drama based on domestic and anecdotal history. It also raises interesting questions regarding gender relations in the domestic sphere.

Tragic drama usually dealt with the fall of the high-born. However 'domestic plays', specifically 'domestic tragedies' featuring middle-class and working-class households made their appearance on the popular stage by the late sixteenth century. Obviously, dramatists were beginning to recognize the tragic potential of these worlds. The tragedies in question often dealt with crime of a titillating nature. They played up the sensational angle, sometimes added a dash of conventional morality and were usually commercially successful. The fact that a second edition of Arden was printed in 1599, just a few years after the first one, attests to the popularity of the play, or at least of the print version.

Even as the Protestant idea of companionate marriage suggested something approaching 'equality' between husband and wife, the home was also visualized as a commonwealth with the man as head. In this structure the female was to be the loyal, loving and obedient subject whose identity was legally subsumed in her husband's. However, the period between 1560 and 1640 saw more and more prosecutions of adultery, fornication, bigamy and violence. The home became the site of complicated change and conflict. Arden's complaint, 'My house is irksome; there I cannot rest' (4.27) is a worrying disruption of the idea that the every man's home is his castle and safe haven.[2]

Arden's 'rest' is disrupted by the illicit longings of his wife Alice and her lover, Mosby. The crime is rendered all the more chilling because of the intimacy between the perpetrators and victim. In reality women and servants were more likely to be victims rather than perpetrators of violent crime, including murder, but the idea of the female killer was more sensational and there were consequently far more popular representations of murders of men by women. The fascination that female violence held for the Renaissance audience was a result of a conflicting attitude to femininity: on the one hand, the ideal feminine nature was supposed to be gentle and averse to bloodshed, but on the other hand, women were believed to be weaker both intellectually and morally and therefore more likely to succumb to their impulses. As Franklin tells Arden, 'it is not strange / That women will be false and wavering' (1.20–21). Alice is married to a good, kind and wealthy man but is most unreasonably besotted with the young Mosby and will do anything, including commit murder, to be with him. The adultery theme enables the dramatist to bring together the intensity of love and sexual desire with questions of morality and social judgement.

While sexual fidelity and chastity were considered the foundations of feminine virtue, women were also considered to be more prone to illicit sexual longings. Male adultery never invited the condemnation that female adultery did. Alice is simultaneously weak-willed, strong-headed and chillingly scheming. Arden is a shrewd and successful businessman who is still 'cuckolded' by his wife. While cuckold jokes depicting the unfortunate husband as weak and unmanly were popular in the period, *Arden* treats the unfortunate mayor of Faversham more sympathetically – he is the innocent man who is marked for an undeserving death.

Alice's adulterous longings become even more problematic because she is in love with the lower-class Mosby. Mosby, says Arden, is a social climber who became steward of a nobleman's house 'by his servile flattering and fawning' (1.28), as opposed to Arden himself who is 'by birth a gentleman of blood' (1.35). Mosby's social aspirations prove to be worse than vulgar – they are dangerous. Class tensions also complicate the relationships between Alice and her lover. They quarrel bitterly at one point in the play and Alice wonders if 'Mosby loves me not but for my wealth . . .' (8.108). She also asserts her social status whenever she is angry with her lover. Arden is a loyal husband, but at least some of his money comes from exploiting men poorer than himself – an aspect of his personality not highlighted in the source material. As Greene, who feels wronged by Arden, says of the latter: 'Desire of wealth is endless in his mind, / And he is greedy-gaping still for gain' (1.474–75). The language of desire for money and sexual and emotional desire constantly intersect with and complicate each other in the play. Class informs almost every relationship. Even the murderers, who are vagrants and displaced men, are driven both by greed and by visions of the relatively high-born Alice curtseying before them in gratitude.

The English domestic play is often criticized for being an aesthetically inferior genre. *Arden* too lacks the finished form and the stirring speeches of the more canonical plays of its time. The epilogue is self-conscious and even somewhat apologetic about 'this naked tragedy' which lacks fine rhetorical figures 'To make it gracious to the ear or eye'. But it closes on a note of something approaching defiance – it deals with truth and 'simple truth is gracious enough, / And needs no other points of glozing stuff' (Epilogue, 14–18). Apart from its claim to represent the 'truth', the play does have some artistic merit that is perhaps easily overlooked. Eschewing the Senecan five-act structure, *Arden* is made up a series of scenes of varying length. The plot is arranged chronologically and ends with the murder of Arden followed swiftly by the detection and arrest of the killers. The audience knows right from the start that Arden will die. In spite of this foregone conclusion, the play has to retain audience interest and create suspense. The focus is not so much on whether Arden dies as on when and how he does. The bulk of the play enacts the hired killers engaging in attempt after attempt to kill Arden and failing to do so. This action is doubtless childish, awkward, ridiculous and even comic (so making this murder story generically confusing – after all crime and comedy rarely mix), but it is also clever. We are appalled by the thought of Arden's death but also, because we know it has to happen, we find ourselves waiting for it. 'Zounds, I was ne'er so toiled in all my life / in following so slight a task as this', protests Shakebag, one of the hired assassins (12.48–49). We find ourselves similarly frustrated and the postponement of the murder complicates our reaction – much as we sympathize with Arden, after a point we are almost waiting for him to be killed.

Alice is the dramatic centre of the play. Desire and violence converge in her in terrible yet fascinating ways. She resists the role of wife and the sanctity of marriage. She is interesting in her restlessness and dissatisfaction with the constraints of the domestic life, somewhat pathetic in her intense, even foolish love for Mosby and chilling in her brutality. Even Mosby is not quite sure of her. "'Tis fearful sleeping in a serpent's bed', he says (8.42). She uses the language of acquisitive desire and resoluteness ('Nay, Mosby, let me still enjoy thy love, / And happen what will, I am resolute'), which is the language usually associated with men (1.218–19). She revolts against the idea of female submission in marriage and asserts her need for self-determination and agency – what right does Arden have to 'govern me that am to rule myself?' she asks (10.84). Alice is admirable in many ways – and yet she is a killer. *Arden*, like other popular texts on domestic crime, does not quite know how to deal with and depict female agency and resorts to linking it either to seductive sexuality or violence. Alice is arrested and executed at the end. Whatever limited freedom she enjoys (and the morally problematic manner in which she exercises it) comes to an end. But the play, unlike homilies and other moralistic texts, does give women like her a face and personality and makes some attempt, however crude, to explore her desires and her motives for the crime. Part of the challenge posed by *Arden* is passing moral judgement on Alice even as we get to know her and understand her. This is what makes the play more than an instruction piece on the evils of adultery and perhaps something more than a piece of sensationalist theatre.

Discussion points

1 Does *Arden of Faversham* with its lurid depiction of a domestic situation and a domestic crime remind you of any modern popular text? Consider a variety of texts including novels, films, TV shows and newspaper features. What generic and thematic continuities do you see between these texts and *Arden*?

2 Read the historical documents in Chapter Two ('Men and Women') alongside *Arden of Faversham*. Consider the points of intersection you detect between the play and the historical documents.

3 Several twentieth-century productions of *Arden*, including Buzz Goldbody's 1970 production and Terry Hands's 1982 one, had star-

actresses at their centre (Dorothy Tutin in the 1970 staging and Jenny Agutter in the 1982 one). Consider why the role of Alice would be a challenging and exciting one for any actress. Think about the multiple personalities Alice puts on and the many roles she plays. Also, think about the moments where Alice is especially assertive and bold (for instance, where she asserts that 'Love is a god, and marriage is but words ...' and Scene 10 where she declares that her husband has no right to 'govern me that am to rule myself ...'). What are the possibilities for the actress in these moments? How would she play these scenes and how would she work on audience support and sympathy?

4 The title page of the 1592 quarto of *Arden*, 'The Lamentable and True Tragedy of M. Arden of Faversham in Kent' describes Alice as 'his most disloyal and wanton wife' and also claims to show 'the great malice and wicked dissimulation of a wicked woman, the unsatiable desire of filthy lust and the shameful end of all murderers'. How does this title page market the book to the potential buyer and how does it direct a reader's response to the play? Questions to consider include: Why the need to insist that the tragedy is based on 'true' events? Is the representation of Alice in the title simplified in comparison to the play itself? Does the evident desire to play up the sensational element sit well with the moralistic declaration?

5 *Arden of Faversham* has not been part of the canon of English literature. Based on your reading of the play and your understanding of how and why certain works are included in the literary canon, why do you think this has been the case? How would you make a case for including *Arden* in a high-school or college course that focuses on Renaissance drama?

11

Doctor Faustus

Christopher Marlowe

Christopher Marlowe's *Doctor Faustus* (first recorded performance 1594) is among the best-known of Renaissance tragedies. This story of a man who sells his soul to the Devil in order to gain knowledge of magic has been read as a morality fable, as the last piece of Christian drama and as a humanist narrative.

The Prologue tells us that Faustus was born into a family of commoners but went on to attend the University of Wittenberg where he excelled as a scholar until he was seized by the ambition to be an all-powerful magician. Written in Marlowe's characteristic grand, even grandiose, style, the play conveys the seductive power of forbidden knowledge. Faustus is 'ravished' by magic and only too aware of the wonders of the 'world of profit and delight, / Of power, of honour, of omnipotence, / . . . promised to the studious artisan!' (1.53–55). Like many of Marlowe's other heroes, Faustus is an 'over-reacher', an aspiring individual whose life is marked by desire: for the unknown, for perfection and for the status of the divine. He is irked by the limits imposed on him, by the fact that he is 'still but Faustus, and a man' (1.23) and is determined to transcend them. From this perspective the play can be read as an illustration of Renaissance humanist philosophy that propounded the semi-divine nature of man and his longings, and as a successful portrayal of the pain and pleasure, struggles and delights of human ambition. The play also captures the restlessness and acquisitive energy of the age itself. Faustus, like the European explorers and world-travellers of the day, dreams of the gold of America being placed at his disposal and of other nations bowing before him just 'As Indian moors obey their Spanish lords' (1.121).

But Marlowe tempers this mood by introducing elements of the medieval morality play into *Doctor Faustus*. Morality drama was a type of vernacular drama produced in the late Middle Ages that was often allegorical (the characters represented moral qualities or abstractions such as Vice, Death or Youth, for example) and that taught moral lessons. Indeed, the play has been considered the last of the morality plays – an example of didactic Renaissance Christian drama dealing with Christian themes of temptation and penitence. The prologue mentions the 'cunning' and self-conceit' (Prologue, 20) that ultimately destroy Faustus and the play ends with the moral lesson that it is best to abstain from doing 'more than heavenly power permits' (13.119). Scenes where Faustus is torn between his own desires and his fear of Heaven and the Good and Evil Angel scenes (where the forces of good and evil both attempt to win Faustus over) are characteristic of morality drama, while the anti-Catholic elements in the play (such as Faustus playing tricks on the Pope and his Cardinals) place it in the context of the Reformation.

This unusual but powerful combination of humanist and morality drama makes *Doctor Faustus* among the most complex of Renaissance plays. Is Faustus heroic in his thirst for knowledge and power, or is he sinful? Do we admire his grit and determination, or do we condemn him for being over-ambitious? Or do we simply sympathize with him for being short-sighted and foolish? Do we censure him, or do we feel his despair and terror as his end draws near and he cries out pleading for 'some end to my incessant pain:' (13.89)? Besides, the play is deliberately spectacular and theatrical. Faustus conjures on stage; he stabs his arm in order to use his blood to sign his pact with the Devil, but in a particularly dramatic moment the blood congeals and he cannot write until Mephastophilis, the Devil's agent, brings fire to make it flow. Notably, Lucifer himself appears before Faustus in order to win him over completely and is greeted with shock and awe as Faustus asks, 'O who art thou that look'st so terrible?' (7.83) – a scene that clearly had an impact on actors and audience alike. More than one report mentions the Devil joining the cast of actors during stagings; the anti-theatricalist William Prynne wrote about

> the visible apparition of the Devill on the stage at the Belsavage playhouse in Queen Elizabeth's days (to the great amazement of both the actors and spectators) while they were prophanely playing the History of Faustus, the truth of which I have heard from many now alive, who well remember it, there being some there distracted with that fearful sight.'[1]

These bold, spectacular scenes have an odd effect. They drive home the fact that Faustus is doing something truly horrific, but by dramatizing Faustus's acts of defiance, the play also renders them impressive and glamorous. In a way, those readers and spectators who enjoy these spectacles of wrongdoing are also implicated in sin. The forces of good and evil that battle over Faustus's soul are certainly reminiscent of morality drama, but they are quite complicated. The Good and Evil Angels are not necessarily spirits outside of Faustus. In at least one version of the play (the 'A Text') they appear to be aspects of Faustus himself, manifestations of his inner psychological conflict. Faustus's relationship with Mephastophilis is particularly fascinating. Mephastophilis's mission is to make Faustus give himself up to the Devil, but it is Faustus who first calls up Mephastophilis of his own free will and asserts himself over the spirit, so raising the question of who has power over whom. Faustus also chooses damnation on his own, quite uninfluenced by Mephastophilis. Indeed, Mephastophilis is something of a tormented soul who even regrets the fact that he is damned. 'Think'st thou that I, who saw the face of God, / And tasted the eternal joys of heaven, / Am not tormented with ten thousand hells / In being deprived of everlasting bliss?', he asks (3.77–80). It is Faustus who urges him to stop thinking about God and Heaven. Later, Mephastophilis paints such a horrifying picture of hell and such a poignant picture of his own damnation that it seems like he is playing good angel rather than evil spirit. Faustus is unmoved by this, however, and actually seems to be annoyed by Mephastophilis's conventional thinking on Hell and Heaven, salvation and damnation. In any case, Mephastophilis is always by Faustus's side and Faustus clings to him as he becomes increasingly isolated from human community. When Faustus is finally dragged off by devils, he cries out for his only companion: 'ah, Mephastophilis!' (13.111).

In contrast to Mephastophilis, the 'good' forces in the play seem to be rather lacklustre and uninteresting. They are largely presented by the Good Angel and by an 'Old Man' who make brief appearances on stage, speak in somewhat clichéd terms on the 'vile and loathsome filthiness' (12.40) of Faustus's actions (in contrast to Mephastophilis's rich, textured language), make what seems like half-hearted attempts to win Faustus over and then leave. God is mentioned quite often but remains a distant figure, unknown and unknowable at best and spiteful and punitive at worst, perhaps indicating that Marlowe was sceptical about all religion and religious belief, viewing traditional religion as based in power struggle and as indifferent to human well-being or fulfilment. The brief and ineffective appearances of the forces of good also raises the question of whether God fights hard enough for Faustus's soul or gives him up too easily. This has led to the conclusion that though Faustus appears to take those fatal decisions that lead to his destruction, his fate is in fact predestined and he will be damned irrespective of his will. This idea that both salvation and damnation was 'predestined' or decided on even before one's birth was one propounded by the French Reformer Jean Calvin. The language of the play occasionally suggests Calvinistic ideas: the Prologue tells us that the heavens 'conspired his [Faustus's] overthrow' (Prologue, 22) and later, when Faustus wonders if God will forgive him if he repents, the Evil Angel replies, 'Ay, but Faustus never shall repent' (7.17). Though this reading has its merits, Faustus is too interesting and complex a figure and too much attention is paid in the narrative to the workings of his mind to suggest that he is simply enacting his pre-set destiny.

Like many plays, this one mingles the tragic and comic modes. The intense and weighty story of Faustus is interspersed with scenes of slapstick humour involving the servants Wagner, Rafe and Robin. Wagner and Robin also (having got hold of Faustus's book) engage in some basic magic of their own to trick others. These actions deliberately parody Faustus's own and imply that Faustus's desires and ambitions are ultimately somewhat ridiculous, so complicating the humanistic celebration of human yearning. Indeed, Faustus who dreams of knowing and conquering heaven and earth in the first few acts degenerates into becoming a mere trickster and conjurer in the latter half of the play, making one wonder if his decision to sell out to the Devil was worth anything after all.

Doctor Faustus is also interesting for quite another reason. The first version printed in 1604 is now known to scholars as the 'A-text' and might have been printed from Marlowe's own drafts. A second edition that appeared in 1616 and now known as the 'B-text' is about 676 lines longer. The additions might have been made by other playwrights after Marlowe's death and a comparative study of the two texts draws attention to the differences between the text as the author might have imagined it and the text as it circulated in the theatre. The B text has more comic scenes and also externalizes the conflict that is mostly psychological in the A text. Faustus largely makes his own moral choices in the A text and is less influenced by Mephastophilis than in the B text.

In both versions, however, the final scene is dramatic as we witness Faustus filled with terror and regret. His language is original and vivid, filled with rich imagery of Christ's blood streaming in the firmament, the 'ireful brows' of God (13.73) and the vast cosmic landscape that will not shelter him. He might be dragged off to hell, but Faustus remains a powerful presence in readers' and spectators' imaginations.

Discussion points

1   Christopher Marlowe is one of the best known dramatists of the period. He is also remembered as being an unconventional man for his time: he won a reputation for atheism (which could have simply implied unconventional religious opinion rather than a disbelief in God), was alleged to have denied the divinity of Christ, indulged in blasphemy and certainly got into trouble with the authorities for violent behavior. Do any of these elements help you better understand *Doctor Faustus*? As you consider this question also think about the strengths and limits of reading a play in light of its author's biography.

2   *Oration on the Dignity of Man* by Pico della Mirandola is often considered a manifesto of Renaissance humanism. It has been reproduced in Chapter Four ('Humanism'). Are any of the ideas put forward by Mirandola on human choice and human dignity and on the freedom given to man to create his own boundaries and limits reflected in *Doctor Faustus*?

3   The discussion above described the forces of good in the play (the Good Angel and the Old Man) as rather dull and lacklustre. Imagine you are directing *Doctor Faustus*. What could you do to render the Good Angel and the Old Man as vivid, original and exciting as the figures of evil in the play?

4   Read Chapter Six of this book ('Books, Authors and Readers') and also consider the fact that there are two versions of *Doctor Faustus* available today. Even though the editor W. W. Greg presented both versions of the play in his 1950 edition, he privileged the 1616 B text because he felt it was closer to the 'original'. Greg's argument is based on aesthetic terms: the B text, he says, is more coherent, with a more 'orderly succession of scenes', while the A text is a jumble of 'merely disjointed episodes' and 'the mutilated remains' of a true original.[2] More recently, Leah Marcus points out that such editorial judgements are relative, i.e. they are based on 'our own tastes and assumptions'.[3] She argues that editors (and subsequently readers) should not focus on identifying the best version or the original one but on recognizing that different versions of a text are produced under different circumstances and therefore equally interesting. Consider the following questions on editorial choices:

   i.   Do you agree with the modern practice of producing parallel editions where both versions of the play are placed alongside each other? Would you pay attention to both versions or would the presentation of two texts be too distracting and bothersome? What do you think you would get out of reading both versions of the play?

ii. What would a reader gain from refraining from making judgements on which is the 'better' version and instead just focusing on the differences between the two texts, as Marcus urges us to?

iii. Look at the two versions of the Old Man's appeal to Faustus as it appears in both versions of the play (Text A 1302–13, Text B 1813–29). Is the tone any different? Is sin portrayed any differently? Does Faustus have a chance to save his soul?

5 How does a play concerned with the sale of a man's soul to the Devil in exchange for knowledge speak to twenty-first-century concerns? Can you imagine a version of the play that would seem relevant and interesting even to audiences who might not necessarily subscribe to the Christian ideas (notably salvation and damnation) that are so essential to *Doctor Faustus*?

12

The Duchess of Malfi

John Webster

John Webster's *The Duchess of Malfi* (first recorded performance *c.* 1613) is based on the real-life story of a young widowed Italian duchess, Giovanna d'Aragana, who had married her chief steward but kept the marriage secret knowing that it would anger her two brothers. However, the marriage was discovered, after which she was killed, her husband banished and then subsequently assassinated. The Duchess's story is first told in an Italian novella, the four-volume *Novelle* (1554–73) by Bandello, and probably reached Webster via William Painter's *The Second Tome of the Palace of Pleasure* (1567), which is an English adaptation of the French retelling of the story by François de Belleforrest.

The Duchess of Malfi is a court story. The action is set in the ducal court; the main characters are aristocrats and those in their service, and the politics and power-play of the court move the plot along. The court is not only a glamorous and seductive space, but is also a degenerate and corrupt one. The play begins with Antonio (the Duchess's steward and now her lover) saying that a court filled with sycophants and people of ill-repute would inevitably result in 'Death, and diseases through the whole land' (1.1.15). These lines echo the Elizabethan humanist Sir Thomas Elyot's *Image of Governance* (1541) that urged for a corruption-free court. They also connect the ducal context of the play to King James's English court, which was notorious for its flatterers and undeserving hangers-on. Not for the first time a foreign, specifically Italian, setting allowed the writer to comment on affairs in England. The Duchess's brothers, the Cardinal and Ferdinand (who will inherit the family title), embody power at its worst. They are calculating, corrupt and surround themselves with 'flatt'ring panders' that feed on them 'like a horse-leech' (1.1.51–52). Both men are masterfully drawn villains. The

Cardinal is a dark, melancholy figure and a dangerous enemy who will ruthlessly destroy those opposed to his will. Ferdinand is a suave but psychotic and frightening personality.

What is most memorable about *Duchess* is Webster's choice of a female protagonist. She is beautiful, wealthy and powerful, the 'great master of her household' (1.1.87), a woman who speaks with force and dignity. The Duchess's role marks the play's departure from the traditional 'great man' model of tragedy which depicts the hero's 'fatal flaw' and his subsequent fall. Instead, *Duchess* examines an unjust social system and how an individual's life is shaped by her social roles – determined by gender and class in this case – and how these can be the source of strength and self-esteem, even as they can render her a victim. The Duchess's downfall is thus caused by neither fate nor her own flaw but is a consequence of defective social structures, specifically the excesses of patriarchal power.

Early in the play the two brothers forcefully warn their sister not to marry. A widow who remarries, they say, is weak and 'whorish' and invites disaster and exploitation. The issue of whether widows should remarry had become a matter of public debate at the time and the criticism of remarrying widows was couched in the language of female depravity and sensuality. In drama widows were usually depicted either as 'merry widows' – bawdy, comic stereotypes – or as unreal, idealized figures. The Duchess distances herself from both types. She is no 'whore', as her brothers imply she is, nor is she as saint-like as Antonio describes her. 'This is flesh, and blood, sir,' she reminds her lover, ''Tis not the figure cut in alabaster / Kneels at my husband's tomb' (1.1.443–45). She boldly defies her brothers by deciding to marry and to marry the man of her choice; she appropriates the rhetoric of male heroism by comparing herself to 'men in some great battles,' who 'By apprehending danger, have achieved / Almost impossible actions' (1.1.335–36); she also disregards tradition by taking the initiative with Antonio and proposing marriage to him. The complexity of the play emerges from changing social structures and the transformation in identities and roles that accompanied it. So the Duchess is high-born and proud of it, but she does not hesitate to marry her steward. She is a public figure, but also is an individual with private needs. Her maid Cariola implies that the 'spirit of greatness' is antithetical to that of 'woman' and that the Duchess should choose between them (1.1.492). The Duchess is thus trapped between contradictory roles and competing ideas regarding appropriate feminine behaviour. Overall, she is a fitting tragic heroine because she fully embodies human possibility and the strength of the human spirit even as she undergoes loss and suffering. We pity her, fear for her and also admire her.

When her brothers discover the Duchess's secret marriage they are furious. The Duchess is puzzled by their reaction but also brave and calm. 'Why might not I marry?' she asks in that memorable scene, 'I have not gone about in this to create / Any new world or custom' (3.2.109–11). She reminds Ferdinand, in lines that are both bold and poignant, that there is no need that she 'Be cased up, like a holy relic' and that she still has 'youth, / And a little beauty' (3.2.138–40). However, Antonio is banished and the Duchess becomes her brothers' prisoner. Ferdinand stages a number of horrific scenes to frighten her: he presents her a hand that is supposedly that of the dead Antonio, displays dead bodies (which he falsely represents as Antonio's and the children's) and stages a grotesque procession of madmen before her. When Ferdinand finally has her strangled, she dies with grace and courage. As she says: 'Necessity makes me suffer constantly, / And custom makes it easy' (4.2.29–30). Although the line 'I am Duchess of Malfi still' (4.2.130), uttered by her at her most vulnerable moment, might seem ironic and pathetic in the face of her powerlessness, it is also an assertion of self. The Duchess dies without delivering the long, heightened speech one expects of tragic heroes and the last one sees of her is a sad, tired woman who is also graceful and dignified. Even Ferdinand, in a moment of penitence or of fear says, as he views her corpse, 'Cover her face. Mine eyes dazzle. She died young' (4.2.250).

The brothers' agent the courtier Bosola is another memorable character. He is supremely cynical, and in a role that is almost chorus-like, comments on and criticizes the degenerate and corrupt practices at court and condemns the Duchess's brothers in particular. Yet he is their henchman, one of the 'flattering panders' he so despises. Moved by his desire for wealth and status and unable to visualize an alternative structure free of exploitative hierarchy and corruption, he knows that 'I must do / All the ill man can invent!' (1.1.265–66). He carries out the Cardinal's and Ferdinand's plans yet is powerless, simply doing what is asked of him. Towards the end of the play he sympathizes with and admires the Duchess and even proclaims that he will save her life. While he does attempt to convince Ferdinand from going ahead with his savage plan ('Faith, end here: / And go no farther to your cruelty' [4.1.113–14]), he does help to execute Ferdinand's orders to have the Duchess killed. After this murder, Bosola realizes that Ferdinand does not intend to reward him for committing the bloody deed or even to support him. He is filled with regret for his wrongdoing and is furious with Ferdinand and the Cardinal. In fact, the Bosola of Act Five, caught between fear for his own life and the desire to do good, enacts the only ethical conflict in the play. In an action-packed ending he attempts to save Antonio but mistakenly kills him instead. He also murders the Cardinal and Ferdinand (who has now turned mad) before meeting his own death suddenly and haphazardly, filled with a sense of despair and hopelessness, the feeling that humans 'are only like dead walls, or vaulted graves, / That ruined, yields no echo' (5.5.96–97)

This sense of unrelieved darkness and unrelenting sorrow pervades *Duchess*. The villainous figures, menacing and almost deranged in their savagery, are almost as impressive as the more sympathetic characters. The play is filled with macabre scenes such as the severed limb scene and the procession of madmen, which add to the sense of a world that is horrific and irrational. It also includes powerfully written scenes such as the one where Antonio hears the echoes, 'so hollow, and so dismal' (5.3.6), from the Duchess's grave – scenes which add to the atmosphere of haunting sadness. But in spite of this sense of all-pervading despair, *Duchess* does not lack a moral vision. The play highlights the injustices of a society where women lack agency. The Duchess herself defies and then courageously endures, and Bosola repents and attempts to right the wrongs he has committed, though too late. Indeed, suffering seems to bring out the best in humans and the play offers some qualified hope in human integrity and human strength.

Discussion points

1 *The Duchess of Malfi* is one of the few Renaissance tragedies with a female protagonist. To what extent does the Duchess conform to the image of the traditional tragic hero?
2 Is there any character in the play who can be considered the male lead?
3 Aristotle argues that the plot of a tragedy is very important to convey the tragic effect. See Chapter Seven ('Genre') as well as the extract from Aristotle reproduced in that chapter, and identify the key elements of the tragic plot in *The Duchess of Malfi*. Especially try to identify the climax of the play and also consider whether the act that follows the protagonist's death really functions as the denouement or resolution to the tragic plot.
4 Consider the section 'Sex, sexuality, marriage' in Chapter Two ('Men and Women'). How does the discussion on courtship, marriage, motherhood and the status of widows alter your understanding of this play? What does this play convey about these issues that the historical information and the historical documents do not?

5   The Modernist poet T.S. Eliot wrote that 'Webster was much possessed by death / And saw the skull beneath the skin . . .'.[1] This sense of the macabre and the grotesque has informed many productions of the play. The Scottish director Philip Prowse's productions of the play in the 1970s and 1980s were inspired by Eliot's lines and depicted the figure of Death looming large over the stage; Peter Hinton's punk/goth interpretation staged in Ontario, Canada in 2006 had the actors swathed in black. These productions in the baroque tradition have been received well by some critics but seen as excessively melodramatic by others. Can you imagine a production of the play that tones down the grotesque and is perhaps more 'realistic' as a result? What would happen to scenes like the dance of the madmen scene, the hand scene and the dead body scenes in such a production? What do you think would be the intended effect of such a staging?

13

Hamlet

William Shakespeare

Hamlet, among the best-known of Renaissance plays, is dated between 1599 and 1602. This most monumental of Western literary works actually exists in three different forms: the first quarto (Q1) of 1603 (which was earlier regarded as a rough draft of the play though many scholars now maintain that it was the version staged by Shakespeare's playing company), the second quarto (Q2) printed in 1604 (which is the longest of the three versions and claims to be 'the true and perfect Coppie' on its title page) and the folio text of 1623, prepared by Shakespeare's fellow actors John Heminge and Henry Condell. Many editors use Q2 with supplements from other versions when preparing modern editions, but Q1, which is significantly shorter, does offer different interpretative possibilities, as we will see.

Hamlet might have been based on a now-lost play called the *Ur-Hamlet*, which we know was a tragedy figuring a ghost who cried 'Hamlet, revenge!' and which was played on the London stage. But the precursor to *Hamlet* that is still available to us today is Thomas Kyd's *The Spanish Tragedy* (see pages 271–76 for a discussion of this play and Chapter Seven for a discussion of revenge tragedy). In both plays a ghost initiates the action, and the protagonist is called upon to take revenge. In the course of the narrative, the protagonist contemplates suicide and either feigns madness or perhaps actually turns mad as the play progresses. Hamlet obsessively remembers the wrong done to his father (who, so Hamlet learns, has been killed by Claudius, Hamlet's uncle); indeed, the act of revenge is possible only if he keeps the memory of the crime in his mind, 'unmixed with baser matter' (1.5.104). As in Kyd's play and other revenge tragedies, Hamlet stages a play to fully identify the murderers.

However, despite a clear invocation of the conventions of revenge tragedy, Shakespeare takes up this more-or-less formulaic genre and rewrites it. In earlier revenge tragedies (including Shakespeare's *Titus Andronicus*) the charge to take revenge is carried out, immediately setting off a chain of murders. Hamlet, however, is an introspective individual who is unable to play the role of the avenging son in the manner expected of the hero of revenge tragedy. Even though the play does not explicitly condemn revenge, by delaying the act it explores the ethics of retribution. Hamlet has no legal recourse (after all, Claudius is the king) and revenge is the only way to right the wrong done to the senior Hamlet. Besides, revenge certainly offers gratification of a kind. However, it can turn the man who was at first the sympathetic victim of a crime into a bloodthirsty villain. One sees this in Laertes who turns from a decent young man into someone who agrees to Claudius's base conspiracies against Hamlet. In short, vengeance blurs the distinction between 'good' and 'evil' deeds. It is also not clear if bloody revenge truly constitutes justice. Rather than speculate on why Hamlet does not act (as much of early criticism was inclined to do), it is more useful to think of the play as raising questions about what constitutes properly informed action, making it an unusually self-reflective revenge tragedy.

The problem with a protagonist who does not act is that there is very little action. What Shakespeare does to fill the gap is to give us a literary representation of his hero's thoughts, feelings and circumstances. Indeed, *Hamlet* has been read as marking a major shift in literature because it is the first work to explore 'interiority', the landscape of the protagonist's mind. Hamlet is interesting because he is tremendously self-conscious, equipped (or burdened, depending on how one sees it) with a full awareness of an inner self that he subjects to exploration and analysis, that he does not always fully understand and that he cannot (or will not) fully communicate to others. The play's famous soliloquies do the work of creating a full and complex literary subjectivity. As Hamlet mourns his father and bitterly condemns himself, when he wonders whether 'To be, or not be' (3.1.56), he uncovers a self that has escaped the scrutiny of the gawking crowds in the royal court and the watchful eyes that are constantly spying on him on the orders of Claudius. But the soliloquies are not just pure self-revelation: they are also a way for Hamlet to understand his inner self and bring that self into being through constant self-examination and self-questioning. Besides, the soliloquies are not always transparent and easy to interpret, indicating that the self presented here is puzzling and complicated. As Hamlet tells his mother, 'I have that within which passes show, / These but the trappings and the suits of woe' (1.2.85–86). Hamlet also despises himself for relying so heavily on language, on being 'like a whore' who does not know what else to do but 'unpack my heart with words / And fall a-cursing like a very drab' (2.2.587–88). But words remains important to Hamlet. Indeed, at the end he requests Horatio to narrate his story, to put what might be the inexpressible pain he has felt into words, to 'Report me and my cause aright / To the unsatisfied' (5.2.346–47).

Hamlet decides to pretend to be mad, to put on an 'antic disposition' (1.5.180). This is a way of diverting attention from his mission to kill the king; it is also a way of hiding his inner self from the public gaze. Hamlet's madness is sometimes playful: it allows him to engage in dark but clever wordplay that either irks or bewilders others in the play. His madness is a puzzle – Polonius interprets it as love-sickness, even as Claudius maintains that it is a 'turbulent and dangerous lunacy' (3.1.4) that is deliberate and directed. While madness is a ruse and disguise early on in the play, as the action proceeds Hamlet might actually go mad, or at least turn into a full-fledged neurotic. Interestingly, because madness was specifically linked to women, Hamlet's association with it, along with his inability to take revenge, renders him fragile and 'effeminate'.

The character who does turn truly mad is Ophelia. She might have been Hamlet's beloved, but she very quickly becomes the hapless witness of his transformation and the victim of the fury he feels against his mother and by extension all women. Although she displays something of an independent spirit when she first appears on stage, she soon becomes an instrument of her father and Claudius. Hamlet's madness is feigned, and even if it is genuine he remains an autonomous individual, fully capable of introspection and coherent speech. In effect, he remains the tragic hero. Ophelia's madness has been read in opposing ways. It has been argued that unlike Hamlet, she simply descends into turbulence and incoherence and that her madness is a sign of and result of her oppression and exploitation and her lack of independent identity. On the other hand, it is significant that the mad Ophelia holds centre-stage, albeit temporarily, singing bawdy songs with a certain licence that was not granted to her earlier. Whatever the case, Ophelia does die at the end. Her death is an accidental one, we are told, and she is described as an ethereal nymph floating down the river – a description that renders her death simultaneously beautiful and pathetic rather than grandly tragic.

Hamlet is also a play about acting. Claudius is a hypocrite and liar to whom deception comes easily. Hamlet too quite successfully plays madness, but he struggles to play the traditional role of avenger. That is why he envies the actors – their personalities are versatile and flexible; they immerse themselves in their roles and work themselves into a passion for a mere fiction. Ultimately, Hamlet turns to drama to 'catch the conscience of the king' (2.2.607). The player scenes tell us something about the Renaissance stage – the fact that players probably still travelled into the countryside and that the rivalry between adult and boys' companies was an ongoing one. They also emphasize the importance of drama. Hamlet insists that the players are 'the abstract and brief chronicles of the time' (2.2.525). Drama imitates life and also affects and shapes human behaviour and action. That is why Claudius reacts so passionately to 'The Mousetrap' and discloses himself to Hamlet.

Even as Hamlet appears to be moved into action in the play's final act, he also realizes that 'There's a divinity that shapes our ends / Rough-hew them how we will' (5.2.10–11). Action and its consequences are determined by a higher power; all he can do as a human is attain a state of preparedness. 'The readiness is all' (5.2.221), he states; this state of 'readiness' is itself a form of action. The final scene is a mess of accidents and mistakes which kill Gertrude, Laertes and finally Hamlet. The killing of Claudius by Hamlet is unpremeditated, an outraged, unthinking response rather than a carefully planned and well-executed act of revenge. Of course, Hamlet too dies. 'The rest is silence' (5.2.364), says the hero whose voice has dominated the play. He requests that Horatio live on to tell his tale. Horatio claims that he can 'Truly deliver' (5.2.393) Hamlet's story, but the little synopsis he provides us of 'carnal, bloody, and unnatural acts' (5.2.387) reads more like a conventional revenge narrative. It fails to capture the turmoil and suffering of Hamlet's life and death or the full depth of the tragedy that Shakespeare has presented us.

Discussion points

1   *Hamlet* is a play about many things, but it is also the story of a young man. Review the section on manhood and masculinity in Chapter Two ('Men and Women') and consider how the complexities of masculinity inform the character of Hamlet, the play's tragic hero.

2   Is *Hamlet* the tragedy of an individual or the tragedy of a society? In other words, does the play deal with the tragic fate of one person (Hamlet in this case), or does it also present a flawed social structure which might even be the cause of the tragedy?

3   Asides are a convention whereby a character's words are unheard by other characters on stage. Asides are interesting, writes Dympna

Callaghan, because they 'reveal a disjunction – sometimes chasm-wide – between what characters say and what they do not disclose'.[1] In Act 1, Claudius refers to Hamlet as his 'son' to which Hamlet responds: 'A little more than kin, and less than kind' (1.2.65). Performances usually make this an aside, but the fact is that it is not indicated as such in any of the texts of the play. Think about how treating this as an aside has a very different effect from treating it as a direct response. Another interesting case is the four lines spoken by Gertrude in Act 4:

> To my sick soul, as sin's true nature is,
> Each toy seems prologue to some great amiss,
> So full of artless jealousy is guilt,
> It spills itself in fearing to be spilt

(4.5.17–20)

Some scholars treat this as Gertrude's only soliloquy in the play, while others treat it as an aside because Ophelia is just entering the stage. Once again, consider the difference between treating this as an aside and as a soliloquy. Further, in the Q2 version each of these lines is prefaced by a quotation mark to signify that these lines are commonplace expressions.[2] What difference does it make that Gertrude might be (at least in this version) mouthing commonplaces and talking in generalities in this seeming confession?

4 *Hamlet* is a story of a prince told by a ghost to avenge his father's death. Most of us are not princes, nor are we visited by ghosts who give us murder assignments. Why then do you think has Hamlet's story been so frequently interpreted as the story of the human condition?

5 The three versions of Hamlet offer different stage directions at points. For example, in Q1 there is a stage direction instructing Hamlet to leap into Ophelia's grave: *Hamlet leaps in after Laertes* (16.145). There are no directions to anyone to leap anywhere in Q2, and in the folio the stage direction directs Laertes to jump into the grave: *Leaps in the grave* (5.1.247). How do the stage directions or the lack thereof govern how we interpret the rivalry between Laertes and Hamlet and the grief they each feel at this point in the play?[3]

14

Henry V

William Shakespeare

As discussed in Chapters One and Seven, the 'history play' was a popular Renaissance genre. These plays combined history and fiction to narrate the stories of past English kings. Even before Shakespeare's play King Henry V was a popular figure who lingered in the national memory as a war hero who led England to victory against France.

The plot of *Henry V* (*c.* 1599) is fast-paced and dramatic. The figure of King Henry dominates. The king is no longer the irresponsible young prince he was in the *Henry IV* plays that preceded this one. He has matured into his royal office and is depicted as the rightful ruler to whom royalty and grace come easily. He is the warrior, statesman and leader; he is both 'Harry', the charismatic 'people's king' and King Henry the 'star of England' (Epilogue, 6). Shakespeare's play is a royalist one on the one hand, paying tribute to the English monarchy, proclaiming it as central to the nation and projecting loyalty to the monarch as a virtue. Henry is the proud ruler who is rightfully angered by the arrogant French Dauphin's insulting message, the stern dispenser of justice and the soldier and orator on the battlefield. The king also disguises himself and goes out among the common soldiers as they wait for battle to begin, providing 'A little touch of Harry in the night' (Chorus 4, 48). On the other hand, we also see more troubling aspects of this public figure. He does not hesitate to have the friend of his youth, the soldier Bardolph, executed for little more than petty theft. We are also reminded that he distanced himself from another old and very dear friend, Falstaff. It is interesting that the play gives no access to the king's thoughts regarding his old friends – we simply know what he does; his feelings remain secret and open to speculation. The one occasion when the audience gets to listen to a soliloquy is when the king is filled with terror and foreboding regarding the impending battle. He prays that the 'God of battles' 'steel my soldiers' hearts' (4.1.285) and that God may forgive his father's murder of Richard to obtain the crown. We also see him burdened by his role and the responsibilities and cares that come with it. In Act Four of the play as Henry is beset by fear and anxiety, he wonders if kingship is nothing but 'general ceremony' (4.2.235) that might create 'awe and fear in other men' (4.1.243). Whether one sympathizes with Henry or not as he questions the meaning of royal power this night before the battle, his doubts and anxieties render him a more complicated figure than the swashbuckling war hero.

Henry V is also a war story. Violence, death and the rivalry between nations are the backdrop against which King Henry is presented. Scheming English churchmen either dupe Henry into war or provide him with an excuse to declare it, but the war against France is still projected as just, fought for 'a well-hallowed cause' (1.2.294) and at the end, after victory is obtained, the king proclaims that 'God fought for us' (4.8.119). War is a glorious patriotic enterprise; it brings men together in fraternal bonds and tests their manhood. Apart from a few isolated fights between individual soldiers, we see very little by way of action on the stage. The thrill and glory of battle is conveyed to us mainly through language. Henry's speeches are dynamic and inspiring as he appeals to his men's honour, patriotism and pride. The famous oratory delivered before the decisive battle of Agincourt speaks of fellowship in battlefield and in death. The soldiers are depicted as the chosen ones, fortunate to fight for their country. They are the 'happy few, we band of brothers; / For he today that sheds his blood with me / Shall be my brother' (4.3.60–62). The speech promises the soldiers fame and everlasting glory with their names etched in history, familiar to all 'as household words' (4.3.52).

But the treatment of war in Henry V is as complex as its treatment of kingship. The play indicates that war is a complicated affair. Not all soldiers are courageous or honourable; nor do all of them fight for the greater cause of the nation. In fact, a number of them, including Henry's old friends Pistol, Fluellen, Nym and Bardolph, are recruited to fight but go forth reluctantly. The second chorus tells us that 'all the youth of England are on fire' (Act 2, Prologue, 1), but the following scene depicts the corporals preoccupied with their own petty quarrels; the king delivers a fiery speech urging the soldiers to rush 'unto the breach' to 'close the wall up with our English dead!' (3.1.1, 2), but this is followed by a scene where Nym urges Bardolph not to press on because 'The knocks are too hot' and 'for mine own part, I have not a case of lives' (3.2.3, 4). The fourth chorus also paints a more grim picture of war. The

English soldiers wait in the dark for battle to begin at dawn. They are uncertain of the outcome and sit 'Like sacrifices, by their watchful fires.' Their worn-out clothing and lean faces make them look like 'So many horrid ghosts' (Act 4, Prologue, 28). Even though they do subsequently win the battle, this image of fearful soldiers awaiting death lingers. Many soldiers do die in battle, including the young boy soldier whom we have caught glimpses of through the play. While Bardolph and his crew can perhaps be dismissed as a bunch of idle cowards, the soldier Williams who meets Henry in the dark presents an articulate critique of war. He doubts if the cause they are fighting for is worthwhile and if death in war is as honourable as it is made out to be. 'I am afeard,' he says, 'there are few die well that die in a battle' (4.1.139–40). It is true that Williams's protest is silenced by the end of the play and that he turns, or at least appears to turn, into the loyal soldier. The guts and glory of battle and the king's speeches are more overpowering than this lone soldier's voice, but this juxtaposition of images of honour and glory in war with a more realistic and critical perspective is an interesting one, with one point of view undercutting and complicating the other.

Henry V is also a product of England's emerging sense of nationhood. In fact, it has been read as the most patriotic of Shakespeare's plays. The words 'England' and 'English' are mentioned over a hundred times. The English are a privileged and exceptional people. The English aristocracy are among the noblest in the world and even the more humble yeoman are also heroes because their 'limbs were made in England' (3.1.26). The sturdy, plainspoken and tough English are contrasted to the dandified and effeminate French. The nation is likened to a hive of honey bees that divide labour amongst themselves and live in unity, harmony and obedience. Thus nature itself teaches the 'act of order to a peopled kingdom' (1.2.189). Even the non-English soldiers in the play – the Scotsman, Jamy, the Irishman, Macmorris, and the Welshman, Fluellen – are loyal fighters, conjuring a vision of a united kingdom. The second chorus presents us with a vision where both wealthy noblemen and poor peasants go forth to fight in unity. But once again, the scenes with the unenthusiastic soldiers and the ones with the treacherous noblemen, along with the questions raised about war, dilute the play's patriotic flavour. 'What ish my nation?' asks Macmorris (3.2.126) and the play, too, subtly wonders: what *is* a nation? Is it really founded on unity and equality? Who belongs to it and who remains an outsider? But perhaps these questions are not obvious ones and the majority of Shakespeare's audience saw the play simply as a stirring, patriotic drama and a thrilling war story. In any case, it is a fact that *Henry V* has been used over the centuries as a patriotic narrative and has served to fortify English pride and patriotism in times of crisis (for example, the 1944 film version starring Sir Laurence Olivier served as a morale booster for England during the Second World War).

Another interesting feature of *Henry V* is its use of a Chorus that appears before every act and at the end of the play. The Chorus provides background information, fills in gaps in the action, sets the tone and provides commentary that occasionally complicates the dominant themes of the play. The Chorus also reminds us that the play is a play, an enactment of reality rather than reality itself. The opening Chorus ponders the limitations of the stage: can a mere 'cockpit hold / The vasty fields of France', and can a little 'wooden O' resound with cannon fire (Chorus 1, 11–12, 13)? The audience's imagination, we are told, makes up for the 'imperfections' (Chorus 1, 24) of the stage. At the end of the play we are offered a vision of a 'bending author' labouring over his script (Epilogue, 2). The Chorus thus serves as a meta-theatrical device, a means by which the play can reflect on itself as a play. Because the Chorus frames the narrative both at the beginning and the end, we are reminded that we are not watching a real king, nor are we actually in the battlefields of France. The sensitive reader is made aware that the history play is a narrative and retelling and like all narratives, the truth it presents is relative and provisional. This might well complicate our response to the play's themes.

Discussion points

1   Review the discussion on history plays in Chapter Seven ('Genre') and Thomas Heywood's defence of drama excerpted in Chapter Five ('The Stage') where he specifically mentions history plays. Keeping *Henry V* in mind, think about whether Heywood is right when he claims that drama teaches the lessons of obedience and loyalty to king and nation?

2   Kenneth Branagh's *Henry V* (1989) is among the best known film versions of the play. Watch the last scene where Henry (played by Branagh) pays court to Princess Katherine (played by Emma Thompson). How do the two actors play this love scene between two aristocrats whose nations have been at war and who, in fact, barely know each other? What does the scene (as played in this film) tell us about the role of the princess in this political story and the connection between gender relations and 'larger' political issues? As you think about this scene keep in mind the same film's quick cut from Henry's

Harfleur speech, which deploys the language of sexual violence, to the princess's bedchamber when she is trying to learn English, the lines from the play that are cut in the filming of this last courtship scene and the fact that Branagh and Thompson were in fact happily married in real life at the time of shooting.

3   The king's meeting with Williams, briefly discussed above, raises important questions about sending soldiers to die in battle. Henry (no longer in disguise) and Williams meet again in Act 4, Scene 8. Williams's attitude is an interesting mix of surprise, defiance, pride and apology. Read the scene carefully and consider the different ways an actor could project Williams in the scene. Also think about how the actor playing Henry would portray the king in that final meeting with his soldier.

4   Consider the role of the common soldiers (Pistol, Bardolph, Nym, Williams and Bates) in *Henry V*. What does Shakespeare's inclusion of such figures contribute to his vision of national community and national history and the figures who are its movers and shakers?

5   Reviewing Branagh's *Henry V* soon after its release, *The New York Times* film critic Vincent Canby contrasts it to Laurence Olivier's *Henry V* (1944). 'Olivier's *Henry V* is a splendid film that is also splendid propaganda', Canby writes. While 'The Branagh *Henry*', he maintains, 'is something quite another. There is less pageantry and less pomp.'[1] Do you agree with this description of the two versions of *Henry V*? Explain your response by comparing specific scenes from both films.

15

The Jew of Malta

Christopher Marlowe

The famous tragedie of the rich Jew of Malta was written sometime between 1589 and 1591 and the earliest recorded performance was in 1592 at the Rose Theatre (with the 'cauldron for the Jew' mentioned in Henslowe's list of stage props probably being brought onto the stage). The earliest existing print edition of *The Jew of Malta* is a 1633 quarto that might well be a revision of Christopher Marlowe's original play. If Marlowe's other play *Doctor Faustus* is about a magician whose ambitions seduce and ultimately destroy him, *The Jew of Malta* is about another marginal figure, a Jewish merchant on the island of Malta whose diabolical plotting and scheming evoke in us a deeply divided response.

Niccolò Machiavelli, the Italian Renaissance philosopher and author of the political essay, *The Prince*, is presented as speaking in the play's prologue. The prevalent stereotypes of Machiavelli as an unscrupulous and godless figure are reproduced here as he declares religion 'but a childish toy' and that there is no 'sin but ignorance' (Prologue, 14, 15). These defiantly cynical lines might have shocked an audience used to the usually self-righteous utterances of drama. Further, we are told that Barabas, the protagonist of the play, resembles Machiavelli. Although Machiavelli never reappears, his shadowy presence persists in this play of intrigue and villainy. Indeed, the same actor who presents Machiavelli in the prologue might have played Barabas.

While the play has no single source, it refers to contemporary events and issues including the Turkish siege of the Mediterranean island of Malta, a siege that ultimately failed. Renaissance Malta was a complicated place, a site of continuous conflict between Christian and Turkish powers, even as it was an important centre of international trade and commerce. Jewish merchants played a key role in this trade. Barabas, we gather, has benefited tremendously from it. His ships ply back and forth on the Mediterranean leaving him with a surfeit of wealth. 'Infinite riches', he says, are crammed 'in a little room' (1.1.37). Money is the source of Barabas's power, as well as his pride and joy. The play caters to stereotypes by linking Barabas's wealth to his religious identity. Indeed, exaggerated rumours of the wealth and power of the Mediterranean Jewish community (who often played the role of middlemen between Christians and Turks) make their way into the play. Barabas boasts that money is one of the 'blessings promised to the Jews' (1.1.104). They might be a dispossessed people and a 'scattered nation' (1.1.120), yet he, Barabas, would rather be a rich Jew than a poor Christian. Like other Jewish characters in Renaissance plays, Barabas becomes a symbol of the energy of the new capitalist economy that characterized the time period – ambitious, risk-taking and governed by self-interest.

We cannot but help sympathize with Barabas when he and his fellow Jews are called upon to give up half their property so that Ferneze, the Christian governor of Malta, can pay tribute to Selim Calymath, the Turkish prince. If any Jew fails to obey the order he would have to convert to Christianity. Barabas resists courageously and there is a certain poignancy to his lines when he says, 'The man that dealeth righteously shall live: / and which of you can charge me otherwise?' (1.2.117–18). His wealth, he says, is not simply money; it is 'the labour of my life, / The comfort of mine age, my children's hope' (1.2.150–51). When Barabas resists the tax, he is accused of 'covetousness' by Ferneze to which Barabas quite convincingly replies that 'theft is worse' than greed (1.2.125, 126) and that if his money is stolen from him, he, in turn, 'must be forced to steal and compass more' (1.2.128). We cannot help but feel sorry for the Jewish merchant who is exploited by a hypocritical Christian society.

However, we are not allowed to pity Barabas for too long. When he is alone on stage he gleefully reveals that he has retained far more money and jewels than he has given away. We might sympathize with his lamentations when he hears that the money might be lost because the house he has hidden it in has been seized by the authorities and we might even support his attempts to get his daughter to help him recover the treasure. But our responses are further complicated by the large-scale and spectacular nature of Barabas's villainy later in the play. He poisons a houseful of nuns (and kills his daughter Abigail in the process); his schemes result in Abigail's young suitors (including the one she loves, Mathias) killing each other; he murders his servant, Ithamore, and finally conspires to kill the Turkish Calymath even as he pretends to be his ally. Like Marlowe's other heroes, Barabas is morally flawed but still energetic, strong-willed and fascinating. Further, his villainy is so excessive and dramatic that it is almost ridiculous. In a long gloating speech he claims to have walked abroad at nights to 'kill sick people groaning under walls' (2.3.174), to have poisoned wells and to have engaged in all manner of evil first as a physician, then as an engineer and finally as a money-lender. His status as outsider in Maltese society requires that he put self-interest first and make both friends and enemies judiciously. As he says: 'Thus loving neither [Christian nor Turk], will I live with both, / Making a profit of my policy' (5.2.111–12).

Barabas is, then, a complicated a figure: do we read him as a wronged Jew who is simply seeking revenge? Or is he a vindictive and naturally villainous figure, the stereotypical monster brought in to frighten yet excite the audience? Is he to be received as grotesquely inhuman, a caricature of evil rather than as a realistic character? Does he play to stereotypes only because he knows that the Christian inhabitants of the island, and we, the audience, want him to? Or is he simply all too human in his greed and cunning? Like the Vice figure of medieval drama (from whom he might have been derived) Barabas invites our condemnation as well as our admiration and laughter as we follow his clever (and funny) plots and machinations. We even become somewhat intimate with him as a character and as he is presented to us in almost every scene, we revel in his malice and maybe even share in his guilt.

Scenes that would be traditionally frightening or poignant and tragic are written to darkly comic effect. The death of the houseful of nuns is thus both horrifying and so excessive that it becomes ridiculous; the scene where Barabas and Ithamore strangle the greedy and unfortunate Friar Barnadine and cause the equally greedy Friar Jacamo to think he is to blame, is both dark and slapstick. The play thus refuses to aspire to tragic grandeur. Instead, it revels in savage, though still serious, farce. The tragic world-view is expressed through cynicism – the world is devious, self-serving and hypocritical, and Barabas is, if anything, not the villainous exception in a society of good men but a representative of a degenerate society.

Barabas is named governor of the island by Calymath, but unsure of whether he has enough support from the people to survive in that role, he bargains with Ferneze to get rid of the Turks. But Ferneze turns against him and the play ends with Barabas at last falling into the trap of his own making. Even as he falls into the boiling cauldron he defiantly calls out, 'And had I but escaped this strategem, / I should have brought confusion on you all, / Damned Christian dogs, and Turkish infidels' (5.5.83–85). He makes no gestures of repentance, nor does he beg for forgiveness. Instead he dies cursing and blaming his misfortune rather than himself or his actions. Spectacularly evil as Barabas has been, it is somehow not easy to read this scene as evil getting its just deserts. This is because we still remember the sympathy we felt for Barabas the persecuted alien in the early scenes of the play and also because the Christian Ferneze is no virtuous hero. He does not hesitate to bargain with Barabas, even as he does not hesitate to betray him when needed. He is crafty, self-serving and generally unscrupulous. It could be argued that in fact Ferneze is the true Machiavellian figure of the play. Unlike Barabas he triumphs and survives – further emphasizing the play's cynical view of politics, society and human nature.

This is a world where 'profit' and 'policy' (self-interest and deviousness) are both sadly prevalent, necessary and interlinked, where alliances, both political and personal, are fragile and constantly shifting. Jews, Christians, and Turks (though Calymath is something of an exception) are all self-serving and religion itself becomes a façade to hide villainy. So Ferneze and the two 'religious caterpillars' (4.1.21), the greedy and grasping friars Barnadine and Jacamo, become sorry representatives of a hypocritical Christianity. Darkly humorous as the play is, the mood is overall cynical and harsh. Unlike other Renaissance tragedies, *The Jew of Malta* is not a story of tragic suffering but is rather a dark spectacle of evil at work. Nor is it, in any real sense, the tragedy of an individual. It is instead the tragedy of a fallen society that cannot redeem itself. Given all that has passed, when Ferneze delivers the play's sanctimonious closing lines: 'let due praise be given / Neither to fate nor fortune, but to heaven' (5.5.122–23), we cannot respond with anything other than scepticism.

Discussion points

1   T.S. Eliot describes *The Jew of Malta* 'not as a tragedy, or as a "tragedy of blood," but as a farce … the farce of the old English humour, the terribly serious, even savage comic humour'.[1] Consider this quote along with the discussions of tragedy and mixed modes in Chapter Seven 7 ('Genre'). Do you think *The Jew of Malta* is a tragedy at all? Or would you call it a tragi-comedy or even a 'comic-tragedy'? What do you think Eliot mean by the 'serious … savage humour' of this play?

2   Edmund Kean's 1818 production of Sampson Penley's adaptation of *The Jew of Malta* rendered Barabas a tragic victim of a corrupt society.

Penley added a prologue condemning anti-Semitism and eliminated scenes such as the poisoning of the nuns and strangling of Bernadine. What do you think such additions and omissions bring to or take away from the play? Are there other ways of playing the role of Barabas (and other characters) that could potentially downplay the stereotype of the Jewish figure?

3 As mentioned above, Malta was the cross-roads of different civilizations. Review Chapter Three ('Travel and Trade') that discusses increasing 'globalization' and 'internationalization' in the time period. How do different societies and cultures interact in this play and to what end?

4 Chapter Three ('Travel and Trade') also discusses 'race' in the time period as well as the representation of Jewish people at the time. How and where does the play invoke stereotypes in the representation of Barabas? As modern readers of this play (who live in a world where stereotypes are still prevalent) do you think these stereotypes reinforce prejudices, or do they lead us to question and laugh at the very idea of stereotyping itself?

5 Compare Doctor Faustus and Barabas, two of Marlowe's protagonists. To what extent are they similar and how do they differ? Consider both characters in light of their ambitions, their positions outside of mainstream society and their respective attitudes to religion.

16

The Knight of the Burning Pestle

Francis Beaumont

The Knight of the Burning Pestle (first performed *c.* 1607, first printed edition the quarto of 1613) by Francis Beaumont features a citizen (as middle-class London merchants were called) and his wife watching a play. However, they constantly and loudly interrupt it, insisting that a romance of their own direction, starring a merchant-hero (played by Rafe, their apprentice), be staged instead.

The Knight was most likely written for the Blackfriars, an indoors theatre with small audiences. Parody and satire were the preferred genres in this venue. One also sees other features of stagings at the Blackfriars in *The Knight*: the dominating presence of boy actors and the staging of interludes involving songs and jigs between the main action. It was also the custom in playhouses like the Blackfriars for some spectators to view the play from seats on the stage. Beaumont's unforgettable characters, the Citizen and his Wife, clamber onstage and proceed to direct the play's action. The play has been read as a satire on the vulgar tastes and ways of the citizen or merchant class. The high-born audience that frequented the Blackfriars would have especially enjoyed such satire. However, *The Knight* was a failure. The publisher's note says that the audience 'not understanding the privy mark of irony about it' 'utterly rejected' the play (Epistle, 4–6). Why did this happen? One plausible explanation is that the audience of the Blackfriars was not restricted to the nobility but included prosperous citizens who didn't quite appreciate the joke.

Even the argument that Beaumont was ridiculing the merchant classes for being coarse and smug is only somewhat convincing. Satire in *The Knight* is more in the manner of gentle mockery than harsh ridicule. As the preface says, the play hopes to 'please all, and be hurtful to none' ('To the Readers', 10). *The Knight* is an interesting combination of satire and celebration. The three different narrative threads – the citizens watching the play, the play that is actually being staged by the actors ('The Merchant's Tale') and the story of the apprentice-knight starring Rafe – destroy any pretence of formal unity. But a delightful energy circulates between the three plots and a very entertaining play emerges from the confusion. *The Knight* is a play where the playing space extends beyond the stage into the world. Spectators participate in the fiction and the play does show sympathy or at least amused tolerance for a variety of tastes. Decorum and probability can and will be violated and the stage can simultaneously accommodate both the real world of the London citizenry and the fantastical 'enchanted valley' of the play being staged.

The Citizen suspects that 'The London Merchant' is a play that 'girds at [mocks] citizens' and objects to it (Induction, 8): 'Down with your title, boy,' he cries (Induction, 9). He and his wife certainly lack literary sophistication – they miss sarcastic references, innocently comment on the bawdy jokes and want the play to gratify their whims and fancies. But they are ultimately charming figures whose naiveté is refreshing. They are certainly more entertaining than the play they interrupt. They insist that their apprentice, Rafe, stars in a chivalric merchant-romance and completely destroy the plot of the original play. The boy who plays the Prologue objects: 'You'll utterly spoil our play, and make it to be hissed, and it cost money; you will not suffer us to go on with our plot' (3.294–96). He alternately pleads with and threatens the Citizen and his wife, but they are insistent. 'Plot me no plots,' the Citizen orders, 'I'll ha' Rafe come out; I'll make your house too hot for you else' (2. 268–69).

The Knight explores the interactions between art and life, the stage and the audience. The reactions of the Citizen and the Wife are varied and quite complex. There are times when the Wife cannot suspend disbelief and immerse herself in the fiction: she is charmed by the boy who plays Humphrey, reminds the audience that Rafe is 'a poor fatherless child' (Epilogue, 4–5) and asks him when he reappears for a new scene: 'Oh, Rafe, how dost thou, Rafe? How hast thou slept tonight? Has the knight used thee well?' (3.137–38). At other times she and her husband are ideal spectators, enthusiastically and fully accepting the world of make-believe: the wife trembles like 'an aspen leaf' (3.132) after witnessing a fight on stage and cheers Rafe on with all her might: 'Run, Rafe; run, Rafe; run for thy life, boy; Jasper comes, Jasper comes'

(2.313–14). She and her husband blur the line between fiction and reality and sometimes insert themselves into the action as when the Citizen rescues Rafe by paying the innkeeper the money owed him and gives him money to tip the princess's servants. They refuse to sympathize with Jasper, the romantic hero of the actors' play whom they see as a rebellious apprentice whom the citizen would 'hang up by the heels' (1.334) if he could. Similarly, the wife does not see Master Merrythought as the comic type he is meant to be and delivers him a ringing rebuke for not behaving like a gentleman of his 'age and discretion' (3.539). The wife's desires and needs are also shaped by what she witnesses on stage. She is moved by Humphrey's courtship of Luce and asks her husband: 'When will you do as much for me, George?' (1.131–2). Their demands are unreal and comic but richly various: they want romance, violence, fantastical settings and apprentices who can court king's daughters. Interestingly, their (and our own) collective imaginations triumph at the end – the actor who plays the innkeeper does accept the citizen's money and alters the course of the play's action, and everyone – including the barber in the Rafe story – pretends that the barber is a giant when he is not. We don't wonder how the Lady Pomiona and Rafe work out their lines together given that the scene was just invented by the Wife. We too begin to cooperate with the Citizen and his Wife and we too blur the distinctions between stage action and 'real life'.

The Citizens want a heroic drama that will simultaneously celebrate citizens. As the husband says: 'I will have a grocer, and he shall do admirable things' (Induction, 34–35). The play they create and direct that stars their apprentice Rafe is 'The Knight of the Burning Pestle' (a title that takes off from court plays with titles like 'The Knight of the Golden Shield' and 'The Knight of the Burning Rock'). Rafe is an apprentice-knight like the heroes of Thomas Heywood's *Four Prentices of London* (1592), a play the Citizen mentions with admiration ('Read the play *The Four Prentices of London*, where they toss their pikes so' [4.49–50]). Not only do the Citizens admire and love the character that Rafe represents, they are also proud of their apprentice's acting abilities and believe that 'for clean action and good delivery they may all cast their caps at him' (2.199–200). The onstage Rafe is as proud of being an apprentice as he is of being an errant knight. A pestle becomes his emblem 'in remembrance of my former trade' (1.264), much to the delight of the citizens who are overjoyed that the hero 'wilt not forget thy old trade' (1.266). Rafe thus gives the Citizens a certain fantasized self-image, the belief that even a shopkeeper or an apprentice has a claim to heroism. He continues to stay loyal to his class when he rejects the princess's protestations of love because his real beloved is Susan, 'A cobbler's maid in Milk Street, whom I vow / Ne'er to forsake whilst life and pestle last' (4.96–97). For a while Rafe the apprentice-knight seems to be humiliated: he is beaten up by Jasper, the hero of the 'main plot', and cannot pay the innkeeper. But he defeats the barber and sets himself on the heroic path. The actor Rafe is also quite admirable – he is given a situation by his demanding audience which he quickly and easily fills out, adds to and improvises. His ability to speak the language of romance, replete with grand flourishes and heroic rhetoric is impressive. At the end Rafe plays the Lord of May, summons a citizen militia and creates an atmosphere of revelry and celebration. His speech is an entertaining mixture of the bawdy and the patriotic before he dies in the approved tragic manner, an ending the citizens see as befitting a romance.

All along the actors have doggedly performed or tried to perform their rather dull play, 'The London Merchant', a formulaic domestic comedy with young lovers rebelling against an unsympathetic patriarch. It is not entirely unlike Rafe's play – both Rafe and Jasper are young apprentices, each embarking on his own adventures (Jasper rejects an inherited fortune, pursues love and engages in mighty quarrels). So, in spite of the actors' disparaging attitude towards Rafe's play, the regular fare they offer for the viewers' consumption is also an unrealistic and idealizing fiction. Jasper's prodigal father, Master Merrythought, is perhaps the most memorable element in 'The London Merchant'. With his wild extravagant ways and indifference to the cares of the world (including the death of his son), he is a satire on the good citizens idealized in plays by other writers such as Thomas Dekker. Merrythought is a Lord of Misrule standing for the play's festive comic spirit. He says that 'mirth' is what 'keeps life and soul together . . . This is the philosophers' stone that they write so much on, that keeps a man ever young' (4.341–43).

It is this festive spirit that prevails at the end of *The Knight*. Life, chaotic and creative, has shaped art and art itself has proved to be adaptable and resilient. Theatre becomes a space of freedom where the audience's imagination and desires reign supreme. The vocal Wife rightly has the last word with her genial invitation to everyone to come to her house 'for a bottle of wine and a pipe of tobacco' (Epilogue, 6–7).

Discussion points

1 Satires can be either cutting and cruel (supposedly in order to reform) or genial, fun and accepting. How would you describe *The Knight of the*

Burning Pestle's satire of the Citizen and his Wife? Focus on the play's depiction of their taste in drama and their behaviour as spectators.

2 Is it significant that the playwright does not present us with the gentlemen in the audience? They stay silent throughout the play and the Citizens' loud interruptions. Why do you think this is the case? Speculate on what the experience was like for them.

3 The first production of *The Knight of the Burning Pestle* was a failure for reasons speculated on above. Imagine you are a member of that first audience (decide on whether you want to be an aristocratic spectator or a middle-class citizen) and write a brief review of the play.

4 The romance was a type of narrative popular in the Middle Ages. These stories were based on chivalric love and adventure and featured knightly heroes and their fair ladies. *Knight* appears to mock the conventions of romance, but the citizens in the play do want a play that features citizens as romance-heroes. What do you think is the appeal of a romance that features a citizen-hero (rather than a knight)? How would this modification alter the traditional genre of romance?

5 Although *The Knight of the Burning Pestle* has been revived by amateur groups, professional performances are still relatively rare. Imagine that you are a director of a small professional theatre group. Make a case for producing *Knight*. Why is the play worth staging in your local community? Why would it be of interest to local theatre-goers? If you think you should adapt the play to make it meaningful to modern audiences, how would you go about doing so?

17

The Roaring Girl

Thomas Dekker and Thomas Middleton

The Roaring Girl (staged *c.* 1611 and printed shortly after) was co-authored by Thomas Middleton and Thomas Dekker, both of whom were professional playwrights with an intimate knowledge of London. Their plays are a celebration of that vibrant, complex and ever-changing city. *The Roaring Girl* is written in the tradition of city comedy and the city is as much a character as any of the colourful personalities who make up the cast. The play is based on real-life character Mary Frith or Moll Cutpurse (1584?–1659) who cut a figure in early seventeenth-century London as both a cross-dresser and petty thief.

The Roaring Girl has a classic comic storyline. The main plot figures Sebastian Wengrave's attempts to outwit his father, Sir Alexander, who will not allow his marriage to the less affluent Mary Fitz-Allard, by pretending to be in love with the notorious transvestite Moll. The sub-plot is typical of citizen comedy with a group of idle gallants attempting to seduce a group of citizen-wives and eventually failing. Moll links the main and sub-plot but does not entirely belong to either of the two worlds represented in the play.

The cover page of the 1611 edition displays the 'roaring girl' dressed in fashionable male clothing and flamboyantly smoking a pipe. It also includes what might have been a proverbial expression: 'My case is alter'd, I must work for my living'. Moll cross-dresses and defies conventional gender roles; she is also a girl who must work for her keep. Perhaps Moll must cross-dress in order to live and work freely in the city. Or perhaps the fact that she is a cross-dresser makes it necessary that she work, since she cannot, like most middle-class women, rely on a husband to support her financially.

Unlike Shakespeare's romantic heroines, Moll is not disguised as a man. She habitually dresses as one. The cross-dressed woman was perceived as disorderly and as disrupting natural and social hierarchies. The Prologue to *The Roaring Girl* indicates that the writers are aware that the subject would shock and also arouse the audience's prurient curiosity. However, we are told that the roaring girl of the play 'flies / With wings more lofty' (Prologue, 25–26). The text refuses to completely cater to audience expectations right from the start – this roaring girl is no sexual deviant or odd perversion of social norms. In fact, the play appears to go out of its way not to normalize Moll but to valorize her. She is, somewhat unexpectedly, an idealized version of the bawdy, drunk pickpocket who was her real-life counterpart. Sir Alexander might be filled with horror at the thought that Sebastian might be in love with 'A Creature' 'brought forth / To mock the sex of woman' (1.2.127–28) and 'a thing / One knows not how to name' (1.2.129–30), but he is not a favourable character in the play; nor are the unsavoury Trapdoor and Laxton, who are certain that Moll is sexually depraved. The young gallants who view Moll with fear, fascination and repulsion, but always with desire, are themselves either conniving or foolish. When we actually see Moll on stage she is certainly unusual, but she is also admirable – bold, plain-spoken, self-reliant and more than willing to help the young Sebastian wed his Mary. She tells Sebastian that she herself has 'no humour to marry' because she is 'too headstrong to obey' (2.2.36, 38–39). There is a deliberate simplicity to her language as she expresses her rejection of marriage and domesticity; she is neither apologetic nor boastful of her unusual lifestyle.

The sub-plot takes us to the heart of commercial London. The shops, owned by a newly wealthy merchant class, are filled with goods to be bought and sold. Interestingly, the prosperous merchants' wives are the ones who transact business. They indicate the entry of middle-class women into the public sphere, a phenomenon that generated some controversy in the period. Class and class relations are as important to *The Roaring Girl* as gender. The wealthy merchants are a reminder of the aristocracy's fears of the rising middle-class, while the young gallants preying on the citizen wives are impoverished, idle and profligate, representing the declining and insecure aristocracy. The slimy Laxton is especially persistent in his pursuit of Mrs Gallipot, the apothecary's wife, and she appears to be vulnerable to his charms. The city space becomes the arena of complex and dangerous sexual transactions. The play makes interesting connections between Moll and the middle-class women. Like her, they too have ventured out of the confines of their homes into the public space of the city and so opened themselves to the preying young men's advances. But while Mrs Gallipot and her associates are not entirely immune to the young gallants, Moll reacts very differently to

Laxton. She agrees to a rendezvous with him but fiercely rejects his advances and beats him up. In this way the 'roaring girl' proves to be more chaste than the citizen wives.

The speech addressed by Moll to Laxton is among the longest in the play. Symbolically attired in male clothing, she speaks out against male dominance. She accuses Laxton and men like him of preying upon vulnerable women and perceiving any woman who happens to be free and open in public as a 'fond flexible whore' (3.1.72). She speaks up for women's right to be seen in public and to laugh and drink without being misinterpreted as sexually loose. In denouncing him, she denounces all masculine power: 'In thee I defy all men, their worst hates, / And their best flatteries, all their golden witchcrafts, / With which they entangle the poor spirits of fools' (3.1.91–93). She attacks particularly Laxton for preying on those women in impoverished circumstances: 'Distressed needlewomen and trade-fallen wives, / Fish that must needs bite or themselves be bitten' (3.1.94–95). Once again, the play draws attention to the complex interplay of gender and class politics. Moll herself speaks up – both as a woman who has chosen to reject traditional female roles and as a woman of the working classes. Even as she speaks out against the exploitation of women, she refuses to use the rhetoric of victimhood and asserts her own agency and power, stating that she is not a prostitute (as many female cross-dressers were thought to be). On the other hand, she claims that she can, if she so wishes, assert her power over men: 'I scorn to prostitute myself to a man, / I that can prostitute a man to me' (3.1.110–11). This episode clearly works to undo the conventional connection between cross-dressing and sexual depravity, a connection made repeatedly in other social texts. Cross-dressing might be unconventional, but sexual exploitation of the less powerful, based on conventionally structured gender and class hierarchies and ideologies, is not only more objectionable but entirely unethical. On the other hand, cross-dressing is associated with the courage to question sexual exploitation and other social injustices.

The play also has an interesting take on masculinity. While Sebastian is clearly the romantic male lead, he is a relatively undeveloped character who fades into insignificance alongside the larger-than-life Moll. Sir Alexander is certainly not admirable; the young gallants are either unsavoury or simply foolish; the citizens, for the most part, while worthy businessmen, appear to be bullied by their wives. Moll, with her 'masculine' qualities of independence and courage, is as close as one gets to ideal 'manhood' in the play. Masculinity becomes a matter of ethical and upright behaviour rather than based on 'natural' gender identity.

The sub-plot ends with the citizens' wives realizing the worthiness of their own husbands and rejecting the gallants. In the tradition of all comedy, domestic harmony is restored, and in the tradition of good city comedy, the citizens – both men and women – unite themselves against the young gallants though we are not certain if Mr Gallipot fully forgives his ever-wily, straying wife. The citizens' newfound economic self-confidence is given voice by Mistress Openwork who declares the well-born young men to be 'Idle simple things' whom 'we shopkeepers, when all's done, are sure to have 'em in our purse-nets at length' (4.2.46–48). The hostile Sir Alexander also repents; father and son are reconciled and the lovers are united, thanks to Moll's help. Shakespearean comedy often signals the reinstatement of social order by having its cross-dressed protagonist shed her disguise and resume her traditional female role. Moll, however, has never really been in disguise and continues to be her unconventional self. The play is an example of 'radical comedy' that interrogates the prevailing social order. Because Sir Alexander and others who have been hostile to Moll recognize her worth at the end, the play also envisions a world founded on principles of acceptance and flexibility, a world where even Moll has a place.

But it is not quite clear what exactly that place will be. Moll is certainly part of the celebrations at the end but also persists in remaining just outside of them. Neither thief nor prostitute, in spite of her earthiness, Moll remains a slightly unreal and disembodied figure. Her personal life and her desires remain unknown, and she seems to live entirely to serve as the voice of justice and goodness. But *The Roaring Girl* remains an interesting play, daring in its choice of protagonist and unusual in its depiction of her.

Discussion points

1 Review the historical document on female cross-dressing (*Hic Mulier*) excerpted in Chapter Two ('Men and Women'). Compare the representation of female cross-dressing in the document and in the play. Also consider the section on cross-dressing on stage in Stephen Gosson's *Plays Confuted in Five Actions* (excerpted in Chapter Five, 'The Stage'). Do you think the fact that a boy actor played Moll makes her more or less interesting?

2 Review the section on comedy in Chapter Seven ('Genre'). What are the features of city comedy and romantic comedy that you can see in

this play? Is it disappointing that, unlike heroines of comedy, Moll does not find romance?

3 *The Roaring Girl* was rarely if ever staged for hundreds of years after the early production. One modern editor of the play states that the 'growth of the women's movement is largely behind the relative frequency with which it has been revived in recent years'.[1] In 1979 the play was put on in the University of Los Angeles with the subtitle 'a feminist infiltration'. Do you think this play's self-consciousness about gender and its depiction of gender roles and relations make it a 'feminist' play? Consider the play alongside Chapter Two ('Men and Women') and think about whether one can even consider the possibility of 'feminist' writing in the Renaissance.

4 Moll is present at the celebrations and general joyousness at the end of the play. However, she indicates she has no interest in marrying. Her last lines are: 'As a musician, I pursue no pity: / Follow the law: and you can cuck me, spare not: / Hang up my viol by me, and care not' (5.2.253–55). How would an actress deliver these lines: Jovially? Carelessly? Defiantly? To convey boredom, indifference or something else? In other words, how do you think Moll, who is not given the traditional comic ending (romantic love, marriage, family), should be represented as feeling at the end of the play? Has she found community or does she remain something of the outsider?

5 If you are interested in creative writing, consider a modern adaptation of *The Roaring Girl*. You could attempt either a play or a short-story. Like Dekker and Middleton, place a cross-dressed woman at the centre of the story and create a plot involving romance and sexual intrigue.

18

The Shoemaker's Holiday

Thomas Dekker

The Shoemaker's Holiday (1599) by Thomas Dekker is a fast-paced, cheery play
that celebrates a particular section of the London citizenry – the artisan or
manufacturing class, in this case the shoemakers. This class is made out to be
energetic, ambitious and central to the social and economic life of the nation.
Based on *The Gentle Craft* by Thomas Deloney, a prose narrative first published
in 1598 which tells three separate stories about shoemakers, and also drawing
from John Stow's *Survey of London* (1598), which includes a brief account of
Simon Eyre's rise, Dekker's play was written at a difficult time. England was
just emerging from wars with Spain, and inflation, poverty and famine were
harsh facts of life. But Dekker's lively comedy is a fantasy of social harmony
and social mobility. The tale of the fantastic rise of a shoemaker, Simon Eyre,
to the position of Lord Mayor and that of the aristocratic Roland and his love
for Rose, a Citizen's daughter, is designed to especially appeal to the artisan
spectators. Though the play is set in medieval times (a historical Simon Eyre
did become Mayor of London in 1445), the setting of the play powerfully
evokes Elizabethan London with its use of the colloquial language of the
shoemakers and references to locations which Dekker's audience would have
been familiar with. The shoemakers are workers first and foremost, men who
labour with their hands. The play celebrates work as a central value and places
those who work on the national stage. So Eyre tells his workmen to 'haste to
work' (4.22) and urges the apparently widowed Jane to use her fine white
hands to 'work for your living' (1.209).[1] The extravagant and foppish aristocrat
Roland Lacy redeems himself by learning the trade of shoemakers and living
by honest manual labour. The shoemakers' workshop is an idyllic space with
none of the tensions and conflicts of a real-life workplace.

In spite of this, there are visible tensions in the city surrounding the workshop. War looms in the background. While Roland has few qualms about dodging the draft, workmen like Ralph need to go to fight. Ralph returns alive but injured and both he and his wife have to face tremendous economic and emotional stress because of his absence. Class conflicts abound as well. Sir Hugh Lacy, the haughty nobleman, opposes his nephew Roland's marriage to the daughter of gentlemen-grocer Roger Oatley and advises Oatley to seek 'some honest citizen to wed your daughter to' (1.36–37). Though Oatley responds with pretended humility, he actually despises aristocrats for their decadence and extravagance. Noblemen, he says, 'will in silks and gay apparel spend / More in one year than I'm worth by far' (1.13–14). Later in the play he tries to persuade Rose to marry Hammon who is a citizen by birth and so a more suitable mate for his daughter. Nor are all citizens united: the shoemakers, for instance, refer to the wealthy and snobbish Oatley, who, as a grocer, must have belonged to one of London's most powerful trade guilds, as 'Sir Roger Oatmeal' (13.29); Hammon, the wealthy citizen with pretensions to aristocracy (as seen in his hunting pursuits and courtly wooing style), is also despised by the shoemakers.

The shoemakers themselves are, however, a united social group. Their shared specialized skill of working with 'St. Hugh's Bones' (as they refer to their tools) is considered manly and unifying. As Eyre says, 'the Gentle Trade is a living for a man through Europe, through the world!' (1.45–46). The shoemakers might be a rambunctious lot and heavy drinkers, but they are still an orderly, disciplined and honourable crew. When Ralph presents Jane with a pair of shoes he proudly describes them as the special product of collective craftsmanship: 'Here, take these pair of shoes cut out by Hodge, / Stitched by my fellow Firk, seamed by myself' (1.228–29). Towards the end of the play, he refuses Hammon's money, indignantly remarking, 'dost thou think a shoemaker is so base to be bawd to his own wife for commodity? Take thy gold, choke with it!' (18.83–84). Besides, the shoemakers always appear on stage together, heroically united to protect the interests of one of their own. As Hodge says when the shoemakers band together to stop Hammon from marrying Jane: 'Shoemakers are steel to the back, men every inch of them, all spirit' (18.33–34). Later, when Firk is offered a bribe by Oatley to reveal Roland's whereabouts, he indignantly asks, 'Shall I betray my brother? No. Shall I prove Judas to Hans? No. Shall I cry treason to my corporation? No' (16.93–94).

Roland enters the fraternity of shoemakers by seeking work at Eyre's workshop disguised as Hans, a Dutch shoemaker. Hodge insists that he be hired because he is 'a proper man' and 'a fine workman' and even threatens to quit 'If such a man as he cannot find work' (4.55–57). So though Hans might be depicted in stereotypical ways and the English shoemakers might call him a 'butter- box' (4.50) and tease him for his Dutch accent (his so-called 'gibble-gabble': 4.45), apparently the unity among shoemakers exceeds national boundaries (though, of course, it helps that Hans is Dutch and so Protestant, indicating an international Protestant brotherhood). This friendliness to the foreign workman ignores the real-life resentment felt against immigrant workers who were accused of agreeing to low wages and so taking away jobs from natives. But in the play Hans is well-liked and soon becomes one of the fraternity.

The outstanding shoemaker is, of course, Eyre, the master shoemaker, jolly patriarch and Lord of Feasts. Though he is master to the other shoemakers, he never projects himself as superior to them. He exuberantly proclaims, 'I love my men as my life' (4.65–66) and generously treats them to drinks and feasts. The play dramatically compresses Eyre's rise from shoemaker to alderman to Lord Mayor. This narrative of rapid upward social mobility is a bit fantastic and even Dekker's audiences must have thought it so. In reality only members of prestigious guilds, mostly Merchant Traders, became mayors. Even the historical Eyre was in fact a draper by trade. In the play, in spite of his newfound status and his newfound wealth, he is always proud of being a shoemaker. Several times in the play he repeatedly proclaims, 'Prince am I none, yet am I princely born' (21.15–16). While Eyre's wife, Margery, becomes somewhat snobbish after her husband's promotion and dons fine clothing, pretends affected speech and attempts to curb her husband's rowdiness, Eyre does not aspire to behave like an aristocrat. He continues to be loud and irrepressible and his language is still earthy and colourful. Though he asks the king to 'pardon my rude behavior. I am a handicraftsmen, my heart is without craft' (21.9–10), this appears to be less an apology than an assertion of his identity as a shoemaker. Eyre might be one of the 'merriest madcaps' in England and come across 'rather a wild ruffian than a Mayor' (19.2, 4), yet he is also intelligent, ambitious and can be 'serious, provident and wise' when needed (19.8).

The play also very conspicuously describes and displays fine clothing and luxury goods. Roland dresses extravagantly before he disguises himself and Margery wants fine clothes like French hoods, farthingales and cork shoes once she becomes mayor's wife. Clothes are markers of status and though Eyre might tease his wife for her 'pishery-pashery' (20.49–50), he too dresses up in an embroidered gown and damask cassock when he becomes alderman.

Clothing is a necessary investment, part of being ambitious and enterprising. In fact, many people might have come to watch the play to see these samples of fine clothing on display. Eyre also makes his money by buying luxury cargo, including almonds, civet, sugar and cambric, off a Dutch ship. Though he disguises himself as an alderman to pull off this transaction, there seem to be no concerns on his or others' part about ethical practice. Eyre's is a worldly brand of Protestantism where wealth and luxury goods are prized and coexist quite easily with love and good fellowship. In a sense the play foresees a capitalist world in which trade, especially in luxury goods, is a means to wealth, social status and even happiness.

Although the play visualizes an increasingly powerful artisan class, that class is still devoted to the king who is just, gracious and at ease with the commoners. Most importantly, he serves as a buffer against social conflict. He urges the reluctant Sir Hugh and Sir Oatley to let the young people marry as their hearts dictate saying that 'love respects no blood, / Cares not for difference of birth or state' (21.103–04). The older men have no option but to agree. He also overlooks, even encourages, Eyre's rather rough demeanour by urging him to be 'even as merry / As if thou wert among thy shoemakers' (21.12–13). The king also names Leadenhall, the building that Eyre has constructed, and so ratifies the energy of the artisan class and their importance to the nation's economy. The king is overall important to the play's comic conclusion, diffusing class-tension and joining in the celebration of Eyre and his like.

Dekker's 'festive comedy' also finds another way to suspend social conflict and bring about the comic resolution of joyous celebration and forgiving laughter. At the play's conclusion Eyre declares Shrove Tuesday a holiday for the shoemakers. Though Shrove Tuesday holidays eventually came to be characterized by riots carried out by disgruntled apprentices, Eyre's holiday is marked in the play by an abundance of food, drink and hilarity. The artisans will go back to work the next day, sure of their place in the nation's story. For that day, they will simply celebrate.

Discussion points

1   What is the appeal, if any, of *The Shoemaker's Holiday* to twenty-first-century audiences? Is there anything about this story about social mobility and wealth made through trade that continues to interest us today? Could Eyre be a modern hero or does he remind you of any

modern public figure or celebrity? Another way to think about this: could the story be transplanted to the twenty-first century and still be interesting and appealing? Are there changes you would have to make (additions or omissions to the story and cast of characters) if you were rewriting this as a 'modern' tale?

2 The play presents a highly idealized vision of manual labour, shoemaking in particular. Are there any discordant notes in it? What kind of historical documents would you want to read alongside this play to more fully understand the lives of shoemakers (and other artisans) in the time period?

3 In Chapter Three ('Travel and Trade') we discussed England's engagement with other parts of the world and English understandings of people who came from these foreign lands. Hans is (supposedly) a Dutch shoemaker in the play. Until he sheds his disguise, he is a lovably comic figure. Is this depiction a limited treatment of foreigners? Could Hans have been represented in more complex ways without making him any less appealing and without forgetting that the play is a comedy? Also, would the play's treatment of Hans have been inevitably different if he had been, for example, Jewish or an African 'moor'?

4 The play is full of material goods. Eyre profits through trade in luxury goods – the consumption of such goods is a mark of status, and some of the more lavish objects might have actually drawn spectators who were keen to feast their eyes on these objects. Make a list of all the physical objects that appear or are referred to in the play. Which of them do you think would have been especially fascinating to people who came to see the play? Jonathan Gil Harris writes that that the 'power of the play's luxury goods is such that they do not just arouse the characters but ultimately erase them.'[2] Do you agree with this argument? Do the goods seem to become more important than people or come to stand for and identify people in the play?

5 While many productions of the play have focused on the play's comic and celebratory elements, it is also possible (as more recent productions have done) to foreground its dark side. Pick out moments in the play that could be interpreted as sad or upsetting (even if they are not represented as such in the text) and as possible moments of class or other tension.

19

The Spanish Tragedy

Thomas Kyd

Composed and first performed between 1585 and 1589, *The Spanish Tragedy* by Thomas Kyd is often regarded as the first revenge tragedy in English and had a tremendous influence on later plays in the genre, notably Shakespeare's *Hamlet*. It was also a very popular play with twenty-five performances in the first five years after its publication in 1592 and ten, or possibly eleven, printed editions in the four decades between 1592 and 1633. The fact that it was added to (probably by Ben Jonson) in 1602 and revived for the stage is further testimony to its popularity.

If the play had a single source, it is now lost. In fact, it is more likely to have been assembled from a variety of borrowings from Latin texts by Virgil, Ovid and Seneca. The debt to Seneca is the most obvious. As discussed in Chapter Seven ('Genre'), 'revenge tragedy' was particularly influenced by Senecan drama. The revenge motive is central to the plot, which moves neatly forward to the actual act of revenge. The narrative usually elicits audience support for the avenger who is torn apart by grief and rage. Hieronimo, a man of law and a loyal subject, vows to avenge the murder of his son, Horatio, by the king's nephew, Lorenzo, and the Portuguese Viceroy's son, Balthazar. We witness Hieronimo's transformation from a peace-loving, content man to one wracked by sorrow and bitterness. He swears that 'I'll not entomb them [Horatio's bleeding wounds] till I have revenge. / Then will I joy amidst my discontent. / Till then my sorrow never shall be spent' (2.5.54–56). On the one hand, Hieronimo's desire for revenge seems but natural – it is after all driven by love and grief. On the other hand, revenge was forbidden both by law and religion. Much of Hieronimo's conflict comes from this opposition. For instance, in the well-known '*Vindicta mihi!*' ('Vengeance is mine') speech he tries to assure himself that heaven will avenge all ill-doing, but after agonized introspection concludes that he has to take the initiative and act (3.13.1–45).

The Spanish Tragedy dramatizes the conflict between law and revenge. In fact, the preoccupation with justice is discernible right from the start when the judges of the underworld are unable to pass judgement on the life of Don Andrea, the young man who was killed in battle by the Portuguese nobleman Balthazar. His ghost then returns to the world of the living accompanied by the spirit of Revenge who promises Andrea that he will soon see his death avenged. Very soon after, in an earthly court, the Spanish king is called to adjudicate between Lorenzo and Horatio. He passes a fair judgement, proclaiming that 'you both deserve and both shall have reward' (1.2.179). However, the idea that justice is always well executed is quickly complicated. The Portuguese Viceroy, too hastily and with inadequate evidence, condemns Alexandro. When it is Hieronimo's turn to seek justice following Horatio's death he quite naturally turns 'to my lord the king' to 'cry aloud for justice through the court' (3.7.69–70). The king is, however, easily misled by Lorenzo and pays no attention to Hieronimo. As Hieronimo's wife, Isabella, says, 'neither piety nor pity moves / The King to justice or compassion' (4.2.2–3). Hieronimo himself is baffled and outraged because 'justice is exiled from the earth' (3.13.137). Although he himself has been an agent of justice in his role as Marshal, he is unsure whether justice has any real meaning anymore and almost has no choice but to seek private retribution. Revenge is thus represented as the product of a corrupt, unjust society and the last resort of the wronged and the powerless, making the play the tragedy of a society as much as it is a tragedy of an individual and a family. As Hieronimo says, the world is a 'mass of public wrongs, / Confused and filled with murder and misdeeds!' (3.2.3–4).

Even as the play is concerned with the moral issues surrounding revenge, it also dramatizes the distress suffered by the grieving father and the enraged avenger from the minute Hieronimo discovers the corpse in the garden to the end when he deliberately enacts his revenge. In the tradition of Senecan revenge tragedy Hieronimo delivers intense, impassioned soliloquies to express his emotion, even as he doubts the efficacy of language in conveying such emotion. 'Where shall I run to breathe abroad my woes . . .?' he asks (3.2.1). His pleas for justice do not penetrate the hard 'walls of diamond' of heaven (3.7.1, 16), yet his grief finds eloquent expression in the play. His famous speech beginning 'O eyes, no eyes, but fountains fraught with tears! / O life, no life, but lively form of death!' (3.2.1–2) is a perfectly crafted oration, but it grows more agitated and chaotic as Hieronimo finds Horatio's bloody handkerchief. Similarly, the language of revenge is itself impassioned and self-motivating. Hieronimo shames himself into destroying his son's killers. 'Then shamest thou not, Hieronimo, to neglect / The sweet revenge of thy Horatio?', he taunts himself (3.13.105–06). His grief is intense and convincing, but the play makes no attempt to make his expressions of sorrow 'natural'. Instead, the language of the play, replete with repetition and antithesis, is deliberately artificial. Subsequently, Hieronimo becomes sceptical of all speech: 'But wherefore waste I mine unfruitful words, / When naught but blood will satisfy my woes?' (3.7.67–68). Finally, in the play he stages at the end, language becomes a surreal babble of tongues alienating speaker from listener. Community breaks down even as communication does, and Hieronimo, in one final gesture, rejects all speech by biting out his tongue. Even as *The Spanish Tragedy* is a masterpiece of rhetoric, it is also a critique of language.

The play has many of the motifs of revenge tragedy. The presence of the ghost (here in the framing narrative) and the increasing alienation of the avenger as he bears the burden of his revenge in solitude are features of the genre. Like other heroes of revenge tragedy, Hieronimo is mistaken for mad by others, and he is, in a sense, actually driven to lunacy by the end. He contemplates suicide as a way out of his conflict but decides that if he dies Horatio will be left unavenged. *The Spanish Tragedy* is also truly 'a tragedy of blood'. Some of the violence is depicted on stage. For instance, Horatio is hanged in the arbour before the audience. Murder follows murder in the last scene in an orgy of killing and finally, in the last gory moment, Hieronimo bites off his tongue. Apart from these scenes – which horrify and shock yet also oddly satisfy, partly because the violence appears to serve the cause of justice and partly because of the extravagantly dramatic rendition of violence – the playwright also explores ways of conveying extreme physical violence through language. So, in the underworld, 'bloody Furies shake their whips of steel / ... Where usurers are choked with melting gold, / And wantons are embraced with ugly snakes, / And murderers groan with never-killing wounds, / And perjured wights scalded in boiling lead, / And all foul sins with torments overwhelmed' (1.1.65–71). Another feast of violence is the battlefield where, we are told, 'on every side drop captains to the ground, / And soldiers, some ill-maimed, some slain outright; / Here falls a body sundered from his head, / There legs and arms lie bleeding on the grass, / Mingled with weapons and unbowelled steeds / That, scattering, overspread the purple plain' (1.2.57–62). Violence and bloodshed are characteristic of this world.

Lorenzo is the Machiavellian villain of the play. High-born and courtly, he is a smooth-talker who manipulates language to serve his own ends. As his sister Bel-imperia wryly says, 'Brother, you are become an orator' (3.10.83). His pleasant demeanour masks the fact that he is a 'savage monster, not of human kind' (2.5.19). He is a ruthless man whose ambition is to further elevate his family by royal marriage and who is indifferent to the suffering he causes others. Apart from the murder of Horatio, he casually orders the death of one of his servants and leaves another to be hanged for a crime committed on his behalf. He displays all the arrogance of rank when he says that 'better 'tis that base companions die / ... For die they shall. Slaves are ordained to no other end' (3.2.115, 119).

Another aspect of *The Spanish Tragedy* is its examination of art as a response to grief. In the painter episode (which is one of the additions made by Jonson to the play), Hieronimo considers finding consolation in art. He asks the painter to 'paint some comfort' (3.12A.73). 'Canst paint a doleful cry?' he wonders (3.12A.125), but soon realizes that painting cannot offer him relief. It is drama that offers him a means to bring things to a closure. In fact, performance and theatricality have been important from the start of the play. The victory parade at the beginning is a performance of sorts and even Horatio's murder almost seems staged – a cruel parody of the crucifixion of Christ. The self-conscious oratory of the soliloquies are also performative, as is Hieronimo's decision to 'dissemble' ignorance and unsuspecting calm. Finally, of course, he stages a play, a 'stately-written tragedy. / ... fitting kings, / Containing matter, and not common things' (4.1.152–54). This final episode of *The Spanish Tragedy* is especially self-conscious about its own theatricality: we watch Andrea and Revenge watch the Spanish king and his courtly companions watch a play. Hieronimo's play is a spectacular staging of death and mayhem and a presentation of his own grief. The play-within-the-play not only reflects the reality of Hieronimo's state of mind but also makes its own reality, leading to the killings of Lorenzo, Balthazar and Bel-imperia.

While the play invites us to see the killings at the end as acts of symmetrical revenge, the chaos and catastrophic violence of the last scene leave the audience troubled. Even the innocent Duke of Castile is killed for no apparent reason and Hieronimo himself seems to be swept away by a passion for violence and becomes part of the circle of destruction. The justice enacted by revenge is haphazard and chaotic. Hieronimo gets his revenge but will never be happy again and kills himself. The stage is littered with corpses as the play ends without really offering a moral resolution. As Hieronimo put it earlier, 'O no, there is no end; the end is death and madness' (3.12A. 159–60).

Discussion points

1 Review the section on revenge tragedy in Chapter Seven ('Genre'). *The Spanish Tragedy* is among the early English examples of this genre. Is it important to know something about the genre to fully understand and appreciate this play? Also, is it merely a formulaic play in that it simply reproduces various elements of the genre? If yes, what is the appeal of this kind of 'formula fiction'? If not, how is this play different from conventional revenge tragedy?

2 One of the issues that need to be addressed in any staging of *The Spanish Tragedy* is whether to leave the play within the play in English or to translate it into the four different languages Hieronimo specifies. Michael Bogdanov's 1982 production for the National Theatre in London had the play within the play translated into Latin, ancient Greek, French and Italian. The Royal Shakespeare Company's 1997 production directed by Michael Boyd also had it performed in two languages. Discuss the effect of this kind of translation and what it could do to alter our understanding of the role of language to communicate and create community.

3 Andrea and Revenge offer an interesting frame to the play. Another decision that needs to be taken by the directors involve these two characters. The stage directions in early editions do not indicate if they remain onstage all the time. In fact, the opening stage direction of Act 3 Scene 15 seems to imply that they have previously left the stage. But most modern editions and productions assume that they remain on stage. What do you think is the significance and effect of having Revenge and Andrea witness all the action? Also think about how you would depict Revenge (innovative depictions include Revenge as female in the Oxford University Experimental Theatre Club production in 1973, as a pageboy who participated in the action by doubling as the Page who carries the empty box in London's Mercury Theatre production directed by Philip Allen-Morgan in 1973, as a hangman with his face covered by a black hood in the RSC's 1997 production directed by Michael Boyd and as a ten-year-old girl in Mitchell Moreno's 2009 London staging).

4 Senecan revenge tragedy had a reputation for sensational spectacles of violence. How does the degree and amount of violent action in Kyd's play condition our viewing of it?

5 The 1602 quarto of *The Spanish Tragedy* announces on its title-page that it is 'Newly corrected, amended, and enlarged with new additions of the painters part, and others, as it hath of late been divers times acted.' These additions (five in number and 324 lines in total) were possibly made by Ben Jonson and might be included in your edition of the play. They occur in Scene 2.5, Scene 3.2, Scene 3.10, Scene 3.12 and Scene 4.4. If you were not aware that these sections were added later would the dual authorship of the play be apparent to you? Select any one of these additions and read it carefully to see if you can detect differences in style and also consider if and why you would retain the addition if you were staging the play.

20

The Tempest

William Shakespeare

First performed in 1611 before King James and first printed in Shakespeare's 1623 Folio where it is the opening play, *The Tempest* is often regarded as William Shakespeare's last play. A couple of years after the play's first performance the playwright retired to his birthplace, Stratford, where he was to die in 1616. *The Tempest* has been read as Shakespeare's farewell to the theatre and even as indicative of the state of serenity and peace he had reached as he approached his later years, a state reflected in the play's rhetoric of redemption and forgiveness.

However, it turns out that *The Tempest* might not be the last play at all, and even the play's themes of forgiveness and mercy can perhaps be cast into doubt. Nevertheless, it remains true that *The Tempest* is among the most fascinating of Renaissance plays. It offers itself to numerous and varied interpretations and has inspired other plays, poems and works of fiction. While the play is categorized as a 'comedy' in the first folio and does have many of the elements of comedy, starting in the nineteenth century, it has been described as a 'romance'. The play's island setting, one apparently removed from the everyday realities of life, has partly prompted this label, as well as the significant role of magic in the plot. The basic structure of an adventure story – the departure, quest, discovery, conflict and final return – are also the typical motifs of romance.

However, 'romantic' as the play might be and as lushly lyrical and poetic as the language is, *The Tempest* is also among the most profound and the most political of literary works. This is partly because the language of the play is inherently nuanced and ambiguous. For example, the play's protagonist, Prospero, can be read in very different ways. He is the nurturing, concerned father and the wronged duke cheated of his title by a devious brother. On the island he is the wise, benign magician, brave and virtuous, using all his powers to save the imprisoned Ariel and right the wrongs inflicted on himself and his child. But he is also the controlling patriarch and a domineering authority-figure. Shakespeare's scripting of Prospero's relationship with Caliban is particularly complicated. Prospero is the strong master who has to punish and control the monster-slave who attempted to molest Miranda, but he is also the usurper who has taken away the island that is rightfully Caliban's and who uses magic to harass and humiliate him and to keep him in his place. Prospero's magic is itself interesting and adds to the ambiguity of the character. It could be virtuous knowledge used for good or could also be knowledge of a more dubious nature. Prospero's famous 'Ye elves of hills' speech (5.1.33–57) paraphrases the witch Medea's speech in the poem *Metamorphoses* by the Roman poet Ovid and makes Prospero's magic darker and more mysterious than it seems at first. Perhaps Prospero the magician is not all that different from his arch-rival Sycorax, the witch who practises the dark arts.

Caliban is among the most extraordinary of Shakespeare's creations. Described variously as a 'freckled whelp' (1.2.283), 'a tortoise' (1.2.317), an 'Abhorred slave' (1.2.352) and a 'mishappen knave' (5.1.269), Caliban is certainly the villain to Prospero's hero, depicted as crude and hostile, half-human, half-beast and wholly monstrous. He is also a potential rapist who crudely and aggressively admits to having already attempted to molest Miranda. But Shakespeare plays one representation of Caliban against others – the 'monster' states his claim to the island in impassioned tones and we cannot but help feel the injustice done to him. He is lyrical and has an exquisitely developed sensibility. His language is characterized by vivid and rich images, especially when he refers to the natural landscape of the island. Even as he is violent and fearsome in some scenes and ludicrous and grotesque in others, Caliban stands for the passion and energy behind all calls for freedom.

The fraught relationship between Prospero and Caliban has prompted many scholars to regard *The Tempest* as Shakespeare's 'colonial play'. The unnamed island is often read as America or the Caribbean though it has also been seen as standing for Ireland or the East Indies. Whatever the play's setting, colonial readings focus on the fact that Prospero is a settler on land that was Caliban's native territory. 'This island's mine by Sycorax, my mother …' (1.2.332), Caliban angrily claims. In turn Prospero dismisses Caliban as inhuman and base, and his fury as merely a savage and irrational outburst of rage. Even as Prospero insists that his version of the past (the events that took place in Milan or his settlement of the island) is true, Caliban produces his own account of the truth to counter and challenge Prospero. We are told that Caliban 'wouldst gabble like / A thing most brutish' (1.2.357–58) until Prospero and Miranda taught him language, but he now makes eloquent and passionate use of that language to express his anger and his sorrow. As he puts it: 'You taught me language, and my profit on't / Is I know how to curse' (3.1.365–66). But Caliban the impassioned rebel and Caliban the dreamer degenerate into Caliban the drunk who pathetically allies himself with Stephano and Trinculo in the second half of the play. Caliban is finally subdued by Prospero and retreats to a cave mumbling that he will 'seek for grace' (5.1.297). While Prospero and Miranda leave the island, Caliban's future is unknown. But the relationship between Prospero and his 'monster-slave' remains complicated right to the end. Prospero points to Caliban and says, 'this thing of darkness / I acknowledge mine' (5.1.276–77), simultaneously taking possession of, claiming responsibility for and even admitting to a strange kind of kinship with Caliban.

The women in the play are equally interesting. Sycorax remains a shadowy figure of the past but is evoked by Prospero with fury and some dread, and by Caliban with longing. The language used to describe her is vivid: she was not only a 'foul witch' (1.1.258) but also has with 'age and envy' 'grown into a hoop' (1.2.258–59), indicating an extreme state of moral and physical deformity. She reportedly came to the island pregnant and gave birth to Caliban on it. In all respects Sycorax, the Algerian witch, evokes dark, deviant femininity. In contrast to her is the young, beautiful and chaste Miranda. When the woebegone, shipwrecked Ferdinand catches sight of Miranda for the first time he is awestruck and filled with wonder, responses reminiscent of the amazement with which Europeans responded to the exotic and unexpected beauty and fertility of the New World. Miranda is among the most solitary of Shakespeare's heroines, brought up on the island with no one but her father and Caliban for company. She is schooled by her father to dislike and fear Caliban. Like the island, she becomes the possession the two men fight over. Caliban wants to molest her to get back at her father, while Prospero wants to protect her. She eventually falls in love with Ferdinand (following a meeting orchestrated by Prospero). But Miranda is unexpectedly assertive too. She insistently pleads with her father on Ferdinand's behalf, disobeys him and reveals her name to the young stranger. She sails off to Italy at the end, but her future is also uncertain as this child of the island prepares to be future queen.

The Tempest is also a comment and a reflection on the theatre itself. Prospero's magic has been read as a metaphor for the art and craft of playwriting, which creates and dismantles reality and moves minds, hearts and imaginations. Prospero is the chief actor as well as the director and writer at the centre of the action who decides the fates of the other characters. He stages a spectacular masque complete with song and dance to bedazzle his audience. But the masque ends abruptly and towards the end of the play, in his famous 'our revels now are ended' speech, Prospero gravely reflects on the nature of his magical-artistic undertakings. He is all too aware that actors will soon melt 'into thin air' and the world he has carefully set up is only a 'baseless fabric' which 'shall dissolve, / And like this insubstantial pageant faded, / Leave not a rack behind' (4.1.146–63). The moment is experienced by the magician-playwright with either disappointment at the emptiness of his accomplishments or with acceptance and calm, depending on how the reader interprets it.

In the tradition of romance (and that of comedy) *The Tempest* ends in marriage, happiness, forgiveness and reunion. Ariel, the charming spirit who has served Prospero for years (with some reluctance perhaps, but still faithfully), flies away to freedom even as his master wistfully remarks that he will miss his 'dainty Ariel' (5.1.95). But the celebration is not untarnished. The two political schemers, Antonio and Sebastian, are caught and rebuked for their wrongdoings (although they never quite apologize or repent). Prospero himself claims to have learnt to forgive, but he doesn't quite forget, interjecting sharp rebukes even into his forgiveness speech. The dazzled Miranda wonders at the 'brave new world' she has stumbled onto when she sets eyes on the king and his party, to which Prospero wryly remarks ''Tis new to thee' (5.1.185), perhaps indicating that the world is, unfortunately, neither brave nor entirely new. The happy ending is thus marked by a touch of cynicism, disappointment, even sadness. But readers and audiences still cannot help feeling that they have experienced something 'rich and strange' (1.2.402) – a powerful and moving work that is somehow, all at the same time, political allegory, meta-theatrical commentary, moral tale and magical artistic experience.

Discussion points

1   As pointed out above, *The Tempest* has long been read as a play about colonialism. It can be seen as an example of the typical operations of colonialist discourse: the occupation of the island is depicted as legitimate and even inevitable; the native is represented as inhuman and savage

and the colonizer as wise and benevolent; and ultimately, the colonizer triumphs over the native who retreats apologetic and shame-faced.

However, not all critics have agreed with this reading. Deborah Willis, for instance, finds post-colonial readings reductive because they ignore the complexities of the text. She argues that unlike typical colonial discourse (if there is anything like that, which is particularly unlikely in the time period, argues Willis) the play does not invite us to endorse Prospero, but actually provokes us to critique him. Caliban is also 'by turns sympathetic and ridiculous' and more 'grotesquely comic than devilish'.[1] In fact, it is Antonio, rather than Caliban, who is the main villain of the play, and he is the one who remains impenitent until the end.

Another critic, Paul Brown, does believe that the play should be read in the context of colonialism. But he argues that it is not an imperialist play in the strict sense because it demonstrates the limits and flaws of colonialism, the anxieties felt even by the triumphant colonizer and the contradictions informing the experience of the colonizer and the native alike. As Brown puts it, *The Tempest* 'declares no all-embracing triumph for colonialism. Rather it serves as a limit text in which the characteristic operations of colonialist discourse may be discerned – as an instrument of exploitation, a register of beleaguerment and a site of radical ambivalence.'[2]

Consider these three views of *The Tempest* (you should probably read the two essays mentioned here). What questions would you ask each of these critics if you wanted further clarification of their ideas? What could you say to challenge or to further support each of these critical arguments?

2 Caliban might be a colonized native whose island has been taken over by Prospero. He is created by Shakespeare, the English playwright. Imagine how writers from colonized cultures might rewrite Caliban. You might also want to research the famous 'appropriations' or rewrites of *The Tempest* by authors from different parts of the world. Consider, for instance, Aimé Césaire's play *A Tempest*, Kamau Brathwaite's poem 'Caliban', Marina Warner's novel *Indigo* and Suniti Namjoshi's poem 'Snapshots of Caliban'.

3 Gonzalo, one of men on the royal ship that is caught in the storm created by Prospero and subsequently wrecked on the island, is certainly typecast in some ways: he is the loyal courtier and good friend. However Gonzalo has some interesting moments in the play. For instance his jokes during the storm in the opening scene seem completely misplaced

in this moment of grave danger. What do you make of them and of Gonzalo in this scene? Also examine Gonzalo's speech outlining his vision of the ideal commonwealth (Act 2 Scene 1 – borrowed from the French philosopher Michel de Montaigne's 1580 essay 'Of the Cannibals'). Are these seemingly profound lines meant to be taken seriously or are they to be read as naïve in their idealism and even rather pointless given the circumstances of the lost court party? Note the other characters' responses to Gonzalo's language in general and to these lines in particular and think about how you interpret Gonzalo and the importance of his world-view.

4   Antonio and Sebastian are oddly silent in the last scene. Caliban, who has been so eloquent throughout, mutters that he will 'seek for grace' (5.1.296) and retreats from the scene. If you were an actor cast in one of these roles how would you play the last scene? What would you want to convey about how the character feels and how he responds to the situation he is in at the end of the story?

5   Nineteenth-century productions (notably Charles Kean's 1857 production) were the first to emphasize the spectacular nature of the play: the gigantic storms, the lush island, the incredible effects of Prospero's magic and Ariel's presence. Some viewers, however, saw this emphasis on spectacle as unnecessary or even as detracting from the play. What is your opinion? What does lavish spectacle bring to the play and what does it take away from it? Also, Caliban has been part of the play's spectacle, with the actors playing him costumed variously as monster, animal/animal-like and 'exotic' native. What kind of costume and make up would you give the actor who plays this role?

21

The Tragedy of Mariam

Elizabeth Cary

The Tragedy of Mariam by Elizabeth Cary is among the first plays written in English by a woman. The play is an example of 'closet drama', plays not intended for production but read by the author's circle of family and friends. However, *Mariam* was published in 1613 and consequently had a larger readership than many other closet plays. Cary's immediate sources for the story of Mariam were Thomas Lodge's 1602 translations of Josephus's *Antiquities of the Jews* and *The Jewish Wars*. The play dramatizes events that took place around 29 BC when Herod was appointed governor of Judea, married the princess Mariam and secured his title to the throne. *Mariam* has often been read in relation to its author's life. Cary, like her heroine, was an intelligent, free-spirited young woman. Married when she was 16 years old in an arranged match, Cary remained the learned and rebellious woman, even as she paradoxically idealized conventional wifely behaviour. Whether these connections between the author and the play's protagonist are relevant or not, the fact remains that Cary's play also engages with larger social themes – indeed, closet plays could do so more easily than plays for the public stage as they were not subject to censorship.

The play is a 'tragedy of state' as well as a 'domestic tragedy'. Herod is the stereotypical tyrant: dictatorial, cruel and murderous, who 'ever thirsts for blood...' (1.2.28).[1] He is also something of a madman; even his doting love for Mariam is 'not love, but raging lunacy' (1.2.46), and like other tyrants, he is insecure and paranoid. Many of the play's characters, notably Mariam, have to choose between obedience to the monarch and the dictates of their conscience (Mariam cannot forgive Herod's murder of her grandfather and brother). But Mariam is Herod's wife as well as his subject. He is her husband as well as her king and hence an embodiment of patriarchal structures. Marriage, particularly a royal marriage, becomes the main site of conflict in the play.

Mariam is the idealized heroine in many ways. She is beautiful, chaste and Herod's 'spotless wife' (5.1.198). However, she is associated with open and free speech, a shocking and unacceptable trait in a woman. The king's advisor, Sohemus, says that Mariam's 'unbridled speech' is her 'worst disgrace' (3.3.65) and Herod complains that 'Her mouth will ope to every stranger's ear' (4.7.78). The play opens with Mariam presenting herself as speaking in public, and though she apologizes for it and for displaying 'too rash a judgment' as women supposedly tend to do (1.1.6), she does continue to speak for a full seventy-eight lines! The first fourteen lines of this opening speech also constitute a sonnet. Mariam refuses to be merely the mistress male sonneteers write to but appropriates the poetic form. She compares herself to the mighty male ruler Julius Caesar and deliberately conflates the world of politics with her own private world. She also uses language to explore and express the ambivalent feelings she has upon hearing of Herod's death. She has not been unfaithful to him, but she cannot forgive him for murdering her family. Although she had often wished her husband dead, she still grieves at the news of his demise. She experiences a similar crisis yet again when she hears that Herod is not dead after all – she now mourns because he is alive. Mariam decides to express the anger and resentment she feels when Herod returns. She has had enough of a life of dissembling and pretence, she tells Herod. Her decision is momentous and final: 'I will not to his love be reconciled! / With solemn vows I have foresworn his bed' (3.3.15–16). Herod is bewildered and then furious at this rejection. He eventually lets himself believe that Mariam tried to poison him and orders her execution. Mariam's crime seems to be simply treachery of thought and speech.

However, it is not easy to determine if the play sets her up as a rebel or simply as a victim. Mariam is certainly more actively heroic than many other women in Renaissance tragedy. Her resolve and her desire for personal integrity are indeed admirable. She prides herself on her 'innocence' and although that was a conventionally valued feminine virtue, her innocence involves courage and integrity. Mariam, who has been accused of speech that is unrestrained and too frank, turns to silence at the end. But her silence too is a form of protest as she goes to her death with 'a dutiful, though scornful smile' (5.1.52). She dies a stoic, martyr-like death, so garnering for herself masculine honour and glory. But, in spite of this, prior to her execution Mariam delivers conventional lines on a woman having to be chaste as well as humble and says that both virtues do 'march with equal paces, hand in hand' (4.8.41). Her martyrdom can also been read as an unsatisfying model of female agency, because, after all, whether she's triumphant or not, the fact is that she dies and is celebrated only after death.

Mariam's sister-in-law Salome serves as a foil to Mariam. Both women reject conventional female roles. But the play represents Salome as treacherous, devious and immoral with her numerous lovers and husbands, in contrast to the chaste and upright Mariam. This could indicate that even an unconventional woman like Cary had internalized certain patriarchal attitudes to women. In spite of this, there is something admirable about the boldness with which Salome rejects conventional notions of women's shame and dishonour – 'Shame is gone and honour wiped away' (1.4.33), she declares. Salome actively rebels and perhaps even tries to affect social change. She protests the fact that only men can divorce women. 'Why should such privilege to man be given?' she asks in proto-feminist lines, 'Or, given to them, why barred from women then?' (1.4.45–46). These questions were bold for the time; Salome will not passively accept her position under patriarchal law. She says that she will 'be the custom-breaker and begin / To show my sex the way to freedom's door' (1.4.49–50). She remains defiant even as her husband, Constabarus, accuses her of dishonouring her name, race and husband and of dangerously rebelling: 'Are Hebrew women now transformed to men?' he asks, and is disturbed at the prospect of a world 'topsy-turned quite!' (1.6.47, 50). Constabarus dies cursing all women, but Salome lives on. She does not hesitate to co-opt patriarchal authority to her own purposes and influences Herod to execute his wife. It is hard to sympathize with Salome in moments like this, but the fact that she stays impenitent and goes unpunished might indicate that we are meant to approve of her boldness and rebellion even as we are uncomfortable with her cruelty and unscrupulousness.

The play is subtitled 'The Queen of Jewry'. The Jewish people here are the ancient peoples of the Old Testament. To an extent, the play romanticizes that world, including the Jerusalem of antiquity that is the setting of the play, a setting whose magnificence is reflected in the figure of Mariam. But Jewish people were also a presence in the world of the Renaissance and were often perceived in stereotypical and racist ways, as we saw in Chapter Three ('Travel and Trade'). Dympna Callaghan suggests that Renaissance England's complex attitudes to the Jewish people inform *Mariam*. While Herod, the Jewish male, is marked as morally and racially debased, the representation of Mariam (as Jewish) is more complicated. Even as she is marked as the 'queen of Jewry', she is conspicuously white. Her light skin not only sets up the standard of beauty, it is also a mark of her morality. Indeed Mariam herself sees her body as signifying her goodness. 'If fair she be, she is as chaste as fair', she says (4.8.58). Herod loves her beauty, yet it also makes him jealous and insecure. He fears that it might conceal the truth about her, that she is a 'fair fiend' who has duped him 'With heavenly semblance' (4.4.55, 56). As he admits at the end, 'If she had been like an Egyptian, black, / And not as fair, she had been longer lived' (5.1.239–40). Salome is also a sensual and beautiful woman, but she is represented as relatively dark-skinned. Her rebelliousness and her sexual appetite are associated with 'voracious blackness'.[2] Mariam talks of Salome's 'black acts' (1.3.38) and Herod says his sister is 'a sunburnt blackmoore' (4.7.106). Salome does not remain silent at these remarks. When Mariam insults her 'baser birth' on the grounds that Salome is of mixed Jewish lineage (1.3.27), Salome challenges her. What real difference is there, she asks, 'betwixt thy ancestors and mine? / Both born of Adam, both were made of earth, / And both did come from holy Abraham's line' (1.3.34–36). Indeed, Salome later resolves to take revenge on Mariam for disparaging her birth and origins.

The complexity with which Mariam and Salome are represented makes *Mariam* a richly ambiguous play. This ambiguity is further heightened by the presence of a Chorus which is generally conservative in its statements regarding female behaviour. It implies that a woman who speaks in public 'doth her glory blot' (3 Chorus, 17) and even disapproves of Mariam's assertiveness, seeing her as being swayed by 'sullen passion' and a base desire for revenge (4 Chorus, 33). The Chorus further seems to advocate that women give up freedom of thought upon marriage. But the Chorus's voice is not necessarily that of the playwright. Besides, the fact that the Chorus often voices its thoughts on women's independence in the form of questions rather than assertions (for example, 'Do they not wholly give themselves away? / Or give they but their body, not their mind' [3 Chorus, 20–21]) leaves open the possibility that women do *not*, in fact, wholly give themselves away after marriage. Even as the play supports patriarchy and condemns women's assertiveness, it still depicts female rebellion and recognizes the challenges in the way of women gaining autonomy and self-fulfilment. *Mariam* is clearly an exploration of, rather than a solution to, the tensions and complexities surrounding women's roles in the Renaissance.

Discussion points

1 *Mariam* has been linked to Elizabeth Cary's life (see the opening paragraph above). Look for further information on the author's life

and see if any aspect of her life-story helps you better understand the play. In other words, what are the possibilities and limitations of a 'biographical approach' to better understand this play? Also, think about whether we tend to turn to biographical readings when we are studying writing by women. If so, why?

2 Certain sections of the play have been described as 'proto-feminist'. However, some critics have argued that its 'feminism' is neither simple nor straightforward. Consider, for instance, Ramona Wray's claim that the play 'exemplifies and elaborates two of the main restrictions imposed upon Renaissance women – the twin doctrines of silence and chastity – in a way that is neither prescriptive nor judgemental'.[3] Do you agree with Wray's point? If so, could a text that is so indirect in its criticism of conventional attitudes and expectations be considered 'feminist' at all?

3 For a long time *Mariam* was not considered one of the 'great plays' of the Renaissance and was certainly not taught very often. Why do you think this has been the case? Consider the play's authorship, its status as closet drama, its theme and style. What kind of argument would you make for the play to be taught and staged more often?

4 Like the Duchess of Malfi (another female protagonist), Mariam dies at the end of the play. In fact, death often seems to be the lot of strong female leads. What do we make of this? Are the deaths of the Duchess and Mariam 'heroic', i.e. befitting tragic heroes?

5 There are few stage directions in the original text of *Mariam*. This is characteristic of closet drama. Some modern editors have, however, added some stage directions. Look through the text and add stage directions that you think might direct the actor. This exercise might help you envisage the play for the stage.

22

Volpone

Ben Jonson

Volpone is a sophisticated and delightful satirical comedy which was performed on the Renaissance public stage for the first time in 1606. The play was also printed in quarto in 1607 and in the folio of Jonson's *Works* in 1616. The story of the wealthy Volpone who dupes greedy men and women by promising to make them heir to his great wealth is broadly based on Aesopian beast fables, many of which figure a sly fox who outwits other creatures – tales extremely popular in Renaissance Europe. Like Volpone, the fox of these tales often plays dead in order to trap the creatures who come to feed off his corpse.

Venice, Europe's major commercial centre, is the perfect setting. Motivated by the desire for gold, all characters of the play are spurred into frenetic activity. Indeed, *Volpone* is a highly energetic and very busy play with its endless plotting and scheming, varied disguises and many exits and entrances. Jonson keeps all this activity going and multiple storylines running in a tightly constructed plot.

Volpone is among the most clever, agile and inventive of Jonson's creations. He is a strangely solitary creature with no family or companions except for his servants, yet there is no regret when he says 'I have no wife, no parent, child, ally, / To give my substance to' (1.1.73–74). He delights in his cleverness and though he does make money from his victims, he schemes against them primarily because he enjoys doing so and to satisfy his intelligent, restless mind. This is what gives the play its peculiar zest. In fact, Volpone's attitude to money too is more complex than is obvious at first glance. His opening speech in which he worships money is a mocking parody of other people who adore gold. The protagonist of the play is not exceptionally greedy or even corrupt – simply because everyone in this world is.

Volpone differs from the others because he is more intelligent than them. His plans are stunningly simple yet always work. He is witty and clever with words. He is cheeky, funny and dazzling in his guise as a dying man, as a street healer and when, with a straight face, he condemns other cheats as 'turdy-facey-nasty-patey-lousy-fartical rogues' (2.2.59). Sir Politic remarks wonderingly about Volpone's speech: 'Ha' you heard better language, sir?' (2.2.68). And indeed, we rarely have. He dismisses conventional morality as 'the beggar's virtue' (3.7.210) and delights in his victims' hostility because 'The fox fares ever best when he is cursed' (5.3.120). Roguery is a form of artistry for Volpone. He plays with his victims' hopes, 'Letting the cherry knock against their lips, / And draw it by their mouths, and back again' (1.2.89–90). He is a master performer: he successfully plays ill, plays dead and plays a doctor. Even the love-agony he claims he feels after seeing Celia for the first time is a parody of traditional Petrarchan love celebrations of the beloved. Volpone becomes the embodiment of a theatrical identity that shapes itself through self-conscious performance. We, the audience, delight in Volpone's performances and laugh with him rather than at him. Since he is often on stage and addresses the audience directly a number of times, we establish a certain intimacy with him and don't want his trickery to stop because it entertains us. As so much of Volpone's scheming is against the greedy scavengers of the city, we don't fully condemn him either. His mockery and exposure of human folly makes Volpone a satirist in the best tradition. It is when Volpone lets his own desires take over the sport and attempts to assault Celia and dupes the young innocent Bonario that we find him more unsavoury.

Volpone's servant Mosca is reminiscent of the wily servant of Roman comedy. He is as much the artist-rogue as his master is, constantly baiting and playing with his victims in cat-and-mouse fashion. He distinguishes himself from inferior parasites who get by with fawning and flattering and doing 'court-dog-tricks' (3.1.20) to please their masters. Instead, he is a 'fine, elegant rascal, that can rise / And stoop, almost together, like an arrow; / Shoot through the air, as nimbly as a star; / Turn short, as doth a swallow; and be here, / And there, and here, and yonder, all at once' (3.2.13–27). These lines are almost lyrical in their celebration of the agility and quickness of the rogue. Mosca and Volpone appear to have a high regard for each other and work together very efficiently until Mosca's greed gets the better of him and he decides to trap Volpone and seize all his wealth for himself. 'My fox / Is out on his hole, and, ere he shall re-enter, / I will make him languish' (5.5.7–8), Mosca declares – and then proceeds to scheme against his master.

Volpone's and Mosca's victims are the 'gulls', foolish victims of tricks whom Jonson delighted in satirizing in his comedies. They are gullible because they are greedy. Volpone says money 'mak'st men do all things' (1.1.23) and it is certainly the reason why the gulls flatter, lie and cheat. Money is a valued possession that also possesses these men and takes over their minds and lives. Volpone is also able to control his victims because of their delusional, self-aggrandizing fantasies. As Mosca comments, 'each of 'em / Is so possessed, and stuffed with his own hopes, / That anything unto the contrary, / Never so true, or never so apparent, / Never so palpable, but they will resist it' (5.2.23–27). Volpone comes to the conclusion that 'To be a fool born is a disease incurable' (2.2.159). Jonson's depiction of the gulls is clearly drawn from the beast fables. Voltore is the vulture, the greedy carrion-seeker; the old man Corbaccio is like the raven, associated with death and with abandoning his offspring and Corvino is the crow, another scavenger bird. 'All my birds of prey, / That think me turning carcass, now they come' (1.2.89–90), gloats Volpone as they hover eagerly over the supposedly dying man. Corvino is caught between his greed and his insane jealousy, but the former wins out as he offers his wife Celia to Volpone. The wretched Corbaccio is a decrepit old man, even older and sicker than Volpone can even pretend to be, but he has deluded himself into believing that he will live for years more and 'hopes to hop / Over his [Volpone's] grave' (1.4.4–5). He disinherits his son without a second thought to please Volpone. The greedy advocate, Voltore, is not a stupid man. On the contrary, he is a shrewd and unscrupulous lawyer who does not hesitate to defend criminals and wrongdoers. However, his greed for money and status make him vulnerable to Volpone's machinations.

Folly also reigns supreme in the sub-plot. The foolish Sir Politic prides himself on being cosmopolitan and invests the most banal incidents in his life with mystery, besides having the most grandiose and unrealistic of schemes. His wife, the over-talkative Lady Would-Be, is described as 'My madam with the everlasting voice' (3.5.4) and her company is dreaded even by Volpone. She is obsessed with decorum and everything Italian. However, these characters are not vicious or corrupt like those in the main plot. But neither Peregrine, the young man who exposes the Politics' folly, nor Celia and Bonario in the main plot can be considered the 'heroes' of the story. While Celia and Bonario are the only truly 'good characters' and certainly have our sympathy, Jonson deliberately overdoes the representation of Celia as the virtuous lady and later as the damsel in distress. Her language is almost a parody of virtue ('Sir, kill me rather: I will take down poison, / Eat burning coals, do anything' [3.7.93–94]). Similarly, even as we are glad that Bonario steps in and prevents the rape of Celia, his rhetoric is so much that of the rescuing hero that it smacks of irony ('Forbear, foul ravisher, libidinous swine / Free the forced lady, or thou diest, imposter' [3.7.266–67]). In any case, both Bonario and Celia are so slightly sketched that they remain virtuous but uninteresting characters and Jonson resists the conventional ending by refusing to hint at the possibility of a romantic bond between them.

What kind of ending does *Volpone* demand? Could the play end with Act 4 where Volpone and Mosca's triumph seems absolute, making the play truly a celebration of the artist-rogue? If we have fully enjoyed Volpone's machinations and performances this would be the fit ending. But if we are uneasy about the morality of some of his actions, one more act and another conclusion are called for. Jonson chooses the latter option. After their last trick Mosca says, 'this is our masterpiece; / We cannot go beyond this' (5.2.13–14). But Volpone is carried away by his success and gets reckless. He not only spreads the news of his death but walks abroad in disguise to taunt his victims. Mosca then decides to outwit his master. The law steps in at the end to punish the gulls for their greed and Volpone and Mosca for their devious scheming. But the *avocatari* (magistrates), in spite of their pious talk of crime and punishment, are also corrupt. For instance, they focus more on gaining Mosca (who they thought had become wealthy) as a son-in-law than in meting out justice. So the portrayal of justice is ambivalent at best. Besides, the harsh sentences delivered by the law take away from the play's playful comic spirit and violate the convention of the traditional comic ending. The play ceases to be a satire and instead becomes an enactment of justice. It is as if Jonson is experimenting with a moralistic ending. Satire is complicated by the demands of justice; wit is set up against morality. Finally, justice and morality win. Volpone does have the last word as he re-enters to deliver the Epilogue. We are thus invited to identify him with the author and to remember the play less for its ending than for the inventiveness and ingeniousness of the author and his wily protagonist.

Discussion points

1 As discussed above, the conclusion of the play could be considered somewhat unsatisfactory. The director of the Bristol Old Vic production of 1972 changed the ending and Tyrone Guthrie in the 1968 National Theatre version played up the comic element by adding a madrigal

between the sentencing and the epilogue to render the ending less harshly moralistic. What do you think of these changes? Do they keep the play interesting even as they try to make it more palatable or at least more consistent with the comic tone? What other changes could one make to the end of the play if one were staging it?

2 Celia is usually performed as the virtuous lady who becomes Volpone's victim. But the actress's tone and body language in her encounters with Volpone from the mountebank scene to the attempted-rape scene hold some interesting possibilities. Consider the different ways Celia could be played in these scenes.

3 Unlike other comic writers, Jonson often refuses to introduce a romantic plot into his comedies. We see this both in *Volpone* and *The Alchemist* (see the earlier discussion of *The Alchemist*). Do you think the absence of romance enhances or takes away from *Volpone*? How would the play change if this element were introduced? If you are interested in creative writing, imagine a rewritten *Volpone* with romantic love as part of the storyline. How does the added element alter the tone of the play?

4 *Volpone* is one the cleverest and wittiest of Renaissance comedies as far as its style is concerned. Review Chapter Eight ('Language and Style') and try to identify and characterize the different styles of speech in the play. Consider how the different styles help to shape individual characters.

5 *Volpone* is set in Renaissance Venice. Reset *Volpone* in any modern-day setting, preferably in one you are familiar with. How would you rewrite or update the characters of Volpone, Mosca and the gulls? Are there elements of the storyline you would change to make it a more modern play?

Appendix

From *Henslowe's Diary* (1591–1609): Modern spelling transcript (see pages 128–29 for the original version)

The Inventory taken of all the properties for My Lord Admiral's Men, the 10 of March 1598.

   Item, One rock, one cage, one tomb, one hell mouth.

   Item, One tomb of Guido, one tomb of Dido, one bedstead.

   Item, Eight lances, one pair of stairs for Phaeton.

   Item, Two steeples and one chime of bells and one beacon.

   Item, One heifer for the play of Phaeton, the limbs dead.

   Item, One globe, one golden sceptre, and three clubs.

   Item, Two marchpanes [models/sculptures made of sugar confections or, more likely, fabricated of pasteboard in imitation of sugar confections] and the City of Rome.

   Item, One golden fleece, two rackets, and one bay tree.

   Item, One wooden hatchet, one leather hatchet.

   Item, One wooden canopy, old Mahomet's head.

   Item, One lion skin, one bear's skin and Phaeton's limbs and Phaeton's chariot and Argus's head [presumably Argus Panoptes, the many-eyed giant who guarded Zeus's heifer].

   Item, Neptune fork and garland.

   Item, One crosier's [bearer of a bishop's staff] staff, Kent's wooden leg.

   Item, Iris's head and rainbow, one little altar.

   Item, Eight visors, Tamburlaine's bridle, one wooden mattock [a digging tool].

   Item, Cupid's bow and quiver, the Cloth of the Sun and Moon.

   Item, One boar's head and Cerberus's three heads.

   Item, One caduceus [wand carried by Hermes, the messenger god], two moss banks and one snake.

   Item, Two fans of feathers, Belendon stables [probably for a lost *c.* 1594 play titled *Bellendon*], one tree of golden apples, Tantelus tree [Tantalus is a figure in Greek mythology subject to eternal punishment; he is made to stand below a fruit tree with low-hanging branches, with the fruit ever eluding his grasp. This prop might have been used in a 1596 play titled *Fortunas*], nine iron targets.

Item, One copper target, seventeen foils.

Item, Four wooden targets, one greve armour [armour for the leg below the knee].

Item, One sign for Mother Redcap, one buckler.

Item, Mercury's wings, Tasso pictures, one helmet with a dragon, one shield with three lions, one elm bowl.

Item, One chain of dragons, one gilt spear.

Item, Two coffins, one bull's head, one philtre [love potion].

Item, Three timbrels [either a percussion instrument like a tambourine or the crest for a helmet], one dragon in Faustus.

Item, One lion, two lion heads, one great horse with his legs, one sack-butt [a large cask of wine or ale].

Item, One wheel and frame in the Siege of London.

Item, One pair of wrought [embroidered] gloves.

Item, One Pope's mitre [ornate headdress].

Item, Three Imperial crowns, one plain crown.

Item, One ghost's crown, one crown with a sun.

Item, One frame for the heading in Black Jone.

Item, One black dog.

Item, One cauldron for the Jew.

Suggested Reading

Chapter 1 – Politics and Society

Beier, A.L. 'Vagrants and the Social Order in Elizabethan England', *Past and Present* 64 (1974): 3–29.

Haigh, Christopher. *English Reformations: Religion, Politics and Society under the Tudors* (Oxford: Oxford University Press, 1993).

Helgerson, Richard. *Forms of Nationhood: The Elizabethan Writing of England* (Chicago: University of Chicago Press, 1995).

Jones, Norman. *The English Reformation: Religion and Cultural Adaption* (New York: Wiley-Blackwell, 2002).

Marshall, Peter. '(Re)Defining the English Reformation', *Journal of British Studies* 48, no.3 (2009): 564–586.

Neill, Michael. 'Broken English and Broken Irish: Nation, Language and the Optic of Power in Shakespeare's Histories', *Shakespeare Quarterly* 45, no.1 (1994): 1–32.

Sharpe, J. *Early Modern England: A Social History 1550–1760* (London: Bloomsbury, 2009).

Chapter 2 – Men and Women

Amussen, Susan. *An Ordered Society: Gender and Class in Early Modern England* (New York: Columbia University Press, 1988).

Bray, Alan. 'Homosexuality and the Signs of Male Friendship in Elizabethan England', *History Workshop* 29 (Spring 1990): 1–19.

Callaghan, Dympna. *Shakespeare Without Women* (New York: Routledge, 1999).

Jardine, Lisa. *Still Harping on Daughter: Women and Drama in the Age of Shakespeare* (New York: Columbia University Press, 1999; first published 1983).

Orgel, Stephen. *Impersonations: The Performance of Gender in Shakespeare's England* (Cambridge: Cambridge University Press, 1996).

Peters, Christine. *Women in Early Modern Britain, 1450–1640* (Basingstoke: Palgrave Macmillan, 2004).

Rackin, Phyllis. 'Why Feminism Still Matters', *Shakespeare in Our Time*, ed. Dympna Callaghan and Suzanne Gossett, 7–14 (London: Bloomsbury Arden Shakespeare, 2016).

Chapter 3 – Travel and Trade

Loomba, Ania. *Shakespeare, Race, and Colonialism* (Oxford: Oxford University Press, 2002).

Singh, Jyotsna. *Colonial Narratives/Cultural Dialogues: 'Discoveries' of India in the Language of Colonialism* (London: Routledge, 1996).

Smith, Ian. 'Barbarian Errors: Performing Race in Early Modern England', *Shakespeare Quarterly* 49, no.2 (1998): 168–186.

Vaughan, Virginia Mason. *Performing Blackness on English Stages, 1470–1800* (Cambridge: Cambridge University Press, 2005).

Vitkus, Daniel. 'Circumnavigation, Shakespeare, and the origins of Globalization', *Shakespeare in Our Time*, ed. Dympna Callaghan and Suzanne Gossett, 167–170 (London: Bloomsbury Arden Shakespeare, 2016).

Chapter 4 – Humanism

Blair, Ann and Anthony Grafton. 'Reassessing Humanism and Science', *Journal of the History of Ideas* 53, no.4 (1992): 535–540.

Bushnell, Rebecca. *A Culture of Teaching: Early Modern Humanism in Theory and Practice* (Ithaca: Cornell University Press, 1996).

Cartwright, Kent. *Theatre and Humanism: English Drama in the Sixteenth Century* (Cambridge: Cambridge University Press, 1999).

Caspari, Frank. *Humanism and the Social Order in Tudor England* (New York: Teacher's College Press, 1968).

Pincombe, Michael. *Elizabethan Humanism: Literature and Learning in the Later Sixteenth Century* (New York: Longman, 2001).

Pincombe, Michael. 'Some Sixteenth-century Records of the Words Humanist and Humanitian', *The Review of English Studies*, 44, no.173 (1993): 1–15.

Chapter 5 – The Stage

Gibbons, Brian. 'The Question of Place', *Cahiers élisabéthains* 50 (1996): 33–43.

Gurr, Andrew. *The Shakespearean Playing Companies* (Oxford: The Clarendon Press, 1996).

Gurr, Andrew. 'The social evolution of Shakespeare's Globe', *Theatre Symposium* 4 (1996): 15–26.

Harbage, Andrew. *Shakespeare's Audience* (New York: Columbia University Press, 1961).

Kinney, Arthur F. *Shakespeare by Stages: An Historical Introduction* (Malden, MA: Blackwell, 2003).

Stern, Tiffany. 'The Study of Historical Performance', *Shakespeare in our Time*, ed. Dympna Callaghan and Suzanne Gossett, 319–323 (London: Bloomsbury Arden Shakespeare, 2016).

Chapter 6 – Books, Authors and Readers

Blayney, Peter. 'The Publication of Playbooks', in *A New History Of Early English Drama*, ed. John Cox and David Kastan, 383–422 (New York: Columbia University Press, 1987).

Brooks, Douglas. *Playhouse to Printing House: Dramatic Authorship and Publication in Early Modern England* (New York: Cambridge University Press, 2000).

Farmer, Alan and Zach Lessor. 'The Popularity of Playbooks Revisited', *Shakespeare Quarterly* 56, no.1 (2005): 1–432.

Kastan, David. *Shakespeare and the Book* (Cambridge: Cambridge University Press, 2001).

Sherman, William H. *Used Books: Marking Readers in Renaissance England* (Philadelphia: University of Pennsylvania, 2008).

Smith, Emma. 'Author v. Character in Early Modern Dramatic Authorship: The Example of Thomas Kyd and *The Spanish Tragedy*', *Medieval and Renaissance Drama in English* 11 (1999): 129–142.

Chapter 7 – Genre

Danson, Lawrence. *Shakespeare's Dramatic Genres* (Oxford: Oxford University Press, 2000).

Leggat, Alexander. *Introduction to English Renaissance Comedy* (Manchester: Manchester University Press, 1999).

Leonard, Nathaniel C. 'Embracing the "Mongrel": John Marston's *The Malcontent*, *Antonio and Mellida* and the Development of English Early Modern Tragicomedy', *Journal of Early Modern Cultural Studies* 12, no.3 (Summer 2012): 60–87.

Rackin, Phyllis. *Stages of History: Shakespeare's English Chronicles* (Ithaca: Cornell University Press, 1990).

Smith, Emma and Garret Sullivan (eds). *The Cambridge Companion to English Renaissance Tragedy* (Cambridge: Cambridge University Press, 2010).

Wells, Stanley. 'Shakespeare and Romance', *Later Shakespeare*, ed. John Brown and Harris Bernard, 49–80 (London: E. Arnold, St. Martins, 1965).

Chapter 8 – Language and Style

Barber, Charles. *Early Modern English* (London: Deutsch, 1976).

Blake, N.F. *Shakespeare's Language: An Introduction* (London: Methuen, 1983).

Houston, John Porter. *Shakespearean Sentences: A Study in Style and Syntax* (Baton Rouge: Louisiana State University Press, 1988).

Jones, Richard Foster. *The Triumph of the English Language: A Survey of Opinions Concerning the Vernacular from the Introduction of Printing to the Reformation* (Stanford, CA: Stanford University Press, 1953).

Lanham, Richard. *The Motives of Eloquence: Literary Rhetoric in the Renaissance* (New Haven, CT: Yale University Press, 1976).

McDonald, Russ. 'William Shakespeare, Elizabethan Stylist', *Shakespeare in Our Time*, ed. Dympna Callaghan and Suzanne Gossett, 295–302 (London: Bloomsbury Arden Shakespeare, 2016).

Notes

PART I

Chapter 1 – Politics and Society

1. All quotations from this play taken from Christopher Marlowe, *Tamburlaine, Parts One and Two*, ed. Anthony Dawson (London: Bloomsbury, 2014).
2. Statute in Restrain of Appeals, 1532.
3. Richard Hooker, *Of the Laws of Ecclesiastical Policy*, ed. Arthur McGrade (Cambridge: Cambridge University Press, 1989), 150.
4. James I, 'Speech of 1609', in *Political Writings*, ed. J.P. Sommerville, 179–203 (Cambridge: Cambridge University Press, 1994).
5. *Elizabeth I: Collected Works*, ed. Leah Marcus, Janel Mueller and Mary Beth Rose (Chicago: University of Chicago Press, 2000), 59.
6. James I, *Basilikon Doron*, in *Political Writings*, 1–61, 40.
7. All quotations from this play taken from Christopher Marlowe, *Edward II*, ed. Martin Wiggins and Robert Lindsey (London: Bloomsbury, 2014).
8. Stephen Gosson, *Plays Confuted in Five Actions* (London, 1582), E1r.
9. David Bevington, *Tudor Drama and Politics* (Cambridge, MA: Harvard University Press, 1968), 302.
10. Temperament, turn of mind.
11. Leniency.
12. An order from the Diocesan Court of High Commission in the North for a letter to be sent to the civic authorities in Wakefield relating to their Corpus Christi play, 27 May 1576.
13. Christopher Haigh, *English Reformations: Religion, Politics, and Society under the Tudors* (Oxford: Clarendon Press, 1993), 20.
14. Haigh, *English Reformations*, 13.
15. Quoted in Norman Jones, *The English Reformation, Religion and Cultural Adaptation* (Malden, MA: Blackwell, 2002), 97.
16. A.G. Dickens, *The English Reformation* (New York: Schocken Books, 1964), 307.

17. One of the oldest festivals of the Christian Church, observed on 24 June.
18. Bound to, compelled to.
19. An Anglican service held in the morning.
20. Church service celebrated shortly after sunset.
21. Generally speaking, certain rituals or ceremonies belonging to the Church.
22. Partakers of communion. More generally, participants in church ritual.
23. Parson. In this Act 'person' often stands for 'parson.'
24. Privately.
25. Room or building for private worship.
26. Disparagement.
27. The act of procuring the release of a prisoner on someone's undertaking to stand surety for his or her appearance in court at a certain time.
28. Once again, second time.
29. By the very fact.
30. Prevent, hinder.
31. Property, land.
32. Decrees, orders.
33. Haigh, *English Reformations*, 19.
34. Quoted in Christopher Haigh, 'The Continuity of Catholicism in the English Reformation', in *The English Reformation. Revised,* ed. Christopher Haigh, 176–209 (Cambridge: Cambridge University Press, 1987), 184.
35. William Perkins, *The Workes of the Famous and Worthy Minister of Christ* (London, 1609), Vol. 1 sig. A2v, 31.
36. Jones, *The English Reformation,* 198.
37. Eamon Duffy, *The Stripping of the Altars* (New Haven: Yale University Press, 1992), 593.
38. 'An Admonition to Parliament', in *Puritan Manifestoes,* ed. W.H. Frere and C.E. Douglas (Society for Promoting Christian Knowledge, 1907), 9.
39. Perkins, *The Works,* Vol. 1, 670.
40. Perkins, *The Foundation of Christian Religion* (London, 1633), 22.
41. See Patrick Collinson, *The Birthpangs of Protestant England: Religious and Cultural Change in the Sixteenth and Seventeenth Centuries* (New York: St. Martin's Press, 1988).
42. John Foxe, *The Acts and Monuments,* ed. S.R. Cartley and G. Townsend (London, 1837), Vol. iii, 720.
43. See Patrick Collinson, 'Literature and the Church', in *The New Cambridge History of Early Modern English Literature,* ed. David Loewenstein and Janel Muller, 374–398 (Cambridge: Cambridge University Press, 2002).
44. Chapbooks and broadsides were cheaply printed popular texts with crude woodcut illustrations. Chapbooks could take up the religious issues of the

day in a variety of genres including folktales and simply written tracts, while broadsides were generally ballads or rhymes.

45. Patrick Collinson, 'English Reformations', in *A Companion to English Renaissance Literature and Culture*, ed. Michael Hattaway, 27–43 (Oxford: Blackwell, 2000).

46. Quoted in Paul White, *Theatre and Reformation* (Cambridge: Cambridge University Press, 1993), 14.

47. William Prynne, *Histrio-mastix* (London, 1633), 63.

48. Collinson, *The Birthpangs of Protestant England*, 95.

49. See Elizabeth Williams, *The Materiality of Religion in Early Modern English Drama* (Burlington, VT: Asghate, 2009).

50. Stephen Greenblatt, *Learning to Curse: Essays in Early Modern Culture* (New York: Routledge, 2007).

51. Thomas Heywood, *An Apology for Actors* (London, 1612), G2v.

52. All quotations from this play taken from John Webster, *The Duchess of Malfi*, ed. Brian Gibbons (London: Bloomsbury, 2001).

53. Tradition of sermons. In the Church of England this specifically applied to the *Book of Homilies* published for use in parish churches.

54. William Hamlin, *Tragedy and Scepticism in Shakespeare's England* (Basingstoke: Palgrave Macmillan, 2005), 3.

55. David Kastan, *A Will to Believe: Shakespeare and Religion* (Oxford: Oxford University Press, 2014), 6.

56. All quotations from this play taken from Christopher Marlowe, *The Jew of Malta*, ed. James Siemon (London: Bloomsbury, 2014).

57. Benedict Anderson, *Imagined Communities: Reflections on the Origin and Spread of Nationalism* (New York: Verso, 1983).

58. Leah Greenfeld, *Nationalism: Five Roads to Modernity* (Cambridge, MA: Harvard University Press, 1992), 14.

59. Act in Restraint of Appeals, 1533. 24 Henry VIII c 12.

60. Richard Hooker, *Of the Laws of Ecclesiastical Policy*, 116.

61. William Haller, *Foxe's Book of Martyrs and the Elect Nation* (London: Jonathan Cape, 1963).

62. J.A. Sharpe, *Early Modern England: A Social History 1550–1760* (London: Arnold, 2007), 123.

63. Edmund Dudley, *The Tree of Commonwealth* (1510), 7.

64. King James I, Speech to Parliament of 1607, in *Political Writings*, 159–178, 169.

65. David Baker, *Between Nations: Shakespeare, Spenser, Marvell, and the Question of Britain* (Stanford: Stanford University Press, 1997), 65.

66. See Richard Helgerson, *Forms of Nationhood: The Elizabethan Writing of England* (Chicago: University of Chicago Press, 1992) and Claire McEachern, *The Poetics of English Nationhood: 1590–1612* (Cambridge: Cambridge University Press, 1996).

67. See Helgerson, *Forms of Nationhood*.

68. Richard Hakluyt, 'Epistle Dedicatory', in *Divers Voyages Touching the Discovery of America*, ed. John Winter Jones, 8–18 (London: Hakluyt Society, 1850), 8.

69. Heywood, *An Apology for Actors*, C1r.

70. Walter Cohen, *Drama of a Nation: Public Theater in Renaissance England and Spain* (Ithaca: Cornell University Press, 1985).

71. Robert Weimann, *Shakespeare and the Popular Tradition in the Theater* (Baltimore: Johns Hopkins University Press, 1978).

72. Heywood, *An Apology for Actors*, B4r.

73. All quotations from Shakespeare plays are from *The Arden Shakespeare: The Complete Works*, ed. Richard Proudfoot, Ann Thompson and David Kastan (London: Bloomsbury, 2011).

74. All quotations from this play taken from Robert Greene, *Friar Bacon and Friar Bungay*, ed. Daniel Seltzer (Lincoln: University of Nebraska Press, 1963).

75. D.E. Underdown, 'The Taming of the Scold: The Enforcement of Patriarchal Authority in Early Modern England', in *Order and Disorder in Early Modern England*, ed. Anthony Fletcher and John Stevenson, 116–136 (Cambridge: Cambridge University Press, 1987), 116.

76. Compulsory.

77. Proclamation of punishment.

78. Happiness.

79. Set up.

80. Realms, kingdoms.

81. Prudent governance.

82. Lacking sound judgement.

83. Most wicked.

84. Exemption from penalty.

85. Unsuitable.

86. Foolish, ignorant, vulgar, crude.

87. William Harrison, *The Description of England*, ed. George Edelen (Washington, DC: Folger Shakespeare Library, 1994), 114.

88. Generally a resident of a city or borough. More specifically, a person elected to represent fellow-citizens in a government body.

89. Thick woollen fabric.

90. Also a coarse woollen fabric.

91. Densely woven woollen cloth.

92. Cotton fabric used mainly for coats and church vestments.

93. Velvet-like fabric used for garments and trimmings.

94. Smooth fabric woven from silk or worsted.

95. Lead ore in its rough state.

96. China.

97. Russia.
98. Northern and Central Asia.
99. Craftsmen, artisans.
100. Pertains.
101. Fought.
102. Used to, accustomed to.
103. Farmers.
104. Tenants.
105. Pleased to.
106. Judicial body. Harrison explains that in the absence of yeomen, members of this fourth social class sit on juries, etc.
107. Assistants to churchwarden.
108. Ale inspectors.
109. Parish officers who function as constables.
110. Sharpe, *Early Modern England*, 213.
111. All quotations from this play are taken from John Webster, *The White Devil*, ed. Christina Luckyj (London: Bloomsbury, 2008).
112. Gosson, *Plays Confuted in Five Actions*, G7r.

Chapter 2 – Men and Women

1. Jacob Burkhardt, *The Civilization of the Renaissance in Italy* (New York: Phaidon, 1950), 240.
2. Joan Kelly, 'Did Women Have a Renaissance?', in *Becoming Visible: Women in European History*, ed. Renate Bidenthal and Claudia Koonz, 137–164 (Boston: Houghton Mifflin, 1977).
3. Laura Gowing, *Domestic Dangers: Domestic, Words, and Sex in Early Modern London* (Oxford: Clarendon Press, 1996), 28.
4. Virginia Woolf, *A Room of One's Own* (1929) (San Diego: Harcourt Brace, 1989).
5. Stephen Orgel, *Impersonations: The Performance of Gender in Shakespeare's England* (Cambridge: Cambridge University Press, 1996), 19.
6. See Gail Kern Paster, *The Body Embarrassed: Drama and the Disciplines of Shame in Early Modern England* (Ithaca, NY: Cornell University Press, 1993).
7. Lawrence Stone, *The Family, Sex and Marriage in England, 1500–1800* (London: Harper and Row, 1977), 610.
8. Stone, *The Family, Sex and Marriage . . .*, 158.
9. William Gouge, *Of Domesticall Duties* (London: 1622), 117.
10. William Whately, *A Bride-bush* [1617] (Amsterdam: Theatrum Orbis Terrarum: 1975), 36.
11. T.E., *The Law's Resolutions of Women's Rights* (1632) in *Renaissance*

Women: A Sourcebook, ed. Kate Aughterson, 150–154 (New York: Routledge, 1995), 53, 152.

12. T.E., *The Law's Resolutions of Women's Rights*, 151.
13. In this context, sexual relations outside marriage.
14. Controlling.
15. Unrestrained.
16. Peace, harmony.
17. Endowed, given.
18. Restless, discontent.
19. Stern.
20. Ignore some errors or lapses.
21. Explain.
22. Cowardice.
23. Contentment.
24. Avoid.
25. Disobedient.
26. Impudent.
27. Hardly.
28. Praise.
29. Strike.
30. Pagans.
31. Treat.
32. Earlier.
33. Perhaps.
34. Lessen in force.
35. James I, *Basilikon Doron* in *Political Writings*, 23.
36. Jonathan Goldberg, 'Sodomy and Society: The Case of Christopher Marlowe', *The Southwest Review* 69, no.4 (1984): 371–378. 371.
37. See Alan Bray, *Homosexuality in Renaissance England* (New York: Columbia University Press, 1996).
38. All quotations from this play taken from *The Roaring Girl*, ed. Elizabeth Cook (London: A&C Black, 1997).
39. Philip Stubbes, *Anatomie of Abuses* (London: 1595), P1r.
40. Valerie Traub, *Desire and Anxiety: Circulations of Sexuality in Shakespearean Drama* (New York: Routledge, 1992), 108.
41. Traub, 'The (in)significance of "lesbian" desire in early modern England', in *Erotic Politics: Desire on the Renaissance Stage*, ed. Susan Zimmerman, 150–169 (New York: Routledge, 1992), 157.
42. Thomas Becon, *Works* (1564) quoted in *Half Humankind: Contexts and Texts of the Controversy about Women in England, 1540–1640*, ed. Katherine Usher Henderson and Barbara F. McManus (Chicago: University of Illinois Press, 1985), 54.

43. Susan Amussen, *An Ordered Society: Gender and Class in Early Modern England* (New York: Basil Blackwell, 1988).

44. King James I, *Daemonology, in Form of a Dialogue* [1599] (London: 1603), 43–44.

45. Christine Peters, *Women in Early Modern Britain, 1450–1640* (New York: Palgrave Macmillan, 2004), 127.

46. All quotations from this play taken from Ben Jonson, *Epicoene or The silent woman*, ed. Roger Holdsworth (New York: Bloomsbury, 2008).

47. See the chapter on *Arden of Faversham* in Part II for details on the play's possible authorship.

48. Stone, *The Family, Sex and Marriage . . .*, 519.

49. *Microcosmographia* (1615) quoted in Anthony Fletcher, *Gender, Sex and Subordination in England, 1500–1800* (New Haven, CT: Yale University Press, 1995), 72.

50. All quotations from this play taken from Ben Jonson, *Everyman in his Humour*, in *Ben Jonson – Vol.3C*, ed. H. Herford and Percy Simpson (Oxford: Clarendon Press, 1927).

51. Gowing, *Domestic Dangers*, 63.

52. All quotations from this play taken from Thomas Heywood, *A Woman Killed With Kindness*, ed. Frances Dolan (London: Bloomsbury, 2012).

53. Sir Thomas Elyot, *The Boke named the Governour* (1532), ed. H.H.S. Croft, 2 vols (London, 1883; reprinted New York, 1967) Vol. I, 236.

54. *Sermons and Homilies Appointed to be Read in Churches in the Time of Queen Elizabeth* (Oxford: Clarendon Press, 1814), 262.

55. Richard Burton, *The Anatomy of Melancholy*, ed. Floyd Dell and Paul Jordan-Smith (New York: Tudor Publishing Co, 1927), 278.

56. Mark Breitenberg, *Anxious Masculinity in Early Modern England* (Cambridge: Cambridge University Press, 1996).

57. Marjorie Garber, *Vested Interests* (New York: Routledge, 1992), 29.

58. A series of puns on the grammatical terms 'gender', 'number', 'case', 'mood' and 'tense' ('case' could also imply clothing).

59. Produced.

60. Historian, one who studies antiquity.

61. Skill.

62. Carriages.

63. Complicated decorative design imitating branches and foliage.

64. Stylized designs foliage and strange creatures.

65. Prostitutes.

66. Caul, a woman's headdress.

67. Woman's close-fitting cap.

68. Upper-garment either sleeved or sleeveless worn by either men or women, here refers specifically to an article of men's clothing.

69. Long outer petticoats.
70. Skirts.
71. Imitative.
72. Damnation.
73. Merits.
74. Laces.
75. Tie up.
76. Woman's undergarment, shift or chemise.
77. Mask, disguise.
78. Virgin priestesses in charge of the sacred fire in the temple of Vesta in Rome.
79. Attractive.
80. Roman gladiators.
81. Patched, multi-coloured.
82. Surface area.
83. Window frame.
84. A military metaphor. The writer advices women to protect their bodies with 'ordinance' or military force.
85. Sanctified or sacred objects.
86. Counterscarp or the outer walls of a ditch.
87. In this second military metaphor the writer describes the female body and female sexuality as a fortification that has to be well-guarded and defended by appropriate clothing.
88. Bizarre or grotesque.
89. Eccentricity, fanciful.
90. A Roman district frequented by prostitutes.
91. Fabulous monsters, half-woman half-bird, who enticed sailors out at sea by their singing.
92. Form, shape.
93. Right or permission.
94. Title or right.
95. A short, crisp, curl.
96. Frills worn at the neck, typical of costume of the era.
97. Ornamental collars or studded necklaces.
98. Items of clothing that covered the breast.
99. Various head-dresses. 'Shadows' projected to shade the face.
100. Corsets and whalebone bodices.
101. The use of cosmetics.
102. Taken by force.
103. The book is possibly Shakespeare's *Venus and Adonis*. In this poem Venus courts Adonis with traditional 'feminine wiles', including tears and sighs.

104. Combats (for sport) between horsemen carrying lances.
105. Dances for two dancers.
106. Unruly, energetic young goats.
107. Made up of.
108. A game similar to badminton.
109. In this context: an agent, or go-between.
110. Daintiness.
111. Greek philosopher (535–475 BC) known as the 'weeping philosopher'.
112. Weakly, childishly.
113. An instrument for measuring height and distance.
114. Confession told privately. The writer means that the foppish young men subject their clothes to close scrutiny and pay great attention to their flaws/defects.
115. Mote, speck or particle of dust.
116. Albrecht Durer (1471–1528), German artist famous for his writings on perspective.
117. Elegance, but here effeminacy or over-daintiness.
118. Caring physicians.
119. Attractiveness.
120. Anything in us rather than.
121. William Prynne, *Histrio-mastix* (London: 1633), 214.
122. John Rainolds, *The O'erthrow of Stage-Plays* (London, 1599) quoted in Tracey Sedinger, '"If Sight and Shape be True": The Epistemology of Crossdressing on the London Stage', *Shakespeare Quarterly* 48, no.1 (1997): 63–79, 69.
123. Stubbes, C3r.
124. See Phyllis Rackin, 'Androgyny, Mimesis, and the Marriage of the Boy Heroine on The English Renaissance Stage', *PMLA* 102, no.1 (1987): 29–41.
125. Samuel Rowlands, 'The Bride' (1617) in *Renaissance Drama by Women: Texts and Documents*, ed. S.P. Cerasano and Marion Wynne-Davies (New York: Routledge, 1996), 161.
126. Richard Levin, 'Women in the Renaissance Theatre Audience', *Shakespeare Quarterly* 40, no.2 (1989): 165–174.
127. Dympna Callaghan, *The Impact of Feminism in English Renaissance Studies* (New York: Palgrave Macmillan, 2007), 7.
128. John Knox, *The First Blast of the Trumpet against the Monstrous Regiment of Women* (1558), quoted in *Renaissance Women: A Sourcebook*, ed. Kate Aughterson, 138–139 (New York: Routledge, 1995), 138.
129. John Aylmer, *An Harborow for faithful and true subjects* (1559), quoted in *Renaissance Women: A Sourcebook*, ed. Kate Aughterson, 140–142 (New York: Routledge, 1995), 140.

130. Queen Elizabeth, 'First Speech before Parliament' (1559), in *Elizabeth I and her Age*, ed. Donald Stump and Susan Fletch, 125–127 (New York: W.W. Norton, 2009).

131. 'Answer to the Commons' Petition That She Marry' (1563), in *Elizabeth I and her Age*, 127–128, 127.

132. 'Speech to the Troops at Tilbury' (1588), in *Elizabeth I and her Age*, 392.

133. Woolf, *A Room of One's Own*, 46.

Chapter 3 – Travel and Trade

1. Thomas Coryat, Prefatory Material to *Coryat's Crudities*, in *Amazons, Savages and Machiavels: Travel and Colonial Writing in English, 1550–1630*, ed. Andrew Hadfield, 28–32 (Oxford: Oxford University Press, 2002), 30.

2. C.G.A. Clay, *Economic Expansion and Social Change: England 1500–1700. Vol. 2* (Cambridge: Cambridge University Press, 1984).

3. J.A. Froude, *Short Studies on Great Subjects* (New York: Charles Scribner and Company, 1868), 361.

4. Richard Hakluyt, 'Epistle Dedicatory', in *The Principall Navigations*, Vol. 1 (Glasgow: MacLehose, 1903), xvii.

5. Edmund Spenser, *A View of the Present State of Ireland*, ed. William Renwick (Oxford: Clarendon Press, 1970), 84.

6. Long hairstyle worn by Irish men.

7. Spenser, *A View of the Present State of Ireland*, 11.

8. Heirs, successors.

9. Pure, unmixed.

10. Stubbornness.

11. A lightly armed Irish foot-soldier.

12. Insult.

13. Disgraceful.

14. Coarse, untidy.

15. Roman Catholic.

16. Turban-like (hence Turkish) head-dresses.

17. Morisco dances were popular dances said to be of Moorish origin.

18. Loud.

19. 'Brehon' is the term for a judicial or mediative role in Irish society. Early Irish law was known as 'Brehon law'.

20. Looting.

21. Taken the virginity of.

22. Nabil Matar, *Turks, Moors and Englishmen in the Age of Discovery* (New York: Columbia University Press, 1999), 3.

23. Edward Said, *Orientalism* (New York: Random House, 1978).

24. *The Famous and Wonderful Recovery of a Ship of Bristol* (1622), in *Piracy, Slavery and Redemption: Barbary Captivity Narratives from Early Modern England*, ed. Daniel J. Vitkus, 96–120 (New York: Columbia University Press, 2001), 119.

25. T.S., *The Adventures of Mr. T.S.* (1670), 161–162.

26. Richard Knolles, *The General History of the Turks* (London: 1603), 1.

27. Henry Blount, *A Voyage into the Levant* (London: 1636), 2.

28. Conyers Read, *Mr. Secretary Walsingham and the Policy of Queen Elizabeth* (Cambridge, MA: Harvard University Press, 125), 3: 226.

29. Edmund Hogan, 'The Ambassage of Edmund Hogan … 1577', in Hakluyt, *The Principall Navigations*, Vol. 6, 289.

30. Thomas Dekker, *Lust's Dominion* (London, 1657).

31. All quotations from this play taken from George Peele, *The Battle of Alcazar*, in *The Dramatic Works of George Peele*, ed. John Yoklavich, 213–373 (New Haven: Yale University Press, 1962).

32. From excerpt in *Race in Early Modern England: A Documentary Companion*, ed. Ania Loomba and Jonathan Burton, 115–119 (New York: Palgrave Macmillan, 2007).

33. A single-decked sea vessel propelled by oars and sails. Commonly used in the Mediterranean, the rowers were usually slaves or condemned criminals.

34. Renegaded (converted).

35. Converted to Islam.

36. Sodomy.

37. Robbery, piracy.

38. Force them.

39. Low, base.

40. Seraglio or palace housing women of the royal household.

41. Luxuriously sensuous.

42. Grandly, extravagantly.

43. Trade.

44. Marranos – Jews living in Spain and Portugal who converted or were forced to convert to Christianity.

45. Early type of portable gun.

46. Sly, cunning.

47. Detestable.

48. Leo Africanus, *The History and Description of Africa*, trans. John Pory (1600), in *Amazons, Witches*, 139–151, 141.

49. 'The Second Voyage to Guinea', in Hakluyt, *The Principall Navigations*, Vol. 4, 57.

50. Quoted in Jyotsna Singh, *Colonial Narratives, Cultural Dialogues: Discoveries of India in the Language of Colonialism* (New York: Routledge, 1996), 324.

51. John Smith, *Travels and History of Virginia*, ed. E.A. Benians (Cambridge: Cambridge University Press, 1908), 125.

52. Bartolome de las Casas, *A Brief Narration of the Destruction of the Indies by the Spaniards*, trans. M.M. S. (1583) in *Amazons, Witches, Machiavels*, 250–255, 252.

53. Samuel Purchas, *Purchas his Pilgrimes* (1625) Vol. 19 (Glasgow: James MacLehose, 1905–07), 231.

54. See T. Alden and Virginia Mason Vaughan, *Shakespeare's Caliban: A Cultural History* (Cambridge: Cambridge University Press, 1993).

55. Arthur Barlowe, in Hakluyt, *Principall Navigations*, Vol. 8, 305.

56. Michel de Montaigne, 'Of the Cannibals' (1580), trans. John Florio (1603), in *Amazons, Witches*, 286–295, 286.

57. Las Casas, *A Brief Narration . . .*, 252.

58. John Cotton, *The Divine Right to Occupy the Land* (London: 1630).

59. Richard Eden, *The Decades of the Newe Worlde, or West India* (1555), in *Amazons, Savages*, 240–249, 241.

60. Victual – food.

61. Cultivate.

62. Cleanses.

63. In Renaissance physiology and medicine the 'humours' referred to the four fluids (blood, phlegm, bile and choler) that determined, by their presence and proportion, a person's heath and temperament.

64. Grievous, serious.

65. Holy.

66. Instruments.

67. Intelligence.

68. Magnet.

69. A kind of early telescope.

70. Details.

71. Tribes of the region.

72. Tudor Royal Proclamations, Vol. 3, 221–222 (January, 1601).

73. See note 63.

74. George Best, *A True Discourse of the Late Voyages of Discoverie* (1578), in *Race in Early Modern England*, 108–110, 108.

75. James I, 'Lepanto', in *Select Poetry of the Reign of King James I*, ed. Edward Farr (Cambridge: Cambridge University Press, 1847).

76. See Loomba and Burton, *Race in Early Modern England*.

77. Kim Hall, *Things of Darkness: Economies of Race and Gender in Early Modern England* (Ithaca: Cornell University Press, 1995).

78. Ania Loomba, *Shakespeare, Race, and Colonialism* (Oxford: Oxford University Press, 2002), 3.

79. All quotations from this play taken from Thomas Heywood, *The Fair Maid of the West*, in *The Dramatic Works of Thomas Heywood – Vol. 2*, ed. John Pearson, 225–423 (New York: Russell and Russell, 1964).

80. Luke Gernon, *Discourse of Ireland* (London: 1620).

81. Sir Walter Raleigh, *The Discoverie of the Large, Rich and Bewtiful Empyre of Guiana* (1596), in *Amazons, Savages*, 279–286, 285.

82. Spenser, *A View of the Present State of Ireland*, 68.

83. All quotations from this play are from John Fletcher et al, *The Knight of Malta*, in *The Dramatic Works of Ben Jonson and Beaumont and Fletcher – Volume III*, ed. George Coleman, 589–621 (London: John Stockdale, 1811).

84. Spenser, *A View of the Present State of Ireland*, 68.

85. Ania Loomba, '"Delicious Traffick": Racial and Religious Difference in Early Modern Stages', in *Shakespeare and Race*, ed. Catherine Alexander and Stanley Wells, 203–224 (Cambridge: Cambridge University Press, 2000).

86. Roger Ascham, *The Scholemaster* (1570), in *English Works of Roger Ascham*, ed. William Wright, 170–302 (Cambridge: Cambridge University Press, 1904. Reprinted 1970), 229.

87. Robert Wilson, *Three Ladies of London*, in *A Select Collection of Old English Plays*, ed. W. Carew Hazlitt (London: 1874–76).

88. Purchas, *Purchas his Pilgrimes*, Vol. 1, 56.

89. Thomas Lee, 'A Brief declaration of the government of Ireland', in *The Elizabethan Conquest of Ireland: A Pattern Established – 1565-1576* (New York: Harvester Press, 1976), 118.

90. See Dympna Callaghan, 'Irish Memories in *The Tempest*,' in *Shakespeare Without Women*, 97–128 (New York: Routledge, 2000).

Chapter 4 – Humanism

1. Paul Kristeller, *Renaissance Thought: The Classic, Scholastic and Humanist Strains* (New York: Harper and Row, 1961), 10.

2. Fritz Caspari, *Humanism and the Social Order in Tudor England* (New York: Teacher's College Press, 1968), 13.

3. See Nicholas Mann, 'The Origins of Humanism', in *The Cambridge Companion to Renaissance Humanism*, ed. Jill Kraye, 1–19 (Cambridge: Cambridge University Press, 1996).

4. Niccolò Machiavelli, *The Letters of Machiavelli*, ed. and trans. Albert Gilbert (Chicago: University of Chicago Press, 1961), quoted in Tony Davies, *Humanism* (New York: Routledge, 1997), 73.

5. Gabriel Harvey, *Pierce's Superogation*, quoted in Mike Pincombe, *Elizabethan Humanism: Literature and Learning in the Later Sixteenth Century* (New York: Longman, 2001), 59.
6. Joanna Martindale, *English Humanism* (Dover, NH: Croom Helm, 1985), 30.
7. Erasmus, *Methodus* (1516), quoted in Anthony Grafton and Lisa Jardine, *From Humanism to the Humanities: Education and the Liberal Arts in Fifteenth- and Sixteenth-Century Europe* (Cambridge, MA: Harvard University Press, 1986), 147.
8. Harmful.
9. Unholy, heathen.
10. Dedicates.
11. Cicero – Roman philosopher, orator, and politician; Virgil and Horace – Roman poets; Aristotle – Greek philosopher; an Academic – a follower of the Greek Sceptic school of philosophy who argued that knowledge of the truth is impossible; Stoic – a follower of the school of Greek philosophy characterized by austerity, endurance and indifference to pain and pleasure; Epicurean – a member of the school of Greek philosophy that celebrates the pursuit of pleasure.
12. An argument based on merely probable grounds. Here associated with the Greek Stoic philosopher Chrysippus.
13. Logical puzzles seen as pagan wiles.
14. Carneades, an academic Sceptic, second century BC, is said to have taken a purge of the herb hellebore to sharpen his mind.
15. In this context 'gentile' implies heathen, pagan.
16. In Greek mythology a skilled craftsmen.
17. In Greek and Roman mythology a race of giants each with a single eye.
18. A tribe in northern Anatolia regarded as the first ironsmith nation in classical antiquity.
19. According to classical tradition, Coroebus of Athens was the inventor of pottery.
20. The process of cleansing cloth by beating and washing.
21. The staff carried by the messenger god, Mercury.
22. The underworld, realm of ghosts.
23. Controversial theologian (AD 185–254) admired by Erasmus
24. Sardanapalus, King of Assyria, was known for his love of luxury.
25. Gnatho is the parasite in Terence's *Eunuchus*
26. Thraso is a braggart soldier from the same play.
27. Followers of the scholastic theologians Albertus Magnus, Thomas Aquinas, Duns Scotus, William of Occam and Durandus.
28. Harmful.
29. Probably Saint Jerome (AD 347–420), the theologian who translated most of the Old Testament from Hebrew into Latin.

30. Pertaining to the linguistic and interpretative study of literature.
31. Priesthood.
32. Anthony Grafton, 'The New Science and the Traditions of Humanism', in *The Cambridge Companion to Renaissance Humanism*, 203–224, 204.
33. Pincombe, *Elizabethan Humanism*, 196.
34. Gabriel Harvey, *Pierce's Supererogationi* (1593) sig iv, quoted in Pincombe, *Elizabethan Humanism*, 84.
35. Elyot, *The Boke Named the Governour*, Vol. 1, 96.
36. Ascham, *The Scholemaster*, 259.
37. Davies, *Humanism*, 79.
38. See Rebecca Bushnell, *A Culture of Teaching: Early Modern Humanism in Theory and Practice* (Ithaca: Cornell University Press, 1996).
39. Familiar with.
40. Crudely, in a coarse manner.
41. Ideas and thoughts.
42. Foolish, simple-minded. Ascham's point here is that foolish thoughts are reflected in poor language. In other words, content and style are connected.
43. A Christian movement with roots in the Reformation. Anabaptists rejected the practice of baptizing infants and believed instead in delaying baptism till an individual has confessed his/her faith.
44. A non-conformist or free-thinker in religion.
45. Crude, ill-bred.
46. Disorders or failings (those referred to in the previous sentence).
47. Baldessare Castiglione, *The Book of the Courtier*, trans. Thomas Hoby (1561), ed. Virginia Cox (London: Everyman, 1994).
48. Grafton and Jardine, *From Humanism to the Humanities*, xiv.
49. See C.S. Lewis, *English Literature in the Sixteenth Century Excluding Drama* (Oxford: Clarendon Press, 1954).
50. Grafton and Jardine, *Humanism to the Humanities*, xiv.
51. See Kent Cartwright, *Theater and Humanism: English Drama in the Sixteenth Century* (Cambridge: Cambridge Univeristy Press, 1999).
52. Bushnell, *A Culture of Teaching*, 17.
53. Francesco Petrarch, *Le Familiari, Vol. 1*, ed. V. Rossi, quoted in Kristeller, *Renaissance Thought*, 125.
54. Italian Renaissance thinking was influenced by medieval Arab philosophy and translation.
55. The supposed author of a set of texts that formed the basis of Hermetic philosophy.
56. Focal point.
57. Ancient Hebrew king credited for writing many of the psalms in the Biblical Book of Pslams.

58. That which cannot be expressed in language.
59. Rough.
60. Most likely a reference to *Timaeus*, a dialogue by Plato mostly consisting of a long monologue by the titular character.
61. Prototype, original pattern or model.
62. Kristeller, *Renaissance Thought*, 20.
63. Kristeller, *Renaissance Thought*, 70.
64. Quoted in Jacob Burckhardt, *The Civilization of the Renaissance in Italy*, trans. S.G. C. Middlemore (Kitchener, Ontario: Baytoche, 2001).
65. Cicero, *De oratore*, quoted in Pincombe, *Elizabethan Humanism*, 23.
66. Arthur Kinney, *Humanist Poetics: Thought, Rhetoric and Fiction in Sixteenth-century England* (Amherst: University of Massachusetts Press, 1986).
67. Unities of time, place and action – central to the plot structure of classical drama.
68. *Gorboduc* was an English play written ca. 1561 by Thomas Norton and Thomas Sackville. Lewis cites it as an example of humanist drama inspired by classical models.
69. A metrical line consisting of six feet. This was the standard metre used in the Greek and Latin epics.
70. Lewis, *English Literature*, 19.
71. David Bevington, *From Mankind to Marlowe: The Growth of Structure in the Popular Drama of Tudor England* (Cambridge, MA: Harvard University Press, 1962) and Weimann, *Shakespeare and the Popular Tradition*.
72. Cartwright, *Theatre and Humanism*, 1.
73. Bruce Smith, *Ancient Scripts and Modern Experience on the English Stage: 1500-1700* (Princeton, NJ: Princeton University Press, 1988), 271.
74. Kinney, *Humanist Poetics*, 23.
75. T.S. Eliot, 'Seneca in Elizabethan Translation', *Selected Essays*, 51–90 (New York: Harcourt Brace and World, 1960), 75.
76. 'To the Readers' (17–19). All quotations from this play taken from Ben Jonson, *Sejanus*, ed. W.F. Bolton, in *Six Elizabethan and Jacobean Tragedies*, ed. Brian Gibbons (London: Bloomsbury, 2014).
77. See Grafton and Jardine, *From Humanism to the Humanities*, 134.
78. Ovid, *Metamorphoses* (Book XV). Trans. Arthur Golding (1567). Available online: http://www.elizabethanauthors.org/ovid15.htm (accessed 2 February 2015).
79. T.S. Eliot, 'Tradition and the Individual Talent', in *Selected Essays*, 3–11 (New York: Harcourt, Brace and World, 1960), 4.
80. Eliot, 'Philip Massinger', in *Selected Essays*, 181–198, 182.
81. Eliot, 'Seneca in Elizabethan Translation', in *Selected Essays*, 64.

82. Eliot, 'Seneca in Elizabethan Translation', in *Selected Essays*, 70, 75.
83. See Cartwright, *Theater and Humanism*, 16.
84. Unless otherwise indicated all quotations from this play taken from Christopher Marlowe, *Doctor Faustus: Based on the A Text*, ed. Roma Gill (London: Bloomsbury, 2008).

Chapter 5 – The Stage

1. John Stow, *Survey of London* (1603 edition); available online: http://www.british-history.ac.uk/source.aspx?pubid=593 (accessed 8 February 2015).
2. Andrew Gurr, *Playgoing in Shakespeare's London* (Cambridge: Cambridge University Press, 1987), 59.
3. Andrew Gurr, *The Shakespearean Playing Companies* (Oxford: The Clarendon Press, 1996), 19.
4. Gurr, *The Shakespearean Playing Company*, 93.
5. Douglas Bruster, *Drama and the Market in the Age of Shakespeare* (Cambridge: Cambridge University Press, 1992), 3.
6. All quotations from this play taken from Ben Jonson, *Bartholmew Fair*, ed. G.R. Hibbard (London: A&C Black, 1997).
7. Arthur F. Kinney, *Shakespeare by Stages: An Historical Introduction* (Malden, MA: Blackwell, 2003), 10.
8. E.K. Chambers, *The Elizabethan Stage, Vol. 3* (Oxford: The Clarendon Press, 1923).
9. All quotations from this play taken from Ben Jonson, *The Alchemist*, ed. Elizabeth Cook (London: A&C Black, 2010).
10. Kinney, *Shakespeare by Stages*, 10.
11. Andrew Gurr, *The Shakespearean Stage, 1574–1642* (Cambridge: Cambridge University Press, 1970); Kinney, *Shakespeare by Stages*.
12. Quoted in Ann Rosalind Jones and Peter Stallybrass, *Renaissance Clothing and the Materials of Memory* (Cambridge: Cambridge University Press, 2000), 178.
13. Stephen Gosson, *The School of Abuse* (London: 1587), D2r.
14. Margreta De Grazia, 'The Ideology of Superfluous Things: *King Lear* as Period Piece', in *Subject and Object in Renaissance Culture*, ed. Margreta De Grazia, Maureen Quilligan and Peter Stallybrass, 17–42 (Cambridge: Cambridge University Press), 34.
15. Gurr, *The Shakespearean Stage*, 49.
16. Thomas Dekker, *The Magnificent Entertainment* (1603), quoted in 'Introduction', in *Staged Properties in Early Modern England*, ed. Jonathan Gil Harris and Natasha Korda (Cambridge: Cambridge University, 2002).
17. Ben Jonson, *Everyman in his Humour*, Prologue, 16.

18. Harris and Korda, *Staged Properties*, 50.

19. Gerard Bentley, *The Profession of Player in Shakespeare's Time 1590–1642* (Princeton, NJ: Princeton University Press, 1982).

20. Bentley, *The Profession of Player*, 9.

21. See Bentley, *The Profession of Player*, 9.

22. Eyases – little hawks whose training is incomplete. The boy actors who supposedly loudly deliver their lines in high voices (and are applauded for it) are being compared to noisy little untrained birds.

23. S.P. Cersano 'The Chamberlain's-King's Men', in *A Companion to Shakespeare*, ed. David Kastan, 328–345 (Oxford: Blackwell, 1999), 342.

24. Quoted in R.A. Foakes, 'Playhouses and Players', in *The Cambridge Companion to English Renaissance Drama*, ed. A.R. Braunmuller and Michael Hattaway (Cambridge: Cambridge University Press, 2003), 38.

25. See Bentley, *The Profession of Players*.

26. Bentley, *The Profession of Players*, 225

27. Harbage, *Shakespeare's Audience*, 36.

28. Thomas Dekker, *The Guls Hornbook, The Non-dramatic Works of Thomas Dekker – Vol. 2*, ed. Alexander B. Grosart, 193–266 (New York: Russell & Rusell, 1963), 246.

29. Dekker, *The Guls Hornbook – Vol.2*, 247.

30. Robert Weimann, *Shakespeare and the Popular Tradition in the Theater* (Baltimore: Johns Hopkins University Press), 174.

31. In Kinney, *Shakespeare by Stages*, 82.

32. Dekker, *The Guls horn-Booke*, 248, and Ben Jonson, *The Case is Altered*, 2.7; in Harbage, *Shakespeare's Audience*, 109.

33. All quotations from this play taken from Ben Jonson, *Everyman out of his Humour*, in *Ben Jonson – Vol. 3*.

34. Harbage, *Shakespeare's Audience*.

35. See Gurr, *The Shakespearean Playing Company*.

36. Gurr, *Playgoing in Shakespeare's London*, 85.

37. See Gurr, *The Shakespearean Playing Company*.

38. Gurr, *The Shakespearean Playing Company*, 27.

39. Prynne, *Histrio-mastix*, 68; Philip Stubbes, *Anatomie of Abuses* (London: 1595), 103.

40. Stubbes, *Anatomie of Abuses*, 105.

41. Fraud, cheating.

42. Restraint, moderation. The writer accuses comedies of being extreme and overwrought.

43. Loving.

44. Little poem written on a sheet of paper or other writing surface.

45. Imitative bearing/deportment.

46. Young male playgoers preying on women are being compared to birds of prey.

47. A variety of apple.
48. Talk all the time.
49. Commonwealth, nation.
50. Rebounds.
51. Worldly (i.e. impious) people.
52. Renunciation of religion.
53. Unrighteous action or conduct.
54. Gosson, *Plays Confuted in Five Actions*, E1R.
55. Short – often light and humorous – plays enacted between the acts of the longer mystery and morality plays of the Middle Ages.
56. Another word for kissing.
57. Both words imply embracing, cuddling.
58. Private rooms.
59. Stubbes implies that men go home with other men after plays and that they engage with sexual activity with each other.
60. Deception.
61. Cheat.
62. To laugh coarsely.
63. To meow – here the writer simply means to make rude and inappropriate sounds.
64. To behave like a rake or playboy.
65. The practice of sexual pleasure.
66. Cheaters.
67. Deservings.
68. Talk sweetly.
69. Heywood means that the spectator would be inspired and moved by the representation of English heroism on stage.
70. The actor became like or embodied the original or real-life person being imitated on stage.
71. Reshape or reconstitute.
72. Raiding.
73. Fleur-de-lis ('the lily'). The flower symbolized French royalty.
74. Greek philosopher associated with Cynic school of philosophy that advocated simple life of abstinence from material pleasure.
75. Pastry of marzipan layered on wafers. The point here is that dour cynics (like Diogenes) cannot enjoy pleasurable things (like drama).
76. Confused jumble of things.
77. Well-structured.
78. Legendary descendent of Aeneas of Troy. According to medieval British legend, Brute was the founder and first king of Britain.
79. All three words connote rebellion and revolt.
80. Dissuading.

81. Julius Caesar (100–44 BC).
82. Pompey (106–48 BC) was a Roman general, first Caesar's ally and then his enemy. Pompey's fortunes declined due to a mix of treachery and his own failings and misjudgements.
83. Alexander the Great (356–323 BC) killed his friend and general Cleitus in a drunken quarrel.
84. Midas, the Greek mythological figure who could turn everything he touched into gold. He came to hate his gift when even food and water turned into gold. Here he is a warning of the dangers of excessive greed.
85. Nero, Roman emperor (AD 37–68), here a prototype of tyrannical rule.
86. Sardnapalus (seventh century BC) was supposedly king of Assyria. His decadent and self-indulgent lifestyle became the subject of legend.
87. Nynus or Ninus was considered the founder of the city of Nineveh in Assyria. There is no single historical figure with that name and he was probably a compilation of several personages. Here Heywood is probably referring to an unknown play or narrative which portrayed Ninus as a symbol of (over)ambition.
88. Several.
89. Coarse, vulgar.
90. Treats (discusses).
91. Lovers.
92. The figure of Pantaloon was typical of Italian comedy. He was a foolish old man, often the butt of ridicule.
93. A type of play set in an idealized countryside.
94. Extravagance.
95. Lying under oath in court.
96. One who broaches or considers rebellion.
97. Plays.
98. See Stephen Greenblatt, *Shakespearean Negotiations*.
99. Steven Mullaney, *The Place of the Stage: License, Play and Power in Renaissance England* (Chicago: Chicago University Press, 1988).
100. See Howard, *Stage and Social Struggle* (New York: Routledge, 1993).
101. Heywood, 'The Author to his Book,' *An Apology for Actors*, B1v.

Chapter 6 – Books, Authors and Readers

1. See Elizabeth Eisenstein, *The Printing Revolution in Early Modern Europe* (Cambridge: Cambridge University Press, 2005).

2. Parchment prepared from the skin of calves.
3. David Kastan, *Shakespeare and the Book* (Cambridge: Cambridge University Press, 2001), 3.
4. Douglas Brooks, *Playhouse to Printing House: Dramatic Authorship and Publication in Early Modern England* (New York: Cambridge University Press, 2000), 177.
5. Jeffrey Masten, *Textual Intercourse: Collaboration, Authorship, and Sexualities in Renaissance Drama* (Cambridge: Cambridge University Press, 1997), 13.
6. Thomas Heywood, *The English Traveller* (1633), 'To the Reader', A3r.
7. Stephen Orgel, 'What is a Text', in *Staging the Renaissance: Interpretations of Elizabethan and Jacobean Drama*, 83–88 (New York: Routledge, 1991), 87.
8. Bentley, *The Profession of Player.*
9. Trevor Howard-Hill, 'Buc and the Censorship of *Sir John Van Olden Barnavelt* in 1619', *Review of English Studies*, n.s., 39 (1988): 39–63, 43.
10. See Richard Dutton, *Licensing, Censorship and Authorship in Early Modern England* (New York: Palgrave, 2000), 6.
11. H.S. Bennet, *English Books and Readers, Vol. 2* (Cambridge: Cambridge University Press, 1970), 271.
12. Peter Blayney, 'The Publication of Playbooks', in *A New History Of Early English Drama*, ed. John Cox and David Kastan, 393–422 (New York: Columbia University Press, 1987), 385.
13. Douglas Brooks, *Playhouse to Printing House.*
14. Thomas Heywood, *Rape of Lucrece*, 'To the reader' (1608), A2r.
15. Kastan, *Shakespeare and the Book*, 15.
16. Heywood, 'To the Reader', *Rape of Lucrece*, A2r.
17. Blayney, 'The Publication of Playbooks', 387.
18. Alan Farmer and Zach Lessor, 'The Popularity of Playbooks Revisited', *Shakespeare Quarterly* 56, no. 1 (2005): 1–32.
19. Brooks, *Playhouse to Printing House*, 177.
20. Marketable.
21. Prynne, *Histrio-mastix*, 3.
22. Kastan, *Shakespeare and the Book*, 26.
23. Leah Marcus, *Unediting the Renaissance: Shakespeare, Marlowe, Milton* (New York: Routledge, 1996).
24. See Jeffrey Masten, 'Pressing Subjects, or the Secret Lives of Shakespeare's Compositors', in *Language Machines: Technologies of Literary and Cultural Production*, ed. Jeffrey Masten, Peter Stallybrass and Nancy Vickers, 75–107 (New York: Routledge, 1997).
25. Kastan, *Shakespeare After Theory* (New York: Routledge, 1999), 72.
26. 'Dedication', *The Knight of the Burning Pestle*. All quotes taken from Francis Beaumont, *The Knight of the Burning Pestle*, ed. Michael Hattaway (London: Bloomsbury, 2002).

27. Brooks, *Playhouse to Printing House.*
28. Joseph Lowenstein, *Ben Jonson and Possessive Authorship* (Cambridge: Cambridge University Press, 2002).
29. *Wits Recreations* (1640), quoted in C.H. Herford, Percy Simpson and Evelyn Simpson, *Ben Jonson* (Oxford: Clarendon Press, 1925–52), 13.
30. Bentley, *Profession of Player,* 55–56.
31. In this dedicatory note, Jonson states that his play, like its hero Sejanus, was rejected by the people, but it survives, presumably in the printed form.
32. Charged with, blamed for.
33. Jonson agrees that his play does not adhere to all the conventions of ancient tragedy, but states that it is like classical tragedy in its grand tone and elevated theme.
34. Henry Condell and John Heminge, 'To the Great Variety of Readers', *Mr. William Shakespeare's Comedies, Histories, and Tragedies* (London: 1623).
35. 'To The Reader', *Comedies and Tragedies Written by Beaumont and Fletcher* (London, 1642).
36. 'The Stationer to the Reader', *Comedies and Tragedies Written by Beaumont and Fletcher.*
37. To examine, judge.
38. Metaphor of legal trial. These plays have been tried and don't need to be judged further.
39. Fake, fraudulent.
40. Deceptions.
41. The editors imply that Shakespeare wrote so naturally and fluently that he barely stopped or hesitated – hence no blot on his papers.
42. David Scott Kastan, 'Print, Literary Culture and the Book Trade', in *The Cambridge History of Early Modern English Literature*, ed. David Loewenstein and Janel Mueller, 81–116 (Cambridge: Cambridge University Press), 112.
43. David Cressy, *Literacy and the Social Order: Reading and Writing in Tudor and Stuart England* (Cambridge: Cambridge University Press, 2006).
44. Francis Bacon, 'Of Studies', in *Essays,* 432–433 (1625; London: John W. Parker, 1956), 432–433.
45. Steven N. Zwicker, 'The Reader Revealed', in *The Reader Revealed,* ed. Sabrina Baron, Elizabeth Walsh and Susan Scola, 11–17 (Washington, D C: The Folger Shakespeare Library, 2002), 15.
46. Thomas Bodley, *Letters of Sir Thomas Bodley to Thomas James, First keeper of the Bodleian Library,* ed. G.W. Wheeler (Oxford: Clarendon Press, 1926), 221–222.
47. Culture, civilized behaviour. The 'Tartar' here stands for uncivilized and barbaric peoples.

48. Thomas Dekker, *The Wondefull Year*, in *The Non-Dramatic Works Vol. 1*, 71–148, 77.

Chapter 7 – Genre

1. See Bevington, *From Mankind to Marlowe*.
2. Weimann, *Shakespeare and the Popular Tradition*, xviii.
3. Mikhail Bakhtin, *Speech Genres and Other Late Essays*, trans. Vern McGee, ed. C. Emerson and M. Holquist (Austin: University of Texas Press, 1986), 65.
4. Philip Sidney, *An Apology for Poetry; or, The Defence of Poesy*, ed. Geoffrey Shepherd (London: Thomas Nelson, 1967), 117.
5. Sidney, *An Apology for Poetry*, 134.
6. Thomas Heywood, *An Apology for Actors*, F2v.
7. Sidney, *An Apology for Poetry*, 117–118.
8. Aristotle refers to the drama competitions in ancient Athens for which many ancient Greek tragedies were written.
9. Clear.
10. An event that possibly took place in Aristotle's life time; Mitys was a man whose statue fell over and killed his murderer.
11. Reference to *Oedipus Rex* (*c*. 429 BC) by Sophocles.
12. In Greek mythology Danaus, king of Argos, orders his daughters to kill their husbands, all of whom are brothers. One of them, Lynceus, escapes and kills his father-in-law to avenge the death of his brothers. Aristotle probably refers to a lost play by the tragedian Aeschylus.
13. A.C. Bradley, *Shakespearean Tragedy* (London: Macmillan, 1905).
14. All quotations from this play are taken from Thomas Kyd, *The Spanish Tragedy*, ed. Clara Calvo and Jesus Tronch (London: Bloomsbury, 2013)
15. All quotations from this play taken from George Chapman, *Bussy D'Ambois*, ed. Maurice Evans (New York: Hill and Wang, 1966).
16. Bradley, *Shakespearean Tragedy*, 279.
17. Sidney, *An Apology for Poetry*, 135.
18. Defective. In this paragraph Sidney admires the early English tragedy *Gorboduc* for its language and moral lessons but states that it is not a model tragedy because it does not adhere to the unities of place and time.
19. Sidney disapproves here of the flouting of the unities of time and place.
20. Understood.
21. 'Princes' here encompasses both genders, so a prince and a princess.
22. Travels, adventures.
23. Coarseness, indecency.
24. Foolishness.
25. Correspondence, agreement.

26. Detestable, abominable.
27. An officious and fussy courtier.
28. Thraso is the bragging soldier in the Latin play *Eunuchus* by Terence. Sidney's point is that certain comic types are truly pleasing (cause 'delight') rather than crudely and inappropriately comic (simply provoke 'laughter').
29. A self-important but somewhat ignorant schoolmaster.
30. A man transformed by foreign travel.
31. Lacks.
32. Sidney, *An Apology for Poetry*, 134.
33. Heywood, *An Apology for Actors*, F4.v.
34. E.M.W. Tillyard, *The Elizabethan World Picture* (London: Chatto and Windus, 1943).
35. Phyllis Rackin, *Stages of History: Shakespeare's English Chronicles* (Ithaca: Cornell University Press, 1990), 10.
36. Lawrence Danson, *Shakespeare's Dramatic Genres* (Oxford: Oxford University Press, 2000), 4.

Chapter 8 – Language and Style

1. Thomas Elyot, *The Boke Named the Governour* (London: 1531) sig. v 51.
2. Roger Ascham, 'Toxiphilus', in *English Works of Roger Ascham*, ed. William Wright, 170–302 (Cambridge: Cambridge University Press, 1904; reprinted 1970), xiv.
3. Ascham, *English Works of Roger Ascham*, x.
4. Philip Sidney, *An Apology for Poetry; or, The Defence of Poesy*, ed. Geoffrey Shepherd (London: Thomas Nelson, 1967), 138.
5. Edmund Spenser, *The Works of Edmund Spenser: A Variorum Edition*, ed. Edwin Greenlaw, C.G. Osgood et al., 11 vols (Baltimore: Johns Hopkins University Press, 1932–57), Vol. 10, 16.
6. George Puttenham, *The Art of English Poesy* ('The First Book'), ed. Frank Whigham and Wayne Rebhorn (Ithaca, NY: Cornell University Press, 2007), 95.
7. Richard F. Jones, *The Triumph of the English Language* (Stanford, CA: Stanford University Press, 1966), 169–70.
8. Heywood, *An Apology for Actors*, F3r.
9. Madeline Doran, *Endeavours of Art: A Study of Form in Elizabethan Drama* (Madison, WI: University of Wisconsin Press, 1964), 25.
10. Thomas Wilson, *The Art of Rhetoric* (London: 1553) Renascence Editions. Available online: http://www.people.vcu.edu/~nsharp/wilsded1.htm (accessed 12 February 2017).

11. Peter Mack, 'Humanist Rhetoric and Dialectic', in *The Cambridge Companion to Renaissance Humanism*, ed. Jill Kraye, 82–99 (Cambridge: Cambridge University Press, 1996), 96.
12. John Houston, *Shakespearean Sentences: A Study in Style and Syntax* (Baton Rouge: Louisiana State University Press, 1988), 219.
13. Jones, *The Triumph of the English Language*,14.
14. Sidney, *An Apology for Poetry*, 102.
15. Ben Jonson, *Timber, or Discoveries Made Upon Men and Matter* (1641) in *Discoveries Made Upon Men and Matter and Some Poems* (London: Cassell, 1892). Available online: http://www.gutenberg.org/files/5134/5134-h/5134-h.htm (accessed 9 February 2015).
16. Jonson, *Timber or Discoveries*.
17. Balance, harmony, symmetry.
18. Vernacular (here English) literature.
19. Act of decoration.
20. Attractive.
21. Attire.
22. Flustered, embarrassed.
23. Perhaps.
24. Skill, learning.
25. Figures of speech.
26. Pleasant.
27. Stephen Gosson, *School of Abuse*, A2 r. The metaphor is of a disobedient hunting dog that leaves the rest of the pack and does its own bidding.
28. Jonson, 'To the Memory of my Beloved Master William Shakespeare', in *The works of Ben Jonson*, Vol. 3 (London: Chatto and Windus, 1910), 287–289.
29. Jonson, *Timber or Discoveries*.
30. Sidney, *An Apology for Poetry*, 134.
31. Like a prostitute.
32. Ostentatious display.
33. Sidney here criticizes the excessive use of alliteration and similar devices.
34. Figures of speech and other rhetorical ornaments.
35. Not fresh or natural. Sidney condemns the use of over-used or clichéd figures of speech.
36. Marcus Tullius Cicero, anglicized as Tully – Roman politician and orator.
37. Ancient Greek statesmen and orator.
38. Figures and phrases of Demosthenes and Cicero collected by Marius Nizolius in 1535. Some rhetoricians believed that correct writing in classical language should draw only from such compilations. Sidney criticizes this method and calls for a more in-depth study and imitation of the classical style.

39. Catiline was a Roman senator who was opposed by Tully (Cicero)
40. 'Lives, Lives? Why comes he into the Senate?'
41. Choler here implies anger or rage (Sidney is also playing with the word to signify 'colour' or to decorate with figures of speech). Sidney's point in this section is that classical writers like Cicero wrote with a passion that came naturally to them. Modern poets try to reproduce the same intense style but don't truly feel the passion, and hence fail.
42. Comparisons.
43. Sidney is criticizing the habit of employing an unnecessary number of comparisons to plants, animals, etc. Such comparisons don't really serve as proof or constitute argument, he writes, and therefore will not serve to persuade those who disagree with the writer's point.
44. The two main speakers in Cicero's dialogue *de Oratore*.
45. Attach importance to it.
46. Figures of speech. Sidney says that the finest orators have been successful because they used figures of speech sparingly and unselfconsciously.
47. Diverse, several.
48. Sounds unnatural or artificial. Courtiers, writes Sidney, have a better literary style than scholars because they write naturally and hence more artfully or pleasingly. Scholars, on the other hand, use stylistic devices too obviously and artificially and hence fail to write elegantly.
49. All quotations from this play taken from John Marston, *Antonio and Mellida – The First Part*, ed. G.K. Hunter (Lincoln: University of Nebraska Press, 1965).
50. All quotations from this play taken from Ben Jonson, *Volpone*, ed. Robert Watson (London: Bloomsbury, 2003).
51. All quotations from this play taken from John Marston, *Antonio's Revenge*, ed. G.K. Hunter (Lincoln: university of Nebraska Press, 1965).
52. Corrosive poison.
53. F.E. Halliday, *The Poetry of Shakespeare's Plays* (New York: Barnes and Noble, 1964), 23.
54. See Eric Partridge, *Shakespeare's Bawdy* (New York: E.P. Dutton, 1969).

PART II

Chapter 9 – *The Alchemist*

1. Elizabeth Cook, 'Introduction', in *The Alchemist*, ed. Elizabeth Cook, vii–xlii (London, A&C Black, 2010), xxxiv.

Chapter 10 – *Arden of Faversham*

1. See Macdonald P. Jackson, *Determining the Shakespearean Canon – 'Arden of Faversham' and 'The Lover's Complaint'* (Oxford: Oxford University Press, 2014). *The New Oxford Shakespeare*, ed. Gary Taylor, John Jowett, Terri Bourus and Gabriel Egan (Oxford: Oxford University Press, 2016) also includes *Arden* among Shakespeare's works.
2. All quotations from this play taken from Anonymous, *Arden of Faversham*, ed. Tom Lockwood (London: A&C Black, 2007).

Chapter 11 – *Doctor Faustus*

1. William Prynne, *Histrio-mastix: The Player's Scourge or Actor's Tragedy* (London, 1633), 556r.
2. W.W. Gregg (ed.), *Marlowe's Doctor Faustus* (Oxford: Clarendon Press, 1950), 20–39.
3. Leah Marcus, 'Textual Instability and Ideological Difference: The Case of *Doctor Faustus*', *Renaissance Drama* 20 (1990): 38–54, 43.

Chapter 12 – *The Duchess of Malfi*

1. T.S. Eliot, 'Whispers of Immortality', in *Poems* (New York: Alfred A. Knopf, 1920), 31–32.

Chapter 13 – *Hamlet*

1. Dympna Callaghan, *Hamlet: Language and Writing* (London: Bloomsbury, 2015), 84.
2. Callaghan, *Hamlet: Language and Writing*, 84.
3. Callaghan, *Hamlet: Language and Writing*, 29.

Chapter 14 – *Henry V*

1. Vincent Canby, 'A Down-to-Earth "Henry V" Discards Spectacle and Pomp'. *The New York Times*, 8 November 1989.

Chapter 15 – *The Jew of Malta*

1. T.S. Eliot, 'Christopher Marlowe', *Selected Essays*, 100–106 (New York: Harcourt, Brace & World, 1960), 104, 105.

Chapter 17 – *The Roaring Girl*

1. Elizabeth Cook, 'Introduction', in Thomas Middleton and Thomas Dekker, *The Roaring Girl*, ed. Elizabeth Cook, xiii–xxxix (London: A&C Black, 1997), xxv.

Chapter 18 – *The Shoemaker's Holiday*

1. All quotations from the play taken from Thomas Dekker, *The Shoemaker's Holiday*, ed. Jonathan Gil Harris (New Mermaids Edition, A&C Black: London, 2008).
2. Jonathan Gil Harris, 'Introduction', in Thomas Dekker, *The Shoemaker's Holiday*, ed. Jonathan Gil Harris, vii–xxix (New Mermaids Edition, A&C Black: London, 2008), xv.

Chapter 20 – *The Tempest*

1. Deborah Willis, 'Shakespeare and the Discourse of Colonialism', *SEL* 29 no. 2 (1989): 277–289, 286.
2. Paul Brown, '"This thing of darkness I acknowledge mine": *The Tempest* and the Discourse of Colonialism', in *Political Shakespeare: New Essays in Cultural Materialism*, ed. Jonathan Dollimore and Alan Sinfield, 48–71 (Manchester: Manchester University Press, 1985), 68.

Chapter 21 – *The Tragedy of Mariam*

1. All quotations from this play taken from Elizabeth Cary, *The Tragedy of Mariam*, ed. Ramona Wray (London: Bloomsbury, 2012)

2. Dympna Callaghan, 'Re-Reading *The Tragedie of Mariam, Faire Queene of Jewry*', in *Women, 'Race,' and Writing in the Early Modern Period*, ed. Margo Hendricks and Patricia Parker, 163–177 (London: Routledge, 1994), 175.

3. Ramona Wray, 'Introduction', in Elizabeth Cary, *The Tragedy of Mariam*, ed. Ramona Wray, 1–69 (London: Bloomsbury, 2012), 2.

INDEX

Italicized page numbers indicate documents reprinted in *The Arden Guide to Renaissance Drama*; bold page numbers indicate illustrations.

and blank verse 202
as homosexual 45
and style 117, 192
and tragedy 172
as 'university wit' 149
works
 Doctor Faustus 22, 115, 118, 134,
  136, 149, 150, 152, 154, 172,
  166, 176, 198–99, 201, 202, 205,
  207, 223–28, 317 n.84
 Edward II 6, 7, 46, 183, 196,
  301 n.7
 The Jew of Malta 23, 66, 67, 74,
  86, 90, 91, 117, 125, 179, 200,
  247–251, 303 n.56
 Tamburlaine 3, 6, 34, 50, 72, 78, 92,
  93, 126, 130, 133, 136, 150, 156,
  165, 176, 178, 187, 192, 201,
  205, 301 n.1
Marshall, Peter 297
Marston, John 152, 169, 170
 Antonio and Mellida 196
 Antonio's Revenge 196, 326 n.49
 The Dutch Courtesan 67, 169
 The Malcontent 7, 179
Martindale, Joanna 98, 314 n.6
Martyr, Peter (*Decades of the New
 World*) 78
Mary (Queen) 3, 10, 59
Mary Magdalene 19
Massinger, Philip 130, 149, 150
 Believe As you List 151
 The City Madam 170
 The Knight of Malta (with John
  Fletcher and Nathan Field)
  72
 A New Way to Pay Old Debts 41
 The Renegado 72, 73, 89, 90, 182
 The Virgin Martyr (with Thomas
  Dekker) 148
Masten, Jeffrey 321 n.5, n.24,
Master of the Revels/Revels Office 131,
 150, 151
Matar, Nabil 71, 310 n.22

McDonald, Russ 300
medieval drama 9, 19, 165–6, 168, 179.
 See also morality plays
Mediterranean 71, 80, 247, 248
merchants 31, 91, 170. *See also* citizens
metaphor 194–96
Middle Ages 96, 188
Middleton, Thomas 130, 149, 170, 192
 All's Lost by Lust (with William
  Rowley) 73
 A Chaste Maid in Cheapside 39, 50,
  169
 A Game of Chess 21, 22–3, 144
 The Revenger's Tragedy 7, 117, 177
 The Roaring Girl (with Thomas
  Dekker) 39, 45, 48, 50, 58, 92,
  127, 129, 135 169, 206, 259–263,
  306 n.38, 328 n.1
 A Trick to Catch the Old One 169
 The Virgin Martyr (with Philip
  Massinger) 148
miles gloriosus 118, 168
Mirandola, Pico della (*Oration on the
 Dignity of Man*) 109–11, 119,
 227
Mirror for Magistrates, A 171
Moghuls 77
Moluccas 77
Montaigne, Michel de (*Essays*) 80, 102,
 111, 282, 312 n.56
moor/moorish 73–4, 76, 85, 87, 88,
 90
morality plays 22, 113, 115, 223–4
More, Thomas (*Utopia*) 61, 102
Moreno, Mitchell 275
Morocco 71, 72, 73, 74
Moryson, Fynes (*Of Ireland*) 68–70
Mulcaster, Richard (*Positions Concerning
 the Training of Children,
 Elementarie*) 103
Mullaney, Steven 145, 320 n.99
music (in plays) 124
Muslims 71, 72, 73, 86, 88, 89
Mustapha (Fulke Greville) 7, 77